16

From the Sociology of Symbols to the Sociology of Signs

Toward a Dialectical Sociology

From the Sociology of Symbols to the Sociology of Signs

Toward a Dialectical Sociology

INO ROSSI

Hyun Kim
Oct. 1985

Columbia University Press
New York   1983

Ino Rossi is Professor of Sociology and Anthropology
at St. John's University

Library of Congress Cataloging in Publication Data

Rossi, Ino.
  From the sociology of symbols to the sociology of signs.

  Bibliography: p.
  Includes index.
  1. Sociology—Philosophy. 2. Symbolism.
3. Structuralism. 4. Paradigms (Social sciences)
5. Dialectic. I. Title.
HM24.R675 1983   301.01   83-5261
ISBN 0-231-04844-0
ISBN 0-231-04845-9 (pbk).

Columbia University Press
New York   Guildford, Surrey

To my wife Irene
and son Paul
for their enduring support

Contents

INTRODUCTION   1

Modern French Structuralism as a Challenge to the
Empiricism of Traditional Sociology   2

*The Empiricism of Traditional Schools of Sociology, 5;
The Theoretical Perspective of Modern French
Structuralism, 9; Intellectual Origins of Modern French
Structuralism, 17; Varieties of Relational Structuralism
and the Continuity of Sociological Tradition, 19*

The Study of Symbolic Systems in the Classical
Sociological Tradition: The Three Classic Paradigms   26

Scope and Organization of This Volume   33

I. THE SOCIOLOGY OF SYMBOLISM AND MEANING IN
TRADITIONAL SOCIOLOGICAL PARADIGMS   37

1. THE SOCIOLOGY OF SYMBOLIC SYSTEMS AND THE
CRITICAL PARADIGM: FUNCTIONS OF IDEOLOGY,
CONSCIOUSNESS, AND LANGUAGE ACCORDING TO MARX   39

Critique of Marx's Paradigm   43

*Marx's Conception of History: The Notion of Totality
and the Relationship Between Infrastructure and
Superstructure, 44; The Undialectic Nature of Marx's
Dialectic Materialism, 48*

2. THE SOCIOLOGY OF SYMBOLIC SYSTEMS AND
MEANING IN THE INTERPRETIVE PARADIGM   54

The Sociology of Culture in Max Weber   54

*The Subjective Orientation of Social Actors Toward
Ideas, 56; The Copresence of the Subjective and
Structural Orientation, 58*

Critique of Weber's Paradigm   63

Weber's Programmatic Dilemma Between Subjective and Structural Orientation, 63; Empiricist Perspective and the Dualism of the Weberian Orientation, 67; The Weberian Perspective and Formal Structuralism, 71

Excursus on Mannheim's Sociology of Culture   76

Symbolic Interactionism and the Study of Situational Meaning   79

Charles Horton Cooley, 81; George Herbert Mead, 83; A Critique of Symbolic Interactionism, 84

3. THE "NATURAL SCIENCE" PARADIGM AND THE STUDY OF SYMBOLIC SYSTEMS   88

Pareto on the Role of Derivations in Social Life   89

The Symbolic Nature of Collective Representations: Durkheim as a Pre-Semiotic Thinker   94

From a Morphological to a Symbolic Perspective?, 96; Symbolic and Constitutive Function of Collective Representations, 104; Durkheim's Principles of Symbolic Analysis, 113; Conclusion, 119

The Sociology of Symbolism in Parsons' "Natural Science" Paradigm   120

Talcott Parsons as a Natural Science Sociologist, 120; The Sociology of Culture and Symbolism in Voluntaristic Theory of Action and the Early Systemic Approach, 122; The Pervasiveness of the Systemic Perspective in Parsons' Approach, 125

II. SEMIOTIC STRUCTURALISM, GENETIC STRUCTURALISM, TRANSFORMATIONAL GRAMMAR   129

4. THE STRUCTURAL AND SEMIOTIC STUDY OF SYMBOLISM   131

The Structural Linguistics of Saussure   131

The Structural Phonology of the Prague School   136

From Structural Phonology to Scientific Semiotics: The Structuralism of Lévi-Strauss   139

The Semiotic Study of Ideology: Roland Barthes and Umberto Eco   146

The Influence of Hjelmslev's Glossematics, 147;
Umberto Eco, 150; Early Barthes, 151

5. THE GENETIC STRUCTURALISM OF JEAN PIAGET 154

Organismic and Formal Assumptions of Piaget's Thought 154

The Antiempiricist Character of Piaget's Epistemology 155

Structure as a System of Transformations 158

Differences Between Piaget's and Lévi-Strauss'
Frameworks and Their Complementarities 160

6. THE TRANSFORMATIONAL GRAMMAR OF NOAM
CHOMSKY 164

Phrase Structure Rules 165

The Transformational Component 166

7. STRUCTURE AND TRANSFORMATION IN LÉVI-STRAUSS,
CHOMSKY, AND PIAGET 170

Priority of Structure Over Transformation in Lévi-Strauss
and Chomsky 170

Integrating the Static Approach of Lévi-Strauss and
Chomsky with the Dynamic Approach of Piaget 173

III. THE IMPACT OF TRANSFORMATIONAL STRUCTURALISM
ON TRADITIONAL SOCIOLOGICAL PARADIGMS 179

8. TRANSFORMATIONAL STRUCTURALISM AND THE
NATURAL SCIENCE PARADIGM: THE CASE OF TALCOTT
PARSONS 181

Convergencies Between Transformational Structuralism
and the Theory of Action 182

A Common Analytical Approach, 182; A Common
Cybernetic Perspective, 184; Classificatory, Elementary,
and Combinatory Principles, 188

Critique: The Empiricist and Antidialectic Bias of
Parsons' Cybernetic and Evolutionary Perspective 191

Subjective Meaning as Unit of Analysis, 191;
Epistemological Roots of Parsons' Empiricist Approach,
195; The Lack of a Transformational and Truly
Cybernetic Perspective, 202; The Systemic Bias of the
Theory of Social Action and the Missing Dialectic, 205

9. SEMIOTIC STRUCTURALISM AND THE INTERPRETIVE
PARADIGM   208

Phenomenological Sociology and the Constitutive View of
Meaning   208

*The Husserlian Perspective, 210; The Sociological
Phenomenology of Alfred Schutz, 212; Substantive and
Methodological Affinities Between Sociological
Phenomenology and Semiotic Structuralism, 214; The
Persisting Empiricism in Phenomenological Sociology,
217; Attempts to Integrate the Structural and
Phenomenological Levels of Meaning, 221*

The Constitutive and Situational View of Interaction: The
Ethnomethodological Paradigm   225

*Harold Garfinkel, 226; Aaron Cicourel, 228; The
Empiricist and Undialectic Nature of
Ethnomethodology, 230*

Goffman's Analysis of Daily Interaction   234

*The Structuralist Perspective of Frame Analysis, 234;
The Persisting Empiricism of Goffman's Structuralism,
239*

10. THE INTERFACE OF SEMIOTIC STRUCTURALISM AND
MARXISM   243

Structural Causality and the Loss of Subjectivity   244

*Structure and History in Marx and Lévi-Strauss, 245;
Althusser's View of Marxist Dialectic, 248; Lévi-Strauss'
and Althusser's Structural Perspectives, 255; The
Structural Marxism of Maurice Godelier, 260*

The Subjective Interpretation of History: Sartre's Critique
of the Notion of Structural Causality   281

The Production of the Subject by Structure in
Poststructural Semiotics   291

*The Production of the Subject by the Signifying Chain:
Lacan's Perspective, 291; The Infinitive Productivity of
Structure and Subjectivity: Barthes and Derrida, 297;
The Positioning of the Subject in the Signifying Practice:
The Negative Dialectics of Julia Kristeva, 303*

CONCLUSION: TOWARD A DIALECTICAL CONCEPTION OF
STRUCTURE AND SUBJECTIVITY   309

   Continuity of Substantive Concerns: The Central
   Importance of Symbolic Systems in Traditional and
   Semiotic Paradigms   310

   Structural vs. Subjective Explanations of Symbolic
   Systems   311

   Dialectical Approach vs. Multiple Paradigm   312

   On Substantive and Methodological Dialectic   314

   On the Dialectic Between Structure and Speech Event in
   Discourse   315

   Praxis as the Locus of the Dialectic Relationship Between
   Structure and Subjectivity   317

REFERENCES   325

INDEX   339

Introduction

French "structuralism" is a term frequently used in reference to the intellectual movement associated with the works of Claude Lévi-Strauss, Michel Foucault, Jacques Lacan, Roland Barthes, Julia Kristeva, and other structuralists and semioticians as well as Jean Piaget. The same term is also used in connection with the works of Louis Althusser, Maurice Godelier, and other structural Marxists. American sociologists are becoming more and more aware of the interdisciplinary breadth and intellectual ambitions of French structuralism, but they have not produced any serious critical or interpretative monographs on structuralist thinkers. Moreover, some sociologists might be tempted to receive a new book dealing with French structuralism as another futile attempt to keep alive an exotic, highly controversial, and vanishing intellectual fad. Social scientists of the so-called rigorous and scientific persuasion might be especially inclined to consider French structuralism as a quasi-philosophical approach, not worthy of the serious attention of "sound" sociologists.

In the present work I do not intend to offer a "blind faith" recounting of the virtues of what is at times labeled a vanishing French vogue. I do not intend either to offer another repetitious outcry against the misdirected nature of the various criticisms and misinterpretations of French structuralism; the latter point has been abundantly and, in my view, satisfactorily dealt with by Benoist (1978), Lévi-Strauss (1972, 1973, 1976), Marc-Lipiansky (1973), Simonis (1968), and recently by myself (Rossi 1977a, 1978a, 1981). On the contrary, in this volume I intend to lay some ground work for a constructive dialogue between sociologists of traditional orientation and French structuralists. Such an undertaking might seem hardly believable considering the intense and cross-disciplinary debates we have been witnessing during the last forty years between modern structuralists and thinkers of traditional orientation. On the basis of these debates one might hastily conclude that the theoretical differences dividing the two camps are so sharp that it is impossible to have any constructive dialogue between them. Far from sharing such a conclusion, I intend to show why and how modern structuralism[1] can greatly contribute, both at the analytical and the substantive levels, to resolve issues which are still very much at the center of sociologists' concerns.

In this short introduction I shall present the major themes of the book by briefly highlighting the basic assumptions shared by the various forms of modern structuralism and the types of continuities and developments they can generate in sociological thought.

Modern French Structuralism as a Challenge to the Empiricism of Traditional Sociology

One cannot fully comprehend the significance of the current debate surrounding modern structuralism much less determine its real place within the sociological tradition without understanding its intellectual origins and the theoretical and methodological challenges it raises against previous intellectual orientations.

I use the term *modern French structuralism* to distinguish the structuralism of Claude Lévi-Strauss from the classical French structuralism of Emile Durkheim and Marcel Mauss. Both Durkheim and Lévi-Strauss have adopted a systemic and structural perspective and both are positivist thinkers of a sort. I refer here to the early or Comtean positivism, which is based on the following principles: insofar as methodology is concerned, introspection must be rejected and the method of natural sciences must be adopted as the *only* acceptable

---

[1] From now on I will refer to French structuralism as *structuralism* or with the designation of *modern* or *recent* or *recent French structuralism*. I will use also the terms *relational* or *transformational structuralism* to distinguish it from traditional (i.e., presemiotic or empiricist) forms of structuralism, such as structural functionalism, exchange structuralism, and the like. I will explain later on in this introduction the terms *relational* and *transformational structuralism* and their various types, such as the semiotic structuralism of Lévi-Strauss, the genetic structuralism of Piaget, the transformational grammar of Chomsky, and the structural Marxism of Althusser.

scientific method; the purpose of scientific knowledge is to formulate universal and immutable laws or principles of explanation. Both Durkheim and Lévi-Strauss share these assumptions, and in this sense Lévi-Strauss is a positivist also. However, Comte made two additional assumptions derived from empiricism: firstly, he maintained that the function of science is simply to describe "how" things are and not why they are the way they are; secondly, Comte asserted that empirical knowledge is the only valid source of knowledge. Empirical knowledge in the Comtean sense of the term entails a twofold canon: "the highest form of knowledge is simple description of sensory experience" (Beck 1969:267) and scientific laws must be verified by the facts of experience. Most sociologists will not find it difficult to understand these notions and to see they are at the core not only of Durkheimian sociology but also of much of the so-called scientific sociology.

Claude Lévi-Strauss, the anthropologist who has for the first time systematically and extensively applied the method of modern structuralism in the social sciences, resolutely rejects the empiricist assumptions of Comtean and Durkheimian postivism to preserve the specificity of the human sciences. I have dealt extensively with this issue during the last decade (Rossi 1974), also in debate with staunch empiricists (Rossi 1977, 1978a). I shall deal systematically with the structuralist position in the second part of this volume. However, for the benefit of the uninitiated reader and to enhance the intelligibility of the argument of part 1, I will now clarify the terms of the confrontation between empiricism and modern French structuralism.

In a relatively recent collection of his own essays, Lévi-Strauss felt the need to prepare a short preface especially for the English-language reader. In an obvious reference to Popper's neopositivism, Lévi-Strauss stated that "the criterion of falsifiability" can only be applied to fully established sciences (1976:viii), whereas human sciences have not yet reached that stage of maturity. Moreover "we may even wonder if this criterion of *falsifiability* can truly be applied to human sciences; . . . the subject of the human science is man. . . . [W]hat is interesting in man is not subject to scientific decision but results and always will result from a choice which is ultimately of a philosophical order" (p. ix). With that statement Lévi-Strauss seems to refer to the "nonscientifically determinable" level of interpretation he has chosen. He has selected to study not what is experimentally verifiable, and hence what is observable through sensory observation, but the logic underlying observable facts: "Structuralists uncover a unity and a coherence within things which could not be revealed by a simple description of the facts somehow scattered and disorganized before the eyes of knowledge" (p. ix). As we can see, Lévi-Strauss rejects the first assumption of Comtean positivism.

Structuralism deals with facts "more economically with a very small number of principles, axioms and rules, which in a variety of domains, have proved their fecundity" (1976: ix). Lévi-Strauss is referring here to "classificatory" principles of social life à la Durkheim and Mauss (1963a) and to the "grammatical" rules of social life. The crux of the issue is that classificatory principles and grammatical rules are far from being synonymous with statistical averages or regularities of observable events (see Rossi 1977, 1978a). They are rather the result of "interpretation" or "understanding", as Lévi-Strauss notes, rather than empiricist induction. Hence, logical or ordering principles or grammatical rules are not directly verifiable through empirical observations or by "simple description of the facts," to use Lévi-Strauss' words. An interpretative explanation can be "disproved," so to speak, by showing that an alternative interpretation offers greater intelligibility to a set of data or can subsume the set under a larger system (Ardener 1971). (On the issue of verification in structural analysis, see Rossi 1973a). The same principle applies to Weber's "ideal typical" explanation, to the phenomenological analysis of conscious experience as well as to the ethnomethodologists' usage of the notion of interpretive rules. (We shall see that even phenomenological sociologists and ethnomethodologists reject the empiricist orientation.)

At this point, the reader might be tempted to formulate in his or her own mind either one or both of the following conclusions: the argument set forth so far implies that there is an empiricist and a nonempiricist side to Durkheim's positivism—one might wonder how this sort of theoretical distinction is pertinent to the proper domain of sociology. Moreover, one might harbor the suspicion that modern structuralism is some sort of phenomenological analysis; hence, what is so new and interesting about it? The first tentative conclusion is correct, but in my opinion it is of crucial importance to determine what is the most effective level of sociological theorizing. The second tentative conclusion is far from the truth because modern French structuralists propose their approach as an alternative to the empiricism of the functional as well as phenomenological orientations.

From what I have said so far, there are two central questions that need to be answered in this introduction: firstly, precisely what do the empiricism of Durkheim, phenomenology, and other traditional schools of sociology consist of (and how is this issue relevant in assessing the adequacy of sociological theorizing)? Secondly, what is the precise nature of the alternative presented by modern French structuralism (and how is it relevant to the development of sociological theory)?

The Empiricism of Traditional Schools of Sociology

Empiricism is the most frequent villain I shall refer to throughout this book; it is a term used in different and often confused ways. To begin with, empiricism is not synonymous with empirical knowledge but is only a particular way to conceive of empirical knowledge. I certainly agree that social sciences do have an empirical foundation in the sense that sociological data are not productions or projections of the sociologist's mind. I foresee some sociologists coming to my aid and rephrasing my statement more precisely as follows: "Sociologists do deal with data external to and independent of the sociologist's mind." My reply is yes and no; it is true the social world exists independent of the sociologist's mind but it does not become a sociological datum independent of the mental activities of the sociologist. Is this a Lapalissean statement or does it contain a profound or arcane meaning? We are already at the crux of the controversy between empiricists and modern structuralists. This controversy has to do with what Parsons has called "the relation of a knowing subject to an object known. The classical statement of this was of course made by Descartes" (Parsons 1978:368). Parsons is correct to find in the Cartesian dichotomy much of the source of the poorly construed and confused thinking on the nature of sociological knowledge.

Parsons clearly states the two basic positions of Western episte-mology:

The great controversy in Western epistemology has been over the question of what contributes, and how, to knowledge of the *external world*, as Des-cartes called it. Empiricists, usually using such phrases as *sense impressions*, have stressed the contribution from outside the knowing subject; some, like Hume, have denied the existence of any other component. Kant, however, insisted that there is another contribution, from the *categories of under-standing*, which have to be conceived as combining with sense data. The Kantian formula for empirical knowledge thus meets the formal requirement of a *two-way* relationship, symbolic or otherwise, between subject and object. (1978:368)

We shall see that Parsons' expression "symbolic or otherwise" be-trays a dichotomous and undialectical perspective, which leads him to an impasse. Suffice it here to say that Parsons goes on to reject the empiricist position and endorse the Kantian one.

But as there are various forms of philosophical empiricism, so there are various forms and degrees of sociological empiricism.[2] One is what Parsons has labeled radical realism (1961:588), a position which holds that theory is or must be a total reflection of reality: "concrete reality [is] reflected in the conceptual scheme, adequately for all scientific purposes" (p. 476). Parsons is correct in rejecting this position for implying the "fallacy of misplaced concreteness" (p. 589).

In my view, Parsons' own analytical realism is another form of un-acceptable empiricism, although a milder one. Analytical realism is a particular strategy to build sociological theory through a "generalized system of concepts" abstracted from reality. Parsons describes these concepts as follows: "At least some of the general concepts of science are not fictional but adequately *grasp* aspects of the objective exter-nal world. . . . These concepts correspond, not to concrete phenom-ena, but to elements in them which are *analytically* separable from other elements. There is no implication that the value of any such element . . . is completely descriptive of any particular concrete thing or event" (1961:730).

---

[2] I am not interested here with the rightful castigation of abstracted empiricism by C. W. Mills, since this notion is not based on the kind of epistemological considera-tions I am pursuing.

Why is this Parsonian conception to be considered a form of empiricism? First of all, because it is based on the concept-reality and knowing subject-known object dichotomies; secondly, because the underlying assumption is that scientific activity should be selectively X modeled after external reality. The task of the sociologist is reduced to selecting one aspect or another of the reality external to him or her. This means that Parsons did not really avoid, as he claimed, what he defined as the positivist position—namely, the belief that "only empirical science is a source of valid understanding" (1978:354). Since Parsons never abandoned analytical realism, we ought to conclude that he remained an empiricist (the way I define the term) throughout his scientific career. Should we, then, consider his professed Kantianism as a last-minute programmatic statement that was never quite systematically integrated in his overall position? We will come back to Parsons' thought in more detail later on.

At least the milder form of empiricism is inherent in Durkheim's positivism as well as in functional, behavioral, and operational sociologies. All these sociological orientations (which we shall see come under the natural science paradigm) maintain that sociological concepts and theories must be verified through their correspondence to the external world, which means that the term of correspondence is external to the knowing subject. In this sense I describe all these sociological orientations as many forms of objective empiricism. By contrast, I consider as many forms of subjective empiricism the interpretive sociologies of Max Weber, symbolic interactionists, sociological phenomenologists, and ethnomethodologists. I use this term because in this case the term of correspondence is subjective meaning, or intentionality, or the interpretive rules of social actors.

Some sociologists will find it objectionable to use the label of empiricism for phenomenological sociology and ethnomethodology. In fact, ethnomethodologists aim at formulating people's "rational methods and strategies," which *underlie* observable interaction and common sense meanings. My objectors can continue their protest by reminding me that the ethnomethodological posture has derived precisely from phenomenologists' rejection of the naturalist attitude,—that is, the attitude of taking for granted social reality as it is presented in sensory experience and common sense understanding.

As we shall discuss in part 3 of this volume, phenomenologists practice an *époché* or phenomenological suspension, which consists of
"bracketing" ordinary experience, or disconnecting our attention from
it, to prevent it from interfering with a genuine understanding of the
real core of subjective experience. Such a genuine understanding is
obtained through the mental operation of introducing all possible
variations of experience and ascertaining what aspects of experience
can be eliminated (contingencies) without destroying it. The invariant
element we are left with is called the essence of primordial experience. Notwithstanding the various interpretations of the Husserlian
époché introduced by A. Schutz, M. Natanson, T. Luckman, E. Tiryakian, J. Douglas, and other phenomenological sociologists, all of them
accept the principle that we must refrain from accepting ordinary
experience at its face value.

"What more antiempiricist attitude would one want?" my objectors
might ask. My reply is that phenomenologists find the locus (and
hence the source) of genuine meaning within consciousness and intentionality. For Husserl, objects are meaningful precisely because they
are "meant" by consciousness, and phenomenological suspension is
used precisely to reach the genuine core of consciousness. Analogous remarks are valid for ethnomethodology; here the aim is to reach
the genuine interpretive processes underlying ordinary interaction;
therefore, interacting subjectivities remain the vantage point of analysis. This is the reason why I consider phenomenology and ethnomethodology to be "refined" forms of subjective empiricism—they
still remain within the realm of subjective experience and subjectively constructed meaning.

When, in the third part of the volume, we deal with the phenomenological method, we will see that it is only apparently similar to
the structuralist method of Lévi-Strauss. However, Lévi-Strauss' aim
is to ascertain the "unconscious categories" which, in his opinion,
Mauss himself had already found to be the determinants "in magic,
religion, and linguistics" (Lévi-Strauss 1976:7). According to Lévi-
Strauss, the task of finding unconscious categories amounts to finding invariants underneath experiential data. This is shown by replac-
ing experiential data with models upon which we can perform experiments (pp. 15, 25)—intellectual experiments, that is. All this sounds

strikingly similar to the phenomenological method of variation. However, the purpose of the structural experiment is to discover the unconscious structure of a set of experiential data: "An arrangement is structured which meets but two conditions: that it be a system ruled by an internal cohesiveness and that this cohesiveness, unaccessible to observation in an isolated system, be revealed in the study of *transformations* through which similar properties are recognized in apparently different systems" (p. 18); the apparent level is, of course, the empirical level of analysis. Lévi-Strauss argues that Mauss anticipated this line of reasoning with the notion of the totality of social phenomena; those social phenomena are total that are simultaneously juridical, economic, religious, and aesthetic. Lévi-Strauss interprets this notion to mean that the "totality resides in the network of functional *interrelations* among all these planes" (p. 6).

Lévi-Strauss is dealing here with a mathematical, hence metaempirical, level of analysis. In a famous essay, in which he took issue with structural functionalism and other empiricist social scientists, he argued that social structure cannot be found in the observable patterns of interaction because observable (and conscious) phenomena all too often appear to be heterogenous and contradictory. The famous example that Lévi-Strauss gives is that of a jigsaw puzzle. The structure of the jigsaw puzzle "lies not at the empirical level" but "in the mathematical formula expressing the shape of the cams and their speed of rotation" (1976:79), which produced the apparently confusing set of pieces.

It is obvious that we cannot reach the mathematical or logical structure of things by merely 'registering,' external observations but only through intellectual and mathematical operations that Lévi-Strauss calls transformations. Then how is the relationship between theoretical explanation and observable reality to be understood?

The Theoretical Perspective of Modern French Structuralism

Not only Claude Lévi-Strauss, but also Jean Piaget and Noam Chomsky concur in rejecting the empiricist conception of scientific knowledge. Piaget, who has produced classical treatises on structural (genetic) epistemology, explains well why the empiricist theory of knowledge is unacceptable. Empiricism views knowledge "as a copy, a passive copy, of reality" (Piaget 1970a:15). Such a position involves a contradiction. In fact, Piaget argues, to copy something you need to know the model of what you copy; but according to the empiricists we cannot obtain our model except by copying it and so we are caught in a vicious circle. Piaget is not an idealist and admits the importance of "knowledge based on experience in general"; such knowledge he calls *physical knowledge*. He concedes that the knowledge of the physical world comes through abstraction from the objects themselves; in this case the claim of empiricism is valid. However, logical and mathematical knowledge derives not from objects but from our activities (operations) on them. For instance, the property of commutativity is not derived by simple abstraction from the objects but through the activity of arranging and rearranging objects; that is, through *reflective abstraction*. The mental process of reflection entails a reorganization of thought, which occurs through a coordination of actions—additive coordination, sequential or ordinal coordination, and so on (Piaget 1970a:15–19).

For this reason Piaget's genetic epistemology rejects both the empiricist and the a prioristic conceptions of knowledge. According to the empiricists, knowledge consists of discovering what was already existing in external reality; therefore, knowledge doesn't produce a new reality. According to nativists (or a priorists), knowledge is already predetermined within the individual and, therefore, no real novelty is attained either. On the contrary, Piaget holds that knowledge produces "inventions," since knowledge is the result of a continuous construction (1970a:77).

At this point we detect an explicit parallelism between Lévi-Strauss and Piaget. Piaget states that what is being constructed is not the content of objects, of course, but models which enable us to make sense of experience. "Knowing reality means constructing systems of transformations that correspond, more or less adequately, to reality. They are more or less isomorphic to transformations of reality. The transformational structures of which knowledge consists are not copies of the transformations in reality; they are simply possible isomorphic models among which experience can enable us to choose.

Knowledge, then, is a system of *transformations* that become progressively adequate" (1970a:15).

We will discuss Piaget's position more extensively in part 2. What I have said so far is sufficient to understand why the structuralist view of knowledge is based not on the interaction but on the inseparability of the known object and the knowing subject. The very notion of knowledge could not be conceived of without the presence of both terms. I have purposely used the term "inseparability" rather than "interaction." The latter is the term used by Parsons, who, we remember, states his opposition to empiricism and adopts the Kantian view that empirical knowledge entails a "two-way relationship between subject and object" (Parsons 1978:368). It is obvious that this formulation implies the dichotomy of independently constituted subject and object. Parsons states that Kant postulated "categories of understanding" which are "transcendental" to empirical knowledge and without which empirical knowledge could not be interpreted. For Parsons "the human actor can come to understand the necessity and role of such categories but he does not determine them. They come to human knowledge from *outside*, in a sense parallel to that in which sense data come from the *external world*" (p. 370). The distinction between the empirical and transcendental component of knowledge betrays the root of Parsons' unresolvable ambivalence between the empirical and abstract modes of theorizing in sociology. We shall see in part 3 that precisely because of the basic "mind-reality" dichotomy Parsons cannot produce a criterion to find the "fit" between the level of empirical generalizations and abstract formulations.

Does modern structuralism provide a way out of this dilemma? Let us follow for a moment the argument of Claude Lévi-Strauss, the thinker I have been involved with for more than ten years and the one whose point of view is the most frequently referred to throughout this volume: "When confronted with a given ecological and techno-economic situation [here Lévi-Strauss is referring to ecological anthropologists of empiricist orientation], the mind does not stay inactive. It does not merely reflect it, it reacts to it and works it out into a system" (1972:10). Again, Lévi-Strauss and Piaget seem to echo each other. We remember that both thinkers conceive of knowledge in terms of "transformations." Lévi-Strauss elaborates that "the mind does not react only to the particular environment which it perceives through the senses"; it reacts as well to environments which are not experienced in a direct way and also considers how other people react to them: "All these environments, both present and absent, are integrated into an ideological system according to mental laws which recur over and over again and manifest themselves in similar ways, although the geographical surroundings and the techno-economic practices may be widely different" (p. 10). For Lévi-Strauss the central task of the social sciences is to map out these laws of the mind as well as the "inner logic" of ecological changes (p. 12). However, it is not sufficient to take into account both types of constraints—ecological and mental—or to show by concrete examples how they "interlock with each other." To begin with, such an outcome would be impossible if mind and ecology were considered "mutually irreducible entities." "Any attempt to set up the mind and the world as separate entities would bring us back to metaphysics" (*ibid.*) and to a "philosophical dualism" which cannot be bridged.

Lévi-Strauss overcomes the dualism by linking mental constraints to human anatomy and physiology. He draws at some length from the natural, linguistic, and psychological sciences to argue that sensory and intellectual apparatus work not by copying or photographing reality but structurally. For instance, "the eye does not merely photograph the outside world. It rather encodes its formal characteristics. These characteristics consist less in the sensuous qualities of things than in the relationships which prevail between them." This kind of structural analysis goes on in the cells of the retina, the ganglion, or the brain. The cells work by responding to "oppositional" stimuli, such as presence or absence of color, motion, light, or such oppositional dimensions as straight-oblique, left-right, horizontal-vertical, and so on: "Out of this roster of information which becomes remarkably well registered in the brain, the mind rebuilds, so to speak, objects which were never actually perceived as such" (1972:13).

We now understand why knowledge does not consist of copying reality but of reconstructing it; we understand also why Lévi-Strauss states that "the raw material of sensory perception . . . properly speaking does not exist, but [only] abstractions of reality" (1972:13). Moreover, "there is every reason to believe that this encoding and decoding process, which translates incoming data from outside by help of several binary codes enfolded in the nervous system, also exists in man." In the last volume of *Mythologiques*, Lévi-Strauss reviews many empirical studies to back up such a claim. I have myself extensively searched through physiological, neurological, linguistic, ✕ and psychological sources to sound out the scientific basis of Lévi-Strauss' claim, and found a lot of evidence for it (Rossi 1978, 1982a). Suffice it here to quote a leading American neurologist who declares that contemporary neurological research supports the structuralist and not the empiricist perspective: "The neurological findings thus lend biological support for the structuralist dogma that explanations of behavior must be formulated in terms of such deeper programs and reveal the wrong-headedness of the positivistic approach which rejects the postulation of covert internal programs as mentalism" (Stent 1975:1055–1056; for more on this see Rossi 1982a).

What inference does Lévi-Strauss draw from this? After reviewing Berlin and Kay's work on basic color terms, Lévi-Strauss concludes that these terms are governed "by logical properties rather than physical ones, since these can be defined as either present or lacking, and thus expressed by help of a simple system of binary oppositions. Here too a simple logical structure underlies and antedates the subsequent complexities of sensory perception" (1972:14). Lévi-Strauss goes on, stating that "both the natural and the human sciences concur to dismiss an outmoded philosophical dualism. Ideal and real, abstract and concrete . . . can no longer be opposed to each other. What is immediately given to us is neither the one nor the other, but something which lies betwixt and between, that is already encoded by the sense organs as well as by the brain, a text which, like any text, must be first decoded to translate it into the language of other texts."

It is here that the constructivist character of knowledge comes in. For Lévi-Strauss the "original text is primitively encoded" by physiochemical processes and later on it is decoded by the mind with analytical procedures which are "not substantially different." In fact, "understanding takes over and develops intellectual processes already operating in the sensory organs themselves. . . . Structural analysis can only take shape in the mind because its model already exists in the body." Lévi-Strauss claims that this kind of materialism reconciles "soul and body, mind and ecology, thought and world" because "the mind, when trying to understand [the world], only applies operations which do not differ in the end from those going on in the natural world itself" (1972:14).

One might find Lévi-Strauss' position a bit simplistic and, perhaps, naïve in its philosophical underpinning, but it has important consequences for a fruitful conception of sociological theorizing. The principle of isomorphic structural mechanisms avoids both Hegelian and Cartesian dualism by recovering the unity of mind and body and eliminating "the long lasting divorce between intelligibility and sensibility that an outmoded empiricism and mechanism have forced upon us." For the same reason, Lévi-Strauss continues, "reality can be meaningful not only on the abstract plane of scientific knowledge but also on the plane of sensory perception" (1972:4).[3] How important it is for sociology to overcome these old-fashioned dichotomies becomes immediately evident upon reading the founding father of the so-called scientific sociology: "We must consider social phenomena in themselves as distinct from the consciously formed representations of them in the mind; we must study them objectively as external things, for it is this character that they represent to us. If this exteriority should prove to be only apparent, the advance of science will bring the disillusionment and we shall see our conception of social phenomena change, as it were, from the objective to the subjective" (Durkheim 1964:28). The mind-external world, subjective-objective duality is expressed here in its full force.

Durkheim is himself aware of the problem inherent in his position: "It will be said that, in defining phenomena by their apparent characteristics, we are allowing to certain superficial properties a significance greater than that of more fundamental attributes" (1964:42). This difficulty is real, Durkheim concedes, "if these external characteristics were at the same time accidental, that is, if they were not bound up with the fundamental properties of things. Under these condi-

[3] The interested reader will find a more systematic discussion of these ideas by Lévi-Strauss himself in the "Finale" of the last volume of *Mythologiques* (Lévi-Strauss 1971).

tions indeed, after science has pointed them out, it could not possibly go farther; it could not penetrate the deeper surface and essence" (p. 43). The problem is well stated, but the solution he proposes is not convincing. Durkheim seems to argue that if certain characteristics are found identical and always in all phenomena, they must not be accidental. But once you have posited a dichotomy of "external vs. mental characteristics," "surface appearance vs. essence," there is no satisfactory way to overcome it; precisely this realization prompts Lévi-Strauss' argument.

Durkheim's own distinction between surface and essence of things does not seem to square with his positivist methodology. I will show in the first part of this volume that Durkheim actually remained ambivalent, at least in the latter part of his career, between a positivist and a symbolic (and perhaps presemiotic) orientation. I here briefly anticipate this issue by commenting on just two passages of *The Rules of Sociological Method.* Durkheim recognizes that social phenomena are also "mental after a fashion since they all consist of ways of thinking or behavior" (1964:xviii). However, he feels constrained by the demand of the positivist methodology: "If sociological phenomena are only systems of objectivized ideas, to explain them is to rethink them in their logical order, and this explanation is in itself its own proof. . . . Only methodical experiments, on the contrary, can extract from things their real secrets" (p. 144). Durkheim does not leave any doubt about what he means by methodical experiment: "Our method is objective. It is dominated entirely by the idea that social facts are things and must be treated as such. No doubt, this principle is found again, under a slightly different form, at the basis of the doctrines of Comte and Spencer" (p. 143).

As we have seen, the Comtean method demands experimental verification, and Durkheim states: "Not only the explanations thus given differ from the preceding ones [the nonsociological ones], but they are differently verified, or, rather, it is only with them that the need of verification is felt" (p. 144). Durkheim seems to reason as follows: since logical analysis does not lend itself to experimental verification, we must consider the "ideational" component of social facts as nonessential. Hence, we must consider the (recurring) external and observable characteristics of social facts as their essential characteristics. This is a clear example of how a preconceived methodological position can determine the very definition and selection of the subject matter studied. As I have mentioned, we will examine later on all the dimensions of Durkheim's positivistic mind-world, mental-external characteristics dichotomy and his ambivalence between positivist and symbolic orientations.

In the light of such impasse, the unique contribution of semiotic structuralism comes forward in its full strength. Semiotic structuralism sees in the ideational element the core component of social facts, and it accounts for observable behavior and other external characteristics (to use the improper language of Durkheim) on the basis of the logical structure of phenomena, which is the essence of things, in Durkheim's language, or their deep structure, in semiotic terms; the two analytical dimensions are not opposed but are linked by transformational rules. (For a discussion of this point, see Parsons' essay in Rossi 1982 and my analysis of Piaget and Parsons' position in this volume.)

The Durkheimian position, however, is not the only epistemological posture adopted in traditional sociology, that is, before the advent of modern structuralism. We have mentioned that Parsons has stated his intention of overcoming the empiricist position (of which Durkheim's positivism is just one form) by endorsing the Kantian approach to knowledge. For Kant, scientific knowledge comes from two sources: from "sense impressions" outside the knowing subject and from a priori "categories of understanding" (Parsons 1978:368). Parsons, however, does not avoid the trap of dichotomous thinking: in fact, following Kant he holds that the categories of understanding are "transcendental" in the sense that the knowing subject does not determine them: "they come to human knowledge from outside, in a sense parallel to that in which sense data come from the external world. Thus, the human actor is a kind of middle man, the combiner" (p. 370).

A twofold duality is present in this statement: the duality between the knowing subject and the two sources of knowledge (empirical and transcendental) and that between the transcendental and empirical sources of knowledge. How can Parsons guarantee that people make a right combination of the two sources? We will see later on in part 3 that Parsons accepts the dichotomy between empirical and abstract sociological theorizing and cannot satisfactorily reconcile the two or choose between them. Such a dichotomy is rooted precisely in the empirical vs. transcendental source of knowledge, which Parsons accepts as the basis of his own framework.

In the light of these issues that I have so far briefly touched upon, we can see the verisimility of Lévi-Strauss' statement that the starting point of his approach was the realization of the shortcoming of both naïve objectivism and phenomenology (Lévi-Strauss 1965:61). We can now add that modern structuralism permits us to overcome not only empiricism in its objective and subjective form but also Kantianism (and Kantian thought has also influenced Durkheim and, as we will see, Max Weber, among other classical sociologists).

What are the sources of modern structural thought—a form of thought which claims to overcome empiricism and nativism (to use Piaget's terminology), the two forms of thought which have so heavily pervaded philosophical and scientific thought for centuries?

Intellectual Origins of Modern French Structuralism

The structuralist challenge against empiricism has emerged not all of a sudden nor through the efforts of one or a few isolated thinkers, but gradually and through the efforts of convergent trends in philosophy, mathematics, linguistics, psychology, and neurophysiology. Elsewhere I have discussed the linguistic, philosophical, psychological, and cybernetic antecedents of Lévi-Strauss' structuralism (Rossi 1973). Here I intend to briefly consider certain trends in philosophical and mathematical thought which directly or indirectly have prepared the way for the structural perspective in all its varieties. I will focus my attention, first of all, on the structuralist conception of scientific explanation and then on structuralism as a strategy of analysis.

Within the discipline of philosophy, the German positivism of the late nineteenth century began a reaction against the dichotomy posited by earlier positivists between the observer and the observed facts. We have seen that early positivists, like Comte, had claimed that science must be based on *facts* and that facts must be determined on the basis of the external or observable characteristics of the world, independent of the mental apparatus of the scientist. One can easily recognize in this position Durkheim's conception of the sociological method. In reaction to this early positivist thinking, E. Mach pointed out in the late nineteenth century that facts are derived from sensory impressions (and therefore from the mind) and that facts are nothing but theories to which we are accustomed. Poincaré has further elaborated this constructive notion of science by stressing that our impressions depend on sociolinguistic conventions, a notion which has greatly influenced French positivist sociology. Poincaré has shown that knowledge consists of determining relationships between sensations, "relationships having an objective" value. Carnap has continued the tradition of those who advocate the constructive notion of knowledge by putting forward the argument that knowledge does not consist of the activity of abstracting concepts from substances but of the description of the properties of objects and of the relationships between objects; these relationships can be transformed according to constructional rules. Accordingly, any type of scientific knowledge consists of formal and structural descriptions, i.e., in the explication of relationships among relations.

Similar relational and structural trends have emerged among philosophers of mathematical knowledge. In Cartesian thought, mathematical notions were understood to derive from abstractions and to reflect substantive properties of the physical world. For Leibniz, on the contrary, knowledge consisted not of abstracting ideas from reality external to the mind, but in determining relationships between ideas; mathematical ideas are conceived to be not reflections or approximations of external objects, but systems of operations. Cassirer also opposed the substantive conception of knowledge and emphasized the priority of functional relationships. According to him, the notions of time and space and mathematical operations are based on operations which are guided not by the characteristics of external objects but by intellectual criteria.

Gestalt psychologists reached similar conclusions when they stated that psychic operations consist of a series of transformations whereby the parts lose their absolute position while remaining in constant relationship to one another. A lengthier discussion of these and related movements can be found in Riegel and Rosenwald (1975), Robey (1973), and Piaget (1950, 1967, 1970).

However, relational thinking, or the priority given to relations among terms rather than to terms, could have not made an impact in the social sciences without the formulation of methodological or analytical tools that have permitted the application of the structural perspective in the analysis of social phenomena.

The operational formulation of relational thinking has materialized with the advent of the Bourbaki school of mathematics and structural linguistics. The Bourbaki school of mathematics has demonstrated that through the methods of combination and differentiation a large number of mathematical structures can be derived from three parent structures (see Piaget 1970:23ff). Way back in the 1940s Lévi-Strauss had asked the mathematician A. Weil to work out an algebraic interpretation of marriage systems (Lévi-Strauss 1969: ch. 14); ever since, Lévi-Strauss has remained faithful to the practice, or at least the spirit (1969a), of the mathematical approach, especially of qualitative mathematics (1971).

Ferdinand de Saussure has revolutionized linguistics by proposing a structural theory of language and by suggesting a science of signs or semiology, an approach applied by Lévi-Strauss in the analysis of cultural systems. As we will see in part 2 of this volume, Lévi-Strauss has borrowed from Saussure not only the semiological conceptualization of culture, but also the paradigmatic and syntagmatic strategies of analysis; he has also adopted some elements of the phonological method as proposed by the Prague school of linguistics. This is the reason why Lévi-Strauss' structuralism is called semiotic structuralism, i.e. a linguistically based form of structuralism. We will see later on that linguistic strategies of analysis also are fundamental in post-Lévi-Straussian semiotics and that mathematical ideas also are important in nonsemiotic forms of relational structuralism.

Varieties of Relational Structuralism and the Continuity of the Sociological Tradition

The philosophical, psychological, mathematical, and linguistic perspectives so far examined concur in the following fundamental notion: the proper object of scientific analysis cannot be the elements or parts of a totality considered separately from one another, but rather the relational constants among the parts, that is, the relationships which are always present in any one of the possible combinations of the parts; the observable phenomena are considered to be a few realizations out of a large number of possible ones. This relational perspective is a central aspect of the mathematical notion of *group*, which plays an important role not only in the semiotic structuralism of Lévi-Strauss but also in the genetic structuralism of Piaget and the transformational grammar of Chomsky. Far from representing identical theoretical positions, these three thinkers belong to different intellectual traditions and study different subject matter. However, they all agree to the notion that the proper object of scientific analysis is not social structures as they are immediately observable, but the underlying system of mathematical transformations that govern the realization of the actualized as well as other possible structures. Lévi-Strauss, Piaget, and Chomsky also share a cybernetic perspective and an interest in building a formal science aimed at codifying the constitutive (transformational) rules of empirical structures.

Such a relational and formal approach is in sharp contrast with the attitude of social scientists of traditional orientation, who are concerned with the description and explanation of observable patterns of interaction or the subjective meaning of social action. Hence T. Bottomore and R. Nisbet are correct in stating that the antiempiricist, antihumanist, and antihistorical perspectives make of recent structuralism "a distinctive type of sociological analysis" (1978:591ff). Relational structuralism is antihumanist because it does not consider the conscious or subjective meaning at its face value as a reliable or scientific object of analysis. Structuralism is antihistorical in that it gives analytic priority to synchronic over diachronic explanation. I will discuss these issues more extensively in the last part of the volume.

The antiempiricist, antihumanist, and antihistorical perspective is shared also by Maurice Godelier, whose structural Marxism has emerged under the direct influence of Lévi-Strauss and has certain affinities with the thought of Louis Althusser and Michel Foucault.

Roland Barthes, Julia Kristeva, and Jacques Derrida, who have criticized certain aspects of Ferdinand de Saussure and Lévi-Strauss, also adopt an antiempiricist, antihumanist and antihistorical perspective. The convergence of this threefold perspective is the guiding criterion for including under my definition of relational structuralism such diversified thinkers as Saussure, Lévi-Strauss, Piaget, Chomsky, Godelier, Althusser, Jacques Lacan, Kristeva, Barthes, and others inspired by their work. It must be clear, however, that I deal with these authors only to the extent that they share the threefold orientation just mentioned without considering the other similarities and the great many differences which exist among them.

The question we must raise now is the following: can relational structuralism be relevant to sociology when sociology has been largely dominated by the empiricist perspective and when relational structuralism has emerged in opposition to empiricism? I have already stated that relational structuralism can make important contributions in sociology both at a substantive and analytical level. My contention is based on the following considerations: 1) relational structuralism can reestablish the study of symbolic systems at the core of sociological analysis where once it belonged; 2) relational structuralism can show that symbolism plays a much more fundamental role in the structure and dynamics of the social system than previously shown by classical sociologists; 3) relational structuralism can fill gaps existing in the sociological study of symbolism by extending the range of substantive issues to be studied and by offering new analytical tools. I briefly illustrate these points to give an indication of the scope and themes of this volume.

First, the important social functions attributed to Marx's ideology, Durkheim's collective representations, and Weber's ideas clearly demonstrate how central was the study of symbolic systems in the classical sociological tradition. Max Weber has combined the macrosociological and comparative study of symbolic and religious systems with a microsociological perspective; this is particularly evident in his analysis of the cultural significance of historical periods and civilizational developments in terms of the types of "subjective meaning" attributable to typical actors (1964:120). The microsociological concern with subjective meaning is central also in the symbolic interactionism of George H. Mead and in the notions of "sympathetic understanding" of Charles H. Cooley, the "humanistic coefficient" of Florian Znaniecki, and "the definition of the situation" of William I. Thomas as well as in ethnomethodology and phenomenological sociology.

Strongly influenced by Max Weber and phenomenology, Karl Mannheim is another sociologist who has combined the macrosociological with the microsociological study of culture. Mannheim deserves credit for having refused to separate the study of social structure from the study of culture. He maintained that the processes of social interaction and group formation cannot be understood apart from the study of meaning that provides bonds or divisions among people; that branch of sociology which studies meaning is called by Mannheim the "sociology of mind" or "cultural sociology."

The cultural system has been located by Talcott Parsons at the highest level of the cybernetic hierarchy of control of the four subsystems of action—the cultural system, the social system, the personality system, and the organismic system. Parsons has continued the sociological tradition of Weber in that he has contributed to both the macrosociological and comparative study of symbolic systems as well as to the microsociological analysis of the subjective meaning attributed to typical actors in specific situations.

The great importance given by classical sociologists to symbols, meaning, and systems of meanings is in sharp contrast to the relatively marginal attention given to them by much of the contemporary sociological literature, with the notable exceptions of Parsonian, Marxist, and interpretative sociologists. The decreased interest in meaning and systems of meanings has been paralleled by a relative decline of historical and comparative macrosociology and an increased emphasis on exact measurement and microsociological analysis. Relational structuralists can reestablish the study of symbolism at the center of sociological analysis because they conceptualize all domains of social life as systems of communication consisting of signs. As we shall see in part 2, all the efforts of relational structuralists are aimed at mapping out the logic of communication systems.

As to the second point, I contend that with relational structuralism the study of symbolism assumes a much more central role than in classical sociology because the notion that relational constants (logical structures) make possible a great variety of possible combinations of signs is applicable to all domains of social life and introduces intelligibility where previously there appeared to be heterogeneity and discrepancies. As I will explain in the second part of the volume, according to relational structuralists a given set of data is fully explained only when both its social grammar and its relationship of transformation with interrelated sets of data are determined.

Third, I maintain that relational structuralism can help us to see various analytical gaps existing within traditional paradigms, gaps which are connected with or produced by the empiricist perspective. Let us briefly examine how fundamental has been the influence of the empiricist perspective on the classical sociology of symbolism by considering the concepts of *symbol, meaning,* and *culture*. The centrality and interrelatedness of these three concepts in the classical perspective is clearly indicated in Clifford Gertz's definition of culture. "Culture denotes an historically transmitted pattern of meaning embodied in symbols, a system of inherited conceptions expressed in symbolic forms by means of which men communicate, perpetuate, and develop their knowledge about and attitudes toward life" (1966:3). This definition is consistent with the distinction between cultural and social systems made by Sorokin, Kroeber, and Parsons, a distinction which has been recently reinstated by Parsons as follows: "By contrast with the cultural system, which is specifically concerned with systems of meaning, the social system is a way of organizing human action which is concerned with linking meaning to the conditions of concrete behavior in the environmentally given world" (1973:36). Geertz asserts that "cultural patterns are *models*, sets of symbols whose relations on one another model relations among entities." Symbols are models *of* and models *for* reality because "they give meaning, i.e., objective conceptual form, to social and psychological reality both by shaping themselves to it and by shaping it to themselves" (1966:7–8). By structuring, that is, giving meaning to reality, symbols make reality understandable and provide guidelines and sources of motivation for social action.

In traditional sociological paradigms, "meaning" is understood as the set of conceptual and emotional, conscious and unconscious associations aroused in individuals by ideological, religious, and other cultural elements in the course of social interaction. When we consider these associations as components of the individual's orientation toward social action, we deal with meaning from a microsociological perspective; this is the case of Weber, symbolic interactionists, phenomenologists, and ethnomethodologists. When we consider collective representations or ideologies as forces affecting the structure and dynamics of groups, collectivities, and total societies, we deal with systems of meaning from a macrosociological perspective; this is the case of Marx and Durkheim. The empiricist perspective of the traditional microsociological and macrosociological perspective consists of the following three points: meaning refers to the cognitive and affective content of cultural items; this content must be directly accessible through external or internal experience; any datum of experience can be analyzed and understood in and by itself, independent of other experiential data.

As we have seen, relational structuralists have replaced such an empiricist notion of scientific data with the notion of systems of transformations governing the combinations of the constitutive elements of empirical data. Briefly stated, the gist of the structural approach à la Lévi-Strauss consists of the following methodological principles: 1) observable data have to be broken down into elementary components; 2) these components are organized into relationships of oppositions or differences so that their positional (objective) meaning can be determined; 3) through the mental experiment of variations we establish the constant relationships (relational invariants) among the basic elements; these relational invariants constitute the unconscious system (or the systemic tendencies) of a given set of empirical phenomena; 4) we formulate the combinatory or transformational principles through which the relational constants can produce an indefinite number of empirical phenomena; the concrete set of data being studied are interpreted in the light of these transformational principles. (For a brief exposition of this method see Lévi-Strauss 1963: ch. 2; 1976: ch. 1; and Barthes 1967; for concrete examples of this method see Lévi-Strauss 1967 and 1963: ch. 11; for a more detailed discussion see part 2 of this volume.)

At this point some sociologists might become more puzzled by my contention that relational structuralism does not entail a rejection of the past sociological traditions but rather permits one to recapture lines of inquiry and central concerns that have remained dormant or unresolved in traditional sociological orientations.

Let me briefly clarify the thrust of my thesis with a few references I shall discuss at length later on. The notion that symbolic structures are constitutive and organizing principles of social systems permits one to rediscover and develop a line of inquiry that began with a classic work of Durkheim and Mauss (1963). Moreover, we shall see in part 1 that in *The Elementary Forms of Religious Life* one can find already clearly anticipated the elementary and combinatory perspective so fundamental in modern structuralism. (On the centrality of the elementaristic perspective in Durkheim see Ekeh's essay in Rossi 1982.) The very same notion of underlying symbolic structures offers an important solution to a central problem which has permeated all classical sociological paradigms (see Hawthorn 1976), i.e., how to explain the relationship between society and the individual. The importance of Lévi-Strauss' structuralism on this issue has been clearly seen by C. R. Badcock (1975), although this British sociologist has too easily dismissed Lévi-Strauss' position because of misinterpretations. I have already mentioned and shall discuss more extensively in part 2 that the notions of the existence of isomorphic structures in the biological, linguistic, and cultural domains and of universally shared symbolic structures among social actors are central to Lévi-Strauss' position. Chomsky's notion of deep structure and the related notions of "performance" and "competence" have further contributed to the solution of the problem of the relationship between society and individual in a much more fundamental sense than suggested by Parsons' empiricist usage (1978) of Chomsky's concepts. Not only Durkheimian and Parsonian sociologies stand to gain from the relational perspective but interpretative sociologies as well; this is true especially because of the notions of unconscious meaning and meta-situational rules of interpretation. Similarly, the argument will be made that the Marxist paradigm can greatly benefit from the theory of the constitutive role of language in the emergence and functioning of ideological systems.

Considering these lines of argument I have just barely touched

upon, one should not be surprised to see that more and more sociologists are becoming cognizant of relational structuralism; see, for
instance, T. Bottomore and R. Nisbet (1978), R. Boudon (1970), A. Cicourel (1974), S. N. Eisenstadt with M. Curelaru (1976), P. Ekeh (1974),
E. Goffman (1974), F. E. Katz (1976), C. W. and V. M. Lidz (1976), P. K.
Manning (1978), T. Parsons (1969, 1975, 1977), A. Stinchcombe (1975),
G. E. Swanson (1973), and E. A. Tiryakian (1970). Unfortunately, many
of these sociological writings are rather tenuously or marginally related to the main thrust of relational structuralism.[4] Moreover, other
sociologists, such as Badcock (1975), Blau (1975), Homans (1975), Jenkins (1979), and Merton (1975), have offered criticism largely based on
misinterpretations of structuralism. Elsewhere (Rossi 1981) I have
presented a critique of Blau, Homans, and Merton's reactions to
French structuralism, and in the third part of this volume I will present a more extended critique of the reaction of Talcott Parsons.

The Study of Symbolic Systems in the Classical Sociological Tradition: The Three Classic Paradigms

To intelligently discuss the interaction of relational structuralism with
traditional paradigms, we must first discuss the paradigms developed by sociologists of traditional orientation in their study of symbolic systems. As we cannot possibly discuss all sociological theories,
nor do we need to, my argument will be based on the consideration
of the major types. A first difficulty is encountered in the lack of an
agreed upon classification of sociological schools, a lack which is immediately apparent from the reading of such commonly referred to
treatises on the history of sociology or sociological theory as P. Sorokin (1928, 1966), Martindale (1960), Timasheff (1967), Jonathan H.
Turner (1978), Bottomore and Nisbet (1978), and so on. Leon H. Warshay has examined fourteen classifications of sociological theories and

[4]Lemert (1979) stands out as a rare exception. A collection of previously unpublished
essays that I have edited for Columbia University Press contains useful and at times
pioneer applications of various forms of relational structuralism by P. and T. N. Clark,
S. N. Eisenstadt, P. Ekeh, M. Godelier, E. Katz, C. Lemert, W. A. Nielsen, C. Lidz, T.
Parsons, A. Stinchcombe, and others (Rossi 1982).

has found that the proposed number of types or groups of theories varies anywhere from three to eleven (1975:15–21). Some sociologists have used Kuhn's notion of paradigm (1970) without reaching an agreed upon classification either, as is evident, for instance, from the classifications of sociological theories produced by Paul Friedrichs (1970), Andrew Effrat (1972), and Derek Phillips (1973).

George Ritzer has reviewed the various applications in sociology of Kuhn's notion of paradigm and has proposed a new classification of sociological paradigms based on the following useful definition of the term, a term used by Kuhn himself in a variety of ways: "A paradigm is a fundamental image of the subject matter within a science. It serves to define what should be studied, what questions should be asked, how they should be asked, and what rules should be followed in interpreting the answers obtained" (1975:7). Lester Hill and Douglas Lee Eckberg (1981) have strongly argued against the applicability of Kuhn's notion of paradigm in sociology. However, I use the term not in a very technical sense but as a short cut for "general sociological orientation," proposed by Merton (1968:141). Ritzer proposes the threefold typology of social fact paradigm, social definition paradigm, and social behavior paradigm. The social factist deals with social structures and social institutions as "real" things and prefers to use the questionnaire and interview as tools of investigation (Ritzer 1975:25–26). According to Ritzer, Durkheim, structural-functionalists, and conflict sociologists are followers of the social fact paradigm. The social definitionist does not start from "real" and already given structures, but deals with the way people define social action and tends to prefer observation as a method of study (pp. 27–28); Weber, Mead, Cooley, phenomenological sociologists, and ethnomethodologists follow this paradigm. The social behaviorist seeks to predict human behavior and has a preference for the experimental method; George Homans is a good example of social behaviorism.

I find Ritzer's classification not altogether satisfactory because it does not clearly differentiate the various sociological schools in terms of the substantive focus of analysis and method. For instance, both social factists and social behaviorists tend to prefer the experimental method and interview techniques to interpretive and critical analysis. In addition, the method most typically used by social definitionists is not just observation, but interpretive observation. From the point of view of the conception of the subject matter of sociology, Ritzer's classification suffers from an even more fundamental shortcoming. For instance, social structures and institutions are "real" not only for functionalists and conflict sociologists, but also for social behaviorists. On the contrary, a significant difference exists between social factists and social behaviorists on the one hand and social definitionists on the other hand. The latter clearly differentiate themselves from social factists and social behaviorists by focusing on the active contribution of the individual's interpretation of the situation to the emergence and maintenance of social structure. Moreover, although Ritzer recognizes that the critical perspectives of Marx, the Frankfurt school of sociology, and Marcuse are markedly different from the three paradigms he describes (Ritzer 1975:225), he fails to present them as a distinct sociological paradigm. On the basis of these considerations, I find Wagner's threefold classification of "positive," interpretive, and evaluative sociologies preferable to the one proposed by Ritzer. According to Wagner, Durkheim, Simmel, Toennies, functionalism, and social behaviorism belong to positive sociology; Weber, symbolic interactionism, and phenomenological sociology belong to interpretive sociology; and Marx and social reform sociologists belong to evaluative sociology (Wagner 1963).

I have already stated that the subject matter of analysis and method should be the criteria for classifying sociological theories. What is the rationale for this assumption? After stating that no classification can be held more logical or systematic than others, Wagner seems to offer a valuable principle to evaluate proposed classifications. He states that a given classification must be "heuristically useful," which means it must be internally consistent, capable of distinguishing among significantly different theories, and applicable to all existing sociological theories. No one will argue with the first and last criteria, but the second criterion can be a matter of dispute, as Wagner himself admits. One can perhaps suggest that the second criterion should be substituted with the criterion of parsimonia and argue as follows: a typology is heuristically useful when it is internally consistent, can classify all existing theories, and can do so most parsimoniously, that is, by producing the smallest number of paradigms. These three criteria, however, are criteria of formal validity that cannot by themselves settle the issue of the heuristic usefulness of alternative classifications. In fact, it can be argued that most of the proposed classifications plausibly satisfy the first two criteria of formal validity. The parsimony principle, however, can hardly by itself be an adequate discriminant criterion. In fact, a threefold typology of theories has been produced by many other sociologists besides Ritzer and Wagner; see, for instance, the mechanical, organic, and process typology of Walter Buckley (1967), the neopositivist, social action, and middle range typology of Roscoe C. Hinkle and Gisela J. Hinkle (1954), the structural, functional, and psychological typology of George C. Homans (1964), the functional, social action, and conflict typology of John Rex (1961), the nomological, interpretive, and critical typology of L. W. Sherman (1974), and, more recently, the lexical, semantic, and syntactic typology of Charles C. Lemert (1979). For this reason we have to pay more serious attention to the other criterion suggested by Wagner, the capacity of a typology to make distinctions whenever differences are significant.

If we accept Merton's statement that all we have in social sciences are "general orientations toward substantive materials" (1968:142), it is logical that one should characterize a given theory by the type of phenomena it studies and the method it follows. Ritzer's conception of the basic elements of a paradigm (what is studied, the questions to be asked, how they should be asked, and the rules to interpret the answers) are logically reducible to the issues of the subject matter and methodological orientation. I use the term "methodological orientation" not in the narrow sense of techniques and procedures of data collection and analysis, but in a more fundamental and general sense. Abraham Kaplan has distinguished four meanings of the term "methodology"; specific techniques and research procedures, a concern with the "scientific" status or acceptability of one's approach, epistemological assumptions, and "middle range techniques and principles" (Kaplan 1964:18–23). The latter are logical principles specific to sciences as distinct from humanist disciplines. In this sense "methods include such procedures as forming concepts and hypotheses, making observations and measurements, performing experiments, building models and theories, providing explanations, and making predictions" (p. 23). Accordingly, the crucial elements of a method are the type of concepts formed (or used), the type of explanation proposed, and the type of theory aimed at rather than the technical procedures one uses.

This definition of method seems consistent with the distinction made between procedural techniques and methods by a variety of sociologists of humanist, empirical, and quantitative orientation, such as Florian Znaniecki, Robert M. MacIver, George A. Lundberg, Felix Kaufman, Paul P. Lazarsfeld and Morris Rosenberg, and Robert K. Merton (see references in Merton 1968:140). Two sociologists who cannot be suspected of an antiempiricist bias, Lazarsfeld and Rosenberg, state that "the term methodology . . . implies that concrete studies are being scrutinized as to the procedures they use, the underlying assumptions they make, the modes of explanation they consider as satisfactory" (1955:4). Such usage of the term "methodology" is in line also with Merton's characterization of an interpretive scheme: "Like all interpretive schemes, functional analysis depends upon a triple alliance between theory, method and data" (1968:73). "Methodology is the logic of scientific procedure" (p. 140) and crucial elements of this procedure are the theoretical orientation selected and its linkage with the data.

Moreover, phenomenologists do not concur with structural-functionalism in making procedural techniques an indispensible or key aspect of methodology. For instance, for Michael Phillipson methodology consists not of the manipulation of research techniques but in the processes by which a sociologist generates an abstract view of the situation, that is, the processes by which a theory is constructed. Basically, methodology indicates how sociologists decide what social phenomena are relevant (Phillipson 1972:79) and, I add, what concepts are appropriate to explain them. In this sense the substantive focus of analysis and the method adopted are two inseparable components of a theoretical orientation. This notion of methodological orientation also seems consistent with Wagner's assertion that "sociological theories shall be distinguished according to the author's conceptions of the general character and the basic purposes of sociology as a realm of intellectual inquiry" (1963:42). There is no doubt that Wagner's distinction among positive or natural science theories, interpretive sociology, and evaluative social theory expresses the most fundamental differences in the existing sociological orientations.

The natural science paradigm is well defined by Emile Durkheim when he states that we must consider social facts as "things." "A thing differs from an idea in the same way as that which we know from without differs from that which we know from within" (1964:xliii). This implies that the legitimate object for sociological analysis is "phenomena defined in advance by certain common external characteristics" (p. 35). To the natural science paradigm belong Pareto, Comte, Spencer, and all sociologists of behaviorist, experimentalist, neopositivist, and sociometric orientations. All these sociologists share in common the assumption that the proper object of analysis is observable data (behavior or verbalization) taken in their external and quantifiable characteristics independent of the meaning attached to them by social actors. Moreover, sociologists of the natural science orientation aim at formulating laws of empirical regularities according to the methods of natural sciences.

Like the natural science paradigm, the interpretive paradigm also encompasses a variety of sociological schools. All interpretive sociologists have in common an interest in the subjective meaning of social behavior. To this paradigm belong Florian Znaniecki, Max Weber, symbolic interactionists, and ethnomethodologists. Znaniecki distinguished between the natural and cultural way of looking at scientific data; "this essential character of cultural data we call the humanistic coefficient, because such data, as objects of the student's theoretic reflection, already belong to somebody else's active experience and are such as this active experience makes them" (1934:37).

The naturalist, even while recognizing that cultural objects are human values and that cultural systems are construed by human activity, believes that human activity can nevertheless be studied as a natural process given to him (like other natural processes) without any reference to how it appears to anybody else. . . . The other way of obtaining an inductive knowledge of human activity would be to use consistently the humanistic coefficient in dealing with it and take it as it appears to the agent himself and to those who cooperate with him or counteract him. (pp. 44–45)

It is apparent, then, that both subject matter (subjective meaning) and method (humanist coefficient and interpretation) are the distinguishing characteristics of the interpretive paradigm.

The third major sociological paradigm is called by Wagner evaluative social theory, a paradigm he considers a residual category in the sense that it encompasses the sociological orientations which do not belong to the previous two paradigms. According to Wagner, evaluative social theories are characterized by their opposition to "value-neutrality" and for proceeding on the basis of ideological presuppositions. However, one can argue that even the first two paradigms are based on ideological premises; the principle of value neutrality itself is considered by some sociologists an ideological principle. Rather than as a residual category, I conceive of evaluative sociology as a category which logically derives from two major goals of sociological analysis. One goal is to explain social data for the advancement of cumulative sociological knowledge, which can be of a natural science or interpretive type. Another goal of sociological analysis is to evaluate social structure or culture in order to determine whether societal rewards are equitably distributed or whether culture provides adequate meaning and orientation to people. In the first case the focus is on the development of systematic sociological knowledge and the growth of a discipline. In the second case sociologists are mostly interested in social criticism or the application of the sociological perspective for policy making or social reforms.

Another way to conceptualize the underlying dimensions of our threefold typology is in reference to the relationship between the individual and society, an issue which has been a central concern of sociologists throughout the history of the discipline. When the focus of attention is directly on society as such, the sociologist practices the natural science mode of analysis. When the attention is on the individual in terms of the meaning he or she attributes to the situation, the sociologist practices the interpretive type of sociology. When the sociologist is interested in the relationship between society and the individual in terms of the individual's adjustment to and participation in societal rewards, he or she practices an evaluative type of sociology. The focus on either social structure or the individual is also fundamental in another sense; when used as analytical principles of explanation, they constitute the two dynamic poles of a dialectical approach, a point I will discuss at length in the conclusion of the volume. The notion that we must preserve elements of both the structural and subjective perspective by using a dialectical framework is the underlying idea of the whole book.

Before closing this section, I will briefly mention that Wagner's typology needs refinements. Ethnomethodology should be added to the list of interpretive sociologies and sociology of knowledge and social-philosophical theories should not be classified as evaluative sociologies because they are found in all three paradigms. In this volume I will discuss a few key representatives of each paradigm. Within the natural science paradigm I will include Durkheim and Pareto as examples of positivist thinking, and Parsons as an example of systemic thinking, although Parsons has attempted to incorporate elements of the interpretive paradigm. As examples of the interpretive paradigm, I will consider Max Weber, some aspects of Mannheim's sociology, symbolic interactionism, phenomenology, and ethnomethodology. As far as the evaluative paradigm is concerned, I will limit my attention to a few basic aspects of Marx's thought, since the latter has inspired many semiotic structuralists and, of course, structural Marxists. On the other hand, the interaction of the Frankfurt school of thought with relational structuralism has not produced major works; for this reason I will not discuss the Frankfurt school as a separate variety of the critical paradigm, but I will refer to it in discussing the limitations of Marx's position.

Scope and Organization of This Volume

The focus of the book is on the interface of traditional and relational paradigms. Neither the discussion of traditional sociological paradigms or the presentation of the relational paradigm can be self-contained given the great number and diversity of the paradigms in question.

First a word of caution about my discussion of traditional sociological paradigms. The reader cannot expect to find a reference to nuances and subvarieties of the three traditional paradigms or frequent references to recent bibliographical items. I shall focus mostly on the task of elucidating the key analytical concepts used by followers of the traditional paradigms in their study of symbolic systems. The central thrust of the book is, in fact, to compare traditional and structural paradigms to find points of integration and complementarity. For the same reason I shall not touch upon many substantive issues discussed by classical sociologists of symbolic systems.

A second word of caution is in order, concerning my discussion of relational structuralism. Given the unfamiliarity of many American sociologists with this recent movement, I have spent a long section of the book on it. However, I will keep my discussion within the limits already indicated, i.e., I consider the various forms of structuralism in so far as they converge on the antiempiricist, antihumanist, and antihistorical perspectives. The reader who needs a fuller explanation of specific structural concepts or authors will have to refer to sources offering a specialized discussion of the various schools of modern structuralism. This volume is written mostly from a Lévi-Straussian and poststructural semiotic perspective, with the use of some elements of Piaget and structural Marxism; on these perspectives the reader will find useful the following volumes: J. Benoist (1978), S. Clarke (1981), R. Coward and J. Ellis (1977), M. Glucksmann (1974), A. Lemaire (1977), M. Marc-Lipiansky (1973), J. Piaget (1970), D. Robey (1973), I. Rossi (1974), A. Sheridan (1981), J. Sturrock (1979), J. Viet (1969). Other specific sources will be indicated later on in the text.

In part 1 of the volume I will discuss the study of symbolic systems as carried out by sociologists of traditional orientation, who will be grouped under three major paradigms—natural science, interpretive, and critical. The aim of part 1 is to show the centrality of the study of symbolism in the classical sociological tradition and to explain its major analytical concepts. Part 1 will lay the foundation for the argument to be carried out in the rest of the volume, namely, the importance of relational structuralism in recapturing the central role of symbolism in social life and strengthening the analytical scope of traditional paradigms.

The critical perspective of part 1 is inspired by two ideas: the need to overcome the empiricist attitude of the traditional sociological paradigms while at the same time attempting to retain and integrate their valid elements. Having already discussed the gist of theoretical reasons to overcome the empiricist attitude, I must briefly discuss the second idea. In part 1 I will start with the Marxist paradigm, from which I will accept the importance of the object-subject dialectical relationship. This principle will be used, first of all, to highlight some inconsistencies of the Marxist position and then to point out the need to preserve and dialectically integrate the subjective and objective principles of social life, principles which are dominant in the interpretive and natural science paradigms, respectively.

I must caution the reader against a possible misunderstanding. In this volume I do not undertake the questionable task of using the Marxist paradigm to evaluate competing paradigms; I do not intend either to build up an impossible hybrid out of different paradigms. On the contrary, my direct goal is to show how the dialectical perspective (as I conceive of it) permits one to avoid the empiricist shortcomings of traditional sociological paradigms while at the same time using and notably strengthening key elements of their analytical apparatus.

In the second part of the volume I will discuss the convergence of the semiotic structuralism of Claude Lévi-Strauss, the genetic structuralism of Jean Piaget, and the transformational grammar of Noam Chomsky on the antiempiricist, antihumanist, and antihistorical perspectives. In part 3 of the volume I will undertake a systematic discourse on the interaction between the three traditional paradigms and relational structuralism. There the discourse will be extended to structural Marxism and to the poststructural semiotics of R. Barthes, J. Kristeva, and J. Derrida, who have attempted to correct the "systemic" bias of Saussure's and Lévi-Strauss' semiotic structuralism.

The intellectual debate originated by poststructural semiotics and structural Marxism will demonstrate the need for elaborating a truly dialectical approach in sociology. In the conclusion of the volume I will outline some major elements of a dialectic approach that uses elements of the structural and subjective perspectives, perspectives which cut across all the traditional paradigms as well as the various forms of relational structuralism. The intent is not to deemphasize the importance of either the structural or subjective forces in the dynamics of social life, but to argue they must be both taken into account. It will be shown that these two forces "constitute" each other through a dialectic of reciprocity that differs from the Marxist notion of the dialectic of opposites and uses various elements of competing paradigms of traditional orientation as well as elements of relational structuralism. The outcome of such an interparadigmatic linkage will be to provide sociologists not with a monolithic or overencompassing paradigm but with a dialectical orientation that enables them to deal with a larger range of sociological issues than previously possible and to use a more articulated analytical apparatus than previously available.

I

The Sociology of Symbolism and Meaning in Traditional Sociological Paradigms

1

The Sociology of Symbolic Systems and the Critical Paradigm: Functions of Ideology, Consciousness, and Language According to Marx

I begin with the Marxist paradigm because Karl Marx is considered by some authors perhaps the most important social thinker of the late nineteenth century, as much of the sociological thought of Max Weber, Vilfredo Pareto, Gaetano Mosca, Robert Michels, Emile Durkheim, and Karl Mannheim has been formulated either in response to Marxist theses or in the context of the debate with Marx's ghost (Zeitlin 1968:111). Much of such a debate has been focusing on the relative importance of the "ideal" factors (religious ideas, ideology, and other symbolic systems) and "real" factors (economic, political, and biological factors) in the dynamics of social processes. Although Marx formulated his sociology partly in reaction to German Idealism, he certainly did not deny the importance of ideas in social life. On the contrary, for Marx social life unfolds as a dialectical relationship between the material basis and human conceptions, between the mode of production and the person's consciousness of himself or herself as a human being. Such a dialectical view of social life has the merit of avoiding a reified and positivist conception of social structure, insofar as social structure is seen as a product of human activity.

However, neither thought nor the symbolic interpretation of social situations is for Marx the most fundamental human activity: "The social structure and the state continually evolve out of the life-process of definite individuals, but individuals not as they may appear in their own or other people's imagination but rather as they really are, that is, as they work, produce materially, and act under definite material limitations, presuppositions, and conditions independent of their will" (Marx 1970 in Easton and Guddat 1967:413–414). Human beings' symbolic activity is the result of their material productivity:

The production of ideas, of conceptions of consciousness is directly inter-woven with the material activity and the material relationships of men: it is the language of actual life. Conceiving, thinking, and the intellectual relation-ships of men appear here as the direct result of their material behavior. . . . Men are the producers of their conceptions, ideas, etc., but these are real, active men, as they are conditioned by a definite development of their pro-ductive forces and of their relationships corresponding to these up to their highest forms. (p. 414)

By productive forces Marx meant both the means of production and relations of production, that is, the property rights over the modes of production. The mode of production, especially the division of la-bor, determines social relationships; in turn, social relationships de-termine people's mode of consciousness. The economic structure is "the real foundation on which rise legal and political structures and to which correspond definite forms of social consciousness. The mode of production in material life determines the general character of the social, political and spiritual processes of life. It is not the conscious-ness of men that determine their existence, but, on the contrary, their social existence determines their consciousness" (Marx 1904 in Feuer 1959:43).

Because of the restrictions imposed by the mode of production, human consciousness is often illusory or false:

The ideas which these individuals form are ideas either about their relation to nature, their mutual relations, or their own nature. It is evident that in all these cases these ideas are the conscious expression . . . of their actual re-lationships and activities. . . . If the conscious expression of the actual rela-tions of these individuals is illusory, if in their imagination they turn reality upside down, this is in turn a result of their limited mode of activity and their limited social relations arising from it. (Marx 1970 in Easton and Guddat 1967:414)

Human consciousness is distorted largely because of the ideological forces operating in society: "With the change of the economic foun-dation the entire universe superstructure is more or less rapidly transformed. In considering transformations the distinction should be made between the material transformation of the economic condition of production . . . and the legal, political, religious, aesthetic, or philosophic—in short ideological—forms in which men become conscious of this conflict and fight out" (Marx 1904 in Feuer 1959:44).

Ideology distorts people's ideas because it serves the interests of the ruling class: "In every epoch the ideas of the ruling class are the ruling ideas, that is the class that is the ruling *material* power of society is at the same time its ruling *intellectual* power. . . . The ruling ideas are nothing more than the ideal expression of the dominant material relationships grasped as ideas, hence of the relationships which make the one class the ruling one and therefore the ideas of its domination" (Marx 1970 in Easton and Guddat 1967:438). Ideology is, then, determined by the economic and political structure of the capitalistic society: "Each new class which displaces the one previously dominant is forced simply to be able to carry out its aim, to represent its interest as the common interest of all members of society, that is ideally expressed. It has to give its ideas the form of universality and represent them as the only rational, universally valid ones" (p. 439).

Since ideology is a distorted expression of social relations, by absorbing ideology the exploited class develops false consciousness about its social situation. This is why Marx states that social praxis produces appearances, appearances being the way human actions manifest themselves.

These appearances and modes of consciousness are not transparent or immediately intelligible, but opaque. For instance, a commodity would appear to be a very simple and transparent thing, but in reality it becomes a fetish separated from the worker's productive activity:

A commodity is a mysterious thing, simply because in it the social character of men's labour appears to them as an objective character stamped upon the product of labour; because the relation of the producers to the sum total of their own labour is presented to them as a social relation, existing not between them, but between the products of their labour. . . . There is a definite social relation between men that assumes, in their eyes, the fantastic form of a relation between things. . . . This I call the Fetishism which attaches itself to the products of labour, so soon as they are produced as commodities. (Marx 1932 in McLellan 1971:108)

The misrepresentation of the real value of the product of labor and the consequent transformation of the relationship between persons into relationships between things derives from ideological trappings which separate labor from its real basis, that is, the social relationships of production: "Selling is the practice of externalisation. As long as man is imprisoned within religion, he only knows how to objectify his essence by making it into an alien, imaginary being. Similarly, under the domination of egoistic needs he can only become practical, only create practical objects by putting his products and his activity under the domination of an alien entity and lending them the significance of an alien entity—money" (Marx 1971:114).

Money becomes a means of universal exchange that has value independent of what it represents, that is, human labor. Moreover, because of its abstract quality and universal value, money becomes a means to control and manipulate social relations; therefore, it reinforces the process of reification and false consciousness.

The separation of consciousness from the social basis of existence gives origin to entire systems of abstract and pure knowledge, such as ethics, philosophy, and religion. In turn, these systems of abstract thought reinforce the distorted view of reality and the production of false consciousness: "The worker's activity, limited to a mere abstraction, is determined and regulated on all sides by the movement of the machinery, not the other way around. The knowledge that obliges the inanimate parts of the machine through their construction, to work appropriately as an automation, does not exist in the consciousness of the worker, but acts upon him through the machine as an alien force, as the power of the machine itself . . ." (Marx 1972:133). A little further on he continues: "In so far as machinery develops with the accumulation of social knowledge and productive power generally, it is not in labour but in capital that general social labour is represented. . . . The worker appears to be superfluous in so far as his action is not determined by the need of capital" (p. 135).

Besides ideology and other systems of abstract thought, Marx also pays attention to language as the vehicle of abstract thought. Language has an important role in the production of opaque ideas and false consciousness. For Marx, language originates from the need of social communication, and it is both the natural and social medium of consciousness. Through it consciousness is formed and exists:

We find that man also, possesses *consciousness;* but, even so, not inherent, not *pure* consciousness. From the start the *spirit* is afflicted with the curse of being *burdened* with matter, which here makes its appearance in the form of agitated layers of air, sounds—in short, of language. Language is as old as consciousness; language is practical consciousness, as it exists for other men, and for that reason is really beginning to exist for me personally as well; for language, like consciousness, arises from the need, the necessity of intercourse with other men. (Marx 1970 in Feuer 1959:251)

If language is practical consciousness and if the latter perceives social praxis in a distorted way, it follows that language becomes alienated language:

We mutually regard our product as the power each one has over the other and over himself. In other words, our own product is turned against us. . . . Our objects in their relation to one another constitute the only intelligible language we use with one another. We would not understand a human language, and it would remain without effect. . . . We are so much mutually alienated from human nature that the direct language of this nature is an injury to human dignity for us, while the alienated language of objective values appears as justified, self-confident, and self-accepted human dignity. (Marx in Easton and Guddat 1967:280)

Critique of Marx's Paradigm

In this brief review we have encountered the key concepts used by Marx to explain the role of symbolism in social life: mode of production, ideology, false consciousness, praxis, language, fetishism, externalization. In Marx's hands these concepts become sharp analytical tools for the critical analysis of capitalist social structure. However, there are certain gaps or tensions built within Marx's framework: how, for instance, can we reconcile the active view of people with the determining role of the mode of production? Is the relation between the mode of production and ideology a purely mechanistic one and based on economic determinism? Is there more to the relationship between ideology and language than Marx cares to elaborate? I concentrate on these issues because they are the focal points around which has developed the contribution of structural Marxism and semiotic Marxism; such a contribution is central to the perspective of this book, especially in part 3 and in the conclusion.

Marx's Conception of History: The Notion of Totality and the Relationship Between Infrastructure and Superstructure

The three questions I have just formulated are at the heart of Marx's conception of history, a conception concisely and clearly summarized in the Preface to *A Contribution to the Critique of Political Economy:*

The general conclusion at which I arrived and which, once reached, continued to serve as the guiding thread in my studies, may be formulated briefly as follows: In the social production which men carry on they enter into definite relations that are indispensable and independent of their will; these relations of production correspond to a definite stage of development of their material powers of production. The totality of these relations of production constitutes the economic structure of society—the real foundation, on which legal and political superstructures arise and to which definite forms of social consciousness correspond. The mode of production of material life determines the general character of the social, political and spiritual processes of life. It is not the consciousness of men that determines their being, but, on the contrary, their social being determines their consciousness. At a certain stage of their development, the material forces of production in society come in conflict with the existing relations of production, or—what is but a legal expression for the same thing—with the property relations within which they had been at work before. From forms of development of the forces of production these relations turn into their fetters. Then occurs a period of social revolution. With the change of the economic foundation the entire immense superstructure is more or less rapidly transformed. (Marx in Bottomore and Rubel 1963:51–52)

I call the reader's attention to the notion of totality and the active conception of people. Through social activity people create themselves and society, so that they and society become inseparable from each other; as much as people are inseparable from other people, so their activity is inseparable from their own minds:

Social activity and social mind by no means exist only in the form of activity or mind which is manifestly social. Nevertheless, social activity and mind, that is activity and mind which show themselves directly in a real association with other men, are realized everywhere. This direct expression of sociability is based on the nature of the activity or corresponds to the nature of mind. . . . My own existence is a social activity. For this reason, what I myself produce, I produce for society and with the consciousness of acting as a social being. The manifestations of this life—even when it does not appear directly in the form of a social manifestation, accomplished in association with other men—is therefore a manifestation and affirmation of social life. . . . Though man is a unique individual . . . he is equally the *whole, the ideal whole*, the subjective existence of society as thought and experienced. He exists, in reality, as the representation and the real mind of social existence, and as the sum of human manifestations of life. Thought and being are indeed distinct, but they also form a unity. (Marx 1932b as translated in Bottomore and Rubel 1963:76–78)

Marx's notion of wholeness clearly avoided the empiricist individual-society, mind-reality dichotomies. But how is such a unity to be conceived of—as a mechanical or as a dialectical one? Here we touch on a much written about and controversial issue in the Marxist literature. We have seen Marx stating that it is not people's consciousness that determines their being but the other way around: the mode of production determines the political, sociological, and legal texture of society. Yet at the same time Marx states that people produce the very means of production:

The premises from which we begin . . . are the real individuals, their activity and their material conditions of life. . . . [Men] begin to distinguish themselves from animals as soon as they begin to produce their means of subsistence. . . . (But) the way in which man produces their means of subsistence depends in the first place on the nature of the existing means which they have to reproduce. . . . What individuals are, therefore, depends on the material conditions of their production. . . . This conception of history, therefore, rests on the exposition of the real process of production, starting out from the simple material production of life, and on the comprehension of the form of intercourse connected with and created by this mode of production, i.e., civil society. (Marx 1970 in Bottomore and Rubel 1963:53–54, 58)

The mode of production comprises four categories of phenomena: 1) the processes of production, such as the agents and means of production, and the products; 2) the productive forces, such as natural resources and technology; 3) the relations of production, such as the relations between agents of production that are based on power and control; and 4) the mode of production, which comprises the relations between the three elements composing the first category (Israel 1971:335–337). An important issue here is how to relate the material basis to the ideological superstructure. We have repeatedly seen Marx declaring that "the economic structure of society [is] the real foundation on which legal and political superstructures arise and to which definite forms of social consciousness correspond" (Marx 1970 in Bottomore and Rubel 1963:51). To explain the relationship between the economic infrastructure and the superstructure Marx states also that the first is the "real basis" and "explanation" of the latter (pp. 54–55).

How does the economic foundation explain the superstructure? M. M. Bober has made a systematic review of Marx's formulations and concludes that at times, Marx simply states that there is a "correspondence" between the two or that they are "conformable" to each other; at other times, he claims that the economic infrastructure determines or conditions the superstructures (Bober 1965:299–301).

Are these formulations compatible with each other? Yes, if the notion of determination is understood as unilineal and monocausal determinism. According to vulgar materialism, people are just a product of social relations, which in turn are products of the mode of production. According to this interpretation, conscious and cognitive systems would be mere reflections of the economic condition (mirror theory). However, Marx himself has rejected economic determinism because, as we saw, he has admitted that people produce and change the means of production. In *The German Ideology*, Marx asserts that "circumstances make men just as much as men make circumstances" (Marx 1970 in Bottomore and Rubel 1963:55).

Are we, then, to conclude that the subjective and structural (objective) elements have equal importance? This certainly is not the case because the structure is more determinant than the superstructure and conscious praxis. The mode of production is the conditioning element of the superstructure, is "the ultimate cause," "the great moving power," the "final cause in the last instance" (see quotes in Bober 1965:301).

Does this mean that there are determining factors other than economic ones, although they are not equally determinant in the "ultimate sense"? The answer is affirmative since the superstructure itself has a feedback influence on the economic infrastructure. This is well expressed by Engels in an 1890 letter to J. Bloch:

According to the materialist conception of history, the ultimately determining element in history is the production and reproduction of real life. More than this neither Marx nor I have ever asserted. Hence if somebody twists this into saying that the economic element is the only determining one, he transforms that proposition into a meaningless, abstract, senseless phrase. The economic situation is the basis, but the various elements of the superstructure . . . also exercise their influence upon the course of the historical struggle and in many cases preponderate in determining their form. There is an interaction of all these elements in which . . . the economic movement finally asserts itself as necessary. (Quoted in Israel 1971:339)

We can thus agree with Bober that Marx rejects two extreme positions: firstly, the notion that the mode of production is the only determining factor (Marx himself has been explicitly opposed to this position); secondly, the mode of production is only one among several dominant and autonomous factors of history. The more plausible interpretation of Marx's position is that the noneconomic factors modify the mode of production "provided two limitations are kept in mind; one, these noneconomic agencies owe their origin to the system of production and are shaped by it, directly or indirectly; two, the combined effectiveness of all the noneconomic forces yields to the sovereign power of the mode of production" (Bober 1965:302).

This formulation does not clear up all the issues: for one thing, what do the terms "shaping" and "conditioning" mean? Why does Marx at times use the notion of determination, a notion which seems to imply a mechanistic causality? (Aron 1967:157). Is perhaps the economic infrastructure the necessary but not sufficient condition? If so, is each one of the noneconomic factors equally important? How do they interact to yield a unified influence? Finally, what does the notion of "ultimate determinant" mean, a notion that R. Aron, among others, finds "all too vague" (ibid.)? If this notion implies causality, Marx would have adopted a framework based on the notion of temporal sequence, but such a framework is antithetical to the dialectical perspective. We shall see in part 3 that the contribution of structural Marxists, like L. Althusser and L. Sebag, has pushed Marxist thought well beyond the boundaries vaguely delineated by Karl Marx.

Structural Marxism has made important contributions to another aspect of Marxist thought, an aspect which needs much clarification: what are the reasons for the predicted inevitability of the conflict between the material forces of production and the relations of production in capitalistic society? (Such a conflict is formulated in Marx's summary of his own theory quoted at the beginning of this section.) Aron does not find at all clear the Marxist notion of contradiction, as he does not find clear the notion of forces and relations of production nor the notions of infrastructure and superstructure.

These queries strike right at the heart of the Marxist perspective, which is programmatically both a historical and a dialectical perspective.

The Undialectic Nature of Marx's Dialectic Materialism

Since we shall discuss in part 3 the structural Marxists' conception of objective contradiction, i.e., the contradiction inherent within the capitalistic social structure, I shall discuss here another important aspect of Marxist dialectic, the subject-object relationship. I have mentioned above that for Marx, people make circumstances as much as circumstances make people. Moreover, Marx has opposed both bourgeois materialism, which reduces mental and spiritual phenomena to material and chemical processes, and Hegelian idealism, which falls into the opposite error. As an alternative to both positions, Marx proposed a form of humanism or naturalism (terms Marx used synonymously), which could preserve and unify the elements of truth contained in the two positions.

The chief defect of all hitherto existing materialism—that of Feuerbach included—is that the thing, reality, sensuousness, is conceived only in the form of the *object* or of *contemplation*, but not as *human sensuous activity, practice*, not subjectively. Hence it happened that the *active* side, in contradistinction to materialism, was developed by idealism—but only abstractly, since, of course, idealism does not know real, sensuous activity as such. Feuerbach wants sensuous objects really differentiated from the thought objects, but he does not conceive human activity itself as *objective* activity. (Marx 1932a in Feuer 1959:243)

We find here clearly stated the importance of the subjective principle in social life.

However, Marx is too keen a social scientist to fall into the mistake of separating subjective from objective forces of social dynamics:

An objective being acts objectively, and it would not act objectively if objectivity were not part of its essential being. It creates and establishes *only* objects because it is established by objects, and because it is fundamentally *natural*. In the act of establishing it does not descend from its pure activity to the *creation of objects;* its *objective* product simply confirms its *objective* activity, its activity as an objective, natural being. We see here how consistently naturalism or humanism is distinguished from both idealism and materialism, and at the same time constitutes their unifying truth. We see also that only naturalism is able to comprehend the process of world history. (Marx 1932b in Fromm 1968:181).

From these programmatic statements one must conclude that the subjective and objective principles are the two essential poles of Marx's dialectic and that they are related to each other in the following way: the two principles are equally important as forces of social dynamics and they constitute each other through their reciprocal interaction; the interaction between the two principles and their own very nature is based on contradictions that are inherent within the object as well as within the subject. I shall briefly argue that neither Marx himself nor later Marxists thinkers have been consistent in their sociological analysis with these two aspects of the dialectical principle.

Object-Subject Relationship. In analyzing Marx's theory of ideology, consciousness, and language we have seen that subjectivities and subjective consciousness are thought to be determined by the economic infrastructure; alienating and exploitative structures produce false consciousness. Such a conceptualization is clearly antithetical to the notion of the inseparability and the way objective and subjective forces constitute each other—as so eloquently stated in the programmatic quotation to which we have just referred. Nor is it consistent with Marx's statement in *The Economic and Philosophic Manuscript* of 1844 that "as society produces man as man, so is society produced by him" (quoted in Walls 1979:216).

The positivist interpretation of Marx has made even more explicit the thesis of the unilineal determination of superstructures by economic infrastructures. Humanist Marxism has not remedied such inconsistency in Marx's thought with the thesis that we must free the subject from alienating social structures. In fact, such a thesis is based on the quasimetaphysical notions of "human essence" and "free subject," notions which are accepted as given and intelligible independent of their dialectical relationship with objective forces.

Reacting against positivist Marxism, Jurgen Habermas has tried to recapture the original Marxist conception of the dialectical relationship between subject and object. Habermas states that such a dialectic is eliminated when the active intervention of the individual is denied or when culture is reduced to an epiphenomenon of the mode of productivity and of physical events. Habermas argues that by turning Hegel back on his feet, Marx fused two Hegelian elements into one: humankind's reflexive experience of being the maker of the human species and history, as well as "the self-constitution of the species through labor." However, according to Habermas "Marx deludes himself about the nature of reflection when he reduces it to labor. . . . By reducing the self-positing of the absolute ego to the more tangible productive activity of the species, he eliminates reflection as such, as a motive force of history" (Habermas 1971:43–44).

Habermas focuses on symbolic communication as the foundation of subjective action and the sense of collectivity. Communication assumed a decisive importance in late capitalism when the latter had to justify itself; this, of course, meant that capitalist ideology attempted to establish false consciousness. For this reason Habermas selects "communication" as the starting point for critical sociology. For Habermas the central problem of critical sociologists is to transform controlled and distorted communication and to establish the conditions of pure intersubjectivity: "Pure subjectivity is determined by a symmetrical relation between I and you (We and You), I and He (We and They). Pure intersubjectivity exists only when there is complete symmetry in the distribution of assertion and disputation, revelation and hiding, prescription and following among the partners of communication. As long as these symmetries exist, communication will not be hindered by constraints arising from its own structure" (Habermas 1970:143). The issue is one of establishing "communicative competence," that is, "the mastery of the means of construction necessary for the establishment of an ideal speech situation" (p. 144).

The realization of intersubjectivity is a precondition "to stabilize the identification of the individuals as well as that of the social group in a given culture or subculture at a given time" (p. 145).

As laudable as Habermas' intent is, in reality the text I am here considering negates the principle of the reciprocal constitutive interaction of the objective and subjective principles. In fact, Habermas speaks of an "I" and "You" as self-evident notions; accordingly, the role of the critical sociologist would consist only of making them transparent: "Communication competence is defined by the ideal speaker's mastery of the dialogue constitutive universals *irrespective of the actual restrictions under empirical conditions*" (my italics) (Habermas 1970:141). For Habermas, "pure subjectivity" is impeded or prevented rather than constituted by the interaction with objective forces. He seems to suggest that to reconstruct pure subjectivity and intersubjectivity we must practice a kind of "époché" from concrete social structures. Such a theoretical posture is not consistent with the dialectical perspective as just presented. (I leave it up to the experts of the Frankfurt school to decide whether Habermas has elsewhere formulated more dialectical views.)

Moreover, what is pure subjectivity, a metaphysical or a psychological notion? Habermas denies that he reduces subjectivity to the individual but, as Michael Brown says, "this denial remains programmatic within the body of Habermas' works. In my opinion its development depends on the establishment of working relationships between critical theory and contemporary French readings of Freud, structuralist and post-structuralist critique" (Brown 1979:266). We shall see in part 3 that poststructural semiotics permits the construction of a theory of a subject based on symbolic (structural) and dialectical principles.

The Principle of Contradiction. I have stated before that Marx's dialectic implies not only the inseparability of object and subject but also the notion of contradiction as the constitutive force of their interaction as well as their own very nature. This second aspect of dialectic is also absent from the bulk of Marxist works and can be recaptured with the contribution of poststructural semiotics. Let us first examine how crucial is the notion of contradiction in the Marxist tradition, at least as a programmatic statement. Marx was very explicit on this point:

Dialectic in its rational form is a scandal and abomination to bourgeoisdom and its doctrinaire professors because it includes in its comprehension and affirmative recognition of the existing state of things, at the same time also, the recognition of the negation of that state, of its inevitable breaking up; because it regards every historically developed social form as in fluid movement, and therefore takes into account its transient nature not less than its momentary existence; because it lets nothing impose upon it, and is in its essence critical and revolutionary. (Marx 1932 in Feuer 1959:146)

In contrast with the positivist interpretation of Marx, mostly fostered by the second, third, and fourth Internationals (Walls 1979:216) contradiction was clearly presented as the kernel of dialectic materialism by Lenin, Mao, and Lukàcs. Mao (1968) enriched the principle of contradiction with the notions of "principal contradiction" and the "asymmetricality of contradictions." Lenin, who like Lukàcs (1971:3) emphasized the dialectical relationship between object and subject, added to the threefold dimension of dialectic—thesis, antithesis, and synthesis—the fourth term of internal negativity as "the necessary liaison and immanent genesis of differences" and the objective principle in "all natural and spiritual life" (Lenin 1972:97).

However, Marxists have not yet produced a theory of the contradictory subject that activates practice; such a theory would logically derive from Marx's notion of contradiction and Lenin's notion of negativity, but it is in strident contrast with the perspective of positivist Marxism. Without the notion of contradictory and, therefore, active and revolutionary subject, Marxism is caught within a mechanistic interpretation of the movement of superstructures.

Yet no theory of the active subject is possible without considering the constitutive role of language. In the Marxist perspective it is through language that consciousness can be detached from immediate and transparent relationship with the reality; language permits the construction of abstractions and theories, like religion, morality, philosophy—that is the ideological superstructure. Through the mediation of language these symbolic constructs deeply pervade and, at the same time, dialectically interact with social reality. What people say derives not from language but from the division of labor and so-

cial interaction (praxis). However, the praxis enters into their consciousness only by the way of language, which then becomes the
consciousness of people. It seems to follow that the notion that language is produced by ideology is consistent with Marx's perspective.
However, we know that ideology is produced by dominant groups to
mask their interests and to prevent consciousness from perceiving
reality as is. We can conclude then that an inextricable interrelationship exists among ideology, language, consciousness, and praxis.
However, as Figure 1.1 demonstrates, for Marx language is not a constitutive force of social praxis but its product. It is only with the advent of semiotic structuralism that the attention became focused on
the constitutive role of language in social praxis, and this was made
possible by the structural interpretation of Freud proposed by Lacan.

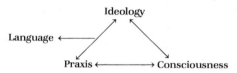

Figure 1.1. Marx's view of language.

Coward and Ellis (1977:92) have expressed well the dilemma of presemiotic Marxist thought. One cannot understand ideology without
a theory of language; this would entail a form of mechanical materialism which denies the input of symbolic systems on the subject
when the latter constructs history and ideology. Yet one cannot analyze language as structure and forget the subject; this would be a
form of metaphysical materialism. Nor can we analyze language without its object; this would be a form of idealism (ibid.). The real dialectic is a dialectic between history, language, and ideology. With Lacan's theory of the subject it became possible to conceptualize the
subject as a materialistic process, and such a conceptualization enabled social scientists to overcome the division between subject and
object and between materialism and Hegelian idealism. We shall see
in part 3 how Julia Kristeva and other poststructural semioticians
have incorporated Lacanian ideas to overcome these critical gaps in
the Marxist paradigm.

2

The Sociology of Symbolic Systems and Meaning in the Interpretive Paradigm

Whereas Marx has emphasized, at least programmatically, the inseparability and constitutive interrelationship of the objective and subjective principles of social life, the followers of the natural science and interpretive paradigms have used the two principles separately and as if each one of them, independent of the other, were an adequate explanatory principle of the totality of social life; natural science sociologists have "objectivized" social life and have heavily relied on structural, functional, and causal modes of explanation. Sociologists of interpretive orientation have chosen "subjective meaning" as the preferred vantage point of a self-contained sociological explanation.

I begin my analysis with the interpretive paradigm, where I will pay particular attention to Max Weber and symbolic interactionism as representative types of interpretive sociology. I shall postpone the discussion of phenomenological sociology, ethnomethodology, and Goffman to the third part of the volume for reasons which I shall discuss later on when they can be better understood.

The Sociology of Culture in Max Weber

Rightly, Max Weber is considered the pioneer of interpretive sociology, especially because of his use of the notions of *verstehen* and ideal type. However, he is at times too hastily set in opposition to Marx for having attributed an important role to ideas in the dynamics of sociohistorical processes. In reality, the dialectical relationship between the works of the two thinkers makes it difficult to adequately ascertain Weber's contribution without understanding his criticism of Marx's position. Irving Zeitlin disagrees with Parsons' view that Weber retreated from an early Marxist position after he became convinced of the important role of ideas in social life. Zeitlin argues that even Marx recognized the importance of ideas in history and that Weber did not reject but supplemented the methodological principles of Marx (Zeitlin 1968:112). In a later work, Zeitlin stressed even further the existence of a complementary relationship between Marx and Weber's sociologies (1973). The fact that the relationship between these two major sociologists is discussed in terms of their conception of the nature and function of ideas in social life clearly indicates the central place occupied by the study of symbolism in much of nineteenth- and twentieth-century sociology.

First, I intend to ascertain the basic elements of the Weberian sociology of culture while at the same time pointing out some points of contact with the Marxist approach. We shall see that Weber had modified Marx's position by attributing to ideas a primary, rather than a derivative, influence upon social processes and by attributing to social interests an influence, not on the origin, but on the interpretation of religious ideas. Naturally Weber's priority on ideas in the development of civilizations entails a different conceptualization of the relationship between material and ideational forces of social life than the one proposed by Marx. What is important from the perspective of this volume is to examine whether Weber's emphasis on the ideational and subjective principles of social life offers a healthy reaction to the strand of economic determinism contained in Marx's works. Weber contends that it is the "subjectively understandable orientation of behavior" to make sociology an interpretive discipline rather than a natural science: "The more precisely [phenomena] are formulated from a point of view of natural science, the less they are accessible to subjective understanding" (Weber 1964:101). We will, however, see that Weber draws also on the structural perspective. Therefore, the central question to be discussed is whether Weber integrates the structural and subjective perspectives, and if so, whether one could find in Weber useful elements for building that theoretical synthesis we have found missing in Marx.

In the critical section I will argue that Weber is caught in a serious dilemma: on the one hand, he defines sociology as an exclusively interpretive discipline and, on the other hand, in his substantive works he uses both the interpretive and the structural approach. Moreover, the Weberian approach suffers, like the Marxist approach, from an empiricist and dualistic flaw that leads Weber to conceptualize and use the subjective principle and the structural principle of explanation as two separate and analytically independent principles.

The Subjective Orientation of Social Actors Toward Ideas

The centrality of symbolism in Weber's sociology stems from his very definition of sociology as a discipline which deals with "historically and culturally important phenomena" (Weber 1964:109). According to Weber the cultural significance of a given period is determined on the basis of the interpretative grasp of the meaning attributed to actors "typical" of that period: "If any object can be found to which the term spirit of capitalism can be applied with any understandable meaning, it can only be an historical individual, i.e., a complex of elements associated in historical reality which we unite into a conceptual whole from the standpoint of their cultural significance" (1958:47;see also 58). For instance, Weber argues that the systematic and rational search for profit is a core component of the ethics of entrepreneurs (typical actors) and of social classes that are the "bearers" of the ethics (1958:65). Similarly, the idea of "calling" is "what is most characteristic of the social ethic of capitalistic culture" (1958:54).

Sociologists cannot make intelligible the cultural significance of historical events by formulating general laws because "the significance of cultural events presupposes a value orientation towards the events. The concept of culture is a value concept" (1949:70). The idea of devotion to labor may appear irrational from the point of view of hedonism and nonreligious rationalism (1958:78), but it becomes rational when related to the idea of calling and religious rationalism. Here Weber deals with what he calls "rational action" in terms of an orientation toward a religious and absolute value (1964:115). Because of its value quality, "cultural or psychic events are *objectively* less governed by laws" (1949:80), and the "knowledge of cultural events is

unconceivable except on the basis of the significance which the concrete constellations of reality have for us in certain individual concrete situations" (ibid.).

The question arises: does the orientation of social actors toward
values mean that cultural factors have an analytical priority and, if
so, how is the orientation of social actors toward culture to be understood—in terms of a connatural and mechanical affinity or in terms
of a dialectical and mutually constitutive relationship? A clear answer
to these questions can be formulated through a close reading of two
seminal essays, the first on the influence of the Protestant ethic on
the development of the economic rationality in Western society (Weber 1958) and the other on the Economic Ethic of World Religions (in
Gerth and Mills 1958).

Let us begin with the first of the two essays. Weber's explanation
of the rise of capitalism is based on socioeconomic, social psychological, and symbolic cultural factors. First, Weber argues that entrepreneurial capitalism presupposes the separation of business from the
household, a system of rational bookkeeping, rational law, and rational administration (Weber 1958:25).[1] These elements seem to indicate as many structural prerequisites for the emergence of capitalism.

Second, the "rational capitalistic organization of free labor" (Weber
1958:21) would not be possible without "the ability and disposition
of men to adopt certain types of practical rational conduct" (p.26).
These personality characteristics constitute the central component of
Weber's explanation. Third, this type of personality is held to be largely
the result of religious ideas. "The magical and religious forces, and
the ethical ideas of duty based upon them, have in the past always
been among the most important formative influences on conduct."
According to Weber one cannot explain the origins of capitalism
without dealing with "the influence of certain religious ideas on the
development of an economic spirit or the ethics of an economic system" (p. 27). Weber intends to ascertain to what extent religious ideas
have influenced "the qualitative formation and the quantitative ex-

[1] All the quotes in this section are taken from the 1958 English translation of Weber's
essay (Weber 1958), a translation which incorporates the changes introduced by Weber
in the second publication of his work.

pansion of the [capitalistic] spirit over the world" (p. 91). Weber defines his task as one of "clarifying the manner and the general direction in which the religious movements have influenced the development of material culture" (pp. 91–92).

The thesis that ideas determine the rational orientations, which in turn determine material culture, could have not been stated more clearly. However, Weber does not exclude the influence on the origin of capitalism of factors other than ideas; he only suggests that "the ethical ideas of duty have in the past always been among the most important formative influences on conduct" (p. 27). Consequently, according to Weber it is advisable to document this influence, first, and then attempt to demonstrate "to what extent the historical development of modern culture can be attributed to those religious forms and to what extent to others" (p. 92). He rejects the thesis "that the spirit of capitalism could only have arisen as the result of certain effects of the Reformation, or even that capitalism as an economic system is a creation of the Reformation" (p. 91). In Weber's words, such a thesis is refuted by "the fact that certain important forms of capitalistic business organizations are known to be considerably older than the Reformation" (ibid.). These passages clearly show that for Weber a monocultural explanation is as erroneous as the monocausal explanation of the economic determinists. Weber is keenly aware of the "tremendous confusion (complexity?) of interdependent influences between the material basis, the forces of social and political organization, and the ideas current in the time of Reformation" (ibid.). Such a formulation seems to go beyond the realm of the interpretive orientation. As a matter of fact, it is clear that the structural perspective is central in Weber's argument even in the two seminal and early essays I have referred to.

The Copresence of the Subjective and Structural Orientation

I argue that Weber's framework contains elements other than prerequisite factors, cultural determinants (ideas), a psychological orientation (economic rationality), and their result, which is the material culture. In fact, Weber states that the notion of making money, not as a means to satisfy material needs, but as a duty which derives from a "calling," an "obligation" toward one's professional activity (1958:54), is mostly responsible for the overcoming of the traditional economic mentality and for providing the "ethical foundation and justification" (p. 75) to the entrepreneurial or capitalistic mentality (p. 63) of the lower industrial middle classes (pp. 65, 69) and modern bourgeoisie (p. 75). We find here a reference to another important variable, class structure. Is class structure to be interpreted as just a structural prerequisite which permits the emergence of a rational mentality? If this is so, religious rationality would be the only direct determinant of economic rationality. Or, rather, is class structure to be understood as an equally important explanatory principle? Moreover, Weber's reference to social class makes one wonder whether he intends to attribute to class interests an influence on the origin of the religious ideas adopted by the bourgeoisie. These issues are clarified in the other classical essay, "The Economic Ethic of World Religions."

This work was written as an introduction to a series of essays on this subject and was published for the first time in 1915 (reprinted in Gerth and Mills 1958). In it Weber deals with the "economic ethic" of Confucianism, Hinduism, Buddhism, Christianity, Islam, and Judaism. Economic ethic is defined as "the practical impulses for action which are founded in the psychological and pragmatic contexts of religions" (p. 267).[2] Once more Weber clearly states that "no economic ethic has ever been determined solely by religion" (p. 268). On the contrary, religion is only one determinant of life conduct, since economic and political factors have a great influence on the life conduct of the social strata that most strongly shape the practical ethic of religion. Weber, however, immediately clarifies that religion can not be explained in terms of the social situation or ideology or material interest of the social stratum that is the bearer of religion. On the contrary, religious ethic "receives its stamp primarily from religious sources, and, first of all, from the content of its annunciation," although it remains true that "each generation adjusts the content of revelation to the needs of the religious community" (pp. 269–270). The Marxist thesis that ideas merely reflect or express material inter-

[2] The quotes in this section and the following sections are taken from Gerth and Mills (1958).

ests is clearly rejected; for Weber there is no preestablished correspondence between the material interests of social classes and the
content of ideas they follow. The original content of revealed religions is not preponderantly originated from the social interests of the
speakers or their followers (p. 270). The interests and ideologies of
social strata, however, influence the formulation of religious doctrines by shaping the form and content of the religious needs of social strata.

The notion of relationship between interests and ideology, on the
one hand, and the interpretation of religious doctrine, on the other
hand, is incompatible not only with a Marxist but also with a psychological explanation of the origin of religion. Weber rejects
Nietzsche's contention that the ethics of duty can be "considered a
product of repressed sentiments for vengeance" on the part of ba-
nausic people who are without power and are forced to work (in
Gerth and Mills 1958:270). Similarly, Weber excludes resentment as
an explanation of the origin of religious ethics. However, he accepts
the notion that certain "motives . . . have determined the different
forms of ethical rationalization of life conduct." For instance, for for-
tunate people religion satisfies the need to know that their fortunes
are "legitimate." Weber does not state that the theodicy of good for-
tune is produced but rather that it is "anchored" in such a need
(p. 271).

For Weber a fundamental function of religion is to satisfy the deep
human need to give meaning to the cosmos, and such meaning, or
religious rationalism, is produced by the stratum of intellectuals (in
Gerth and Mills 1958:281). Religion contains a system of rational
meanings as well as irrational presuppositions that are accepted as
given: "What these presuppositions have been is historically and socially determined, at least to a very large extent, through the peculiarity of those strata that have been the carriers of the ways of life
during its formative and decisive periods. The interest situation of
these strata, as determined socially and psychologically, has made
for their peculiarity, as we here understand it" (ibid.).

Given his *verstehen* approach, it is not surprising that Weber places
a great emphasis on psychological elements. In discussing magical
asceticism, Weber states that chastisement, abstinence, and suffering

"awaken or at least facilitate" or "are avenues for the attainment of superhuman, that is magical, powers" (pp. 271–272). A similar kind of reasoning must also hold true for religion, since Weber states that "among these 'less favored social strata' religiosity has either been a substitute for, or a rational supplement to magic" (p. 274).

However, as in the case of sociological factors, psychological explanations cannot account for the origin of religion and the initial formulation of the religious message. Not the origin of religion but "the development of a rational religious ethic has had positive and primary roots in inner conditions of those social strata which were less socially valued" (Weber in Gerth and Mills 1958:276). Like sociological explanations, psychological explanations help explain the interpretation and following of religious ideas. For instance, a psychological need of a social group can become the object around which the religious message is reformulated; "resentment could be significant as one factor, among others, in influencing the religiously determined rationalism of socially disadvantaged strata" (p. 276) and to explain why the redemptive interpretation of religion finds a "permanent locus among less favored social strata" and why "the suffering of a people's community . . . becomes the object of hope for religious salvation" (pp. 273–274). In conclusion, their "social locus," or following, can be explained in terms of social and socialpsychological factors.

The central point I want to emphasize is that social psychological factors are rooted in the class structure. In both of the classical essays, social strata are considered as the locus of the link between ideas, social interests, and social action. In *The Protestant Ethic and the Spirit of Capitalism*, Weber attributes to the middle class a crucial role in the emergence of economic rationality because of an elective affinity between the disposition of the middle class to adopt a "practical rational conduct" and the calling to religious rationality. Similarly, in the essay we are presently analyzing Weber attributes to leading social strata the role of fostering the interpretation and development of those ideas which have affinity with their life style and interests. During the routinization of the revealed message, the followers of the religious leader select and reinterpret those ideas that have affinity or convergence with their interests; the part of the message which does not find followers falls into extinction. For instance, although not originated from the interests and needs of literati, Confucian ethics was followed by the literati because such ethics had an affinity with their life style. Similarly, warrior class leaders rejected emotional religions and endorsed religions with powerful gods. Peasants have leaned toward the worship of nature, whereas the urban bourgeoisie has leaned towards Christian piety (Weber in Gerth and Mills 1958:283).

We must conclude, then, that the class structure at least mediates the connection between religious ideas and the psychological orientation of the entrepreneurs. After my close reading of Weber's two essays, I have glanced at some recent Weberian literature and found out that various sociologists concur in the notion that the structural orientation is important in Weber's sociology. For instance, Jonathan Turner states that Weber understands social phenomena at the level of meaning *and* at the collective level that emerges among groups of actors (1978:34). Weber focuses on social and cultural structures and their mutual impact (p. 311). In the words of two authoritative interpreters of Weber, H. H. Gerth and C. Wright Mills, Weber's analysis extends to various social structures, such as society, association, community, bureaucracy, capitalism, and social stratification (class, status, party). In doing so he follows the principles of structural explanation because he explains social structures "by their functions as going concerns rather than by the subjective contentions of the individuals who act them out" (Gerth and Mills 1958:57).

Guenther Roth (1977:1354) agrees with David Beethan on the existence of a duality in Weber's perspective; he insists on such scholarly concerns as the construction of typologies and causal analysis, yet in his political writings he aims at an understanding of the "the interaction between the major features of a particular social and political process, conceived as a whole. . . . It is possible to find in Weber's political writings a sense of interrelationship of forces in society which is frequently lacking in his academic work" (Beethan's words as quoted by Roth 1977). Stated differently, in Weber's political writings the functional and structural perspective are predominant.

Randall Collins (1980) finds that the early theory of the origin of capitalism presented in *The Protestant Ethic and the Spirit of Capi-*

talism is only a fragment of Weber's full theory. Collins argues that a more mature theory can be found in the "General Economic History" and that such a theory is "a predominantly institutional theory, in which religious organizations play a key role in the rise of modern capitalism but especially in conjunction with particular forms of political organization" (p. 296). Collins also finds a dichotomy between Weber's methodological writings, in which he discovered explanations in the forms of general causal principles, and Weber's substantive writings, in which one finds "implicit generalizations about the effects of institutional arrangements upon each other and statements of cause-and-effect" (ibid.).

In my view, Collins' systematization of Weber's theory of capitalism consists of a structural explanation of "the institutional structures of rational capitalism" (p. 932)—an explanation presented in the form of a causal chain whose elements consist of ultimate background, and intermediate conditions of the characteristic features of capitalist rationality. To put it in the words of a contemporary German interpreter of Weber, "Constellations of historical and sociological factors determine for Weber, whether a particular type of rationality in fact found clear expression as a mental process alone or also as regularities of action . . ." (Kalberg 1980:1160). This formulation also seems to point out the analytical priority of structural over interpretative factors of explanation. Without attempting to resolve this issue, I focus my analysis on the question of whether the structural and interpretive perspectives are essential elements of Weber's theoretical, i.e., programmatic, formulations. Then I shall raise the question of whether the presence of the two perspectives indicates a theoretical inconsistency and, if so, what are the reasons for such an inconsistency.

Critique of Weber's Paradigm

Weber's Programmatic Dilemma Between Subjective and Structural Orientation

Weber emphatically reiterates that "subjective understanding is the specific characteristic of sociological knowledge" (1964:104) and that one can speak of "sociological generalizations" "only when they can be regarded as manifestations of the understandable subjective meaning of a course of social action" (p. 100). Weber states also that "sociology . . . is a science which attempts the interpretive understanding of social action in order thereby to arrive at a causal explanation of its course and effects" (p. 88).

How are both interpretive understanding and causal explanation possible?—Doesn't the notion of causality presuppose generalizations? In a lucid vindication of Weber's methodology, David Zaret has tried to restore the special significance of causal explanation: Weber does not refer to nomothetic causal explanations as many of his commentators claim, but to serial and concrete causality, whereby the attempt is made to integrate a particular fact into a concrete text and hence to explain its genesis (Zaret 1980). Zaret argues that Weber could integrate "interpretation" and "explanation" (which entails the notion of causality) because of the special methodological tool he had invented, namely, the ideal type. "They [ideal types] causally relate formal features of social life to their culturally significant elements, to typified subjective meanings seen as antecedent causal factors." Hence, "ideal types facilitate explanatory and interpretative analysis while maintaining a subjective point of view because empirical generalization never achieves nomological status." Such a theoretical posture derives from Weber's concern with the uniqueness of historical events (Zaret 1980:1187–1188). According to this interpretation, Weber has always remained consistent with his own programmatic interpretive orientation, since the latter is not incompatible with elements of causal explanation.

However, I maintain that a close reading of Weber's texts reveals the presence of an unresolved dilemma. Weber admitted the necessity of reckoning with a set of data which do not fit the scope of interpretive sociology; this is the case, for instance, of "statistical uniformities" such as death rates, crime rates, occupational distributions, and similar "statistice of processes." Statistical rates and "uniformities" are not understandable, in the Weberian sense of the term, and, therefore, cannot be the proper object of sociology, which for Weber must be restricted "to subjectively understandable phenomena" (1964:100). Yet, Weber concedes that these "processes and uniformities" are not any the less important for sociology since "they become conditions, stimuli, furthering or hindering circumstances of action" (p. 100). Undeniably, Weber is here referring to structural constraints of subjectively oriented action. Weber continues that "such phenomena, however important, are simply treated by a different method from the others" (p. 100).

The question immediately arises: what kind of methodology does Weber refer to and should such a methodology be considered a sociological methodology? Weber maintains that "a subjectively understandable orientation of behavior exists only as the behavior of one or more individual human beings." However, an individual can be considered "as a collection of cells" or as a psyhic life made up of "a variety of different elements." When we consider the individual from this point of view, we are developing knowledge about the behavior of elements, and such a knowledge is expressed in terms of uniformities and causal relations. Obviously, the notion of uniformities and relationships among parts refers to a structural type of explanation. For Weber this kind of explanation belongs to the natural science paradigm: "To obtain a causal explanation of individual phenomena [is] to subsume them under uniformities" and this is to deal with them from the point of view of natural science (1964:101). Apparently here Weber refers to nomothetic causality—at least if we want to be in tune with Zaret's line of reasoning. Functional analysis, which typically deals with "the relation of *parts* to a *whole* also belongs to the realm of natural science; but the functional frame of reference is "not only useful but indispensable" (Weber 1964:103) as a provisional orientation, that is, as "only the beginning of sociological analysis." Weber argues that we "must go beyond merely demonstrating functional relationships and uniformities" (p. 103), the latter being the typical accomplishment of natural sciences.

The question, then, is whether the study of social structures and structural explanations can properly belong to the realm of mature sociological analysis. By social structures, I refer to what Weber calls social collectivities, such as "states, associations, business corporations, foundations" or "nation, army" (1964:101–102). Weber is not prepared to write them off altogether from the realm of interpretive sociology, and therefore he focuses on the concept of people's orientation toward normative structures. "The subjective interpretation of action must take account" that these collective entities "have a meaning in the minds of individual persons, partly as something actually existing, partly as something in the normative authority. . . . Actors thus in part orient their action to them, and in this role such ideas have a powerful, often a decisive, causal influence on the course of action of real individuals. This is above all true where the ideas concern a recognized positive or negative normative pattern" (p. 102). It is precisely because "the action of various individuals is oriented to the belief" that collectivities exist or should exist (ibid.) that sociologists must go beyond the level of functional relationships and reach the level of "the subjective understanding of the action of the component individuals" (p. 103).

However, Weber seems to reduce collectivities to individuals; for instance, he states that "it may be convenient or even indispensable to treat social collectivities . . . as if they were individual persons" (1964:101). Far from being deterred by psychological reductionism, Weber seems to offer a rationale for a substantive and a methodological form of it: "But for the subjective interpretation of action in sociological work these collectivities must be treated as solely the resultants and modes of organization of the particular acts of individual persons [substantive psychologism], since these alone can be treated as agents in a course of subjectively understandable action [methodological psychologism]" (p. 101). Weber justifies his at least apparent substantive psychologism by the following reasoning: when in sociology a reference is made to collectivities "what is meant is only a certain kind of development of actual or possible social actions or individual persons" (p. 102).

Weber seems forced to such a conclusion by the premise that because sociology deals only with the subjective interpretation of action "collectivities must be treated as solely the resultants . . . of the particular acts of individuals" (1964:101). Consequently, Weber's methodological assumption has the twofold consequence of reducing structural and functional explanations to a subordinate role and, worse, of reducing social structures to psychological entities. The conflict between structural explanation and interpretation is programmatically resolved with the elimination of structural explanation.

Weber's solution, however, is merely a verbal one because he leaves two problems unresolved. Firstly, there remains a theoretical problem: Weber does not offer methodological tools to deal in their own terms with the social (structural) properties emerging out of social interaction; this remains true even though he has conceded that structural factors "condition" social action. Secondly, there remains a de facto inconsistency in Weber's works; as we have already mentioned, Weber has dealt in his substantive analyses with social structures as intelligible units of sociological analysis; especially in his political writings he has focused on social institutions and explained them structurally and functionally as well as causally. In conclusion Weber seems caught in the conflict of choosing between the structural and the interpretative orientation. What are the roots of such a dilemma?

Empiricist Perspective and the Dualism of the Weberian Orientation

Weber's analysis suffers from an inadequate epistemological assumption. In fact, Weber considers subjective meaning, ideas, and statistical uniformities to be self-evident and self-contained data of analysis. But once these data are accepted as legitimate and reliable at their face value, one cannot adequately deal with the issue of the scientific validity of concepts and explanations, nor can one integrate interpretive and structural analyses, nor meaningfully argue that functional analysis is important only as a "beginning of sociological analysis" (Weber 1964:103) and as a "preliminary preparation for the investigation" (p. 107).

That Weber, like other empiricist social scientists, takes sociological data at their face value is overwhelmingly clear from his own formulations. Just a few quotes will be sufficient to make the point clearly. Weber declares that in studying the spirit of capitalism he was dealing "with the question of whether a particular type of religiosity produced a psychological vehicle that tended to create a typical conduct"; in his own words that vehicle consists of "praticalpsychological motives with which a particular religion imbues actual ethical conduct" (Weber 1978:1113). These particular formulations reflect not only the initial but also the late period of Weber's career. In fact, the passage I have just referred to was written in 1910 in a polemic against detractors of his essay on the origin of the spirit of capitalism. In that essay Weber explains that he was dealing with the "psychological tendencies" that sprang from religion, that is, with a "habitus" that emerged among people which prepared them to live in a specific way, or with the "inner ethical core of the personality" (p. 1124). At the same time, he was interested in the "objective political and objective economic prerequisites" of that spirit. These formulations reflect the empirical conceptualization of traditional sociological orientations. Weber could have not been more explicit on this point. Since his own study encompasses "a very complex historical phenomenon," "it is possible to begin only with *the apparent givens* and gradually attempt, by sorting and abstracting, to grasp the concept through the exclusion of that which is nonessential" (my italics) (p. 112). Weber relied, then, on "the apparent givens" of sensory information to formulate his own concepts.

Such an empiricist position had serious implications for his own understanding of sociology as a "generalizing science" (Weber 1964:109). Weber agrees with the principle that no one can make a claim of scientific knowledge unless he or she can demonstrate the adequacy and validity of the concepts used and the conclusions reached. Accordingly, Weber claims that a given course of social action becomes comprehensible when it is "shown to be both adequately grasped at the level of meaning and at the same time the interpretation is to some degree causally adequate" (p. 99). The interpretation of meaning can be achieved through a "direct observational understanding" of actions and utterances (p. 95) and through an "explanatory understanding" which implies that "we understand in terms of motive the meaning an actor attaches" to actions (ibid.).

The issue of the adequacy and verification applies to causal explanation as well. The interpretation of a sequence of events is causally adequate when "according to established generalizations from experience, there is a probability that it will always actually occur in the same ways" (1964:95); this explanation is based on the notion of "statistical probability according to verified generalizations from experience" (*ibid.*).

David Zaret argues that Weber is concerned with "genetic accounts of unique configurations at a high level of generality" rather than with analytic laws which are not compatible with the analysis of cultural significance. Weber's usage of ideal type demonstrates a "balance between generalizing abstraction and concrete analysis" (Zaret 1980:1187). My contention is that the empiricist conceptualization of historical data has prevented Weber from achieving a satisfactory formulation of the relationship between abstraction and concrete data. As a result, the scientific validity of both interpretation and causal explanation are put into question. Firstly, how can one prove the adequacy of interpretive understanding if it is based on direct observation and on the "observational understanding of action?" (Webster 1964:95). Weber argues that "for the verifiable accuracy of interpretation of the meaning of a phenomenon, it is a great help to be able to put one's self imaginatively in the place of the actor and thus sympathetically to participate in his experiences" (p. 90). Formulations of subjectively understandable action constitute "sociological types of empirical process only when they can be empirically observed with significant degree of approximations" (*ibid.*). However, Weber must immediately admit that such an internal observation (opposed to the "external observation" of causal and functional analysis) has a "price" in that it possesses "hypothetical and fragmentary character" (p. 104). Like any other empiricist sociologist, Weber cannot produce a satisfactory solution of the "correspondence" rule "between the theoretical interpretation of motivation and its empirical verification" (p. 98).

A similar problem exists with the notion of the adequacy of causal explanation, since it is based on "statistical probability according to verified generalizations from experience" (Weber 1964:99).

These criticisms are not intended in the least to undervalue the monumental achievement of Weber's historical and comparative analyses. I am here taking issue only with the theoretical foundations of Weber's methodology, an aspect of his sociology which is far from being a marginal one; in fact, Weber's contribution to sociological methodology is considered a milestone in the history of sociology. The problem exists not only in the reliability of the appearances of experiential data but also in the notion of generalizations from experience and in the process of concept formation (ideal type) from experiential data. I am aware of Zaret's complaint that Parsons has dehistoricized Weber, who was not at all interested in general laws. However, even Weber's ideal type entails a process of concept formation and a type of analysis that is conducted "at a high level of generality" (Zaret 1980:1187). In fact, like other empiricist social scientists, Weber claims that sociology as a generalizing science is characterized by the abstract character of his concepts, which lack the "fullness of concrete content." In this passage Weber clarifies that the process of "sorting and abstracting" employed to form a concept entails "the exclusion of that which is nonessential" (1978:1112). The process of abstracting just the essential features of a historical phenomenon entails a level of formalization which is clearly different from the level of empirical generalizations based on statistical patterns and uniformities.

In discussing Parsons' position elsewhere I have precisely pointed out the existence in Parsons of an impasse between the level of empirical generalizations and the level of abstract formulations, or an impasse between an empiricist and a formalist level of analysis (Rossi 1981:56–60). By the same token, and for the same reasons discussed here, Parsons cannot offer either a satisfactory solution to the problem of empirical verification (Rossi 1981:61–62). In dealing with Parsons, I have mentioned that transformational structuralism offers a positive solution to the issue of concept formation and verification with the notion of transformational rules. I will discuss these issues in part 2 of this volume.

I shall briefly mention also that the empiricist perspective introduced not only a dichotomy between the concrete level of historical data and social concepts but also an unbridgeable dilemma between structural explanation and interpretation. In fact, either one reduces social structure to psychological entities, as Weber seems inclined to do in his methodological writing, or he accepts social structures as data to be explained in their own terms. In the first case, structural explanation is virtually eliminated and in the second case it remains analytically distinct and independent from interpretive understanding; as a consequence the problem of the fit or correspondence or subordination of the two forms of explanation remains a moot question.

Transformational structuralism avoids such a theoretical dichotomy with the notion of transformational links between the epiphenomenal level of subjective meaning and observable patterns of interaction, on the one hand, and the underlying logical matrix of their various possible actualizations, on the other hand. The discussion of these notions will also have to await the second part of this volume.

Before closing the chapter on Weber it is worth mentioning some Weberian perspectives and ideas which, to Weber's credit, seem to have somewhat sensed certain shortcomings of the empiricist perspective and even anticipated some concepts of transformational structuralism, embryonically at least.

The Weberian Perspective and Formal Structuralism: A Case of Affinity?

Eisenstadt (1981:173) has argued, and Blau echoed (1981:5), that Weber has provided some initial answers missing in the structuralist approach of Lévi-Strauss, expecially the identification of institutional mechanisms which link deep structures to overt social organization. According to Eisenstadt, Weber's *wirtschaftsethik*, or general religious ethic orientation, is to be considered the equivalent of the notion of deep code in structuralist thought, except for the formalist quality that this notion has in Lévi-Strauss' works. Moreover, Eisenstadt considers Weber's demonstration of the influence of religious ideas on economic and political spheres examples of institutional mechanisms missing in Lévi-Strauss.

No one can deny the existence of analogies between the Weberian paradigm and transformational structuralism. I for one argue in favor of such a thesis but for different and, I believe, stronger reasons than the ones suggested by Eisenstadt. To begin with, Eisenstadt's castigation of the formalist and abstract quality of the structuralist notion of code and his insistence on identifying the institutional loci of the code and the institutional mechanisms linking the deep structure to overt behavior betray an empiricist orientation. In fact, Lévi-Strauss' whole effort consists of going beyond the empiricist level of analysis by formalizing the logical matrix of observable institutional loci and mechanisms. These logical matrixes are not merely abstract codes but both "logical operators" (Lévi-Strauss 1969:181), or operational procedures for analysis, and constitutive mechanisms of institutional structures. The need for an empirical identification of the institutional loci and mechanisms of the structural codes is not a controverted issue. Structuralists rely on ethnographical and statistical analyses of institutional mechanisms and loci of symbolic codes only as a preliminary phase of analysis. For structuralists the crucial issue is to identity the relationship of logical transformations that link the various cultural orders so as to map out what Lévi-Strauss calls the "order of orders." Hence, what Eisenstadt dismiss as formalistic categories are nonetheless the key elements of the structuralist approach, which is a formal but not a formalist approach.

Let us revert to the issue of whether Weber's approach contains elements of relational structuralism. The formal perspective is certainly present in Max Weber. Let us, for instance, consider the notion of "status group"; whereas class is defined by Weber in terms of the market situation, or market control, of economic goods, status group is defined in terms of symbolic properties, i.e., in terms of "the probability of certain social groups receiving positive or negative social honor. The chances of attaining social honor are primarily determined by differences in the styles of life of these groups, hence chiefly by differences of education" (Weber in Gerth and Mills 1958:300). Weber argues that social interaction implies "mutual esteem among equals;" therefore, the absence of interaction among certain people signifies the existence of "status differences" among them (ibid.). "Status stratification influences the economic structure by barriers or regulations of consumption, and by status monopolies [and] . . . through the bearing of the status conventions of the respective ruling strata who set the example. These conventions may be in the nature of ritualist stereotyped forms, which to a large extent has been the case with the status stratification of Asia" (p. 301).

Weber could not have been more explicit in asserting that life style, social conventions, patterns of consumption, and ritualist forms are the defining characteristics of status groups. This means that for Weber symbolic forms and "regulations" are important constitutive principles of social stratification. The importance of symbolic forms in Weber's sociology emerges also in his discussion of "modes of orientation of social action," or types of action which correspond to a "typically appropriate subjective meaning attributable to the same actors" (Weber 1964:120). There are three modes of orientation to social action—those based on the belief in "legitimate order," those based on "self-interest," and those based on "usage." Usage is closely related to fashion and "convention," both of which "usually spring from a desire for social prestige" (Weber 1964:121).

It is Weber's contention that, because of increasing rationalization, matters of style and art are more and more considered "independent values which exist in their own right." Art would rescue us from the pressures of everyday life, and especially "from the increasing pressures of theoretical and practical rationalism." In such a climate there is "a shift from the moral to the aesthetic evaluation of conduct" (in Gerth and Mills 1958:342). A clear example of how aesthetic forms can be constitutive principles of social ranking can be seen in the "status honor" enjoyed by Chinese literati and in the "gentleman ideal" which prevailed at their time: "The princely man and once the hero was the man who had attained all around self-perfection, who had become a work of art—in the sense of a classical, eternally valid, canon of physical beauty. . . . Benevolence tempered by classical [canonical] beauty was therefore the goal of self-perfection" (p. 436). Weber goes on to explain a little further that the Chinese prebendary official demonstrated his status—that is, his charisma—"through the canonical correctness of his literary forms." For this reason a great importance was given to these forms in official communications (p. 437). Here artistic norms become social norms and the criterion which defines the group one belongs to as well as its "status." These quotes clearly indicate that Weber's symbolic sociology dealt not only with symbolic content (ideas) but also with symbolic forms. These considerations, however, are not sufficient by themselves to make of Weber a relational structuralist inasmuch as formal considerations can be incorporated within an empiricist framework.

One can, however, detect in Weber's works certain tendencies toward, or affinities with, key elements of the metaempiricist formalism that are at the core of relational structuralism. Firstly, Weber has proposed the conception of sociology as a form of logical analysis, the definition that Lévi-Strauss himself has given of the structuralist approach (Lévi-Strauss 1963:217). Both Lévi-Strauss and Weber have been influenced by Kantian and neo-Kantian thought, which are essentially antiempiricist movements. Werner Stark has stated that the concept of "elective affinity" was construed by Weber as a theoretical alternative to "mechanistic causalism and quasi-organological functionalism," two preeminent forms of empiricism (Stark 1958:256). Richard Herbert Howe has argued that the concept of elective affinity is an idea in the Kantian sense of the term. In Kant's *Critique of Pure Reason*, affinity denotes a canon to be followed by the intellect in the process of concept formation: the "law of the affinity of all concepts bids a continuous transition from every single species to every other via the stepwise increase in multiplicity" (Kant quoted in Howe 1978:376). Logical or analytical affinity indicates properties common to a given set of concepts.

It is my contention that Weber's analysis unfolds within such a framework. For instance, he claims that given the complex web of reciprocal influences in the case of the origin of the spirit of capitalism "one can proceed only by first of all inquiring as to whether and in what points definitive elective affinities between certain forms of the religious faith and its work ethic are discernible" (Weber quoted in Howe 1978:368). Howe makes the following comment on the underlying rationale of Weber's methodology: "Within the chaos that the social scientist confronts, there is an order; this order exists not only for himself but also for the actors in history and largely affects history's course. The logic of history would be the logic of the elective affinities" (1978:368). Here one finds explicitly stated the key ontological assumption of structuralism—the existence of an "immanent" rationality within the universe (Lévi-Strauss 1971:614).

There is another important affinity between Weber and relational structuralism. Any concrete phenomenon is best understood as a particular realization among a large number of other possible realizations; hence, to fully understand the significance of a given phenomenon one must map out the logic of all possibilities. Such a combinatory logic is germane to Kant's notion that nothing is possible unless its predicate includes all possible predicates of things in general (Howe 1978:376). The logical analysis of all possibilities is clearly implied in Weber's explanation of historical phenomena. For instance, in *The Social Psychology of World Religions*, Weber avers: "All the great religions are historical individualities of a highly complex nature; taken all together, they exhaust only a few of the possible combinations that could conceivably be formed from the very numerous individual factors to be considered in such historical combinations" (in Gerth and Mills 1958:292). The same consideration applies to Weber's definition of the ideal type: "The great majority of empirical cases represent a combination or a state of transition among several such pure types" (pp. 299–300).

According to relational structuralists, only after the logic of the possibilities has been determined can one determine the deep structure of a phenomenon or the relational constants among its elementary components. Such a notion does not seem alien from Weber's perspective, since he wrote: "Not ideas but material and ideal interests, directly govern men's conduct. Yet very frequently the world images that have been created by ideas have, like switchmen, determined the tracks along which has been pushed by the dynamic of interest" (Weber in Gerth and Mills 1958:280). Obviously, the notion of world images has strong affinities with the notion of structural constraints and deep structure.

We can speak also of a methodological affinity between the Weberian ideal type and the structural notion of mechanical model, a notion which has been the stumbling block for many empiricist critics of Lévi-Strauss. Whereas statistical models are based on averages of empirically observable frequencies, mechanical models are formulated to isolate only the structural tendencies of the system (see Rossi 1973a, 1977, 1981). Perhaps the empiricist critics of Lévi-Strauss would better understand the structuralist position if they carefully read the distinction made by Weber between "average types of an empirical statistical character" and "ideal or pure types." Rightly Weber maintains that statistical averages are precise when a given action remains qualitatively the same and the differences are only differences of degree. "But in the majority of cases of action in history and sociology the motives which determine it are qualitatively heterogeneous. Then it is quite impossible to speak of an average in the true sense. The ideal types of social action . . . are thus unrealistic or abstract in that they always ask what course of action would take place if it were purely rational and oriented to economic ends alone" (Weber 1964:110–111). The methodological elimination of nonrational factors from the ideal type is rendered necessary by the need to formulate models completely adequate on the level of meaning (p. 110). Hence, Weber rightly states that ideal types are unrealistic in the sense that social actors are usually moved by a combination of motives.

Unfortunately, Weber uses subjective meaning as the core element of the ideal type and, therefore, he cannot go beyond the empiricist level of analysis. In other words, since Weber has chosen "subjectively understandable meaning" as a level of analysis, he cannot deal with the relational constants which are constitutive of a given historical situation or with the transformational relationships connecting different historical periods. We shall see that the contribution of relational structuralism on this point is crucial. In this sense, relational structuralism brings to full fruition important Weberian concepts which have been forced by the empiricist orientation to remain latent.

Excursus on Mannheim's Sociology of Culture

Mannheim was an eclectic thinker influenced, among others, by Simmel, Marx, Lukàcs, Scheler's phenomenology, Gestalt psychology, and the neo-Kantianism of Rickert and Windelband. Mannheim had as a teacher Alfred Weber, whose sociology of culture had a special influence on his thought. I shall briefly analyze Mannheim's conception of sociology of culture and a few other aspects of his thought which seem to anticipate or have affinity with certain ideas of transformational structuralism.[3]

Consistent with the distinction between ideal and real factors,

---

[3] Mannheim was also heavily influenced by the Marxist theory of ideology, which he both generalized, by proposing the notion that all knowledge is existentially determined, and also modified, by stressing the notion that ideas are both material and spiritual. However, since Mannheim did not offer a new paradigm for the sociological study of ideology, I shall not discuss this and related aspects of his thought that underwent various stages of development.

which was traditional in German social thought, Mannheim distinguishes between the spiritual, or intellectual, and historical, or temporal, elements of social phenomena. He echoes Max Weber's notion of sociological explanation when he states that social phenomena must be explained through causal analysis, in so far as they are historical occurrences, and through interpretive "understanding," in so far as they are intellectual or ahistorical phenomena (Wolff 1971:xxivff).[4] However, such a distinction does not imply a positivist dichotomy between the mental and historical aspect of social phenomena or between mind and society:

It is senseless to pose questions as to whether the mind is socially determined, as if mind and society each possessed a substance of its own. The sociology of mind is not an inquiry into the social causation of intellectual processes, but a study of the social character of those expressions whose currency does not reveal, or adequately disclose their action context." Mannheim 1967:20)

By focusing on situational meaning the sociologist can study both aspects of social phenomena in an integrated way. The sociologist must make sure that "the content analysis of the utterances is resumed in the restored context of the original interaction, and their complete situational meaning is reconstructed" (Mannheim 1967:54). Mannheim uses the notion of social interaction and situational meaning not in a behaviorist sense but in a cultural sense, as is clear from the following passage: "Inasmuch as society is the common frame of interaction, ideation and communication, the sociology of mind is the study of mental functions in the context of action" (p. 20).

Because of its cultural or symbolic significance, the study of social interaction must always include the study of meaning, which has both a conscious and unconscious dimension (Mannheim 1967:55). Elsewhere, he states that the "sociology of mind" studies "meanings and symbolic acts" and equates the "sociology of mind" with "cultural sociology" or the "sociological study of symbolic acts" (p. 58). The notions that social interaction has a symbolic or cultural significance and that it must be studied both in terms of conscious and

[4] The quotes from Mannheim's works are taken from Wolff (1971) unless otherwise indicated.

unconscious meaning are pioneer contributions, which have been developed by symbolic interactionists and phenomenological sociologists. More recently, they have found a new interpretation with the notion of symbolic structure as developed by transformational structuralists.

We have stated that Mannheim rejects the positivist dichotomies between mental and social processes; he proposes this important concept when he discusses the relationship between the function and meaning of ideas. Having noted that ideas assume new meaning when they change social function, he argues that "the sociology of mind does not seek to relate two discrete sets of objects—the social and the mental—to one another, it merely helps to visualize their often concealed identity" (Wolff 1971:lxxxviii).

This view seems to anticipate or at least be consistent with the notion of isomorphic relations between mental, social, and biological structures postulated by transformational structuralists.

Mannheim makes a distinction between the idiographic, comparative, and ahistorical or axiomatic forms of sociological analysis. The task of the "ahistorical axiomatic" explanation is to identify "constants" in social life (Wolff 1971:lxxvi). Structural sociology explains "the specific, separate constellations which the universally possible, ultimate elements of society assume in different societies in history" (p. lxxxvii). Elsewhere, Mannheim argues that "immanent structural analysis" must show the a priori possibility of a system of thought "by a logical analysis of structure" (p. xxiv). Again, this perspective is consistent with transformational structuralism, which is a form of logical analysis used to explain apparently contradictory or heterogeneous data in terms of few underlying logical structures.

Mannheim distinguishes in any system of thought three elements—systematization, system, and architectonics. Systematization is the "first ordering of the elements of experience," a "constitutive ordering of all theoretical notions which are conceptualizable only as systemic entities." Such a perspective is shared also by Lévi-Strauss, who holds that the perception of relationship is the fundamental operation by which mind organizes (structures) social reality. For Mannheim, system is a "methodological form" and "architectonics" is the "mere mode of presentation" (Wolff 1971:XXIII). One may argue that the intermediate position occupied by the system between systematization and architectonics is analogous to the notion central to transformational structuralism that transformational rules provide the link between the surface and deep structure of culture.

Mannheim seems to adopt a combinatory view of social phenomena when he declares: "General sociology construes rather than describes its subjects, and it proceeds typologically from elementary to complex phenomena. Elementary are those acts which enter into all or many relationships, while complex are those phenomena which present combinations of elementary acts" (Mannheim 1967:56). Mannheim quotes Simmel, Park, and Burgess as proponents of a combinatory view of social phenomena: "On this level [of general sociology] the singular phenomena of history are construed as particular combinations of suprahistorical tendencies" (p. 57). We shall see that the combinatory view of social phenomena is at the core of Lévi-Strauss' perspective and that this perspective allows transformational structuralists to overcome the dichotomy between the subject of investigation and the object investigated, and to construct a scientific language common to linguistic, social, and natural sciences.

Before we can deal with this question (in the third part of this volume), we must consider the post-Weberian and post-Mannheimian developments of the interpretive paradigm.

Symbolic Interactionism and the Study of Situational Meaning

Weber's programmatic concern with "subjectively understandable meaning" has given rise to the theoretical justification for developing the microsociological perspective in sociology. According to Weber, "action is social in so far as by virtue of the subjective meaning attached to it by the acting individual (or individuals), it takes account of the behavior of others and is thereby oriented in its course" (Weber 1964:88). "Social action may be oriented to the past, present, or expected future behavior of others" (p. 112). Central to this conception of social action is a reference to the "reciprocal orientation" of social actors, so that the study of social action becomes the study of the process of interaction among reciprocally oriented social actors.

The concern with social interaction has been investigated in a systematic way by symbolic interactionists, whose most distinguished representatives are Charles Horton Cooley (1864–1929) and George Herbert Mead (1863–1931).

We must, however, acknowledge that the European sociologist Georg Simmel has pioneered the systematic study of sociability, or social interaction. What is interesting is not only the formal aspects of Simmel's sociology but also his symbolic character. The influence of the German tradition of Kant and Dilthey is clearly visible in Simmel's distinction between the form and content of social interaction and his insistence that sociologists should be concerned with the forms or "underlying uniformities" of interaction (Coser 1965:7). Even more interesting to me is Simmel's idea of "pure form," which comes close to Weber's notion of ideal type, as was discussed in the previous section. The symbolic aspect of Simmel's sociology is evident in his contention that sociology must deal not only with forms of interaction but also with the invisible world of symbols and perceptual forms through which people perceive the world. These forms are transmitted through language, ideology, institutions—in a word, through culture, which is a constraining force on the individual.

The American school of social interactionism has undertaken the systematic study of the interacting links between symbolic systems and the individual as well as the processes through which the human personality emerges out of such an interaction. In these brief pages I limit my consideration to the key elements of the interactionist approach as developed by Cooley and Mead without entering into an extended discussion of the various representatives of American interactionism, such as Robert Park, E. C. Hughes, and W. T. Thomas, or the difference between the Chicago and Iowa schools of interactionism.

Charles Horton Cooley and George Herbert Mead were influenced by pragmatist philosophers, especially by certain ideas of William James regarding the importance of subjectivity in social life and the nature of the mind. William James had proposed the notion that consciousness is to be considered as a continuous flow of conscious states and that the mind continuously expands on the occasion of new experiences. He also introduced the distinction between the I, or the self as a knower, and the Me, or the self as a known object; in an innovative way, James considered not only the external world but also the self as an object of study and distinguished a material, a social, and a spiritual self.

Charles Horton Cooley

Charles Horton Cooley proposed the view that social interaction is mediated by mental processes. He argued that social relations take place among "personal ideas" we have of real persons: "My association with you evidently consists in the relation between my idea of you and the rest of my mind. . . . The immediate social reality is the personal idea. . . . Society, then, in its immediate aspect, is a relation among personal ideas" (Cooley 1964:18–19).

Consistently with the emphasis he placed on the "mental" aspect of social interaction, Cooley argued that to understand social interaction is not sufficient to observe behavior and to collect verbal explanations of behavior; one must also interpret behavior through a sympathetic understanding: "The perception or imagination of the external trait is accompanied by sympathy with the feeling, sentiment, or idea that goes with it" (Cooley 1926 in Manis and Meltzer 1967:72). Cooley distinguishes between the knowledge of external traits and human knowledge. The knowledge of external traits is "spatial, material," (p. 69) "external" and "behavioristic" knowledge (p. 72). Human knowledge is "personal or social knowledge," and is "sympathetic" knowledge because it presupposes a communication with the minds of other men, "which sets going a process of thought and sentiment similar to theirs and enables us to understand them by sharing their states of mind." Human knowledge is also "dramatic," because it consists of "a visualization of behavior accompanied by imagination of corresponding mental processes" (p. 69).

In explaining human or social knowledge Cooley stresses the notion that experience, consciousness, meaning, symbolism and language are essential elements of social interaction. The experiential and affective aspect, or empathy, which accompanies the perception of behavior is the distinctive element of dramatic knowledge. In fact, dramatic knowledge "is based ultimately on perceptions of the intercommunicating behavior of men, and experience ot the processes of mind that go with it. It also consists of inner sentiments which you yourself feel in some degree when you think of him in these situations, ascribing them to him" (p. 72). "Dramatic" and "sympathetic introspection" is a form of "mental analysis through the probing of consciousness and memory" (p. 77). But one cannot introspect into the content of consciousness without the mediation of gestures and symbols because thought and feelings are expressed through gestures as well as verbal and written symbols (p. 74). Symbols are vehicles and recording devices of meaning: "As we perceive and remember sensuous images of gesture, voice, and facial expression, so at the same time, we record the movements of thought and feeling in our consciousness, ascribe similar movements to others, and so gain an insight into their minds" (p. 75).

Cooley's thesis is that sympathetic introspection cannot take place without the mediation of language. In fact, language stimulates and organizes the process of introspection: "When we have come to use understandingly . . . words recalling motions of the mind as well as of the body, it shows that we have not only kept a record of our inner life, but we have worked up the data into definite conceptions which we can pass on to others by aid of the common symbol" (p. 75). In summary, according to Cooley, ideas and conscious states are essential constituents of social interaction that cannot be understood without the mediation of symbols and language.

I omit here the discussion of the refinements brought by Cooley on the notion of self, the process of "looking-glass self," the role of primary groups, and so on. However, I want to mention that the emphasis on subjective meaning and consciousness is characteristic also of McIver's idea of "dynamic assessment," W. I. Thomas' "definition of the situation," and Florian Znaniecki's concept of "humanistic coefficient." Znaniecki contends that the cultural aspect of data is the distinguishing element of sociological analysis and that cultural data cannot be separated from human experience, which he labeled the "humanistic coefficient." Znaniecki distinguishes two types of sociology. First, there is the natural science orientation of the sociologist who studies human actions "as a natural process given to him without any reference to how it appears to anybody else. . . . The other way of obtaining an inductive knowledge of human activity would be to use consistently the humanist coefficient in dealing with it and take it as it appears to the agent himself and to those who cooperate with him or counteract him" (Znaniecki 1934:44–45).

George Herbert Mead

The sociologist who proposed the most systematic view of the symbolic nature of social interaction and of the interrelationship between social interaction and the emergence of self was George Herbert Mead. Mead intended to correct the introspective and mentalistic view of the self proposed by Cooley by stressing the notion that the self and society are not merely mental phenomena but belong to the objective social experience. Mead was influenced by pragmatism, which gives priority to behavior over experience and explains meaning in terms of behavior. Like Weber and Cooley, Mead considered meaning the distinguishing characteristic of human behavior, but he did not consider meaning an idea superimposed on action or as a quality intrinsic to objects; rather, he defined meaning as the totality of the responses people make to objects. Although humans can respond to an object without being conscious of it, they usually are endowed with consciousness of meaning and thought.

From the Meadean point of view, symbolism is what distinguishes human from animal communication. In the infrahuman world, communication takes place through gestures without the mediation of meaning, whereas humans respond to each other on the basis of meaning they attribute to gestures. Gestures which contain meaning are called symbols. Mead defines symbols as "the means whereby individuals can indicate to one another what their responses to objects will be, and hence what the meanings of objects are" (1934:61). Gestures with a common or shared meaning are "significant symbols."

Symbols have an important threefold function. Through symbols we understand reality, develop our thought, and regulate our behavior. First of all, the function of language is not simply to symbolize an object which is already out there or given in advance; rather language "makes possible the existence or the appearance of a situation or object, for it is a part of the mechanism whereby that situation or object is created" (Mead 1934:78). Secondly, "mind" is constituted through the interpretation of symbols, which implies the internalization of meaning, and through the organization of responses, which implies the examination of alternative courses of action. Finally, human behavior consists of the response determined by our interpretation of the situation.

A Critique of Symbolic Interactionism

Mead's notion that people respond by "constructing" their own response rather than reacting in a mechanistic way introduced a radical change in sociological thinking. In much previous sociological thinking the analytical priority was attributed to such societal characteristics as structure, culture, and collective representations, which were understood to determine the way people behave. Social interaction was understood as an expression of these societal characteristics. On the contrary, for symbolic interactionists the behavior of individuals is not an expression of societal forces or psychic drives but a constructive process, since social behavior largely derives from the way people interpret the situation. According to Blumer (1962), the structures of society and culture provide the frameworks within which the symbolic construction of interaction takes place but they do not directly determine the process of symbolic construction.

George Herbert Mead was an influential sociologist who synthesized different traditions of thought. Some sociologists emphasize the behavioral aspect of his thought, which is especially evident in the early phases of his career (for a recent example see Lewis 1979) and others emphasize the phenomenological aspect, which became evident in the later stages of his career. Some sociologists have argued that the two aspects of Mead's thought are not irreconcilable, and others have attempted to synthesize them.[5]

The resolution of this controversy is not important for the argument I am developing in this volume, since both the phenomenolog-

[5] For a discussion and bibliography on this point see Douglas (1970:16ff) and the recent controversy between Herbert Blumer (1980), on the one hand, and Clark McPhail and Cynthia Rexroat (1979, 1980), on the other.

ical and the behavioral interpretation of G. H. Mead are weakened by the empiricist perspective. In fact, the gist of the phenomenologically oriented interactionism is that solid phenomena must be studied "on their own grounds," "as experienced in everyday life" and not as "created by (or strained through) experimental situations." Phenomenological interactionists maintain that "human actions are highly situational, and that human actors act in accord with their constructions of meanings for the concrete situations they face" (Douglas 1970:7). The emphasis on meaning as experienced and constructed by the social actors and on situation-specific and concrete actions make phenomenological interactionism vulnerable to the same criticism of intuitive and "approximate" approach leveled against Max Weber's methodology. In fact, the basic method for reconstructing the "experiential meaning" remains *verstehen* and empathy. Moreover, phenomenological interactionists do not explain how it is possible that different actors in different social positions produce coherent patterns of intersubjective communication of experience and meaning. Phenomenological interactionists take for granted what they ought to demonstrate, the very core of their perspective.

Behavioral interactionists do not fare any better, notwithstanding the claim that their own position is theoretically more fruitful and methodologically more applicable than the phenomenological interpretation of interactionism. One can appreciate Lewis' ingenious discussion of the various feedback mechanisms which link the transitions from symbol to attitude and from attitude to response. One is surprised also to see a behaviorist stating that "the social act is a series of four [alternating] unconscious and self-conscious moments" (Lewis 1979:284). However, I cannot see how "unconscious moments" can be studied through those reliable and experimental procedures on which behaviorists so much insist. Moreover, the real issue is to explain how the individual reliably accomplishes the itinerary through conscious and unconscious moments. It was up to phenomenological sociologists and ethnomethodologists to initiate the study of the constructive rules used by social actors to interpret a variety of situations.

A final criticism of symbolic interactionism is its inadequate consideration of the influence of structural constraints on social interaction. E. Lemert suggested that Mead had a vague conception of the "group" (Lemert 1974) and L. Reynolds (1969) claims that symbolic interactionism exhibits "astructural bias" (see also Reynolds and Reynolds 1973). When we limit our attention to Blumer's version of interactionism, we encounter in the literature a more pointed criticism. I. Zeitlin, for instance, argued that Blumer has dropped Mead's "dialectical view" to present a one-sided interpretation of Mead which "denies altogether social relationships, social structure, and social organization" (Zeitlin 1973:218). Lewis Coser concurred with Zeitlin's criticism and stated that Blumer's "orientation prevents the understanding of social structures and their constraining characteristics or of patterns of human organization such as class hierarchies or power constellations" (Coser 1976:156–157).

David R. Maines counterargued that Blumer acknowledged the presence of social organization mechanisms that have a constraining influence on the individual. According to Maines, Blumer even holds a Durkheimian conception of "social fact," although his contribution consists of showing that "these very constraining processes are composed of and expressed through interacting individuals" (Maines 1977:238). However, it is not enough to assert the presence of constraints; the important point is to offer the proper conceptual tools for analyzing the interface between structural and interpretive processes. Having stated that nothing in symbolic interactionism precludes the analysis of social structure, Maines concedes that not all symbolic interactionists have attended to this issue. It is Maines' view that most symbolic interactionists would agree with the conception of social structure as a continuous process and a changing reality produced by processes which at times have nonstructural sources. However, without an adequate conceptual apparatus one cannot make much of this statement nor of Maines' and Bottomore's contention that social structure is "simultaneously a *producer* and a *product*" (Maines 1976:256).

I shall discuss whether one can find elements of such a conceptual apparatus in the phenomenologists' and ethnomethodologists' concern for the constructive rules used by social actors in attributing meaning to particular situations. However, this discussion will be postponed to part 3, since phenomenologists and ethnomethodologists claim to be antiempiricist, a claim also put forward by relational structuralists, as I shall discuss in part 2.

Having examined the important role that two schools of interpretive sociology attribute to subject in social life, I consider next the natural science paradigm.

3

The "Natural Science" Paradigm and the Study of Symbolic Systems

I have explained in the introduction the criteria for including under this paradigm such diverse approaches as the positivist sociology of Pareto and Durkheim, the social behaviorism of G. H. Homans, and the operationalist and quantitative orientations that prevail in American sociology. In this volume I limit my attention to three of the most influential representatives of the natural science paradigm: Vilfredo Pareto, Emile Durkheim, and Talcott Parsons. All three thinkers share a marked systemic perspective and a tendency toward mathematical formulations, a tendency common also to Lévi-Strauss, Piaget, and Chomsky. Pareto deserves special consideration because he influenced the early Parsonian thought. Parsons himself has acknowledged that Henderson and Pareto were the two thinkers who more than anyone else sensitized him to the concept of system. Parsons attributed to Henderson the "statement that perhaps Pareto's most important contribution to sociology was his conception of the social system, a dictum which I myself took so seriously that I used the phrase as the title of a book some years later" (Parsons 1970a:830). I will not extensively deal with Pareto since no contemporary school of sociology claims him as the main master. I will limit my attention to the role of "derivations" in Pareto's sociology to highlight the importance of symbolism in his systemic orientation and at the same time to point out certain affinities with modern structuralism.

The well-known importance of Durkheim and Parsons in contemporary functional thought absolves me from a lengthy justification for discussing them rather than other sociologists of natural science orientation. Durkheim deserves special attention because, notwithstanding his all too often stressed positivist orientation, he clearly perceived in the latter part of his scientific career the constitutive role of symbolic systems in social life (Durkheim 1912). Moreover, we shall see that he clearly anticipated certain basic elements of modern semiotic structuralism, and his collective work with Marcel Mauss can be considered the first attempt at structural analysis in sociology (Durkheim and Mauss 1963). Lévi-Strauss himself stated at the beginning of his career that he was nearer to the Durkheimian tradition than any one of his colleagues (Lévi-Strauss 1963:63). For this reason I will deal more extensively with Durkheim than Pareto.

The influence of Parsons in contemporary sociology does not need elaboration. Besides his systemic orientation there are two additional reasons for an extensive discussion of Parsons' thinking both in part 1 and in part 3. First, he shares with Lévi-Strauss, Piaget, and Chomsky a cybernetic orientation and, second, he is a thinker who has attempted to incorporate elements of the interpretive and systemic approaches of traditional sociological thought. For this reason, Parsons is a central figure who better than any other contemporary sociologist permits one to determine the differences as well as possible relationships of complementarities between traditional paradigms and modern structuralism.

Pareto on the Role of Derivations in Social Life

Pareto was trained in natural sciences, mathematics, and mathematical economics and exposed to the positivist thought of Spencer, Comte, and J. S. Mills. It is not surprising, then, that he viewed society as a system of interdependent variables that determine human action and held that sociology should follow, as much as possible, the methods of natural and physical sciences.

Fundamental in Pareto's sociology is the distinction between logical and nonlogical actions. Logical actions are the "actions that logically contain means to ends not only from the standpoint of the subject performing them, but from the standpoint of other persons who have a more extensive knowledge" (1963:paragraph 150).[1] Human ac-

---

[1] The paragraph numeration is taken from Pareto (1963).

tions almost always have a logical purpose from a subjective point of view because "human beings have a very conspicuous tendency to paint a varnish of logic over their conduct" (paragraph 154). Actions which are logical from the objective point of view are found mostly in the realms of arts, sciences, and political economy. Nonlogical actions are the subject matter of sociology and logical actions are the subject matter of political economy.

Symbolism and symbolic human activity occupy a central place in Pareto's sociology because of the central assumptions he made about the source and nature of social life. He holds that a person is prompted to action by "sentiments,"[2] but at the same time "he wants to explain how that comes about, to *demonstrate* that in doing what he does he is prompted by force of logic" (paragraph 799). The "hunger for thinking" leads people to construct "concrete theories," some of which are "logico-experimental theories" and most of which are "pseudo-experimental reasonings" (paragraph 1401) or rationalizations. Theologies, ethical systems, philosophies, and political theories are all grouped under the category of rationalizations. Rationalizations rarely determine human conduct, but have the function of masking sentiments and giving conduct an appearance of rationality. The sociologist carries out the important task of unmasking rationalizations by distinguishing, in theories, a constant and changing element (*ibid.*). People can use more than one rationalization to justify a given course of action, but underneath a variety of rationalizations one can discover recurring imperatives or motives, such as "do not steal" or "believe in God." These constant imperatives are called "residues" of action and are not observable realities, but analytical concepts needed to link actions and rationalizations to sentiments, which are not directly observable. Residues are not a sort of fundamental instinct, but either are sentiments that give origin, for instance, to theories of sexual morality or respect for property or are deeply internalized values. The residue of sociality is an example of value res-

---

[2] Pareto uses the terms "instinct," "sentiment," "appetite," "taste," and "motivation" to refer to the spontaneous tendency of people toward objects and goals satisfying their needs. All these terms seem to indicate states which spontaneously originate in the mind; the term "interest," however, refers to psychic tendencies which originate from a reflective and calculated activity.

idue as it includes, among others, the residue of "self-sacrifice for the good of others" and "sentiments of social ranking."

The changing elements of theories are called "derivations," a term which refers to the variety of reasonings that can be used to rationalize a given course of action. These reasonings can take a great variety of forms because they "reflect the play of imagination" (Pareto 1963: paragraphs 850–851). Pareto makes a distinction between pseudoscientific theories, which are rationalizations of psychic elements, and "theories transcending experience." Preeminent among the latter are religious theories and religious rituals, which do not claim a scientific status but provide human conduct with values and cultural significance. Like Marx, Weber, and Durkheim, Pareto attributes to symbolic and other cultural elements an important role in social life. He argues that people share a number of descriptive or preceptive propositions which, combined by logical or nonlogical nexus, "with factual narrations of various sorts, constitute theories, theologies, cosmogonies, systems of metaphysics and so on. . . . The image of social activity is stamped on the majority of such propositions and theories and often it is through them alone that we manage to gain some knowledge of the forms which are at work in society—that is, of the tendencies and inclinations of human beings" (quoted in Duncan 1969:104–105). "The image of social activity" indicates that "descriptive and preceptive propositions" have an important function in the normative structure of society which is analogous to the normative function played by ideas and collective representations, respectively in Weber and Durkheim's sociology. In fact, according to Pareto, rationalizations provide human action with a "varnish of logic," and, according to Weber, ideas have the function of satisfying the basic human need for meaning. Far from being useless rationalizations, derivations have the function of intensifying the force of residues by making them conscious and coloring them with emotionality. This social psychological orientation is absent from the perspective of Durkheim, who insists that collective representations must be considered as if they were independent of the psychic activity of individuals.

The notion of derivations as masks of the real reasons for people's conduct also has some affinity with the Marxist notion of ideology.

According to Pareto, ideology encompasses not only ideas, which derive from economic and class interests, but any thought which masks any human motive. There is, however, an important difference between Pareto and Marx on this point. According to Pareto, derivations originate from the innate tendencies of an unchanging human nature, whereas for Marx consciousness and "false" consciousness are determined by social praxis.

In his early works, Pareto used the notion of class but in *The Treatise of General Sociology* he replaced it with the notion of elite, which is largely explained in terms of residues. Two of the six classes of residues are particularly relevant in explaining the nature and circulation of elites, the instinct for combinations, and the persistence of aggregates. The instinct for combinations accounts for the logical development of ideas through the combination of ideas with things and the combination of ideas with other ideas. People primarily moved by this residue elaborate pseudological systems and magical practices, thrive for economic and political control, and attempt to manipulate people and promote change even through deceptions; in short, they are like foxes. People primarily moved by the persistence of aggregates, however, tend to reject new combinations of ideas and things and to resist change; like lions, they are ready to defend with force their loyalty to their family, nation, religion, class. In economic institutions there exist two corresponding classes: the speculators, who like foxes are primarily responsible for change and progress, and the rentiers, who are interested in preserving the status quo and fight like lions to preserve it.

Once again, this conceptualization of social class reveals a social psychological perspective that also is present in Weber. As we have seen, Weber's ideal type of the "capitalist entrepreneur" implies a personality structure characterized by rationality. According to Pareto, the personality type which prevails in different groups of people determines the system of social stratification and the process of social change. The various types of residues are not evenly distributed throughout social groups, as the higher social strata absorb the less vital elements and the lower strata absorb the more vital ones. The resulting social imbalance provokes a replacement of the dominant type of elites, that is, the circulation of lions and foxes. Whereas according to Marx the fundamental fact of social structure lies in class conflict, in Pareto's sociology the fundamental distinction lies between the masses and the professional, economic, political, or governing elite.

The idea that the type of ruling elite depends on the distribution of residues seems to indicate that, like Marx, Pareto holds a monocausal explanation of social stratification, with the difference that Marx's explanation is based on economic factors and Pareto's on psychological ones. On the contrary, Pareto avoids a merely psychological as well as a merely economic approach and explains social stratification in terms of the interaction between residues, interests, and derivations or ideology. Like Marx, Pareto makes room for interests, but only as one element of the dynamics of social structure. By "interest" Pareto means the human tendencies toward material gain, political power, social honor, and, therefore, to calculated and purposeful behavior. Since social strata are the results of a differential distribution of residues, they must be considered "constellations of consciousness." However, social strata can pursue their own interests more effectively by concealing them with the help of ideology. For example, the ruling class tries to make it appear that its own interests ("utility of the community") would benefit the whole society ("utility for the community") (1963: paragraph 2134). In summary, residues, social interests, and ideology act in a combined way as constitutive principles of social stratification.

We must, then, conclude that symbolic forces are fundamental explanatory variables in Pareto's view of society because the thrust of his sociology is to explain society through an analysis of its psychological foundations and the symbolic systems which emanate from them. Like other conventional sociologists, Pareto deals with symbolism in terms of content and function, but he also anticipates elements of transformational structuralism. For instance, Pareto's distinction between constant forces in society (residues) and the changing derivations in a sense parallels the structuralist distinction between the surface and deep structure of social phenomena. Also, Pareto's notions of aggregation and combination of aggregates have some affinity with the structuralist notion that social phenomena are constituted through the combination and recombination of elementary units, as we will see in the second part of this volume. What one finds missing in Pareto is the explanation of how constant elements (residues) are related to varying elements (derivations). We will see that the notion of transformational rules adopted by transformational structuralists attempts to provide an answer to this question.

The Symbolic Nature of Collective Representations: Durkheim as a Pre-Semiotic Thinker

No sociologist will doubt that Durkheim has attributed a central importance to symbolism in social life, especially if we think of the social function that Durkheim has attributed to collective representations. Most sociologists also agree that Durkheim is a most distinguished representative of positivist sociology. Positivism is a theoretical perspective based on naturalist, determinist, and phenomenalist assumptions in the study of social facts. Naturalism holds that human society operates according to laws similar to those which govern the natural world; as a consequence, social facts can be explained independent of human will. This is the reason why positivism is also a form of determinism. Positivism also is based on phenomenalist assumptions because it assumes that the external world can be reliably understood through the phenomenal appearances that come to us through our sensory perceptions. Consistent with these three assumptions, Durkheim upheld the principle that social facts should be studied as if they were independent of the psychological life of the individuals. The notion that social facts should be studied as if they were natural objects or "things" is a methodological principle which derives from all these assumptions.

In this section I argue that the prevailing empiricist interpretation among sociologists has led them to emphasize the structural (and functional) aspect of Durkheimian sociology without perceiving the precise nature and role of symbolism, at least in late Durkheimian thought. More specifically, I shall raise the issue of whether Durkheim can be understood as a precursor of semiotic structuralism and, if so, what theoretical and methodological principles of transformational structuralism he has explicitly or implicitly anticipated. I shall argue that the combinatorial perspective so central to semiotic structuralism is consistent with Durkheim's notion of elementary forms (on the principle of elementarism see Ekeh's paper in Rossi 1982). Moreover, I shall contend that, for Durkheim, "social facts" are symbolic in nature for two reasons: firstly, symbolism not only expresses but also constitutes collective representations; and secondly, collective representations are constitutive principles of social organization. Besides, I shall also demonstrate that Durkheim has spelled out certain methodological principles which are fundamental in semiotic structuralism.

We must first clarify what Durkheim means by symbolism, since this term has been used in a great variety of ways. Durkheim views symbols as "artifices" and "labels attached to representations already created" (1961:231). Such labels are needed because collective representations and "collective ideals can only be manifested and become aware of themselves by being concretely realized in material objects that can be seen by all, understood by all and represented to all minds. Drawings, symbols of all sorts, formulae whether written or spoken, animate or inanimate objects provide examples of such realizations" (1954:94). As we can see, for Durkheim "symbol" encompasses a symbolizing and symbolized element (a distinction which is central in Saussure's perspective). The symbolizing element consists of material or concrete objects, people, events which are used as labels, artifices, vehicles to express beliefs and sentiments; the symbolized element is "beliefs," "sentiments," and "ideals," among which those of a moral and religious nature have a special importance.

Durkheim's usage of the term "representation" encompasses both elements of the term "symbol." When in the rules of sociological method Durkheim states that collective representations are expressed by symbols (1964:xlix), he uses the term "representations" to refer both to what is represented and to the way it is represented. In fact, he defines collective representations as "myths, popular legends, religious conceptions of all sorts, moral beliefs, etc." (p. 1). Yet also states that "what collective representations convey is the way in which the group conceives itself in its relation to objects which affect it" (xlix). "Concepts are collective representations. . . . [T]hey are as

concrete representations as an individual could form of his own personal environment: they correspond to the way in which this very
special being, society, considers the things of its own proper experience" (1961:483). When in this section I speak of the symbolic aspect
of Durkheim's sociology, I usually refer to the characteristics and
functions attributed by Durkheim to the content of representations;
that is, ideas, beliefs, and sentiments.

In *Suicide* he noted that "essentially social life is made up of representations" and that "social environment is fundamentally one of
common ideas, beliefs, customs and tendencies" (1963:302). How can
he reconcile this definition of the subject matter of sociology with his
positivist precept that social facts must be studied as "things," that
is, realities external to the individual, independent of his or her will
and ascertainable by external observations and empirical indicators?
(*The Rules of Sociological Method*, passim). Since this fundamental
rule implies that collective representations are legitimate objects of
sociological study only to the extent that they are externally observable, one may raise questions about the adequacy of the positivist
perspective for the sociological analysis of symbolism and therefore
wonder whether Durkheim subordinated the scope of sociological
analysis to methodological precepts.

From a Morphological to a Symbolic Perspective?

Interpreters of Durkheim have spoken of a basic ambivalence between a Kantian and a positivist attitude in his works. Perhaps one
can more accurately speak of a certain tension between Durkheim's
conception of social facts as collective and objectivized beliefs and
sentiments, on the one hand, and his positivist orientation on the
other. If this is correct, another question inevitably comes to mind:
did Durkheim deemphasize the symbolic component of social facts
(for instance, the way collective representations attract and repel each
other and their "laws of association") to pay attention to observable
patterns of behavior and facts of social morphology? Social facts for
Durkheim are of three kinds: morphological facts, institutionalized
collective representations, and "social currents." Morphological facts
refer to the number and nature of "component segments," the degree

and permanency of their fusion or arrangement, types of habitation, methods of communication, territorial distribution of population, and the like (1964:12). Religious, literary, political, and occupational groups and associations are also morphological facts (p. 3). These morphological facts are crystalized, established, and form what he calls the "social substratum" of social facts; I will use the term "structural factors" to refer to morphological facts, since it is in current use.

The second class of social facts is "legal and moral regulations, religious faiths, financial systems etc.," which "consist of established beliefs and practices" whose origin and "substratum" is either the whole society or some of its groups (1964:4, 3). "Established beliefs" refer to crystalized and, therefore, normative and constraining collective representations. Third, there are social currents like "movements of enthusiasm, indignation" and crowd movements, which are not definitely crystalized, molded, and consolidated (pp. 4, 12). As we can see, Durkheim makes an analytical distinction between collective representations and "social substratum" or structural factors. I refer to the superstructural level, or collective representations, both with the general term "culture," which is in current use in the sociological literature, and with the term "symbolism" to mean what is symbolized by symbols, namely, ideas, beliefs, and sentiments. The issue to be examined here is whether Durkheim attributed analytical priority to the structural or morphological aspect of social facts or to their symbolic aspect.

Some social scientists have labeled Durkheim an "organistic" and "utilitarian" thinker because he explained social institutions in terms of their contribution to social integration, which is assumed to be a major need of the social "organism." Radcliffe-Brown clearly attributes to Durkheim a utilitarian and functionalist perspective, which he himself has applied in anthropology.

Yet, another British anthropologist, Evans-Pritchard, has stated that "Durkheim was not nearly so deterministic and materialistic as some have made him out to be. Indeed, I should be inclined to regard him as a voluntarist and idealist." Evans-Pritchard makes the point that, for Durkheim, once religion has arisen out of social life or collective actions, it gains a certain autonomy and proliferates in a variety of ways that cannot be explained only with reference to the social structure from which it has originated (Evans-Prichard 1965–56).

In *The Structure of Social Action*, Talcott Parsons argued that Durkheim was caught between positivism and Kantianism, determinism and voluntarism (1961:409–450). In that work Parsons asserted that in *The Division of Labor*, published in 1893, and *The Rules of Sociological Method*, published in 1895, Durkheim upheld a positivist posture insofar as he considered social actors constrained by external social realities. Durkheim, according to Parsons, would have broken away from positivism with the publication of *The Elementary Forms of the Religious Life*, published in 1912, and in subsequent works, when he viewed social actors as guided by internalized social norms and began to give importance to the subjective states of the actors. Disputing Parsons, Pope claims that Durkheim was never a positivist in the sense of attributing a rational, calculating, and scientific attitude to humans in society, but was interested in treating society as a reality distinct from individuals and in stressing the importance of the constraining strength of the social factor, its content being of secondary importance. In Pope's view, Durkheim used the notion of internalization from the beginning of his works and was a positivist only in the methodological sense of stressing the use of objective variables analyzable according to the method of natural sciences (Pope 1973:414).

In replying to Pope, Parsons has stated that Durkheim was ambiguous on the issue of positivism but that he was a positivist in insisting "that society should be treated as part of nature and subject to the same order of causal determinism as other parts of nature." Parsons concedes that "the idea of the internalization of cultural components" had been present in Durkheim's works from the beginning. In fact, from the beginning he was interested in the role of morality in human societies and made room for subjective categories, that is, phenomena internal to the individual. "For me, the view that society is both a part of nature and an expression of individual motives is fundamental. Durkheim held this view from the beginning but had difficulty in clarifying his position." According to Parsons, the main reason for the difficulty was that Durkheim remained caught between the Kantian and the positivist perspectives. Parsons saw a progressive improvement in Durkheim's notion of the internalization of culture, but such an improvement led him too close to idealism; the idealist tendency is for Parsons especially evident in *The Elementary Forms of the Religious Life*, where Durkheim went as far as stating that society exists solely "in the minds of individuals" (Parsons 1975a:108).

To clarify this controversy it is useful to determine whether Durkheim gives analytical priority to the symbolic or the structural aspect of social facts. Consistent with the fundamental rule of considering social facts as things, that is, as realities external to individuals and constraining their behavior, Durkheim advocated the objective method of explaining social facts not in terms of psychic or organic elements but in terms of other social facts (1964:145–146) and according to causal and functional principles (p. 95). The efficient cause of social facts must be sought in preceding social facts; their function must be sought in the correspondence between social facts and "the general needs of the social organism" (*ibid.*) or "some social end" (p. 111). However, the notions of causal and functional explanation do not specify whether structural or symbolic variables have analytical priority and it is, therefore, not surprising to see a dilemma surfacing in Durkheim's methodology. After having stated that "ways of thinking and acting constitute the proper domain of sociology" (p. 4), Durkheim concedes that he does not possess a method to scientifically analyze social facts *both* as ideas and as observable behavior. As a result he distinguishes between a logical method, which deals with social facts as ideas, and a "methodical method," which deals with social facts as things: "If sociological phenomena are only systems of *objectivized ideas*, to explain them is to rethink them in their logical order, and this explanation is in itself its own proof; at the very most, it will require confirmation by a few examples. Only methodical experiments, on the contrary, can extract from things their real secret" (p. 144).

It is well known that by the terms "objective method" and "methodical experiment" Durkheim refers to the scientific method of natural sciences. One notices throughout his works an insistence on the "methodical" study of social facts "as things" and a neglect for the "logical order" of "objectivized ideas"; this makes one conclude that for Durkheim only methodical experiment deserves the full attention of the sociologist, no matter whether the latter studies the "structural" or "symbolic" aspect of social facts. Such a positivist methodological perspective is not only followed de facto in his works but is also a programmatic position. In fact, he states that "the ideas are not immediately given. They cannot be perceived or known directly, but only through the phenomenal reality expressing them" (1964:27). Conceivably, such a principle would apply to symbolic as well as structural aspects of social facts. However, the important issue is whether the nature and degree of logical integration of collective representations and their classificatory function in the social system are recognized as an important sociological concern. The insistence on accepting as legitimate sociological data only "what is perceived or known directly" and on the imperative of handling the data only through methodical experiments could have easily lead Durkheim to ignore the two aspects of symbolism I have just mentioned and, perhaps, even to reject them as a legitimate object of sociological analysis.

This seems to be the conclusion that Radcliffe-Brown reached when he defined "social anthropology as a branch of natural science" (1965:188) whose object of study is human society and not culture. In his view, the social scientist must be concerned with "concrete, observable facts," whereas culture "denotes not any concrete reality, but an abstraction, and as it is commonly used as a vague abstraction." After stating that the social scientist can observe only "relations of associations between individual organisms" (ibid.), he defines the task of social anthropologists as the study of social structure, which he defines as the "network of actually existing relations" (p. 190). Radcliffe-Brown distinguishes between "structure as an actually existing concrete reality, to be directly observed, and structural form" (p. 192). Structure "can only be described by reference to the reciprocal behavior of the persons related. The form of social structure has therefore to be described by the patterns of behavior to which individuals and groups conform in their dealings with one another" (p. 198).

Was Durkheim also led by positivist methodological assumptions to a similar conception of sociological analysis? It would appear that a positivist conception of social facts might have lead Durkheim to focus more readily on structural facts as objects of sociological analysis and select them as explanatory variables, the reason being that they are "directly knowable" and easier to be studied through "methodical experiments." As a result, the symbolic facts would be readily accounted for in terms of structural factors and analyzed primarily in terms of observable referents, neglecting their logical integration and classificatory function. It is clear that in his early works Durkheim explains social facts, including symbolic ones, in terms of morphological (structural) factors. For instance, in *The Division of Labor*, he treats the division of labor as the independent variable whose functions or effects are not only a variety of political, economic, and religious institutions, but also a certain type of solidarity and collective consciousness. Mechanical solidarity and a homogeneous and strong form of collective consciousness are associated with a low division of labor; on the contrary, a high division of labor produces an organic form of solidarity and a heterogeneous and weak form of collective consciousness. When Durkheim explains the causes of the increased division of labor, he states that an increase in population density causes competition among the members of the same occupations. The competition is decreased by diversifying the occupations, that is, by increasing the division of labor. In this analytical framework, the explanatory variables are morphological (structural) factors. However, in the same work one notices an ambiguity: Durkheim argues against Fustel de Coulange's contention that social arrangements (morphological factors) explain the power and nature of religious ideas.

In *The Rules of Sociological Method* Durkheim's position seems to become even more ambiguous. On the one hand he states that the forms of association are the determining conditions of social phenomena. The greater the number of people in association and the greater the social density, the greater is the intensity of social interaction and of social stimulation, which produces an emerging sense of social solidarity and a need to express it through collective representations (1964:112–114). On the other hand, whereas in *The Division of Labor* moral density is explained by material density, in *The Rules of Sociological Method* it is attributed to the fact that a "number of individuals are effectively related not merely commercially but morally, that is, who not only exchange resources and engage in competition, but live a common life" (p. 114). Moreover, he states that morphological phenomena are of the same nature as other social facts, that public law determines social organization, that political divisions are moral in nature, and that people concentrate in towns because of currents of opinions and collective pressure (pp. 11, 13). Consequently, it is not clear whether cultural (collective consciousness and representations) or structural variables have an analytical priority or whether both types of variables are explaining variables, albeit in a different and complementary sense.

In *Suicide*, the explanation of social facts no longer seems to be structural because it is held that the "victim's moral predisposition" to voluntary death is determined by "the moral constitution of society," "a collective force" or inclination (1963:299–300). Durkheim states that the social environment is the same for all individuals and affects them all in the same way but "the social environment is fundamentally one of common ideas (beliefs), customs and tendencies" (p. 302). While in this passage the analytical priority is attributed to cultural rather than structural factors, later he argues that "a people's mental system is a system of definite forces . . . [which] depends really on the grouping and organization of social elements. . . . The nature of the collective existence necessarily varies depending on whether its composite parts are more or less numerous, arranged on this or that plan, and so its ways of thinking and acting change" (p. 387).

Durkheim clarifies this apparent ambiguity in a review of a Marxist work published in the same year as *Suicide*. He argues that once they emerge from their substratum (or associations of groups and other aspects of social morphology), collective representations have an effectiveness and influence of their own and react upon the substratum itself (1897:n.p.). Clearly, this formulation assumes a partial autonomy of collective representations from the social substratum from which they originate. In an 1898 article, Durkheim illustrated this relative autonomy by comparing it to the autonomy of mental phenomena from the brain, although in later works he used biological and chemical analogies to make the same point (see Lukes 1972:233). Collective representations initially depend on the number, distribution, and forms of various social elements, but then they become "partially autonomous realities which live their own life." Collective representations have "the power to attract and repel each other and to form amongst themselves various syntheses, which are determined by their natural affinities, and not by the state of the environment in the midst of which they evolve."

Clearly, then, the "logical order" of collective representations has a lot to do with their logical properties. In this sense the organization and, partially, the content, of collective representations are explained by other collective representations rather than by "this or that characteristic of the social structure." For instance, "the luxuriant growth of myths and legends, theogonic and cosmological systems, etc. which grow out of religious thought, is not directly related to the particular features of the social structure" (Durkheim 1954:51ff). We can conclude, then, that from a mechanistic conception held in *The Division of Labor* and a belief in the primary and determining causal influence of social morphology, Durkheim moved toward the conception of social morphology as a precondition but not as a total explanation of the content or organization of collective presentations.

As to *The Elementary Forms of the Religious Life*, Talcott Parsons has recently stated that the book is couched at the level of the general system of action, which includes the social system, cultural system, personality system, and the behavioral organism. Parsons declares that "human society and the cultural framework of the human condition, including knowledge, have evolved concomitantly from a common basis" and become differentiated only at later stages of sociocultural development. Parsons maintains that this conception of a common origin is very different from the "one way conception of determinism, namely that of society as an independently existing entity, determining the nature of the organization of knowledge" (1973a:157–158). This passage rightly excludes the notion of a causal influence by the structural on the symbolic facts, but it does not dispense altogether with the issue of the analytical status of the two components; in fact, their process of differentiation still has to be explained. The explicit thesis of *The Elementary Forms* is that collective ideas are produced by and modeled after specific forms of social organization. For instance, people use the category of class because society is divided in groups.

The idea of class is an instrument of thought which has obviously been constructed by men. . . . But in constructing it, we have at least had a need of model. . . . [The only models] known from experience are those formed by men in associating themselves. . . . We would never have thought of uniting the beings of the universe into homogeneous groups, called classes, if we had not had the example of human societies before our eyes, if we had not even commenced by making things themselves members of man's society, and also if human groups and logical groups had not been confused at first. (1961:172)

Whereas the explicit thesis is that symbolism arose out of society and, therefore the social has priority over the symbolic, the implicit but fundamental thesis of Durkheim's work is that society cannot exist without symbolism. Society is held to be essentially composed of collective and symbolic representations. In a 1911 essay, Durkheim stated that "society cannot be constituted without creating ideals. These ideals are concepts, the ideas in terms of which society sees itself. . . . To see society only as an organized body of vital functions is to diminish it, for this body has a soul which is the composition of collective ideals" (1911:135–136). In a 1912 letter to Bouglé he stated that *The Elementary Forms of the Religious Life* had "the ideal for its domain" and that "ultimately this is what is essential in sociology" (quoted in Lukes 1972:236). It is more and more apparent that in this book as well as in the preface to the second edition of *The Rules* and in *Primitive Classifications* Durkheim gives an analytical priority to collective representations, that is, to symbolic or cultural facts. The preliminary analysis I have presented in these pages warrants the hypothesis that perhaps Durkheim's thought evolved from a morphological (structural) to a symbolic conception of social life; this hypothesis, however, has to be submitted to a more thorough historical sociological analysis.

At this point we must closely examine Durkheim's conception of the nature and function of collective representations to assess the exact nature of his symbolic perspective, and more specifically, to determine whether it contains elements of a presemiotic orientation.

Symbolic and Constitutive Function of Collective Representations

We have seen that for Durkheim collective representations are one of the three classes of social facts and we have also stated that collective representations consist of ideas, beliefs, and sentiments. The issues to be examined are the ideational nature of collective representations and the relationship of ideational factors to structural ones.

Ideational Nature of Social Facts. "[Social facts] consist of ways of acting, thinking, and feeling external to the individual, and endowed with a power of coercion by reason of which they control him" (Durkheim 1964:3). There are two elements in this definition: social facts consist of thoughts, feelings, and actions, and they have an external and coercive quality. The prevailing post-Durkheim sociological tradition permeated by positivist and behaviorist assumptions has largely identified the study of symbolic phenomena (and meaning) with symbolic interactionism and phenomenology and it has considered the study of observable structures of social interaction as the proper subject of structural-functional analysis. Yet Durkheim has been mostly explicit in emphasizing the mental component of social facts. Having stated that social facts differ from psychological facts, he continues: "This does not mean that they are not also mental . . . after a fashion, since they all consist of ways of thinking or behaving" (p. xlix). "Social things are actualized only through men. . . . They appear to be nothing but the overt manifestation of ideas, perhaps innate, contained in the mind. . . . The ideas therefore become the proper subject matter of sociology" (pp. 17–18). "Whereas we had expressly stated and reiterated that social life is constituted wholly of collective representations, we were accused of eliminating the mental element from sociology" (p. xli). On the contrary, "to treat the facts of a certain order as things is not to place them in a certain category of reality but to assume a certain mental attitude toward them" (p. xliii). "That social facts must be treated as things, it is not necessary to maintain that social life consists of other than representations" (p. xliv).

The mental aspect of social facts is called representation because "concepts express the manner in which society represents things" (1961:487). Religion is "a system of ideas with which the individuals represent to themselves the society of which they are members and the obscure but intimate relations which they have with it" (1961:257).

Rightly, Bellah notes that two of the fundamental terms of Durkheim are conscience and representation, which refer to mental reality. Durkheim referred to social facts as moral, mental, spiritual, or ideal and was always preoccupied with mind, consciousness, and conscience (Bellah 1973:xx–xxi). In reviewing the first volume of the work of the organicist A. Schäffle, Durkheim stated that society is integrated "not by material relations but by the ties of ideas" (1885:85); he even declared that social facts are essentially ideals and values (1911).

Durkheim fostered what he himself called an "essential idealism," which consists of two elements. The first is that it is an error "to derive all social life from its material foundation (either economic or territorial)" because "here [in the social kingdom] more than anywhere else, the idea is the reality." Durkheim does not claim that human minds create reality; after all, human mind needs material things to express ideas and produce symbols. "But here the part of matter is reduced to a minimum. The object serving as support for the idea is not much in comparison with the ideal superstructure beneath which it disappears, and also, it counts for nothing in the superstructure" (1961:260). This passage does not leave doubts on the relative independence of the *ideal* and symbolic component. The second element is that "collective representations are [realities and] forces even more powerful than individual representations." "Social thought . . . by the power which it has over our minds, it can make us see things in whatever light it pleases; it adds to reality or deducts from it according to circumstances" (*ibid.*). This notion that the great influence of ideas in society derives from their collective nature is of paramount importance in Durkheim's thought. It should be noted that both principles are fundamental in Lévi-Strauss' structuralism.

Constraining Properties of Collective Representations. "It is the collective aspects of the beliefs, tendencies and practices of a group that characterize truly social phenomena" (Durkheim 1964:7). "Above private ideas, there is a world of absolute ideas according to which [the individual] must shape his own" (1961:485). "A collective representation presents guarantees of objectivity by the fact that it is collective. A collective representation is necessarily submitted to a control that is repeated indefinitely" (p. 486). "The states of the collective consciousness are different in nature from the states of the individual consciousness; they are representations of another type. . . . The mentality of groups is not the same as that of individuals; it has its own laws" (1964:xlix).

Some authors have wondered whether the notion of collective representations implies the existence of a group mind, but Durkheim dispels any doubt about it. "If one can say that, to a certain extent, collective representations are exterior to individual minds, it means that they do not derive from them as such but from the association of minds, which is a very different thing." Collective representations are "produced by the action and reaction between individual minds that form the society" (Durkheim 1954:24–26). In an early writing, Durkheim also had stated that the collective conscience is "a composite the elements of which are individual minds" (1885:92).

Because of their supraindividual nature, collective representations have a constraining quality. "Social beliefs and practices act on us from without; the influence exerted by them differs fundamentally from the effect of habit" which "rules us from within." "[The idea of 'social constraint'] implies that collective ways of acting or thinking have a reality outside the individuals, who at every moment of time, conform to it. These ways of thinking and acting exist in their own right" (1964:lv–lvi).

We have seen that humans need symbols to concretely express collective representations. Durkheim more than other classical sociologists has emphasized the fundamental importance of symbolism in social life.

Symbolism as a Constitutive Element of Collective Representations.
The idea of totem and the idea of social unity are expressed in "a material form" or emblem. The emblem is a means to make an idea "more obvious," it is "a convenient process for clarifying the sentiment society has of itself; it also serves to create this sentiment, it is one of its constituent elements" (Durkheim 1961:262). Usually, symbols are understood as vehicles for expressing and communicating the content of collective representations; however, Durkheim contends they partially constitute the content itself. Collective representations are products of the interaction among individual minds, and this interaction cannot take place without "material intermediaries"

or emblems. "The latter do not confine themselves to revealing the mental status with which they are associated; they aid in creating it." How do emblems aid in creating mental states to which they are associated? Individual minds can communicate with one another by coming out of themselves through movements. "It is the homogeneity of these movements that gives the group consciousness of itself and consequently makes it. When this homogeneity is once established and these movements have once taken a stereotypical form, they serve to symbolize the corresponding representations. But they symbolize them only because they have aided in forming them" (p. 263).

Symbols endure and so they constantly bring to mind and arouse the collective sentiments to which they are connected. Without symbols, collective sentiments would become feebler and feebler and the individual sentiments would gradually take over. "Thus these systems of emblems, which are necessary if society is to become conscious of itself, are no less indispensable for assuring the continuation of this consciousness" (Durkheim 1961:263).

Symbols are an integral part of collective representations for another reason: "Even the fact that collective sentiments are attached to things completely foreign to them is not purely conventional; it illustrates under a conventional form a real characteristic of social facts, that is, their transcendence over individual minds. In fact, it is known that social phenomena are born not in individuals, but in the group" (Durkheim 1961:263). When we represent social phenomena with material objects, such as totems and emblems, we do not mean that they "come from the specific things to which we connect them" but that they originate from outside of ourselves as individuals. "The objectivity of its symbol only translates its externalness" (p. 264). In other words, the objective, that is, the supraindividual and constraining, property of symbols is aptly expressed and maintained by the use of symbolizing objects that are external to individuals. Durkheim's position is clear. Symbols not only are tools for expressing and clarifying representations, but they also make possible group consciousness and consequently help in creating and constituting collective representations. This is why "social life, in all its aspects and in every period of its history, is made possible only by a vast symbolism" (ibid.).

In a 1911 essay, Durkheim makes an important distinction between two types of ideals—"concepts" and "ideals of value." The concept is "a symbol of a thing and makes it an object of understanding." The function of a concept is "to express the reality to which they adhere" and to enable to make judgment "limited to the faithful analysis and representation of reality." In the case of the ideal of value, "the thing itself symbolizes the ideal and acts as the medium through which the ideal becomes capable of being understood." The function of the ideal of value is "to transfigure the realities to which they relate" and to enable one to make judgments expressing "that novel aspect of the object with which it is endowed by the ideal. This aspect is itself real, but not real in the same way that the inherent properties of the object are real" (Durkheim 1954:96). Concepts are the basic ingredient of scientific symbolism that seem to be a specific component of religious symbolism. In Bellah's opinion, this passage of Durkheim obscurely offers a *position* of *symbolic realism* in so far as it attributes to religious symbolism an active and formative role. Bellah explains that Durkheim never fully and clearly developed this point because he saw a continuity between two types of ideals and because of his devotion to science and "the real" (Bellah 1973: lii). Perhaps the positivist conception of science and reality has something to do with this gap in Durkheim's thought.

We can agree with Tiryakian that Durkheim was interested in social facts as cultural facts (1962:17–18). The analytical distinction between social and cultural systems was not institutionalized in Durkheim's time, but the definition of social facts as collective representations of mental and symbolic nature is congruent with Parsons' definition of the cultural system.

Transformational structuralists, like Lévi-Strauss and Piaget, have explained how symbolism is a constitutive principle not of the content but of the structure of collective representations, and so they develop a trend of thought that began with Durkheim.

Collective representations not only have the function of influencing the behavior of individuals but as symbolic principles of classification they have also a crucial role in the organization of the whole society.

Collective Representations As Organizing Principles of Social Structure. To avoid social chaos and collision between groups, the social space has to be divided among different groups. "Generally, society presupposes a self-conscious organization which is nothing other than a classification" (Durkheim 1961:492). Organization is an essential property of society because society consists mainly of collective consciousness and "collective consciousness is the highest form of the psychic life, since it is the consciousness of the consciousness" (ibid.). Some ideas, like space, time, class, cause, substance, and personality, are the basic categories of understanding because they dominate all our logical thought (pp. 21–22, 488).

That for Durkheim collective representations are constitutive principles of social organization can be shown as follows:

A. Collective representations are conceptual tools (logical symbols) of classificatory nature.

The individual intellect has "the power to perceive resemblances between objects of which it is conscious" and classify things on the basis of their similarity of opposition (Durkheim 1961:170). "This opposition of things has extended itself to persons; the logical contrast has begotten a sort of social conflict" (p. 171). "Certain intuition of the resemblances and differences presented by things has played an important part in the genesis of these classifications," that is, animals or natural elements placed in different clans (ibid.).

Rightly, Durkheim distinguishes between sensory images and abstract ideas.

The feeling of resemblances is one thing and the idea of class is another. The class is the external framework of which objects perceived to be similar form, in part, the contents. Now the contents cannot furnish the framework into which they fit. . . . The framework, on the contrary, is a definite form, with fixed outlines, but which may be applied to an undetermined number of things, perceived or not, actual or real. . . . The generic image is only the indistinctly bounded residual representation left in us by similar representations, when they are present in consciousness simultaneously; the class is a logical symbol by means of which we think distinctly of these similarities and of other analogous ones." (Durkheim 1961:172).

Durkheim has an essentialist frame of mind. Thinking by concepts or "conceiving something is both learning its essential elements better and also locating it in its place; for each civilization has its organized system of concepts which characterizes it" (Durkheim 1961:484).

"Thinking conceptually is not simply isolating and grouping together the common characteristics of a certain number of objects; it is relating the variable to the permanent, the individual to the social" (p. 487).

Durkheim's intellectualist bias is clear: "A logical classification is a classification of concepts. Now a concept is the notion of a clearly determined group of things; it is fluid and inconsistent . . . naturally refractory to analysis" (Durkheim and Mauss 1963:87–88). According to Durkheim, the history of scientific classifications is "the history of stages by which social affectivity has progressively weakened and made room for reflective thought" (ibid.). It is clear that both Durkheim and Lévi-Strauss share a neo-Kantian, hence intellectualist, perspective. Because of their logical nature, concepts and categories are communicable and permit the communication of minds, from which collective representations originate.

B. Collective classifications are ordering principles of social structure.

Durkheim and Mauss were concerned with symbolic classifications of moral or religious nature and not with classification intended to facilitate action or for other practical purposes. The classifications they studied have a "speculative purpose," as their function is "to make intelligible the relations which exist between things" and so are of the same nature as scientific classifications" (Durkheim and Mauss 1963:81). The principle of classification is indispensible for the organization of society in distinct and coordinated groups. In fact, to classify things is to arrange them in groups which are distinct from each other and are separate by clearly determined lines of demarcation" (p. 4).

Durkheim and Mauss discuss various systems of classificatory concepts, such as the dualistic Chinese principles of yang and yin, the division of society in two exogamous halves, in clans, in cardinal directions, or in terms of both clan and cardinal principles. Durkheim and Mauss' thesis is that various systems of social classifications have left in us "mental habits by which we conceive things and facts in the form of coordinated or hierarchized groups" (Durkheim and Mauss 1963:88).

It can be asserted that Durkheim and Mauss discovered the principle of structural explanation when they stated that the clasificatory principle of society tends to persist notwithstanding later developments of the social substrata. They also seem to have assumed a formal correspondence between symbolic forms and forms of social organization; semiotic structuralists demonstrate a structural correspondence between symbolic classification and social organization simply by showing that they have in common a similar system of relationships. The notion of homologous relationships among social institutions, understood as a system of constant relationships among their constitutive elements, is now also being applied in sociology (see the essays by Stinchcombe, Eisenstadt, Ekeh, and others in Rossi 1982).

C. The unconscious is a constitutive principle of social facts.

We have stated that the explicit or apparent thesis of *The Elementary Forms of the Religious Life* and of *Primitive Classifications* is that classificatory ideas are a reflection of social groups; in other words, mental ideas are shaped after existing forms of social organization. For Lévi-Strauss just the opposite is true. Without appropriate conceptual categories social classifications would not be possible. For instance, it is the notion of class which made possible totemic classifications because the notion of class permits one to perceive a species through particular animals. In fact, animals lack individuality and are identified by the name of their species (Lévi-Strauss 1969:151). All social institutions are logical structures built out of perceptions of relationships of similarities and differences among the raw elements of the physical habitat, and the animal and human world (*ibid.*). These perceptions are organized in binary pairs of oppositions, which are combined and recombined (Lévi-Strauss 1966:131) according to transformational rules.

We have seen that even Durkheim stresses the perception of similarities and differences as a constitutive element of class. Moreover, even Durkheim attributes a certain role to the unconscious as a source of social phenomena. "Social facts are almost too complex to be embraced in their integral aspect by a human intellect, no matter how vast it may be. Thus the majority of moral and social institutions are due, not to reasoning and calculation, but to obscure causes, to unconscious feelings, to motives having no relation to the effects which they produce and, which consequently, they cannot explain" (Durkheim 1887:118). Social phenomena are collective psychological phenomena which at times take the form of collective currents or forces. At a deeper level, social reality is the collective unconscious, which is the progenitor of collective beliefs and social currents (from *Suicide*, paraphrased in Tiryakian 1962:23). Given Durkheim's programmatic refusal to consider psychological variables as explanatory variables, the reference to the role of the unconscious as a partial source of collective representations has a special significance.

However, Durkheim does not believe in the unconscious as an aggregate of mental structures or internal constraints of mental functioning, a notion fundamental to Lévi-Strauss' semiotic structuralism. Semiotic structuralists conceive of structure as a set of relational and logical principles which generate the surface structure of sociocultural phenomena. Semiotic structuralists have developed specific methodological principles to analyze the constitutive role of deep symbolic structures in social life. Durkheim has explictly or implicitly anticipated some methodological principles of semiotic structuralism.

Durkheim's Principles of Symbolic Analysis: Preliminaries to the Semiotic Approach

According to a well-received interpretation of Lévi-Strauss' approach, the structuralist method consists of the following principles: 1) the object of study must be the totality of social facts, and the parts composing the totality receive their meaning from the place they occupy and the function they play within the totality 2) social facts must be explained in terms of immanent and not external factors; 3) the priority should be given to synchronic and not to diachronic explanations; 4) sociological explanation ultimately consists of discovering the constant relationships of similarities and differences which unite the parts composing the totality (Marc-Lipiansky 1973). It can be shown that these principles are contained in Durkheim's work, the first three explicitly and the last one implicitly.

The Notion of "Total Social Fact"; Priority of the Totality Over the Parts Constituting the Totality. The notion that the object of sociological study must be the totality of social facts rather than isolated facts is clearly contained in Durkheim's work, where the social whole is seen as "emerging" out of the union of component parts and is accepted as a primary explanatory concept (Piaget 1970:8, 98). The same is true of the principle that the parts receive their meaning from their place and function within the totality; this principle is a corollary of the previous one. Lévi-Strauss has explained this principle in the following way: anthropology has discovered that the economic, political, aesthetic, and religious aspects of life "make up a significant complex and that not one of these aspects can be understood unless it is considered together with all the others. It, therefore, tends to work from the whole to the parts, or, at least, to give the former logical precedence over the latter" (Lévi-Strauss 1963:358).

Durkheim clearly anticipated these principles when he rejected the associationist principle, according to which what is complex can be explained by what is simple and the totality can be explained by its parts through the association of elementary units. Durkheim argues that through this explanation we could not explain why the whole has properties not present in its parts. The idealistic approach, which derives the parts from the whole, is equally invalid because the whole is nothing without the parts of which it is composed. Durkheim states that social facts are the results of *sui generis* combinations of simpler elements (Durkheim 1954:28–32), and, consequently, they have "emergent" properties of totalities which are different from those of the composing parts. However, he does not explain the law of composition of this emerging totality—an explanation contained in the semiotic structuralism of Lévi-Strauss and the genetic structuralism of Jean Piaget (see part 2 of this volume).

The Principle of Immanent Explanation. Since Durkheim's explicit thesis was that association determines social phenomena, the latter should vary according to the ways the constitutive parts are grouped together. From this follows that "the first origins of all social processes of any importance should be sought in the internal constitution of the social group" (Durkheim 1964:113). Durkheim has rephrased this principle in terms of causal and classificatory explanation: "Since the constitution of the social milieu results from the mode of composition of the social aggregates . . . we now have the proof that there are no more essential characteristics than those assigned by us as the basis of sociological classifications." On this basis he rejects the accusation that his method seeks the source of social facts in conditions external to them. "On the contrary, the considerations just stated lead us back to the idea that the causes of social phenomena are internal to society" (pp. 120–121).

Priority of the Synchronic Over the Diachronic Explanation. This principle is a logical corollary of the previous one. For Durkheim the crucial factor which explains a great number of facts is the social milieu. He insists that without this factor sociology cannot establish relations of causality because "if we eliminate this type of cause, there are no concomitant conditions on which social phenomena can depend. . . . The principal causes of historical development would not be found among the concomitant circumstances; they would all be in the past. . . . The present events of social life would originate not in the present state of society but in prior events, from historical precedents; and sociological explanations would consist exclusively in connecting the present with the past" (Durkheim 1964:117).

Durkheim made an abundant use of historical data because historical development permits a deep knowledge of collective consciousness. However, history as a discipline does not explain but only describes society: "To describe the evolution of an idea or an institution is not to explain it" (Durkheim 1887:282). In fact, "it is impossible to conceive how the stage which a civilization has reached at a given moment could be the determining cause of the subsequent stage. The stages that humanity successively traverses do not engender one another (1964:117). "The antecedent state does not produce the subsequent one, but the relation between them is exclusively chronological" (p. 118). Moreover, history is concerned with the description of particular events, or, at most, "with the general direction in which humanity orients itself" (p. 119), whereas for Durkheim sociology has to be concerned with regularities, causal relations, and laws.

The Principle of Elementarism and the Relational Perspective. The principle of elementarism logically derives from Durkheim's notion that social facts are constituted through associational processes.

We know that societies are composed of various parts in combination. . . . The nature of aggregates depends necessarily on the nature and number of component elements and their mode of combination. The constitutive parts of every society are societies more simple than itself. . . . If, then, we understand the most simple society that has ever existed, to make our classification [of social types] we should have only to follow the way these simple societies form compounds and how these compound societies combine again to form more complex wholes. (Durkheim 1964:80–81)

The horde is for Durkheim the simplest social segment, and the next largest social unit is the clan composed of several families. Then comes polysegmented societies, like Kabyle tribes, which consist of many clans. Finally, we have doubly composed segmental societies, exemplified by the Greek and Roman city-states.

Consistent with this perspective, when Durkheim wants to explain why the primitives arrange their ideas in systems of classifications and where they find the plan for them, he proposes "to investigate the most rudimentary classifications made by mankind in order to see with what elements they have been constructed" (Durkheim and Mauss 1963:9).

This approach antedates and gives support to the basic methodological procedure of semiotic structuralism, which consists of breaking down a phenomenon under study into its smallest meaningful units and in determining the laws of combination and variation through which these units constitute concrete phenomena.

Semiotic structuralism has shifted the analysis from the study of concrete phenomena, each one of which is considered independent of one another in its observable characteristics, to the study of relational constants uniting the elementary relationships; this seems to be the fundamental methodological program of *The Elementary Forms of the Religious Life,* as described in its introduction. There Durkheim clearly formulates both the elementary principle and the relational perspective:

We cannot arrive at an understanding of the most recent religions except by following the manner in which they have been progressively composed in history. In fact, historical analysis is the only means of explanation which is possible to apply to them. It alone enables us to resolve an institution into its constituent elements, for it shows them to us as they are born in time, one after another. . . . It is necessary to commence by going back to its most primitive and simple form . . . and then to show how it developed and became complicated little by little. (1961:15)

Having determined the elementary units, one can see the relationships which unite them: "But primitive religions do not merely aid us in disengaging the constituent elements of religion; they also have the great advantage that they facilitate the explanation of it. Since the facts there are simpler, the relations between them are more apparent" (1961:19). Durkheim's definition of social class also seems to clearly imply the relational perspective of semiotic structuralism: "A class is not an ideal, but a clearly defined group of things between which internal relationships exist, similar to those of kindred" (p. 172).

The Notion of Deep Structure. Durkheim seems even to anticipate the notion of universal structures as sets of relational constants when he states that "the fundamental relations that exist between things cannot be essentially dissimilar in the different realms" (1961:31). Here Durkheim refers to the social and natural realms; therefore, he fosters a principle very similar to that of isomorphic structural levels underlying organic, linguistic, and cultural realms (see Lévi-Strauss 1963).

In a review of a Marxist work, Durkheim wrote: "We regard as fruitful this idea that social life must be explained, not by the conception of it held by those who participate in it, but by profound causes which escape consciousness" (1897:648). Durkheim has maintained that if external characteristics are identical in all phenomena they must be connected with their essential properties. "And if to a given group of acts there is attached also the peculiarity of a penal sanction, an intimate bond must exist between punishment and the intrinsic attributes of these acts" (1964:43).

Durkheim seems to clearly anticipate the distinction between surface and deep structure. He states that to define phenomena by their apparent characteristics is not to give a greater significance to superficial properties than to fundamental attributes; this would be true only if the former were accidental properties not connected with the latter. In fact, under these conditions "[science] could not penetrate the deeper layers of reality, since there would be no necessary connection between surface and essence" (1964:43). Durkheim was aware that it is not sufficient to establish a distinction between surface and deep structures; there was also the problem of conceptualizing and explaining their reciprocal relationships.

For in order that collective representations should be intelligible, they must come from something and, since they cannot come from a circle closed upon itself, the source whence they derive must be found outside them. Either the collective consciousness floats in the void, like a sort of inconceivable absolute, or it is connected with the rest of the world through the intermediary of a substratum on which, on consequence, it depends. On the other hand, of what can this substratum be composed if not of the members of society as they are socially combined. (1897:648).

In an undated letter to Bouglé, Durkheim wrote that "a phenomenon of individual psychology has an individual conscience for its substratum, a phenomenon of collective psychology a group of individual consciences" (quoted in Lukes 1972:234).

What was missing in Durkheim was the notion of transformational and generational rules; these were introduced later on by transformational linguistics and applied by semiotic structuralists to the study of social and cultural phenomena. However, far from being totally alien to Durkheim's work, this notion is very consistent and a much needed complement of the following passage: "[Religion] was the source, through *successive transformations*, of all other manifestations of collective activity; law, morality, art, science, political forms etc. In the beginning, all is religious" (my italics) (1897:650). The real difference between the Durkheimian, Lévi-Straussian, and structuralist Marxist conceptions of deep structure is that for Durkheim the deep structure does not consist of the unconscious constraints of mind (Lévi-Strauss) or the economic infrastructure (Marxists), but "in the way in which associated individuals are grouped" (1961:172). The other major difference is that Durkheim has not formulated the constitutive rules that give origin to collective consciousness. On these points the contribution of semiotic structuralism has been truly novel and of critical importance.

Conclusion

At the end of this section we can state that the symbolic perspective is truly a fundamental one in Durkheim's sociology and that there are important elements of continuity between the Durkheimian and the semiotic perspectives.

Contemporary structuralists, such as Peter M. Blau (1975:1), list Durkheim among the intellectual antecedents of empirical structuralism. If at all, such an interpretation is correct for the morphological (structural) phase of Durkheim's thought, but it does not do justice to two important contributions of Durkheim on the constituent role of symbolism in the content of collective representations and on the classificatory function of collective representations in society.

As Bellah notes, collective consciousness is "symbolic consciousness for it cannot exist without symbolism (1973:xlviii). This is what makes Durkheim's analytical framework ultimately a symbolic one. Durkheim's framework is structural when it explains the origin of collective representations by associational factors, but even then it is not merely positivist or behaviorist in the sense of denying the irreducible symbolic component of social facts. He is definitely not a behaviorist or a structuralist in the empirical sense of Blau and Merton's (1981) term, since he attributes a constitutive role to symbolism in the origin of collective representations and a classificatory role of collective representations in relationships to social structure.

Lévi-Strauss is one of the major thinkers who carries to the fullest development the notion of the symbolic constitutive principles of cultural and structural phenomena by introducing the basic hypothesis of the symbolic functioning of the human mind. For Lévi-Strauss the symbolic mode of functioning makes possible social exchange and significance. Symbolism is a fundamental given, as humans cannot function otherwise, even if they are not aware of the symbolic laws of their mental activity. This unconscious function gives meaning or structure to the physical world, reconciles social oppositions by giving meaning and coherence to social facts, and establishes the rules of the economic, marriage, and linguistic exchanges. For Lévi-Strauss the basic structural laws of the mind make communication possible, and symbolism is more real and determinant than what it symbolizes. The unconscious becomes the regulating principle of all human institutions (Lévi-Strauss 1969:101), and once we have discovered its structural laws we can explain why social phenomena have to be studied as totalities, which has to be done from an immanent and synchronic perspective. One can see a natural, almost logical, progression from the Durkheimian to the Lévi-Straussian paradigm. We examine next the Parsonian framework, since Parsons claims to have derived some of his important ideas from Durkheim, and in some recent works he has used certain ideas of Piaget, Lévi-Strauss, and Chomsky.

The Sociology of Symbolism in Parsons' "Natural Science" Paradigm

Talcott Parsons as a Natural Science Sociologist

Talcott Parsons has contributed to the macrosociological analysis of the structure and evolution of social systems as well as to the microsociological ("voluntaristic") Theory of Social Action. In a biographical account of his own intellectual itinerary, Parsons singled out Weber, Durkheim, and Freud as the three thinkers who exercised the most important influence on his work (1970a:873) and regarded Durkheim and Freud as his two paramount role models (p. 875). Parsons also claimed that his "first major synthesis" of the General Theory of Action formulated in 1937 must be considered the basic framework for more than forty years of sociological theorizing. Much has been written pro and con the existence of a discontinuity between Parsons' early voluntaristic Theory of Social Action and his later concerns with the systemic aspects of social action (see, for instance, Scott 1969, Turner and Beeghley 1974, Gerstein 1976, and Turner 1978:40). I do not intend to take a stand on this controversy because it is not essential for the thrust of my argument. I do not contest the claim of some of his followers that in Parsons one finds not only elements of both the interpretive and natural science paradigms but also a unique attempt to reach a conceptual balance between the two. Here I am arguing that the conceptual balance that Parsons has tried to reach has been cast in a sociological mode of theorizing that is mostly consistent with, if not inspired by, the natural science paradigm.

In the first work in which Parsons presented his voluntaristic theory of action, he criticized empiricism in its positivist and intuitionist forms (1961:728–730, 773) and proposed analytical realism as a genuinely scientific conception of sociology. Ever since, Parsons' notion of science has been explicitly in line with the natural science paradigm: "it cannot be denied that the cultural systems have the status of science if by that is meant a body of objectively verifiable propositions" (p. 763). After all, analytical realism consists of the formulation of a few central concepts that grasp important aspects of social reality. By abstracting common analytical elements one can theorize about reality without being hampered by its concreteness and complexity. The strength of analytical realism is that one can order a system of interlinked concepts which grasp the systemic element of reality and leave out empirical particularities. As Parsons saw it, at the present stage of development of the sociological theory the priority ought to be on developing systems of concepts rather than systems of propositions. However, at a mature stage "theory proper is confined to the formulation and logical interrelations of propositions containing empirical facts in direct relation to the observation of the facts and thus empirical verification of the propositions" (p. 24). Such a scientific conception of sociological theory modeled after the natural science paradigm has been predominant throughout Parsons' intellectual history.

In *The Structure of Social Action* Parsons identified the basic units of voluntaristic action: implicitly, at least, these units were seen to be in systematic relationship to each other, that is, to constitute the basic "system" of social action. In that work Parsons made an explicit reference to "the organic property of action systems" (1961:745) and to the inadequacy of an atomistic conception of the properties of the units of social action (p. 748–749).

We shall see in the third part of this volume that the systemic view became more and more prominent in the development of Parsons' thought; the natural science orientation became more and more pronounced with the growing emphasis Parsons placed on the systemic and cybernetic perspectives. For instance, in 1949 Parsons defined a theoretical system as "a body of logically interdependent generalized concepts of empirical references," whose function is "to bring out the functional relations involved in the facts already descriptively arranged" (pp. 212, 49). Such a conception is consistent with a natural science orientation and with his declared intention to follow Pareto's logico-empirical method (Parsons 1945, Loubser et al. 1976:37). According to F. Van Zyl Slabert, the following principles are fundamental to the logico-empirical approach: 1) the events are explained only when they are subsumed under general laws; 2) explanation and prediction have the same structure; 3) the same criteria are applicable to explanation in natural and social sciences; and 4) refutation or confirmation of explanations must be based on publicly observable evidence (Slabert 1976:46). These scientific canons constitute the core of the scientific method elaborated by the neopositivist philosophers of science, such as G. Bergman, R. B. Braithwaite, C. G. Hempel, and E. Nagel (p. 57). Some disciples of Parsons claim their master did not fully accept this position. However, it remains significant that such a programmatic statement should be emphasized by his followers in a volume they prepared about recent developments of the theory of social action.

Next we must discuss Parsons' natural science paradigm, and in particular the role that symbolism plays in it.

The Sociology of Culture and Symbolism in the Voluntaristic Theory of Action and the Early Systemic Approach

Parsons has distinguished four major phases in the development of his thought (1970a), which correspond to as many theoretical paradigms he has proposed: the theoretical framework proposed in *The Structure of Social Action* (1961), the pattern variables scheme (Parsons 1951), the four-function paradigm (Parsons 1953), and the interchange paradigm (Parsons 1963 and 1970). Parsons has argued that the original conceptual scheme has endured a considerable continuity notwithstanding various revisions, extensions, and generalizations it has been submitted to; his claim is that the original paradigm has continued to serve as a reference point in dealing with a variety of empirical and theoretical problems (1970a:868). My view is that there are two important elements which account for such a continuity: the unchanged pervasiveness of both the symbolic and systemic orientation in Parsons' thought. These are the two points I shall deal with in the rest of this section.

We know that the notions of meaning, culture, and symbolism played an important role in Parsons' first major work, in which he presented his voluntaristic theory of social action. There Parsons criticized positivism, utilitarianism, and idealism, but he also retained some valid elements of these approaches—the notions of constraints of social action, goal-seeking social actors, and the influence of ideas in social action, respectively. The voluntaristic character of the theory of social action stems from Parsons' focus on the subjective decision-making process of social actors who must select among alternative means to achieve their goals. The subjective decisions of social actors are affected by two kinds of situational elements—the external conditions imposed by the biological organism and the environment, on the one hand, and the normative order, that is, values, norms, and other ideas, on the other hand (Parsons 1961:44). Social action involves a state of tension between the external conditions, which are beyond the control of individuals, and the normative order (p. 732), which governs the relationships between ends and means (p. 736). Symbolism has a central place in this early Parsonian paradigm:

Concrete spatial objects and temporal events may have a cultural aspect, . . . but in so far as they are physically understandable, it can only be as symbols. External objects constitute the meaning of symbols. As objects they exist only in the minds of individuals. They in themselves are not to be found by external observation, only their symbolic manifestations. (p. 763)

Here symbols are considered vehicles and visible manifestations of cultural meanings.

Symbolism has remained a pervasive force even when the consideration of the plurality of social actors has led Parsons to accentuate the functional prespective and to focus on the issue of social integration. The social actor is seen as striving toward the attainment of goals in concrete situations and in interaction with others. The actor's "cognitive orientation is subject to standards of corrections and adequacy," which are provided by "cognitive patterns of ideas, symbols and other elements" of culture (Parsons 1964:228–229). The cog-

nitive understanding of goals by the social actor and the interpretation of the meaning of situations are essential components of the
theory of action.

At the time of the formulation of the pattern variable scheme Parsons had made a systematic distinction between the social system,
personality system, and culture. Again, the concern with meaning
and symbolism is preeminent: "various elements of the situation come
to have special *meanings* for ego as *signs* or *symbols* . . . [which]
acquire common meanings and serve as media of communication
between actors. When symbolic systems which can mediate communication have emerged we may speak of the beginnings of a *culture* which becomes part of the action systems of the relevant actors"
(1951:5). Culture is seen as a system of meaning expressed by symbols that are formulated and agreed upon in the process of interaction. What is the relationship between culture and the action system?

Culture . . . consists . . . in patterned or ordered systems of symbols which
are objects of the orientation of action, internalized components of the per-
sonalities of individual actors and institutionalized patterns of social systems. . . . There is . . . always a normative aspect in the relation of culture
to the motivational components of action; the culture provides standards of
selective orientation and ordering. (p. 327)

By cultural patterns Parsons means "belief systems, systems of expressive symbols, and systems of value orientation" (*ibid.*). The "ideas"
contained in culture patterns are shared by people; therefore, they
are important preconditions for the maintenance and integration of
social order.

Parsons does not hold an intellectualist conception of culture because he considers culture a system of ideas, expressive symbols,
and value orientations which provide the solution to the cognitive,
cathetic, and evaluative aspects, respectively of the motivational orientation problem (1951:21). "Symbols are ways of orienting which are
embodied in or controlled by the external symbolic objects." Symbolic objects control not only the system of cognitive symbols [beliefs]
and expressive symbols, but also value-orientation standards (p. 163).

The repeated emphasis on the notions of meaning, interaction, situation, and symbols is clearly consistent with the Meadian approach.
Not only does Parsons give credit to Mead for dealing with "the prob-

lem of meaning and, hence, the functions of signs and symbols in the elementary processes of social interaction" (Parsons 1965:979, see also p. 1167), but he also declares that the Meadian perspective remains "the focal point of departure for considering the cultural level of meaning" (p. 979).

There is no doubt that the analysis of symbolic systems has a central place and is a distinguishing feature of Parsons' sociology. In one of his latest statements he has declared himself a follower of the tradition of Durkheim, Weber, Freud, Piaget, and Mead in that he has emphasized "the distinctiveness of the involvement of symbolic processes" in human behavior (1978:353). Parsons shares with symbolic interactionists and Durkheim the notion that symbols are vehicles useful for expressing and communicating meaning. Moreover, Parsons concurs with the symbolic orientation of later Durkheim (see previous discussion) and semiotic structuralists assigning an analytical priority to the symbolic system in the explanation of social life. The point to be emphasized here is that by focusing on the meaning (content) of symbols as well as on their social functions, Parsons uses traditional sociological categories, that is, categories which prevailed before the advent of transformational structuralism.

At the same time, however, Parsons and transformational structuralists share systemic perspectives; this is a point which deserves close attention since it is germane to the main ideas of this volume.

The Pervasiveness of the Systemic Perspective in Parsons' Approach

At the beginning of this section I alluded to the controversy over the consistency between Parsons' original concern with the voluntaristic theory of action and his later focus on the fourfold system of action. We remember that in his first major work (1961) Parsons grounded his voluntaristic theory of action on the theoretical orientation he called analytical realism. It is indicative that in his recent discussion of the intellectual history of analytical realism he made a reference to the "closely related . . . conception of system" (1970a:830). Parsons seems to suggest that the notion of system is built within the voluntaristic theory of social action, and one can easily see that the notions of social actor, end-means relationship, goal-seeking actors, and situational constraints cannot be adequately understood except in systematic interrelationship to one another. Parsons asserts that analytical realism is congruent with the perspective of Schumpeter and Pareto, from whom he took the concept of system (p. 830); he also adds that the notion of system "has been central to [his] thinking from a very early stage" (p. 849).

Parsons' systemic perspective has evolved from a mechanical to an organic to a cybernetic conception. At the time of the intellectual influence of Henderson and Pareto, Parsons adopted a mechanical notion of system modeled after the physicochemical system; the notion of mechanical system implies that the whole is equal to the sum of its parts and that the functioning of the whole is identified with the functioning of its parts. Since the parts do not influence each other, a mechanism functions in exactly the same way, no matter how the parts are arranged. Once placed in their position, the parts continue to function in a stable way; accordingly, a mechanism is a system in a continuous state of equilibrium. It is natural, then, that the adoption of the notion of a mechanical model led Parsons to focus on "the internal environment and its stability" (1970a:830).

Soon Parsons switched to an organic or physiological conception of equilibrium, which is more appropriate for explaining the functioning of living organisms. W. B. Cannon's notion of the homeostatic stabilization of physiological processes is responsible for this evolution of Parsons' thought, an evolution reinforced later on by Alfred Emerson's works (Parsons 1970a:831, 849). Seen from the organic perspective, a system is a totality greater than the sum of its parts and a totality possessing its own structure, function, and law of growth. The structure of the organism embodies the function of its parts, none of which can be put to other functions without destroying the organism. Parsons (p. 849) contends that the homeostatic view of the system became essential to the structural-functional phase of his thought, which culminated in The Social System (1951a).

From the organic and homeostatic conception of the system, Parsons gradually moved toward the cybernetic view, an evolution paralleled by a shift from a structural-functional to a markedly functional view of the four-function paradigm (1970:35–36; 1970a:849; 1975:67–69). Living systems are open systems, as they are in continuous transaction with their environment; the same holds true for social systems. According to cyberneticians and information theorists, open systems are "programmed" to behave within a range of contingent situations and to react to feedback deriving from environmental changes as well as from the consequences of their own behavior. For these reasons, self-controlling systems are not static, but grow and change with changes in the environment. Parsons has stated that under the influence of W. B. Cannon and Alfred Emerson cybernetics "became a dominant theme" in his thinking (1970a:831). After his exposure to cybernetic and information theory, Parsons began to focus on the information and communication aspects of culture (1970:35). ✗

This phase of Parsons' thought is of particular interest for us because the cybernetic and communication perspective is fundamental not only in Parsons' conception of culture but also in the views of cultural, psychological, and linguistic processes proposed by Lévi-Strauss, Piaget, and Chomsky, respectively.

This similarity raises the question of whether there exists possible convergencies, or at least complementarities, between the traditional natural science paradigm and semiotic structuralism. This issue cannot be adequately dealt with without discussing first the systemic and cybernetic perspective of semiotic structuralism; we shall do this in the second part of the volume. The relationship between the natural science paradigm à la Parsons and semiotic structuralism will be discussed in the third part of the volume.

In closing this section I suggest that more than accomplishing a "true" synthesis of the interpretive and natural science approaches, Parsons has used in an idiosyncratic way some elements of both approaches; however, the natural science and systemic view has always been predominant. The question of whether Parsons has neglected the free and creative input of subjectivity in the dynamics of social life will be examined in the third part of the volume in the light of the theoretical issues raised by poststructural semiotics. ✗

II

Semiotic Structuralism, Genetic Structuralism, Transformational Grammar

4

The Structural and Semiotic
Study of Symbolism

So far we have seen that conventional sociologists, regardless of whether they follow the interpretive, critical, or natural science paradigm, all deal with symbolic systems in terms of their meaning and social function. Moreover, whether they deal with ideology or collective representations or culture or symbolic interaction, sociologists of traditional orientation share a common definition of symbol. Symbol is any event or object used to express and convey cultural meanings, such as ideas, beliefs, or values, or to express affective and cognitive aspects of the subjective experience of people engaged in social interaction. Social facts are symbolic in nature because they are endowed with "meaning" in the Weberian and Meadian sense of the term. The relationships between the symbolizing element (the signifier, in Saussurean terminology) and the meaning that is symbolized (the signified, in Saussurean terms) as well as the relationships of similarity and difference among the various symbols of a given cultural system have not been subjects of analysis in traditional sociology.[1]

The Structural Linguistics of Saussure

Ferdinand de Saussure initiated a new approach to the study of symbolism. The meaning of a symbol is no longer determined on the

[1] Whereas Weber and Simmel pay attention to symbolic forms, they do not analyze the constitutive elements of symbolizing forms much less the systematic relationships among the symbolizing constituents of symbols.

basis of the cultural content or the subjective experience of social actors it embodies (intrinsic meaning), but on the basis of its similarities to or differences from other symbols. In traditional sociological paradigms, the cultural content or the subjective meaning conveyed by symbols can be determined by considering each symbol separately. For Saussure, however, the meaning of a symbol can be determined only by considering its position within a set of symbols. The objects of study are not specific symbols, but whole complexes of symbols conceptualized as systems of differential contrasts. The positional meaning is called objective meaning because the relational position of each symbol within a system of symbols is independent of the people's awareness of it. The shift from an intrinsic and subjective notion of meaning to a relational and objective notion of meaning marks the advent of semiotics, or the science of signs.

The term "semiotics," which is now used more frequently than the term "semiology," originally meant the medical observation of symptoms, or "semeiotic.[2]" Locke introduced the term in philosophy to designate the study of signs used by the mind to understand things and convey knowledge; a similar use of the term is found in Leibniz. Outside of Europe, the science of semiotics has been systematically developed by the philosophers Charles Sanders Peirce, Charles Morris, and Rudolf Carnap, and has been later strengthened by the input of linguistics. Semiotic ideas have been used also in mathematics and information theory and have been introduced into social sciences by Jurgen Ruesch and Gregory Bateson, and in psychiatry by Harry Stack Sullivan. In France, semiology has received a major impulse from the linguistics of Saussure, and in Russia from mathematical and structural linguistics, psycholinguistics, and the structural typology of language.

[2] Saussure used the term "semiology," whereas John Locke used the term "semiotiché" and C. S. Peirce the terms "semiotic, semeiotic, semeotic." Until recently the first term has been preferred by French writers and the second one by Anglo-Saxon and Russian writers. However, after the International Society of Semiotics was established, the second term was used more frequently by French (see Greimas 1976) and Italian writers (see Eco 1976). A small number of authors, whom I do not follow, prefer to use the term "semiotics" for the general science of all signs and the term "semiology" for the science of signs which are intentionally used for the purpose of communication. In this restricted sense, semiology is the science of transverbal and postverbal signs (see, for instance, Rossi-Landi 1973). Whenever I use "semiology" I use it as a synonym of "semiotics."

We deal here with the theory of signs as it principally derives from the linguistics of Saussure because Saussurean ideas have been widely applied to the study of social and cultural phenomena. Saussure has defined semiology as "a science that studies the life of signs within society." He remarks that "semiology would show what constitutes signs, what laws govern them" and that "linguistics is only a part of the general science of semiology" (1966:16).[3] From the methodological point of view, language offers a model for building the science of semiology: "Language is a system of signs that express ideas, and is therefore comparable to a system of writing, the alphabet of deaf-mutes, symbolic rules, polite formulas, military signs, etc. But it is the most important of all these systems" (*ibid.*).

Saussure introduced the distinction between language as a system, *la langue*, and language as spoken by individuals, *la parole* (speech). This distinction has remained fundamental in much of linguistics and semiology. Language as a system "is a storehouse filled by the members of a given community through their active use of speaking, a grammatical system that has a potential existence . . . in the brains of a group of individuals. . . . Language is not a function of the speaker; it is a product that is passively assimilated by the individual. . . . It is the social side of speech, outside the individual who can never create nor modify it by himself; it exists only by virtue of a sort of contract signed by the members of a community" (pp. 13–14). The various speech and styles of speech of individuals are particular applications ("executions") of the grammatical system shared by a given community (p. 13).

The often mentioned influence of Durkheim on Saussure is quite evident in the Saussurean distinction between *langue* and *parole*. The *langue* is "a social fact" constituted by a "social bond" (p. 13). "In separating language from speaking we are at the same time separating what is social from what is individual and what is essential from what is accessory and more or less accidental (p. 14).[4] The influence of Durkheim on Saussure also is apparent in Sassure's contention

[3] Unless otherwise indicated the references in this section are all taken from Saussure 1966.

[4] This Saussurean distinction somewhat parallels the distinction between grammatical rules and linguistic behavior, and the distinction between code and message used by geneticists and by Jakobson and Halle.

that linguistics must study the social aspect of language (*la langue*) if it pretends to be a science.

Language, unlike speaking, is something that we can study separately. Although dead languages are no longer spoken, we can easily assimilate their linguistic organisms [system]. We can dispense with the other elements of speech [la parole]; indeed, the science of language is possible only if the other elements are excluded. [p. 15]

The positivist perspective is of paramount importance in Saussure's argument. Because speaking is an individual act, "it is wilful" (p. 14) and heterogeneous (p. 15). On the contrary, language is homogeneous because it is constituted by "social bond" (p. 13), social convention "or contract" of people (p. 14), or "collective approval" (p. 15). *La langue* can be studied scientifically because it is "a system of signs in which the only essential thing is the union of meanings and sound-images. . . . In language there is only the sound-image" (*ibid.*). There is an additional reason why language can be studied scientifically. "Linguistic signs . . . are not abstractions" but "tangible" entities, and "it is possible to reduce them to conventional written symbols" (*ibid.*).

Why does Saussure prefer the term "sign" to "symbol"? He conceives of all social relations as relations of signs and all systems of signs, like the grammatical system or the food system, as composed of the two dimensions of language and speech. For Saussure, sign is the union of a concept (signified) with a sound image (signifier), whereas in the pre-Saussurean terminology the word "sign," and often the word "symbol," were used to indicate the signifier. Saussure restricts the use of the term "symbol" to those signs based on the "rudiment of a natural bond between the signifier and signified." The "symbol" is "motivated," whereas the "sign" is "arbitrary," or unmotivated, because "it actually has no natural connection with the signified" (p. 69). Some signs are absolutely arbitrary, while others "may be relatively motivated" (p. 31).

Sign is a merely relational entity because it is "the whole that results from the associating of the signifier with the signified" (p. 67), and this association is usually arbitrary, since "even in the most favorable cases motivation is never absolute" (p. 132). If language as the *langue* is a system of signs and if in the sign "the only essential thing is the union of meaning (signified) and sound-image (signifier)," it follows that language is just a system of relational contrasts.

A linguistic system is a series of differences of sounds combined with a series of differences of ideas. . . . In language there are only differences without positive terms. Whether we take the signified or the signifier, language has neither ideas nor sounds that existed before the linguistic system, but only conceptual and phonic differences that have issued from the system (p. 120).

This Saussurean relational perspective is fundamental in structuralism, and it has produced the shift from the traditional sociological perspective, according to which the meaning of a symbol is determined on the basis of the cultural content or subjective meaning it conveys, to the semiotic perspective, according to which the meaning (or rather the value) of a sign, is determined from its position within a system of relational differences and oppositions (objective or positional meaning).

The positional or relational value of signs is determined in terms of two types of relationships that are fundamental in structural linguistics and in all semiotic approaches derived from it. The value of terms, let us say of a sentence, is determined by syntagmatic and associative relationships, the latter also called by other authors paradigmatic relationships. "In the syntagm a term acquires its value only because it stands in opposition to everything that precedes or follows it, or to both" (p. 123). Saussure defines syntagms as "combinations supported by linearity" (*ibid.*). Syntagmatic relationships unite terms which are actually present in a given chain of speaking and have a bearing on the possibility of combination, implication, and compatibility among the terms. Linguistic terms, however, also acquire their value on the basis of their difference from other terms that are not present in the discourse but that could be used as alternative terms. "The associative relations unite terms in absentia in a potential mnemonic series" (*ibid.*). When we make "mental comparisons" between one term and others, "although none of these elements is present in space, the relation is associative" (p. 124). Paradigmatic relationships determine the possibility of substituting some terms with others.

We can see, then, that combination, substitution, commutation, and permutation are the operations by which the positional meaning (value) of linguistic terms is determined. Permutation is an operation which puts into evidence the pertinent character of the linear nature of the auditory signifiers. "Their elements are presented in succession, they form a chain" (p. 70); their elements stand in "different oppositions to what precedes and what follows" (ibid.). The fact that certain letters can never occur at the end of a word means that "their presence or absence in a definite position counts in the structure of the word and in the structure of the sentence" (p. 131). We shall see that the notions of combination, permutation, and substitution are fundamental in Lévi-Strauss' and Barthes' semiology.

Saussure also introduced the distinction between the synchronic and diachronic study of language. Synchronic study is the study of a "language-state" (p. 81) or "the logical and psychological relations that bind together coexisting terms and form a system in the collective mind of speakers" (pp. 99–100). Whereas synchronic linguistics studies language at a given point in time, diachronic linguistics studies the evolution of language across time. Saussure seems to imply that a real *scientific analysis* must be a *synchronic analysis* because "diachronic events are always accidental and particular" (p. 93). This is true if one limits oneself to a syntagmatic study of events considered in their temporal and linear succession. However, if we analyze series of events from a paradigmatic perspective, we can interpret the historical succession of contingent events in relationship to other possible sequences of events. In this sense the paradigmatic approach introduces a systematic viewpoint into the study of history.

The Structural Phonology of the Prague School

The emphasis on the paradigmatic approach comes from the Prague school of phonology, whose main representatives are Roman Jakobson and Nikolai S. Troubetzkoy.

Roman Jakobson has accepted Saussure's notion of language as a system of differential contrasts and the distinction between the synchronic and diachronic study of language. He has advocated a historical linguistics, in which the synchronic perspective would play an important role. His contention is that to understand why sounds change we have to understand the relationship of a sound to the whole set of sounds; what matters is the succession of whole stages of sounds rather than of individual sounds.

Jakobson also has accepted Saussure's distinction between syntagmatic and paradigmatic relationships, which he has recast under the terms "metaphoric relationships," or relations of similarity, and "metonymic relationships," or relationships of contiguity.

We have also seen that, together with his colleague Marcel Halle, Jakobson has proposed the notion of linguistic code, which Parsons borrowed from them and used in his recent writings. Saussure himself anticipated the notion of code when he spoke about "the combinations by which the speaker uses the language code for expressing his own thought;" he made a distinction between these combinations and the psychological mechanism by which they are realized (Saussure 1966:14).

According to Jakobson and Halle, the linguistic code includes "all the distinctive features to be manipulated, all their admissible combinations into bundles of concurrent features termed phonemes, and all the rules of concatenating phonemes into sequences" (Jakobson and Halle 1956:5). Besides the concept of combination, recently used by Parsons, we find in this passage also the idea of distinctive features. Jakobson and Halle intended to "dissolve language into its ultimate components" (p. vi); first, into elementary units of meaning, or morphemes, and then into smaller characteristics which distinguish morphemes from one another (distinctive features).

For instance, *unfaithfulness* is composed of the four minimal grammatical units *un-faith-ful-ness*, which can be used either as many independent words or as component parts of other words; think, for instance, of the words *un-orthodox, art-ful, stubborn-ness*. Morphemes are clusters of sounds, but not every sound has the same importance in terms of determining the meaning of words. Some sounds are common to more than one morpheme, while at the same time they distinguish one morpheme from another. For instance, z and s in *zeal* and *seal* have in common the sound features of being a consonant, fricative articulated, no stops, not vowel, not nasal.

However, *z* is voiced and *s* is not; voice is therefore called a distinctive feature. Similarly, *r* and *l* are distinctive features because they distinguish various pairs of words such as *right-light, rot-lot, ramp-lamp*. Jakobson proposed the notion that in all languages the phonemes are organized into a system of binary contrasts, such as *p-b, t-d, s-z*. These bundles of distinctive features are called phonemes. In 1956 Jakobson and Halle organized the distinctive features in twelve binary oppositions on the basis of acoustic and articulatory qualities of sound, such as voiced-voiceless, nasal-nonnasal, grave-acute, etc. Jackson was influenced by Troubetzkoy, who attempted to establish a taxonomy of the phonetic characteristics of the distinctive contrasts of languages. Another theory of distinctive features was proposed by Chomsky and Halle in two different versions (1965, 1968). (For a detailed exposition of the three approaches to distinctive features, see Hyman 1975).

The notion of distinctive features and Saussure's relational conception of language entail that we cannot establish the value of linguistic units without determining their minimal constituents and without establishing the relational constants among them. This is in sharp contrast with the previous descriptive linguistics begun by Franz Boas and Edward Sapir and developed by Leonard Bloomfield and Zellig C. Harris. Descriptive linguists analyze language in terms of immediately observable constituents, such as phonemes and morphemes. On the contrary, Saussurean linguistics and structural phonology have shifted the study of language from the level of observable patterns of meanings and behavior to the level of *deep structures* or relational constants that unite the elementary constituents of observable data. The elementary units and their relational constants are not detectable through direct observation but only through structural analysis.

From the combined influence of the linguistics of Saussure, the Prague school of Jakobson and Troubetzkoy, and, we shall see, the Copenhagen school of Hjelmslev have emerged three major types of semiotics, which have been labeled by Roland Barthes as follows: signaletic semiology or semiology of ideology, such as that of Barthes himself; scientific semiology, such as the structural analysis of Lévi-Strauss; and textual or critical semiology, such as the semanalysis of J. Kristeva. Actually, as we shall see in part 3, Barthes has made a transition from the scientific (or structural) semiotics of Saussure and Lévi-Strauss to the poststructural semiotics of Kristeva and others. The latter approach will be discussed in part 3, whereas the scientific semiology of Lévi-Strauss will be discussed here. In fact, Lévi-Strauss has laid the foundations of the applications of semiotics to social sciences.

From Structural Phonology to Scientific Semiotics: The Structuralism of Lévi-Strauss

Claude Lévi-Strauss has applied the basic ideas of Saussure and certain principles of the structural phonology of Troubetzkoy and Jakobson to the study of social organization and culture. Like Saussure, Lévi-Strauss was influenced by Durkheim, but Lévi-Strauss intends to overcome his positivist and functionalist shortcomings and develop an approach to symbolism which uses Freudian, Marxist, psychoanalytic, cybernetic, and especially linguistic ideas. (The intellectual antecedents of Lévi-Strauss have been discussed in Rossi 1973 and his reasons for rejecting functionalism in Rossi 1974.)

Lévi-Strauss accepts Saussure's distinction between *la langue*, or the essential and necessary aspect of language, and *la parole*, or the secondary and accidental aspect of language, and so he inevitably perpetuates the positivist dichotomies between necessary and contingent, rational and arbitrary, structure and history, structure and event, and unconscious and conscious level of meaning. Lévi-Strauss claims that anthropology is a semiological science in the sense defined by Saussure and occupies that domain of semiology not yet occupied by linguistics. "For anthropology, which is a conversation of a man with man, all things are symbols and signs which act as intermediaries between two subjects" (1976:11). Anthropology deals with "domains . . . pregnant with meaning" (*ibid.*) and meaning, we know, is the realm of the sociology of symbols. For Lévi-Strauss, however, anthropology should be concerned with signs, "the sign being, according to Pierce's famous definition, that which replaces something for someone. What, then, does a stone axe replace, and for whom?" (p. 10). A given technology cannot be explained if considered in and by itself, but only in the context of the inventory of the tech-nologies of all other societies. From this perspective a given set of techniques are as many "equivalents of so many choices, from all the possible ones which each society seems to make. . . . In this sense, it is conceivable that a stone axe could be a sign. . . . It stands for the different implement which another society would use for the same purpose" (ibid). This is a clear example of paradigmatic analysis à la Saussure, the predominant approach used by Lévi-Strauss.

Saussure influenced Lévi-Strauss via the Russian formalists, who applied Saussurian ideas to the study of artistic and literary works. By studying the relationship of individual works of art to the formal structure of the genre from which they arise, the Russian formalists follow the distinction between *langue* and *parole;* they also accept the distinctions between syntagmatic and paradigmatic analysis and between the synchronic analysis of an artistic work and its dia-chronic location in the history of art. The Russian formalists have shifted the focus of analysis from such traditional questions of when and why a given work was composed, by whom and what it is about (content), to the formal characteristics of the artistic content. The most distinguished representative of the Russian formalists was Vladimir Propp, whose morphological study of the folktale was published in 1928 (Propp 1970). Through the synchronic study Propp showed that the Russian tales contain constantly recurring functions, or invariant actions played out by the characters of the story. These "recurrent constants" are limited in number and governed by a narrative logic that is responsible for the occurrence of identical sequences of func-tions in the tales. Propp discussed thirty-one narrative functions, their distributions among the characters of the tales, and the patterns of sequences of these functions.

Lévi-Strauss has pointed out two methodological shortcomings in Propp's approach—a neglect of the cultural context of the tale and an exclusive emphasis on syntagmatic analysis, which is performed by arranging the sequences of events into a temporal and linear or-der (1960). Lévi-Strauss has corrected both shortcomings by taking into consideration the ethnographic context of data and by adding a paradigmatic dimension of analysis. He has observed that the exclu-sive emphasis on syntagmatic analysis is responsible for Propp's con-cern with the surface structural features of the tales, and the consequent neglect of the deep structure from which surface features generate. In an early and well-known structural study of the Oedipus myth, Lévi-Strauss dissected the myth in basic mythemes or small meaningful stories and organized them in four different columns according to four different themes the myth deals with (1955). The myth, then, is read syntagmatically (vertically), or column by column, according to the temporal succession of the events, and paradigmatically (horizontally) to compare the central theme of each column. The paradigmatic reading reveals a deep structure of binary oppositions or a basic meaning which underlies what otherwise would appear to be an incoherent series of events.

In "The Story of Asdival" Lévi-Strauss has shown that Tsimshian mythology cannot be understood separately from the rest of the culture because of the relationship of "dialectic representation" which exists between myths and culture (1960a). This kind of analysis is an important corrective of Propp's neglect of the ethnographic and psychological context of the narratives.

Also predominant in Lévi-Strauss' works is the cybernetic perspective, which we have already discussed. Lévi-Strauss refers to Wiener's notion that society "can only be understood through a study of its messages and the communication facilities which belong to it (1954:16). As early as 1953 Lévi-Strauss had stated that "it can be said that society is, by itself and as a whole, a very large machine for establishing communication on very different levels between human beings" (1953:321). In *The Savage Mind*, Lévi-Strauss argues that both the physical and human world are closed systems of communication signals (1966:267–269). The perspective introduced by information theory makes Lévi-Strauss hopeful that one day we might be able to build a

general theory of society implying a vast system of communication among individuals and groups with several perceptible levels: that of kinship, perpetuated by the exchange of women among group of affines; that of economic activities, wherein goods and services are exchanged between producers and consumers; and that of language, which permits the exchange of messages among speaking subjects. (1976:66)

According to Lévi-Strauss, to interpret society as a whole in terms of the theory of communication is equivalent to a "Copernican Revolution" (1963:83).

Lévi-Strauss' view of society is based on a combination of cybernetic and linguistic ideas. For instance, he proposes to treat "marriage regulations and kinship systems as a kind of language, a set of processes permitting the establishment, between individuals and groups, of a certain type of communication." This does not mean, however, as certain facile critics have suggested, to "reduce society or culture to language" (1963:83). "To derive from language a logical model is in no sense equivalent to treating the former as the origin of the latter" (p. 83). Both in the exchange of linguistic signs and women, Lévi-Strauss distinguishes the twofold aspect of value and sign (p. 61). "These three forms of communication [kinship, economic activity, and language] are also form of exchange" (p. 83). Whereas communication cannot take place without sign, exchange cannot take place except with "complementary values" or items which "are simultaneously perceived as having a value both for the speaker and a listener" (p. 62). Analogously, women are perceived as values by all groups exchanging marriage partners: "Therefore, it should be kept in mind that culture does not consist exclusively of forms of communication of its own, like language, but also (and perhaps mostly) of rules stating how the games of communication should be plaid both on the natural and on the cultural level" (p. 296).

Culture is basically a set of rules for the communication of signs. It is true that in marriage what is exchanged is persons, and in economics what is exchanged is goods and services, i.e., values. However, "though neither symbols nor signs, they [economic values] require symbols or signs in order to be successfully exchanged when the exchange system reaches a certain degree of complexity" (1963:10).

In communication theory, the objects of study are signs that are "much more numerous than those of classical mechanics and much less than those of thermodynamics." As a consequence, the subject matter has been simplified and it has been possible to introduce a rigorous methodology. A similar situation holds true in linguistics, where language is explained with a limited number of morphemes and few "significant regularities in phoneme frequencies." Structuralists argue that the same method can be applied to the study of social structure whose phenomena are "of the same kind as those which in strategic and communication theory, were made the subject of a rigorous approach" (1963:315). In fact, kinship, economic, linguistic, religious, and other cultural data can be studied through a combinatory approach. "One is led to treat the various forms of social life within a given population, and the forms on the same level in different populations, as the elements of a vast combinatory system submitted to rules of compatibility and incompatibility. This makes certain arrangements possible, excludes others, and brings about a transformation of the general balance each time that an alternation or a substitution affects any of the elements" (1976:67).

In the area of totemism and kinship systems Lévi-Strauss has accounted for a variety of empirical data by showing they are as many realizations of various possible combinations of the elementary constituents of the phenomenon under study. Before Lévi-Strauss, anthropologists had offered a variety of explanations of totemism, each one accounting only for certain types of totemism and not others. By extending and reversing Durkheim's perspective, Lévi-Strauss has shown that the apparently irrational use of many insignificant insects or animals as totems is explained by an underlying logic of the natives who use them to conceptually organize the social world. Totemic species are used as intellectual devices to conceptualize not only the differences but also basic similarities and complementarities among different social groups; these intellectual devices are very useful for conceptualizing the similarities and differences clearly and concretely, and therefore for reinforcing or maintaining social differences and similarities.

For instance, the totemic animals are often pairs of animals, such as eagles and hawks, which belong to the same species. As the eagle and the hawk are two different birds, so the eagle clan and the hawk clan are two different clans. The members of the different clans are not related to each other and, therefore, are in exogamic relationship. At the same time, the two clans belong to the same tribe just as the two animals belong to the same category, "bird." We can, then, understand why the two clans exchange marriage partners with each other. Moreover, the variety of totemic systems themselves are shown to be generated by the combination of the natural order with the social order, both of which are dichotomized, the first into animal category and particular animals, and the second one into social category and persons. When a natural species is combined with a social group (clan, moiety, etc.) we have social totemism, when a natural category is combined with a person we have individual totemism, and so on. All the known forms of totemism are expressions of one or another of these possible combinations (Lévi-Strauss 1967:16–17).

Lévi-Strauss has applied not only the Saussurean combinatory and paradigmatic approach but also Troubetzkoy's phonological method, which Lévi-Strauss conceptualizes as follows: the aim is to discover general laws by using the concept of system, and selecting as units of analysis the relationships between terms rather than the terms themselves; this method implies a shift of analysis from the conscious and surface level of the phenomena to that of their unconscious infrastructure (1963:33). (For some critiques of Lévi-Strauss' use of linguistics, see Mounin and Durbin's essays in Rossi 1974.) A well-known application of these criteria is found in Lévi-Strauss' explanation of the varieties of relationships between the maternal uncle and nephew found in different societies. Lévi-Strauss observes that when the father is an authority figure, the uncle has a warm relationship with the nephews, and vice versa. The observable instances of this relation are governed by an unconscious system of relational constants, which consists of a bundle of features, or two sets of attitudes organized in two pairs of oppositions. The selection of the opposition is determined by the principle of descent; in a society with a matrilineal descent, the maternal uncle is the authority figure, whereas in patrilineal societies the reverse holds true. This relationship is illustrated in figure 4.1.

Principle of Descent	Authority, Austerity	Familiarity
Matrilineal	+	−
Patrilineal	−	+

Figure 4.1. Comparison of descent in matrilineal and patrilineal societies.

This twofold set of binary oppositions, however, does not explain all the ethnographic facts because it is incomplete. The avuncular relationship is composed of a larger system of oppositional and symmetrical relationships comprising not only two but four terms—

brother, sister, brother-in-law, and nephew. The various possible relationships among these four terms are governed by the following law: "The relation between maternal uncle and nephew is to the relation between brother and sister as the relation between father and son is to that between husband and wife" (Lévi-Strauss 1963:42). Since the system must be in balance, such law is a predictive one: if we know the relationship between the elements of one pair, we can infer the relationships existing in the other pairs. The same is true in phonology, where, for instance, from the relationship between b and p we can infer the relationship between d and t. By using this approach, Lévi-Strauss has explained a great variety of kinship systems not in terms of ad hoc explanations, such as historical, psychological, or other forms of "contingent" explanation, but as concrete manifestations of the elementary symbolic structure, which he calls the "atom of kinship." Any observable kinship system is one among other possible combinations of the invariant relationships which unite the four basic terms.

Lévi-Strauss has not limited his analysis to the phenomenon of the avunculate, but has analyzed numerous kinship and marriage systems and has shown that a previously unexplained variety of heterogenous marriage systems can be explained as empirical instances generated from two elementary structures of exchange—the restricted and the extended (see Lévi-Strauss 1963:122–125; 1969). He also has reconciled apparently contradictory explanations of observable structures proposed by different social actors by showing that social systems, which on the surface appear to be of a dualistic type, in reality are based on an underlying tripartite structure (1963: ch. 8). By using this kind of analysis, which was in part adumbrated by Durkheim and Mauss (1963), Lévi-Strauss has shown that collective representations are structured systems built out of few logical principles (see his *Mythologiques*). The function of a myth and entire systems of myths consists of mediating and resolving oppositions found in the natural and cultural realms and in reconciling conflicts or apparent contradictions between mythological and experiential knowledge. (For a more detailed explanation of this point see Rossi 1974.)

Some authors have argued that Lévi-Strauss does not follow the method of structural phonology but that he continues to operate within the boundaries of the Saussurean paradigmatic analysis. These authors argue that Jakobson and Troubetzkoy have proposed a dynamic structuralism which goes beyond the synchronic and static framework of Saussure; moreover, these two linguists have applied structural analysis to the dynamics and historical development of language. The same critics argue that Lévi-Strauss' distinction between history and structure goes against this program and ends the Durkheimian ambivalence between the logical and historical explanation by opting for a logical and synchronic analysis. (See, among others, Remotti 1971 and Granger 1960.) These critiques, which all too often are based on a too narrow interpretation of Lévi-Strauss' analysis, are not discussed here. (They are discussed in Rossi, ed. 1974.) My main intent is to show that Saussure and the Prague school agree on the notion of system as a set of invariant relationships among the basic components of a phenomena and on the use of combinatory and paradigmatic analysis. Moreover, I wanted to show that the basic tools of semiological analysis applied in social sciences have been largely provided by linguistics.

Later on I will discuss the possibility of integrating some elements of the Piagetian developmental approach with Lévi-Strauss' perspective.

The Semiotic Study of Ideology: Roland Barthes and Umberto Eco

The linguistic model of Saussure has influenced not only the social sciences but also literary criticism. Some French semioticians have approached literary works as cultural "texts" that are useful for studying the nature of cultural systems, and especially for decoding the ideological component of culture. Since the study of ideology has been of central importance in traditional sociology, I shall briefly examine the contribution that semiotics has made to the study of ideology from the methodological point of view as well as from the point of view of substantive findings. I will limit my attention to a few aspects of the works of Roland Barthes and Umberto Eco, since they have offered two of the most interesting applications of semiotic ideas to the study of ideology. Eco and the early Barthes share with Lévi-Strauss the perspective of scientific semiology; this means they study culture as a system of signs in the same sense that Saussure has studied language, as a system of signs (*langue*) rather than on the usage of language (*parole*).

Roland Barthes has achieved a reputation as a literary critic with such works as *Writing Degree Zero* (1970), *On Racine* (1964), *Critique et Verité* (1966), *The Pleasure of the Text* (1975), and so on. He has been influenced by Saussure[5] more through the Russian formalists than Lévi-Strauss. In fact, like two other French semiologists, Alexander J. Greimas and Tzvetan Todorov, Roland Barthes is concerned with the surface structures rather than with the deep structures of narrative texts. Barthes distinguishes between the story (*histoire*), or the sequence of events as they presumably occurred, and the discourse (*discours*), or the sequence of events as organized by the narrator. The structure of discourse does not depend on unconscious constraints but on the conscious control of the narrator or artist. Barthes distinguishes "action" from "function," function being the role played by actions in the story. He deals with two types of functions— cardinal functions, or metonymic plot events, and indexical, or metaphoric functions. In Barthes' view these two types of functions combine in a hierarchical way to produce the surface organization of the discourse. We may notice that the analysis of narratives in terms of these two types of functions is consistent with the syntagmatic and paradigmatic analysis of the texts, the hallmarks of structural analysis. In fact, the terms *metaphoric* and *metonymic* are Jakobson's rendition and elaboration of the Saussurean notions of "syntagmatic" and "paradigmatic" relationships.

The Influence of Hjelmslev's Glossematics

Besides using the structural notions of binarism and classification of oppositions, Barthes makes great use of the notion of "connotation"

[5] The reader should be aware that there are two competing views of semiology, both of which claim to derive from Saussure. Barthes' semiotics has been called the "semiology of signification" and it is connected to Saussure via Hjelmslev and Merlau-Ponty. This semiotic perspective defines systems of signs in terms of "signification" and extends the semiotic perspective to all conventional facts. Another interpretation of semiotics derives from Saussure via the phonological school of Prague and the functional linguistics of A. Martinet and is called the "semiology of communication." According to this view, the system of signs is defined by its function, i.e., "communication," and semiology encompasses only those signs which are used for the purpose of communication. Leading representatives of this second view of semiology are Mounin (1970) and Prieto (1968).

and "detonation" proposed by the Danish linguist Louis Hjelmslev. Hjelmslev proposed a view of language called "glossematics," which is a development of Saussure's formal view of language. Hjelsmelev acknowledges the influence of Saussure and the similarity between his scientific view of language and Saussure's formal view of language, but he claims to have arrived at the notion of a "scientific description" of language independently of Saussure. By "scientific description" Hjelmslev means a description in terms of relations between units; the notion of relationship is independent "of any properties which may be displayed by these units but which are not relevant to the relations or deducible from the relations" (Hjelmslev 1959:27). Hjelmslev states that linguistics studies the "relational pattern of language without knowing what the relata are." It is the task of phonetics and semantics to determine what the relata (the things which are related) are; but phoneticians and semanticians can do so "only by means of describing the relations between their parts and parts of their parts" (p. 33).

Hjelmslev distinguishes between the expression (or signifier) and the content (or signified) of linguistic signs, where *content* is not to be identified with *meaning*, since some content can be meaningless. Whatever is used to express some content, it is called a *sign*. Hjelmslev calls the relation (R) between the plane of expression (E) and the plane of content (C) "sign function" (1961:48–49). In turn, the sign function can become the plane of expression (or signifier) of a second and wider system of meaning, which is called a *connotative system*. These ideas are graphically represented in figure 4.2.

2d system	E	C	Connotation
1st system	EC		Denotation

(1967:89–90)

Figure 4.2. Graphic representation of connotative and denotative systems of meaning.

In these pages I am directly concerned with the denotative system of meaning. Hjelmslev states that denotative semiotics is concerned with a language whose meanings are referential and not connotative.

Denotation consists of identifying objects or events to which linguistic terms directly refer. Denotative meaning or referential meaning is also called base or first language. Connotation is a system of secondary meanings which people associate with the basic or linguistic meanings of the terms. Connotation is a system composed of signifiers (connotators) and signifieds. Hjelmslev discusses a variety of connotators, such as stylistic forms, media of communication, tones of voice, and idioms (1961:115). The signifieds of connotation refers to ideas, feelings, or affective evaluations which are implicitly or explicitly associated with the basic or denotative meaning of terms. The association between denotational and connotational meanings is specific to different cultural contexts; this is why Barthes is correct in stating that the signifieds of connotation are related to the "culture, knowledge, history" of a society, and are "fragments of ideology" (1967:91). According to Barthes, it is important to elaborate a semiology of connotation because society continuously develops second order or (connotational) signifying systems. The connotational, and largely ideological, system mediates and permeates any element which enters into the semiotic system. For this reason ideology is "the *form* (in Hjelmslev's sense of the word) of the signifieds of connotation, while *rhetoric* is the form of the connotators" (p. 92).

A level of form and substance must be distinguished both in the signified (or content) and the signifier (or expression). *Form* is what can be described adequately and coherently in linguistic terms. *Substance* refers to the rest of linguistic phenomena, which can be described only with extralinguistic criteria. Accordingly, the form of the signifier consists of syntactic and paradigmatic rules, and the substance of the signifier consists of the phonetic aspects. The substance of the signified consists of the emotional and ideological aspect of the signified, and the form of the signified refers to its organization in terms of the presence or absence of semantic markers.[6]

---

[6] Markers are elements on the basis of which we can isolate the units of meaning. For instance, *boy* is unmarked or neutral, while *boys* is marked or positive because of the final *s*. Usually, the unmarked form is more general and has a wider distribution than the marked form. By extension *dog* is semantically unmarked or neutral in respect to sex, whereas *bitch* is marked under the same respect.

Umberto Eco

Umberto Eco has applied these and related semiotic notions to the study of culture. He has suggested that culture can be viewed as a communication process, a system of signs. The idea that a sign is composed of the coupling of the signifier and the signified can be extended to the semantic level. Culture can be seen as a set of semantic units combined according to combinatory rules, with units of expression matching units of content. For instance, *mouse* and *rat* are two units of the form of content that match two units of the substance of content, a small and a big rodent, respectively. Any cultural item receives its meaning from its relationship to other items of the semantic field. For instance, the meaning of *whale* is established by contrasting terrestrial/marine, fish/mammal, and so on. In turn, each one of these terms generates other items and the meaning of each semiotic item is established by the systematic relationship and opposition to the other semiotic units (Eco 1973).

Eco illustrates the usefulness of the semiotic study of culture with an example taken from Karl Marx. An object with "use value" becomes a sign when it acquires an "exchange value." When we state that a commodity has an exchange value, we express its value in terms of the value of another commodity. By establishing a system of correspondence among various semantic axes (goods), we establish a code of commodities. Commodities take meaning from their reciprocal relationship because they are parts of semiotic systems or systems of oppositions and relationships. (A more systematic and further presentation of Eco's semantic views can be found in Eco 1976.) We can see, then, that the semiotic method can be helpful in determining the logical structure of ideological systems and the precise significance of each aspect of ideology. Semiotic analysis can explain in what sense the significance of a given aspect or segment of ideology derives from its systematic relationships to other aspects or segments of ideology.

The semiotic perspective can add theoretical and methodological refinements to the traditional notion of "the definition of the situation." George H. Mead's position can be restated as follows: by formulating a system of significant symbols, we structure the social universe into a system of semiotic signs, where each sign contributes to determine the semantic position of the other sign. Semiotic analysis can be applied to discover the inner organization of *all* cultural items and the way they reciprocally determine their semiotic function. This is what makes the study of the "form of expression" of the signifier of paramount importance for the sociology of ideology.

Early Barthes

Roland Barthes has asserted that we have to free ourselves from the preoccupation with content and pay more attention to the signifier to be able to grasp the "inalienable sense of things." For Barthes, structuralism is not a school or a movement, but an activity or a set of mental operations which reconstruct an object in order to reveal the rules of its functioning (functions). Structuralism finds in history "not only certain contents but also certain forms, not only the material but also the intelligible, not only the ideological but also the aesthetic" (1967a).

An example of Barthes' substantive contribution to the study of ideology can be found in his analysis of Brecht's theatrical works. Barthes starts from the premise that "revolutionary art must admit the arbitrariness of signs, must allow a certain formalism in the sense that it must treat form according to the proper method, which is semiological method" (1964a:87). Berthold Brecht proposes an important notion of alienation that he calls estrangement effect. For Brecht the fundamental distinction is not between natural and manufactured social products but between what is perceived as changeless or eternal and what is perceived as changing in time and as historical. Our alienation derives from the fact that we are habituated to believe that the present is eternal and the institutions we live in are "natural" and permanent. The purpose of Brecht's theory of extrangement effect is to make us perceive that social institutions are the result of historical changes and, therefore, they are changeable by nature. It goes without saying that this kind of analysis is consistent with the intent of Marx's *Theses on Feuerbach* and it clarifies certain aspects of the Marxist notion of ideology.

Barthes has systematically studied the ideological aspect of various cultural systems. In his *Système de la Mode* (1967b) he has argued that in our society myths and rituals have taken the form of reasoning and speech; therefore, language is not only a model for meaning but also the foundation of meaning. Fashion cannot exist without speech, but speech is interposed between the object and the user of the object for the purpose of economic profit. Industrial society interposes a simulacrum of images and reasons between the buyer and the product to be sold to obfuscate the awareness of the buyer. The result is that a simulated image of the object is substituted for the real one; it is not the object but its artificially manipulated image which is sought and bought out. To understand the real meaning of messages we have to decipher the cultural codes governing the structure of messages and their mode of signifying and we have to map out the denotational and connotational systems. Since any communication takes place within an ideological context, we cannot understand the messages without identifying the ideology. A lasting contribution of Barthes' works is having shown the pervasiveness and structure of codes in various areas of cultural experience, such as clothing, furniture, food, architecture, and cars. (For a more elaborate discussion of the semiotic study of ideology, consult Rossi-Landi 1968, 1973.)

Barthes has argued also that the French style of writing is forged and used by the bourgeoisie to shape society in its own image. For this reason, the writing style is not an innocent means of communication but a carrier, transmitter, and encoder of the bourgeois world view. This is the second stage of Barthes' semiotics, where he moved away from scientific semiotics and joined the new semiotics represented by the theories of schizophrenia of Gilles Deleuze and René Girard, the Russian semioticians, and Jacques Derrida. Barthes, then, has shifted his attention away from the formal aspect of language (*langue*) to the problem of the creativity of reading and writing (*parole*). Julia Kristeva is another preeminent representative of the new semiotics, which deserves special attention for having combined the psychoanalytical and Marxist (sociological) approaches and for having given attention to the pragmatic dimension of semiotic analysis. We shall discuss this new (or poststructuralist) semiotics in the third part of the volume, after first completing the discussion of other forms of structuralism, or scientific semiotics, to use Barthes' terminology.

At this point one may wonder what the difference is between semiotics and structuralism and whether it is appropriate to equate structuralism with semiotic structuralism, as Pettit (1975) and Culler do (1975). I refuse to equate these two terms for the simple reason that semiotic structuralism derives its methodology from linguistics and therefore does not apply to Piaget, who adds important elements to the structural paradigm of Saussure, Lévi-Strauss, and other semioticians.

5

The Genetic Structuralism of Jean Piaget

Piaget's early training was in biological sciences and psychology. Organismic assumptions are evident in his early works, and the same assumptions also are paramount in Lévi-Strauss. The organism is seen as an organized whole composed of parts, none of which can be changed without producing changes in the other parts; human behavior is explained as a byproduct of biological structures and psychological functioning.

Organismic and Formal Assumptions of Piaget's Thought

In Piaget's psychological training particular importance must be attributed to Pierre Janet and Alfred Binet. Very early Piaget became interested in studying the logic present in children's behavior and language. Although he had some exposure to psychoanalytic thought, Piaget became mostly concerned with the biological explanation of knowledge. Methodologically, Piaget combined the use of observation—typical of experimental psychologists—with the clinical interview of psychiatrists.

Up to 1940 Piaget had no explicit contact with structural linguistics nor had he shown a clear orientation toward formal thinking, a way of thinking so marked in the notions of differential contrasts and binary oppositions of structural linguistics. After he became the director of the psychology laboratory in 1940, Piaget expanded his research activity into the figurative aspects of language, which deal with the perception of time, space, and movement, and into the formal aspects of knowledge, which deal with the perception of quantity and numbers. Piaget began formalizing his findings on the mental operations of children and adolescents in logical and mathematical terms. For instance, he has shown that the mental operations implied by additive and multiplicative classes, relations, formal combinatory operations, and propositional operations are logical and mathematical in nature. In his more recent works on the sequences of the child's psychological growth, Piaget has shown a marked inclination toward the logical and mathematical conceptualization of his findings. In this sense one can find in his works a certain similarity to the formal aspects of structural linguistics and the early semiotics. However, the notions of binary contrasts and distinctive features have never become basic analytical tools in Piaget's works.

The Antiempiricist Character of Piaget's Epistemology

After 1950 Piaget's concern with epistemology developed into an inductive study of the psychological mechanisms common to the construction of various forms of knowledge. His genetic epistemology is the best systematic discussion of the epistemological foundations of transformational structuralism, and especially of its antiempiricist conception of scientific explanation. A brief discussion of Piaget's epistemology is essential to clarify certain theoretical assumptions which are fundamental both in Piaget and in Lévi-Strauss' structuralism, and, more specifically, to elucidate the reasons for their common opposition to the empiricism prevailing among Anglo-Saxon social scientists.

In Piaget's own words, "genetic epistemology deals with the formation and meaning of knowledge and the means by which human mind goes from a lower level of knowledge to one that is judged to be higher" (1969:xliii). Whereas both Piaget and Lévi-Strauss are interested in the human mind, Piaget is primarily interested in the structure underlying the *dynamics* of the human mind. Moreover, Piaget's concern extends beyond the intellectual or rational dimension of psychic activity: "The fundamental hypothesis of genetic epistemology is that there is a parallelism between the progress made in the logical and rational organization of knowledge and the corresponding psychological processes" (1969a:xlii).

Piaget attributes a genetic priority to the logic of coordinated *action*, so that the logic of thought is considered to derive from the logic of action. This position is in direct opposition to the priority attributed by logical positivists to language. The priority given by Piaget to prelinguistic structures is apparent in his contention that "the genetic analysis of logico-mathematical structures" has shown that "their roots are anterior to language and are situated in the coordination itself of actions." Piaget states the following:

In studying the intellectual development of the child one finds in the sensory-motor levels anterior to language a schematism of actions which already implies structures of relations (especially relationships of order intervening in the coordination of means and ends, and so on); these structures prepare the classifications and inferences which at times entail an elementary transitivity. On the other hand (and this is a second fundamental finding) these actions, whose coordination is already a sort of logic, are at the starting point of what will become operations of thought. . . . These [operatory] structures whose psychological criterion is the constitution of invariants . . . consist in classifications, seriations, numerical correspondences etc., but they still ignore the logic of propositions and essentially remain concrete. (1967:95–96)

One is not surprised, then, to see Piaget arguing that "from linguistic logic . . . we must go back to the deeper logic of coordination of actions" (1967:96). In this quote are contained all the basic tenets of Piaget's structuralism: the fundamental unit of analysis is activity or "operation"; the emphasis is on the intrinsic intelligibility and logic of psychological activity; this logic consists of invariant structures of relation, order, and classification; and these invariant structures are self-sufficient and can be understood independent of considerations external to them.

Fundamental to transformational structuralism is the assumption that the structures of biological, mental, and cultural reality are isomorphic. This hypothesis has a direct bearing on the theory of knowledge and, more specifically, on the conceptualization of the relationship between the subject and object of scientific activity; similarly, this hypothesis shows why the notion of transformation is important in explaining the structure of both scientific knowledge and reality. Piaget distinguishes between the figurative and operative aspects of thought. The figurative aspect is the imitation of the static aspects of reality; that is, for instance, the key characteristic of the cognitive processes called perception, imitation, and imagery in the cognitive area. The operative aspect of thought deals with transformations from one state to another. Piaget argues that the operative aspect of thought is more fundamental than the figurative one for the reason that any given state is either an outcome or a point of departure of transformations. The operative aspect of thought "includes action . . . which transform objects or states, and intellectual operations, which are essentially systems of transformations. . . . Human knowledge is essentially active. *To know is to assimilate reality into systems of transformations.* To know is to transform reality in order to understand how a certain state is brought about" (1969:xliv).

Such a position is consistent with Lévi-Strauss' notion that culture emerged with people's symbolic function; that is, with people's capacity to organize reality into sets of binary oppositions. However, Piaget carefully avoids mentalistic and idealistic positions:

Knowing reality means constructing systems of transformations that correspond, more or less adequately, to reality. They are more or less isomorphic to transformations of reality. The transformational structures of which knowledge consists are not copies of the transformations in reality; they are simply possible isomorphic models among which experience can enable us to choose. Knowledge, then, is a system of transformations that becomes progressively adequate. (1969:xliv)

It is quite clear, then, that for structuralists, the human mind does not produce reality, as idealists argue; the human mind produces only models isomorphic to reality through which we can interpret experiential data. Structuralists also reject the notion that knowledge consists of copying immediately observable characteristics of data, as empiricists contend, because the data are known through the mediation of progressive transformations or models. It is a basic tenet of structuralists that both the subject and the object of scientific activity have an input into knowledge. Therefore, structuralists reject the reification of the object operated by positivists and other empiricists. Piaget must be credited for having systematically explained and emphasized the interaction between the subject and object linked through progressive transformations.

We have stated previously that transformation is also a key aspect of the structure of reality. This concept brings our attention to the question of whether genetic structuralism can be considered a form of dialectic structuralism. One thing is unquestionable: Piaget attributes an analytic priority to the notion of genesis over structure and he conceives of the latter as a system of transformations.

Structure as a System of Transformations

Piaget has provided a classic definition of social structure, consisting of three elements: 1) structure is a system of transformations; 2) the transformations are self-regulatory in nature; and 3) structure is a totality whose properties are distinct from the properties of its constitutive elements.

First of all, structure is "a system of transformations" or a "closed system under transformation" (Piaget 1970:5). The term "transformation" is used by different authors in different ways. By transformation Piaget means "an intelligible change, which does not transform things beyond recognition at one stroke, and which always preserves invariance in certain respects" (p. 20); "the transformations inherent in a structure never lead beyond the system, but always engender elements that belong to it and preserve its laws" (p. 14). The Piagetian meaning of transformation derives from mathematics; Piaget has stressed the importance of the discovery made by the Bourbaki school of mathematics—that through combinations and differentiations we can construct particular structures from certain general or "parent" structures (1973:22).

The elements of a structure change but the laws according to which the constitutive elements of structure transform are stable; this, however, does not mean that such laws are necessarily innate, as Chomsky maintains; on the contrary, it means that the system of transformations is self-regulatory and self-maintaining and that transformations remain within the boundaries of the system. The self-regulatory aspect of transformations points at the cybernetic aspect of Piaget's thought, an aspect he shares with Lévi-Strauss and, we shall see, with the theorists of social action in sociology.

The third aspect of the notion of structure is totality. Piaget convincingly argues that totality is a key concept of the structural perspectives, a perspective which has permeated linguistics, the social sciences, mathematics, logic, biology, Gestalt psychology, and philosophy. According to Piaget (1970), the concept of group of nineteenth-century mathematics is one of the oldest structural ideas, and has become central in the recent mathematics of Nicolas Bourbaki. In reaction against the compartmentalization of mathematical domains, Bourbaki has shown that algebraic structures, topological structures, and order structures are the three fundamental (parent) structures out of which all other structures derive. The notion of group has also been used in physics in reaction against a positivist and merely descriptive notion of scientific explanation. Similarly, in biology the cybernetic study of evolution has emerged in reaction against a segmented notion of the organism and as an attempt to discover the organizing principle of the whole organism. In human sciences, Saussure has reacted against an excessive emphasis on historical explanations and has formulated synchronic laws of equilibrium which are independent of the history of particular linguistic elements. In psychology, the Gestalt school has reacted against the associationist notion that mental realities are constituted by the aggregation of already given elements, and it has attempted to discover the original totalities of psychic activities.

In summary, to state that structure is a totality means that structure is more than an aggregate of preformed elements and that it possesses properties and systemic laws different from the laws of its elements. For this reason the notion of totality is antithetical to the associationist perspective, which emphasizes the notion of genesis but lacks the notion of structure. Associationists have the notion of genesis because they explain phenomena by prior and simple elements; however, they do not have the notion of structure because they reduce phenomena to their simple elements and the laws of totality to the laws of the constituent elements of structure.

Durkheim and Gestalt psychology foster a type of static structuralism that reverses the position of associationists. In the works of Durkheim and Gestaltists one finds the notion of structure but not the notion of genesis. Durkheim conceives of totality as a property emerging from the association of the elements and with properties independent of the properties of the elements. However, structure is assumed to be the first and self-explanatory datum; all the scientist has to be concerned with is to describe the totality, without having to be concerned with the laws of composition of the totality (Piaget 1970:8).

Piaget claims that only genetic structuralism can explain the holistic character of phenomena, because it conceives of the whole as "the product of the composition of formative interactions" (1973:22). The relations among the elements are constitutive of the elements themselves, and since the constitution of elements takes place according to precise laws of composition, the latter are prior to and more fundamental than the elements themselves.

The emphasis on the constructive or compositional laws of structure differentiates Lévi-Strauss' structuralism from that of Piaget. For Lévi-Strauss the basic elements and their relational constraints are the first and most fundamental aspect of reality. For Piaget the most fundamental aspects of reality are the constitutive laws of totality, not the properties of the elements of totality. For this reason, some authors have differentiated between Lévi-Strauss' elementary structuralism and Piaget's holistic structuralism (Overton 1975:66ff). Such a distinction leads us to a systematic discussion of the differences between Lévi-Strauss' and Piaget's structuralism.

Differences Between Piaget's and Lévi-Strauss' Frameworks and Their Complementarities

We have already pointed out certain basic convergencies between Piaget's and Lévi-Strauss' perspectives. Both thinkers assume that phenomena have an intrinsic intelligibility and should be explained in terms of their internal relationships. Both Piaget and Lévi-Strauss conceptualize the phenomena they study as systems of relationships among their constitutive elements and consider these relationships as constitutive of the elements themselves. Both adopt the notion of structure as a system of reversible transformations. Both foster the use of formal models as tools of analysis and both uphold an antiempiricist conception of scientific explanation. However, Lévi-Strauss operates at the level of culture and, consistent with his linguistic orientation, he conceptualizes the underlying cultural code in terms of cultural grammar; culture is defined as a system of signs and as human beings perceivers of binary oppositions and patterned relationships among signs. (For a detailed discussion of Lévi-Strauss' intellectual antecedents, see Rossi 1973 and 1974.) Methodologically, Lévi-Strauss emphasizes the "distinctive features" approach and stresses the notion of bundles of oppositions, which he studies through logical and intuitive analysis and a form of "mental experimentation" with the help of formal models.

Piaget operates at the level of individual action and is interested in the way individuals construct knowledge in interaction with the environment. We have seen that for Piaget, knowledge consists of the construction of systems of transformations that are not just copies of reality but transformations that progressively become more and more adequate (homologous) to the transformations of reality (1970a:15). The system of transformations governing psychological activity does not affect only the relationship among the elements internal to the psychological system but also entails an interchange with the environment (1973:36–37). It is a distinctive mark of Piaget's perspective to have conceived of structure as a dynamic link between subject and object, system and environment, genesis and function. Piaget wants to explain how the formation (genesis) of structure insures an optimum functioning in mutable conditions and, because of this concern, he links the functional to the structural perspective. This is the reason why Piaget expresses his opposition to Chomsky's antihistorical and antigenetic conception of structure. We shall also see that the functional view of Piaget has found strong sympathizers among some Parsonian sociologists who attempt to demonstrate a basic affinity and complementarity between the Piagetian paradigm and the paradigm of the theory of action (Lidz and Lidz 1976).

Given the importance that Piaget attributes to the notion of function, it is not surprising that he disagrees with Lévi-Strauss' dismissal of functionalism. In Piaget's view, Lévi-Strauss rejects functionalism because he has a static notion of structure and because he neglects historical factors (1973:36–37).

Lévi-Strauss and Piaget differ not only on the notion of structure but also on the conception of scientific explanation. Because of his emphasis on the static properties of social structure, Lévi-Strauss considers analysis as the paradigm of scientific explanation. A scientific understanding of social phenomena is reached by breaking down the phenomenon into its components and by determining the relational constants among them; these relational constants are considered properties of physical reality, which means that structure refers to objective characteristics of physical reality. The emphasis on the genesis or construction of structure leads Piaget, however, to follow a different form of explanation. Since structure is constructed in interaction with the environment, the first task of scientific explanation is to specify the adaptive function of the phenomenon, then to represent its organization, and finally to examine the relationship between structures and between the system and the environment. From this perspective, structure is a construct or an explanatory concept rather than a property of physical reality (Overton 1975:66–67).

However, these theoretical and methodological differences do not warrant the conclusion that Piaget and Lévi-Strauss' opositions are fundamentally irreconcilable. Howard Gardner has argued that Roman Jakobson has offered elements of a synthesis between the developmental perspective of Piaget and the static perspective of Lévi-Strauss. In his work *Child Language: Aphasia and Phonological Universals* (1968), Jakobson has used the structural notions of code, binary oppositions, and distinctive features together with the Piagetian notions of differentiation and integration, structural stages, progression, and regression. Gardner argues that there are other elements of potential complementarity between Piagetian and semiotic structuralism. For instance, if Piaget were to focus on the objects upon which the individual operates, he might find useful the notion of distinctive features to characterize the properties by which the child identifies objects. Conversely, if Lévi-Strauss, or semiotic structuralists, were to focus on the relationship between the cultural codes and the activity of the individual, they would find useful certain elements of the Piagetian developmental perspective (Gardner 1973:60ff).

Condon and Wieting suggest a useful application of Piaget's ideas in sociology. They argue that although Piaget has been concerned with the development of intellectual structures rather than with the sociocultural context of such a development, the perspective he had developed helps explain important aspects of the socialization process. Parsons notes that through the internalization of the value system culture comes to exercise a cybernetic control over the social system. A theory of the construction of normative order is needed to explain how the process of internalization takes place and to reconcile the free and creative input of the individuals with the normative guidelines that enable individuals to make their choices. Condon and Wieting show the shortcomings of the empiricist approach and the advantages of a structural developmental approach à la Piaget to link the input of the individual and that of the normative order. The biological competence, which points at a "necessary" element, is seen to provide interacting individuals with a sense of social structure, which is viewed as a "contingent" element; the genetic component has a greater determining influence at the early stages of child's development (in Rossi 1982).

The notion of genetic component is similar to the notion of a basic structural code, and calls to mind Chomsky's notion of competence. Rawls borrows Chomskian and Piagetian concepts to formulate the principles of the construction of social structures capable of linking both the individual and societal inputs. Such a conception counteracts Durkheim's view that morality and even reason are merely social products. Rawls' view also counteracts the opposite Kantian view that norms are altogether inborn categories. We can see, then, that the notion of genetic and linguistic competence offers the possibility of filling important gaps in classical sociological thinking. For this reason, and because the notion of competence is also used by Cicourel, Goffman, and certain theorists of social action, we must consider the basic elements of the Chomskian perspective and its relationship to Lévi-Strauss' and Piaget's perspectives.

6

The Transformational Grammar of
Noam Chomsky

As Saussure has revolutionized the science of linguistics with his structural view of language, so has Noam Chomsky revolutionized contemporary linguistics with his theory of transformational grammar. Both Saussure and Chomsky are concerned with the study of language as a system of rules (*langue*) rather than with the use of linguistic rules (*parole*), and both have proposed a formal interpretation of language. Chomsky, however, provides explanatory notions which are much more powerful than the notions of permutation as well as the notions of syntagmatic and paradigmatic relations proposed by Saussure and the notion of distinctive features proposed by the Prague school of linguistics. Like Saussure and the linguists of the Prague school, Chomsky conceptualizes the linguistic system in terms of deep and surface structure. However, the major novelty of his approach consists in proposing a syntactic view of the underlying structure and in linking the deep and surface structure through transformational rules, hence the term "transformational grammar."

Whereas Saussure saw language as an inventory of items in systematic relationship to each other, Chomsky sees language as a system of rules which account for our capacity to produce and interpret an indefinite number of sentences (surface structures). Chomsky calls the conscious or unconscious capacity to apply these rules "linguistic competence," and the way people use their linguistic competence "linguistic performance." The distinction between linguistic competence and linguistic performance can be considered an extension and elaboration of Saussure's distinction between the *langue* and the *parole.*

Chomsky's theory has undergone various phases of development and it is still being modified and subjected to various criticisms. Here I briefly illustrate a few key ideas of Chomsky's transformational grammar inasmuch as it is needed to understand the terms "syntax," "transformation," "generative rules," "rewrite rules," and "competence," which have found application in the writing of Cicourel, Goffman, and certain theorists of social action (see Loubser et al. 1976).

The term "grammar" for Chomsky includes the whole linguistic apparatus of a speaker, i.e., the system of sounds (phonology), the system of meaning (semantics), and the rules for the formation of sentences (syntax). The syntactical rules are those grammatical rules which enable one to transmit meaning through the combination of morphemes into larger units. In his major early work, Chomsky attempted to explain the entire language on the basis of syntax; the semantic and phonological aspects of language were understood to derive their meaning from the syntactic relationships of the system (1957). According to this early Chomskian view, the grammar of language consisted of a phrase structure component, a transformational component, a morphophonemic component, and a sound component, as shown in figure 6.1.

Phrase Structure
↓
Transformational Component
↓
Morphophonemic Component
↓
Sound Level

Figure 6.1. An early Chomskian view of language.

Phrase Structure Rules

The phrase structure rules determine the basic constituent slots of a sentence and the relationship among them. Following are some basic phrase structure rules:

1. S → NP   VP

2. NP → Pro
         N Prop
         Art (Adj) N
3. VP → V   NP

The arrow means "rewrite as." The initial symbol S (sentence) is re-written as a noun phrase (NP) and a verb phrase (VP). The noun phrase can be a pronoun (Pro) or a proper noun (N Prop) or a noun pre-ceded by an article (Art) and an adjective (Adj). The verb phrase may consist of a verb alone or a verb and a noun phrase.

The elements at the left of the arrow produce the elements at the right of the arrow; the latter constitute the underlying and abstract structure of language. The underlying structure is organized by phrase structure rules in a linear and hierarchical structure, called alterna-tively structure tree or phrase structure tree, or phrase marker, as shown in figure 6.2.

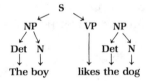

Figure 6.2. A phrase structure tree.

The Transformational Component

Phrase structure rules are not sufficient to account for all possible grammatical structures. For instance, the sentences *the boy puts the bicycle away* and *the boy puts away the bicycle* have the same mean-ing but different structures.

Transformational rules account not only for sentences that are sty-listic variations of each other, but also for ambiguous sentences that possess a common identical phrase structure. Transformational rules specify which changes (transformations) have to be made in the com-mon phrase structure to obtain unambiguous surface sentences. Transformational rules also specify changes needed to express one basic meaning in negative, passive, and interrogative forms. Usually transformational rules are represented with a double shafted arrow ($\Longrightarrow$) to distinguish them from phonological and from phrase structure rules.

Chomsky's 1957 model did not prevent the possibility of generating ungrammatical sentences. For this reason Chomsky had to introduce selectional rules, which subcategorize the syntactic units in terms of which ones can co-occur and which ones cannot co-occur. The outcome of this effort has been a more complex model of language, which Chomsky proposed in 1965. In the new model, the syntactic structure is composed of a phrase structure and a lexicon, both of which concur in producing the deep structure. Through transformations and additional lexical insertions, the underlying structure produces surface structures. The deep structure is processed by a semantic component, which produces semantic interpretation, and the surface structure is processed by a phonological component, which produces a phonetic interpretation. The 1965 model of language can be represented as in figure 6.3. (Besides Chomsky, Katz and Postal (1964) have also contributed to the codification of this theory, which is called "standard theory.")

According to this model, language is a formal device which relates the phonological to the semantic level. The model, however, still centers on syntactic rules because the sequential organization of the components and the directionality of the arrows clearly indicates the primacy of syntax. This assumption has prompted the criticism of

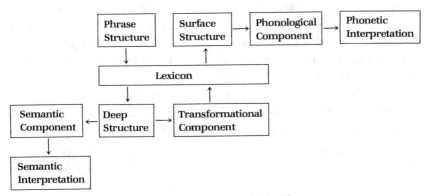

Figure 6.3. Chomsky's 1965 model of language.

other linguists, who argue that language should be based on semantics because it is a system devised to express meanings. Chomsky has replied that the directionality of the arrows is a mere graphic artifact. As a matter of fact, the directionality of the relationships can be understood any way one wants; what is important are the relationships specified by the model.

Notwithstanding this explanation, one cannot escape the conclusion that according to Chomsky the semantic component interprets, but does not generate, the deep structure. The leading exponents of generative semantics, such as McCawley, Ross, and Lakoff, argue that semantics should be considered the generative component of language because semantics provides the ultimate criterion of the nonambiguity of a sentence. For instance, the sentence *the shooting of the animal upset them* is not ambiguous because it wouldn't make sense to consider the animal as the subject of the action expressed in the sentence. The exponents of generative semantics also argue that syntax is concerned not only with the rules of the proper formation of sentences but also with providing the semantic representation of the sentence; for this reason their description of grammar includes such categories as human, terrestrial, and inanimate. The intent of the exponents of generative semantics is to produce more abstract categories than Chomskian categories in such a way as to formulate an abstract syntax that can be equated with semantics. In this way the linguistic grammar resembles the propositional logic developed by philosophers.[1]

Generative semantics is not without its critics. Some anthropologists argue that the linguistic model provided by generative semantics is so abstract that it cannot be verified. Moreover, the distinction between semantics and syntax becomes blurred. Chomsky (1972) has put forward the argument that generative semantics is nothing but a notational variant of the standard theory.

As to Chomsky himself, he has kept modifying his own theory. He first proposed an extended standard theory, in which semantic interpretation rules apply to both deep and surface phrase markers. Then,

[1] Contemporary linguists, however, argue that there is no pretheoretical way of distinguishing semantic from syntactic primitives, so that the distinction between the two is of no practical and theoretical value.

in 1975 he offered a revised extended standard theory, in which all
semantic interpretation occurs at the level of the surface structure.
However, J. J. Katz has argued that this new model must enlarge the
surface structure so much as to be able to contain all the syntactic
structures necessary to predict the semantic properties.

T. G. Bever, J. J. Katz, and D. T. Langendoen argue that the standard theory is the most clear formulation of transformational grammar and the one which indicates the most narrow constraints on the
types of possible grammars (1976).[2]

The discussion of these issues, which are at the center of contemporary linguistic controversies, is beyond the scope of these pages.
What is important from our point of view is that nearly all linguists
have accepted the notion of a *generative* model of language, a notion
originally proposed by Chomsky. Common to the various versions of
generative grammar as well as generative semantics is the notion that
a central component of language "generates" the whole linguistic
system through transformational rules.

We have seen that the notion of transformation together with that
of structure is also important in the works of Lévi-Strauss and Piaget.
Given the centrality of these notions not only in the works of these
three thinkers but also in contemporary sociological applications of
their perspectives, we should briefly examine whether they are used
in the same sense. The intent is to determine the existence of basic
differences and, perhaps, complementarities between the approach
of Lévi-Strauss, Chomsky, and Piaget, and to provide useful suggestions for the formulation of a more articulate structural-transformational approach in the social sciences.

[2] For a clear and not too technical exposition of generative grammar see Fromkin
and Rodman (1974) and for a discussion of generative semantics see Steinberg and
Jakobovitz (1971) and Seuren (1974). Charles Fillmore has proposed another approach
called case grammar, which still falls within the framework of transformational grammar. Recently, however, the theory has lost much of its support.

7

Structure and Transformation in
Lévi-Strauss, Chomsky, and Piaget

Both Lévi-Strauss and Piaget consider Gestalt psychologists pioneers of the structural approach and both of them are directly or indirectly influenced by the notion of gestalt. Wertheimer, Koffka, and Köhler maintain that gestalt is the most fundamental datum of visual perception and psychological experience. The idea of gestalt implies more than the sum of parts; it implies the existence of invariant structural properties of the whole, no matter what changes affect its parts. For instance, the perception of an object is affected by endless transformations because the observer's sensory organs and his or her relative position to the object are undergoing continuous changes. Notwithstanding these endless transformations, the object is perceived as a gestalt. Gestalt psychologists explain this apparent anomaly by stating that psychological activities in general and perception in particular consist of sets of invariant transformations internal and external to the organism rather than of fixed characteristics of either the perceptual apparatus or the object. Whereas the absolute positions of the parts can be transposed or "transformed," their relative positions remain invariant. For this reason Gestalt psychologists attribute an analytical priority to the notion of gestalt over the concept of transformation. Lévi-Strauss and Chomsky share the same position on this point.

Priority of Structure Over Transformation in Lévi-Strauss and Chomsky

Like Piaget, Lévi-Strauss rejects the associationist and substantivist perspectives to adopt the viewpoint of Gestaltists; in fact, he sets for

himself the task of explaining social phenomena as "meaningful totalities" (see Rossi 1974:71). Lévi-Strauss starts from the premise that
social phenomena should be studied with a rigorous method and as
gestalts; then he concludes that only modern mathematics, especially mathematical logic, the theory of group, and topology can provide a rigorous approach to the study of phenomena which do not
permit metrical solutions (Lévi-Strauss 1963:310). In his early major
work, Lévi-Strauss used algebraics and the mathematical theory of
group to study Murngin marriage systems (1969:194–225). A group is
a mathematical structure consisting of a set of operations of whatsoever nature and performed on whatsoever elements as long as the
operations preserve certain invariant relationships; these invariant relationships constitute the structure of the group. One of the indispensible conditions for the existence of a group is the reversibility of
the operations. By adopting the mathematical notion of group, Lévi-
Strauss conceives of structure as a set of merely relational properties
of constant and reversible nature; moreover, he attributes a priority
to structure over transformation.

The mathematical perspective is preeminent also in the structural
linguistics of Saussure and the transformational grammar of Chomsky. Saussure uses the notions of substitution and permutation as
devices to establish the value of linguistic terms. A permutation is the
operation of defining the meaning of linguistic elements by relating
them to the other elements that are present in the same sentence
(syntagmatic relations) or to elements that could be used as their
substitutes (paradigmatic relations). These operations are similar to
the permutational and reversible operations implied by the notion of
group.

Lévi-Strauss adopts the paradigmatic approach of Saussure; although he uses the terms "permutation," "transformation," and "substitution" somewhat loosely and interchangeably, his basic intent is
clear. Lévi-Strauss wants to determine the meaning of a term by per-
muting it in all the contexts in which it can be used. This permutational or transformational approach is in reality a paradigmatic approach. Such an approach allows Lévi-Strauss to prescind from the
content as a "content"; he can then translate mythical data into geometric terms, and transform the geometric terms into one another

through algebraic operations (1966a:407). By this procedure, Lévi-Strauss can compare the structures of different orders of phenomena, such as myths, ritual, art, culinary customs, and so on, and determine the relationships of transformation among these various structures. The notion of invariant and reversible relationships allows him to reconstitute the raw data from which he starts his analysis; this is a form of verification of explanations based on paradigmatic analysis (Rossi 1973a). The notion of invariant transformational relationships also enables Lévi-Strauss to predict the existence of systems that are variants, through transformations, of already discovered symbolic systems. He begins from the existence of a structure as a totality, which makes possible transformational processes as well as transformational analysis. Rather than focusing on the constitutive and genetic processes of structure, as Piaget does, Lévi-Strauss focuses on the transformational process linking various structures that are assumed to be given totalities.

The same priority of structure over transformation, or of the static over the dynamic and developmental point of view, holds true for the transformational grammar of Chomsky. In 1957 Chomsky used the term "transformation" to refer to a type of nonsymmetrical rules which relate the logical precursors of sentences to actual sentences. Since these rules could alter the meaning, they are considered to contribute to the semantic interpretation of linguistic elements. In 1965 Chomsky used the term "transformation" to refer to a set of rules which link the underlying structure to surface syntactical structures. These rules alter the syntactical structure and the phrase structure tree also, but they do not change the meaning, because meaning is produced by the semantic component. The underlying structure is acted upon both by transformational rules to produce surface syntactic structures and by interpretive rules to produce semantic interpretation. Therefore, the underlying structure provides the link between the form and meaning of language and, in this sense, is properly called deep structure. Transformations operate on the deep structure to produce surface structures, but they do not produce the deep structure; on this point Chomsky concurs with Saussure and Lévi-Strauss; that is, like them, Chomsky assigns a priority to structure over transformation. Not surprisingly, some transformational linguists have hypothesized the existence of a deep structure common to all languages and have connected such a structure to the innate mental apparatus of human beings.

Integrating the Static Approach of Lévi-Strauss and Chomsky with the Dynamic Approach of Piaget

The idea of invariant relationships is fundamental not only in Gestalt psychology and Lévi-Strauss but also in Piaget. As we have already seen, Piaget defines structure as a system of transformations which exhibit invariant and reversible properties. However, the novelty of Piaget's approach is focusing on the constitutive or genetic processes of structure. Structure is constituted by the adaptive functions of the system through a series of diachronic transformations which are internal to the system. In this way Piaget reverses Lévi-Strauss' and Chomsky's notion of deep structure.

However, the static and dynamic approaches are not mutually exclusive, but rather can complement each other. Piagetian psychologists may find useful Lévi-Strauss' methodology and his findings about the structure and transformational process of symbolic systems. Similarly, the Chomskian notion of transformational rules may be useful in understanding the structure and development of language, which is intimately connected with the development of thought and moral judgement. The question of the relationship of affinity or complementarity between Lévi-Strauss' structuralism and Chomsky's and Piaget's approaches deserves a close scrutiny.

Notwithstanding certain criticisms of Piaget, Lévi-Strauss has argued that there is an affinity between his own perspective and Piaget's. Piaget has claimed that Lévi-Strauss' thesis of "the permanence of the human intellect" is not reconcilable with the basic principles that "there is no structure apart from construction" (1970:140–141). Lévi-Strauss has replied that Piaget's criticism is based on a misunderstanding; he accepts Piaget's notion that "the ultimate nature of reality consists in being continuously under construction rather than in the accumulation of already made structures." (This is Lévi-Strauss' paraphrase of Piaget.) However, Lévi-Strauss contends that "it is structures which through transformations generate other structures. . . . [T]he existence of structure is the first datum" (1971:561). Lévi-Strauss claims that he has never postulated preestablished and immutable structures, but only "matrices from which structures are generated" (ibid.).

At first it would seem that the difference between Lévi-Strauss and Piaget is only a difference of methodological strategy. In a sense it would seem irrelevant whether one starts from the structural or from the transformational aspect of reality as long as neither of these two fundamental aspects is ignored. (See the conclusion of this book.)

However, the difference between Lévi-Strauss and Piaget is much more than a difference of strategy. By stating that structure is first, Lévi-Strauss assumes the existence of structure as a given without explaining how it comes into existence. Piaget faces this issue and convincingly demonstrates that the structure is produced by transformations internal to the system; he concludes that "there is no structure apart from construction" (1970:140). Piaget's assessment that the early version of Lévi-Strauss' structuralism is "relatively static and ahistorical" would seem uncontrovertible. However, Lévi-Strauss seems open to Piaget's point of view. For instance, in the last volume of the *Mythologiques*, Lévi-Strauss has defined structures as follows: "Structures exhibit the character of absolute objects: [they are] generative matrices through successive deformations of types which can be ordered in a series" (1971:33). By underlining the notion of generative matrix and successive deformations, Lévi-Strauss has made a theoretical overture to a dynamic perspective. As his orientation can complement Piaget's perspective, so Piaget's perspective can complement Lévi-Strauss'. In fact, one does not provide an adequate explanation of social and psychic phenomena unless one explains both the processes by which structure is constituted (Piaget's view) and the processes by which a structure generates other structures (Lévi-Strauss' viewpoint).

Lévi-Strauss' notions of generative matrix and successive deformations bring us to discuss the issue of the relation between his own perspective and Chomsky's. Both men distinguish between observable or surface structures and a deep structure of phenomena. Similarly, both use the term "transformation" as a key analytical concept.

However, Lévi-Strauss' notion of transformations refers to paradigmatic relationships between different structures and not to precise and technical rules which can generate surface or observable structures out of deep structures. The already mentioned fact that Lévi-Strauss uses the notions of combination and transformation interchangeably clearly indicates that he practices a paradigmatic analysis like Saussure rather than a transformational analysis like Chomsky. No social scientist has yet been able to formulate precise transformational rules which generate the observable aspects of cultural phenomena. That both Lévi-Strauss and Chomsky use the terms "transformation" and "matrix" indicates that they share a mathematical orientation rather than the notion of competence.

What we have previously stated about the influence of mathematical concepts in Saussure and Lévi-Strauss also applies to the transformational orientation of both Chomskian and non-Chomskian linguistics. In linguistics the term "transformation" has been used in at least three senses (Householder 1972). For Zellig Harris a transformation is a symmetrical relationship between one set of sentences and another set, where neither of the sets has a priority over the other. For instance, the active and passive forms are related to each other, but neither is prior to the other and both forms can convey a same or different meaning. Such a definition of transformation clearly echoes the notion of reversibility, which, as we have previously discussed, is an essential characteristic of the mathematical notion of group.

The mathematical perspective is also preeminent in Chomsky's generative conception of language; this is of no surprise given his strong training in mathematics. As mathematical rules can generate infinite sets of numbers, so linguistic rules should enable one to produce an infinite set of sentences. Chomsky's precise goal is to formulate a set of rules which can generate *all* the grammatical and *only* the grammatically correct sentences of a language. It is in this sense that the Chomskian use of the terms "generate" and "rule" have to be interpreted from a mathematical point of view and that his terms "grammar" and "rule" have to be understood as formal and quasi-mathematical mechanisms constitutive of the whole language.

We have already discussed that the mathematical orientation is common and fundamental to the frameworks of Lévi-Strauss, Piaget, and Chomsky. All three thinkers emphasize the importance of the mathematical formulation of scientific findings, pay special attention to the formal aspect of the phenomena they study, and use formal tools of analysis.

It follows that from the methodological point of view, a major avenue to integrate elements of the structural, semiotic, Chomskian, and Piagetian perspectives is to refine their mathematical concepts and interrelate their mathematical or quasimathematical formulations. The work of formalization in social sciences is at an incipient stage. Lévi-Strauss has admitted that his own mathematical language is vague and the formalization of his findings rudimentary (1969a:31). Even the Chomskian use of the notion of transformation has been criticized for its ambiguity. Whereas mathematicians rigorously describe the invariant properties of numerical systems, linguists emphasize various modifications but they rarely spell out the invariant properties of these modifications.

However, structuralists must be credited for having pioneered the structural transformational approach in the social sciences. By so doing they have remained abreast of modern scientific thinking. As a matter of fact, structural and transformational thinking appears more and more fundamental in the contemporary perspective of the physical, biological, psychological, and linguistic sciences and gives some hope for the formulation of a unifying language and a common framework in the natural as well as social sciences (Rossi 1978a).

It is implicit in my previous discussion that it may be possible to integrate certain Lévi-Straussian, semiotic, Chomskian, and Piagetian ideas. As we have seen, Lévi-Strauss has emphasized the notion of structure as a system of transformations but he has not taken into account the generative processes of structure nor has he formulated the precise transformational rules of these generative processes. Chomsky has formulated precise transformational rules, but they are static and descriptive rules that do not render the real generative processes of the linguistic system. Piaget's notion of diachronic transformations is the only concept which has introduced a dynamic perspective. The works of these three thinkers seem to stress as many components of a thorough structural-transformational approach.

Social scientists of transformational orientation must seriously pursue a twofold task: they must study the applicability of the notion of transformational rules to the analysis of social phenomena and they must adopt a dynamic and historical viewpoint and perhaps make a serious application of the notion of diachronic transformation. The first task is being now tackled by Parsonian sociologists, Goffman, and ethnomethodologists, especially Cicourel. The second task has been at the center of the efforts of structural Marxists.

I now turn my attention to some of these attempts and to the interface between transformational structuralism and the interpretive, critical, and natural science paradigms. I consider first the interface of semiotic and transformational structuralism with the natural science approach of Talcott Parsons. Since Parsons shares a systemic and cybernetic perspective with Lévi-Strauss and Piaget, the Parsonian approach seems an appropriate starting point to undertake a systematic comparison between the traditional paradigms and transformational structuralism.

The Impact of Transformational Structuralism on Traditional Sociological Paradigms

8

Transformational Structuralism and the Natural Science Paradigm: The Case of Talcott Parsons

In this section we examine the most recent phase of Parsons' works, where one can see traces of the influence of transformational structuralism. Lévi-Strauss, Piaget, Chomsky, and poststructural semioticians have formulated their own approach in opposition to the empiricism of traditional approaches. It would, therefore, appear useless to search for elements of similarity or potential complementarity between such antithetical approaches as traditional paradigms and transformational structuralism.

This is a foregone conclusion if by traditional approaches one means natural science approaches in the strong sense of the term, such as, positivism, behaviorism, and operationalism. The distinction between a strong and a moderate version of the natural science approach demands a clarification of the terms "positivism" and "empiricism." Lévi-Strauss, Chomsky, and even Althusser have been accused of positivism because they believe in objective and universal structures and tend to explain social life from the structural point of view, ignoring or unduly underrating the role of subjectivity. I would prefer to use the terms "structural" or "systemic" or "objective" approach to qualify this aspect of their work. However, if we accept the just mentioned use of the term "positivism," we must distinguish between a structural and empiricist version of positivism, depending on whether so-called positivist social scientists hold an empirical or a structural (metaempirical) notion of social structure. I call natural science sociologists in the strong sense of the word those system-oriented sociologists who endorse an empiricist notion of social structure. There are, however, two forms of empiricism: the crude empiricism rejected by Parsons in *The Structure of Social Action* (1961) and the more moderate version of Parsonian empiricism that goes under the name of analytical realism, which is the Parsonian version of the natural science approach.

In discussing the relationship between transformational structuralism and the natural science paradigms, I limit my attention to Talcott Parsons precisely because he represents a moderate form of empiricism. The reason for doing so is that I criticize the Parsonian approach because of its empiricism, and such a criticism holds with greater cogency for other natural science approaches, since they represent stronger forms of empiricism. There is one more reason for selecting the theory of Talcott Parsons as an example of natural science paradigm. Amidst natural science sociologists, Talcott Parsons is the one who has been most aware of the importance of transformational structuralism for sociological theory, and in his more recent essays he has repeatedly referred to and used ideas taken from structural and transformational linguistics.

I shall discuss first the roots of certain basic affinities between transformational structuralists and the Parsonian paradigm and then their fundamental differences, which are rooted in their different posture toward empiricism. I will show how structural and truly cybernetic ideas could notably strengthen the Parsonian paradigm once it is freed of the empiricist bias. I will conclude the section with the issue of the "systemic" bias and the lack of the dialectic perspective in Parsons' paradigm.

Convergencies Between Transformational Structuralism and the Theory of Action

A Common Analytical Approach

Parsons has shown his interest in Lévi-Strauss' structuralism through his participation, together with S. N. Eisenstadt, E. A. Tiryakian, and M. Levy, in a seminar entitled "Structuralism and the Study of Complex Societies" that I organized at the 1975 annual meeting of the American Sociological Association. He has also expressed his interest in Lévi-Strauss in some recent essays (for instance in Parsons, Fox, and Lidz, 1972:370 and in Rossi 1982). In a personal communication to me about his feelings toward Lévi-Strauss' structuralism, Parsons called my attention to an article written by Adrian C. Hayes in which a systematic comparison is established between his own and Lévi-Strauss' theoretical orientation (Hayes 1974). This article deserves special attention, since it clearly outlines some basic features of the analytical approach of both thinkers in contrast with the empirico-inductive mode of analysis. Hayes, however, does not pursue the discussion up to the epistemological foundations of Parsons' analytical approach. He is correct in classifying Parsons under the rationalist paradigm next to Lévi-Strauss, Piaget, and Chomsky rather than under the empiricist paradigm prevailing in Anglo-Saxon sociology. The rationalist approach attributes primacy to the human mind over behavior, to structural and formal methods over quantitative and descriptive methods, to deduction over induction, to a synchronic rather than diachronic perspective. Both Parsons and Lévi-Strauss explain contingent phenomena by locating them within a system of logical possibilities and attempt to deduce properties of things from our theoretical activity on them rather than from the raw data themselves (pp. 102–3).

These points are well taken, and since they are a break with the empiricist tradition, we must consider for a moment their meta-theoretical foundations. Both Lévi-Strauss and Parsons feel the need to establish an a priori analytical scheme or a system of universal categories to classify and interpret phenomena. This approach to knowledge derives from the Kantian or neo-Kantian perspective, which has influenced both Lévi-Strauss and Parsons, as well as Weber, as we have seen. In the autobiographical account of his intellectual itinerary, Parsons referred to his early reading of Kant (Parsons 1970a:76), and in his latest work he has claimed the existence of parallel structure and method between the theory of action and Kantian philosophy (Parsons 1978:713). With such strong statements Parsons differentiates himself from the positivist claim that "only empirical science is a source of valid understanding of the human condition" (p. 354). Were this true, Parsons states, Weber's sociology of religion wouldn't make sense (and we have discussed some of the reasons why this is so). Parsons avers that without transcendental categories knowledge of particular phenomena is not possible (p. 355). Human knowledge takes place through a combination of transcendental categories with empirical facts (p. 344).

Consistent with this position, Parsons declares that analytical realism is construed as an interpenetration of empirical observations with the framework provided by a priori categories (1978:727–728). He makes plainly clear that a priori categories are not empirical categories nor arbitrary conventions but the very conditions of meaningfulness (p. 343). They are not invented by man but "given to man" (p. 374); in Parsons' words man is only a "combiner" (p. 370). Parsons uses the Kantian framework to interpret Chomsky's distinction between the deep structure and surface structure, and the biologist's distinction between genotype and phenotype. In the same vein of reasoning, Parsons claims that the Telic system gives meaning to the Action system. Since the Telic system consists mostly of religion (pp. 356–357), it is external to and cybernetically controls the Action system. Precisely because of its metaempirical nature, the Telic system can informationally give meaning to the Action system.

These clarifications of Parsonian thought seems to offer a healthy reaction to the empiricist conception of knowledge. However, Parsons has not totally freed himself from empiricist positivist assumptions, as we shall see later. At this point I intend to demonstrate that the cybernetic perspective is the vantage point from which other important convergencies between Parsonian and structuralist thought can be best understood.

A Common Cybernetic Perspective

In an article that he entitled "The Present Status of Structural-Functional Theory in Sociology" (1975:67–83), Parsons argued not only in favor of the continued validity but also for the central importance of the functional perspective. He also stated that the label of functionalism is more appropriate than that of structural-functionalism to qualify his own approach (pp. 67–69). His argument in defense of the functional perspective draws heavily from developments "in biological sciences and, to a lesser degree, in linguistics" (p. 80). He asserts

that there is a basic analogy between physiological and social processes because they have a similar function, although this function is
fulfilled through different mechanisms. Both physiological and social
systems have to fulfill the four functions of adaptation, integration,
goal attainment, and pattern maintenance. The recent Parsonian explanation of the pattern maintenance function owes much to molec-
ular genetics and recent linguistics. The role played by the genetic
code and linguistic code in physiological and linguistic systems, respectively, is analogous to the role played by the cultural code in the
social system. This is to say that Parsons establishes the analogy at
the genotypical level (the level of the cultural system), since he locates the social system at the phenotypical level (p. 76): "What is
common between the genetic code and the gene pool, on the one
hand, and the linguistic code and other aspects of human culture,
on the other hand, is that they can function as cybernetic mechanisms which in certain fundamental respects control life processes"
(p. 77).

The cybernetic notion of control has played a central role in the
recent formulations of the four-function paradigm and the generalized media of interchange, which constitute the third and fourth
phases of his thought. The notion of cybernetic control permits Parsons to order the four subsystems of action according to a hierarchy
of cybernetic control in which the higher system transmits information and therefore controls the lower system. In terms of information,
the cultural system controls the social system, which informationally
controls the personality system, which in turn controls the behavioral system. In reverse, the lower system in cybernetic control supplies energy to the higher system; the behavioral system supplies energy to the personality system, the personality system supplies energy
to the social system, which supplies energy to the cultural system.
The fundamental role of the cybernetic perspective in the conceptualization of "the generalized symbolic media of interchange" is made
immediately clear in Parsons' formulation: the media have a "function of control"; they are "mechanisms for the exchange of information, not energy" (1975:79).

What does the cybernetic perspective entail? Is it used in the same
sense by transformational structuralists and by Parsons? Cybernetics,

whose father is widely held to be Norbert Wiener (1954, 1961), is a systematic approach in communication engineering that has emerged as a result of technological developments and converging trends in neurophysiology, psychology, mathematics, and statistics. Parsons has been exposed to the cybernetic ideas of Wiener and Karl W. Deutsch, who has applied cybernetics to social sciences (Deutsch 1963). No system, be it organism or group, can exist without coordination of activities, and no coordination or organization of any kind is possible without communication or transmission of information. Messages are initially available only to the senders of messages; therefore communication, or transmission of messages, implies a form of control.

The gist of the cybernetic perspective consists of the following ideas: First, the notion of "drive" is replaced by that of "steering" or "governing" as a fundamental process. Cybernetics is interested in systems of decision-making, regulation, and control; these systems are dynamic rather than static, whose organization and functioning depend on their ability to store, transmit, and react to information. Second, the emphasis is on self-steering mechanisms, as machines are capable of adjustive reactions to the environment as well as to their own activity; the self-steering process is based on feedback, or action produced in response to the action produced by the system itself. Third, because they are endowed with self-steering mechanisms, systems can adapt to changing environments and so persist over time.

Self-controlling mechanisms presuppose feedback transmission of communication and communication is transmitted according to a commonly shared code. Information cannot be transmitted without a minimum of power and energy, but the amount of information transmitted is largely independent of the quantity of energy needed for its transmission.

The distinction between energy and information derives from the fundamental distinction between power engineering and communication engineering. "Power engineering transfers amounts of electric energy; communication engineering transfers information. It does not transfer events; it transfers a patterned relationship between events" (Deutsch 1963). What is important is the pattern carried by the signal and the relationship of this pattern to the pattern stored in the receiver. For instance, the distribution of lights and shades of a landscape is matched by the distribution of electric impulses in the television cable (p. 146). The notion of information is best rendered with the terms "form," "pattern," "gestalt," "state description," "distribution function" (p. 83).

This emphasis on relationships and patterned relationships is central to the notion of code as used in cybernetics, linguistics, and semiotic structuralism. Communication theorists define code as an "agreed transformation, or set of unambiguous rules whereby messages are converted from one representation to another" (Cherry 1957). We have seen that the concept of transformation is also central in structural and transformational linguistics. This is not surprising, since communication theorists and linguists borrow each other's concepts; for instance, Wiener makes a distinction between the grammar and content of communication: "While human and social communication are extremely complicated in comparison to the existing patterns of machine communication, they are subject to the same grammar; and this grammar has received its highest technical development when applied to the simpler content of the machine (1955, quoted in Deutsch 1963:77)

Not only does Parsons refer to the notion of genetic code but he explicitly refers to the notion of code as proposed by R. Jakobson and M. Halle (1956:23); when he mentions the linguistic code he also refers to Chomsky's notion of deep structure (Parsons 1975:76).

What is the precise meaning of the term "code" in biology and structural linguistics? F. H. Crick, a leading figure in the discovery of the genetic code, defines it as "the *dictionary* used by the cell to translate from the four-letter language of nucleic acids to the 20-letter language of protein" (1966, in Jorgensen 1972:60). The four letters are read three at a time so that 64 triplet combinations are possible. The genetic code consists of these 64 triplets. The notion of code, then, implies a set of rules by which elementary units combine and recombine to constitute larger units. Consequently, the concepts of information and code of information refer directly not to macromolecular and observable phenomena, but to the set of relations among their elemental constitutive units. The emphasis on *relationships* among terms rather than on the terms themselves is fundamental to the notion of information, code, and grammar as used by biologists, cyberneticians, structural linguists, and semiotic structuralists.

Since Parsons uses cybernetic ideas and quotes Jakobson and Halle, the question arises whether Parsons has shifted his focus of analysis from the content of communication (the subjective meaning of traditional sociologists) to the constant relationships and combinatory rules of the elementary units of content (the objective meaning of semiotic structuralists). In the paper published in the collection of essays I have edited (Rossi 1982), Parsons spells out clearly the fundamental analogies he sees among the genetic, linguistic, and action systems. Firstly, in all three systems we can distinguish a level of code in terms of which information is transmitted; the level of code is to be found in the genetic code, the deep structure of language, and the basic system of meaning. Second, in all three systems there is a mediating agency which translates the information contained in the code; the role of mediating agency is played by enzymes in biology, transformational rules in linguistics, and the institutionalization process in the system of action; through the institutionalization process some elements of the cultural system are translated into the social system. Third, Parsons extends his notion of symbolic mediating agency to explain the interchange among the four functions of each subsystem of action; this notion goes under the concept of generalized symbolic media of interchange.

This relatively recent perspective has permitted another major development in Parsons' thinking.

Classificatory, Elementary, and Combinatory Principles: Cybernetics and Evolutionary Theory

Parsons has contended that the cybernetic perspective has enabled him to focus on problems of control both in terms of "stability and change in action system" (Parsons 1970a:850); consistent with this line of thinking, Parsons has made a distinction between "the processes by which a system pattern is maintained and those by which its major structure is itself altered" (p. 851). Parsons seems to claim a direct continuity between systemic and evolutionary concerns. Such a linkage became possible after he came into contact with "Emerson's idea that the system of cultural symbolic meaning played a role analogous to that played by genes in biological heredity" (p. 850). By analogy Parsons here means a "functional similarity between the role of the genetic constitution in the organic world and that of the cultural system in the world of human action" (Parsons 1971:98). Parsons directly links this idea to the four-function paradigm whereby the pattern maintenance occupies "a special place as relatively invariant, i.e., changing by something like evolutionary processes on a long-time scale rather than by short-run adjustive processes" (ibid.). As the gene in biology is relatively insulated from change, so the Latency subsystem is relatively unaffected by change because of the stability given by the value system. Linguistic developments parallel to biological developments have shown that language is organized around a symbolic code (p. 93). The code makes language resistant to change: "The code element of the language (its syntax, grammar, vocabulary) make possible an indefinite variety of specific utterances, which are adaptive" (Parsons 1970:34). Similarly, in the action system, which is cybernetically controlled by the cultural system, "the most important structural components are the symbolic codes by the use of which detailed adaptive activities take place" (p. 36).

Such genetic and linguistic notions are the theoretical springboard for Parsons' theory of evolution as elaborated in *Societies* (1966) and in *The System of Modern Societies* (1971a). Language cannot any longer be considered an aggregate of symbols; rather "it is a system of symbols which have meaning relative to a code. A linguistic code is a normative structure parallel to that composed of societal values and norms" (Parsons 1966:20). Parsons developed a classification of evolutionary stages—primitive, intermediate, and modern—on the basis of "critical developments in the code elements of the normative structures. For the transition from primitive to intermediate society the focal development is in language, which is primarily part of the cultural system; in the transition from intermediate to modern society, the crucial change took place within the institutionalized codes of normative order internal to the societal structure and centers in the legal system" (p. 26).

Such a development of the Parsonian framework is of particular

interest because it is centered like semiotic structuralism on the notion of code. Parsons also shares with Lévi-Strauss a classificatory,
elementary, and combinatorial perspective. In fact, Parsons defends
his usage of the four-function scheme by stating that in the history
of science "very generally simplification through abstraction has been
a central feature of empirically fruitful theory. The fruitful path has
not been to avoid simple schemes but to use them to define elementary systems, and then to treat more complicated systems in terms
of combinations of more elementary components on various different
levels" (Parsons 1970:35; see also Parsons 1966:20–21). We seem to find
here a clear echo of Durkheimian and Lévi-Straussian principles. The
institutionalization process itself is understood by Parsons as a process of selection and combination of certain elements of the cultural
system that then became part of the social system (Parsons 1982).

Parsons clearly also endorsed the binary principle. His early theory
of action centered on a set of elementary and binary units (Parsons
1961:731). The binary principle is in full evidence in the more recent
evolutionary theory as well; they key process of social evolution is
"differentiation," which in the living system follows "the binary principle" exemplified by the cell division. Parsons notes that such a
principle is congenial to the theoretical schemes he has been working out, "such as the dichotomous character of pattern-variable pairs
and the conception of four primary system functions" (1971:100). The
extensive usage of the binary principle in Parsons' evolutionary theory is apparent, for instance, in the notions of high vs. low differentiation (1971:104) and mechanical and organical solidarities (p. 106)
and in the usage of sex and generation as the two axes of differentiation of the nuclear family (p. 105); from the latter idea Parsons derives
"the familiar four-fold table of two dichotomous variables" (1972:373).
In the essay coauthored with Renée C. Fox and Victor M. Lidz, Parsons concedes that his inspiration had come from Lévi-Strauss and
certain structural essays of Edmund Leach (Parsons, Fox, and Lidz
1972).

At this point we must raise a fundamental question: did Parsons
use the structural perspective as a descriptive analogy, as a strategy
to strengthen or refine his functional—hence empirical—perspective,
or was he in the process of moving his perspective from the level of

subjective meaning to that of objective and constitutive meaning, from the level of empirical to that of metaempirical—and perhaps semiotic—level of analysis?

Critique: The Empiricist and Antidialectic Bias of Parsons' Cybernetic and Evolutionary Perspective

Subjective Meaning As a Unit of Analysis

A close examination of Parsons' cybernetic formulations clearly indicates that his focus of analysis remains the "subjective meaning" of traditional sociological orientations. Parsons argues that the notion of cultural code permits a new interpretation of the role of ideas and collective representations in Weber's and Durkheim's sociologies, respectively. Culture legitimizes the normative order by providing reasons for the rights and duties of individuals (1969:11–12). The components of cultural systems are values, empirical knowledge, and expressive symbolic structures of religious systems. Value patterns are especially important as sources of legitimation, since the normative order is legitimized by grounding it in such ultimate realities as religious orientations, arts, and science (pp. 12–13). Cultural systems are organized around the characteristics of complexes of symbolic meanings, "the codes in terms of which they are structured," the clusters of symbols they employ, and the conditions of their utilization, maintenance, and change (p. 35).

The term "code," then, for Parsons indicates the structuring component of the cultural system. "A code is a normative structure, often described as a set of rules, within which messages . . . may be formulated" (1969:482) and interpreted. However, the components of the Parsonian cultural code are not elemental units, as is the case with the notion of code used in linguistics and genetics. "We consider value-patterns to be elements of the codes which "program" the patterning of action" (p. 447). Since values are "conceptions of desirable, . . . a value-pattern defines a direction of choice, and consequent commitment to action" (p. 441). "Authority," for instance, is "the code in terms of which the use of power is the class of messages that have meaning within the code" (p. 482). The codes of generalized media are composed of a value principle, such as the concept of utility, and a "coordinative standard, such as the concept of solvency" (p. 402). This conception is consistent with the definition of code provided in the paper published in my edited volume: a code is "a framework of symbolic categories or patterned arrangements" (Rossi 1982:58).

These few quotes clearly show that Parsons does not endorse a relational notion of code in the metaempirical sense. In fact, his most elemental units of analysis are the units of analysis of prestructural sociologists, that is, symbols and meanings are studied in terms of the subjective meaning, which is directly documentable through empirical observation. On the contrary, we have seen that transformational structuralists decompose observable data in terms of their elemental constituents and determine the constant relational properties and combinatory rules through which the elemental units are understood to constitute observable phenomena.

In the very same work in which Parsons refers to the linguistic concepts of Jakobson and Halle and uses cybernetic ideas, he declares: "Human action is organized through and in terms of the patterning of the meanings of objects" (Parsons et al. 1965:963). The study of the function of signs and symbols in the elementary process of interaction remains the starting point for studying cultural meaning (p. 979). Parsons uses the term "symbol" to indicate objects with generalized meaning, the latter "being superadded to the intrinsic significance" of the properties of the object (pp. 975–976). He sees a direct association between the terms "meaning," symbolism, and culture. "Action consists of the structures and processes by which human beings form meaningful intentions and, more or less successfully, implement them in concrete situations. The word meaningful implies the symbolic or cultural level of representation and reference" (1969:5).

A little further on Parsons continues: "Human action is *cultural* in that meanings and intentions concerning acts are formed in terms of symbolic systems (including codes through which they operate in patterns) that focus most generally around the universal of human societies, language" (1969:6). Although Parsons refers to Jakobson and Halle's linguistic notions, he does not share their metaempirical view of language: "We shall attempt to apply the above outline of the dimensions of cultural systems to the cultural phenomenon of language" (1961:971). "If language is considered first as a semantic system in terms of categories of meaning, there is a general correspondence with our way of analyzing culture" (p. 974). Parsons is interested in language primarily as a mechanism of communication and social integration (p. 971). Communication takes place through the communication of messages from one unit of the social system to others (*ibid.*). "Messages, therefore, constitute a kind of circulating medium" (p. 972). Language is the principal mechanism which mediates the interchange between the cultural and social systems. Culture provides the social system with culture patterns or systems of meaning that are institutionalized by the social system and accepted by social actors as the way to think and communicate. Language contributes to the cultural system with its pattern structure, like linguistic "form-patterns," which influence the categorization of experience (Whorf hypothesis), and syntactical structures, which are described by Jakobson and Halle (p. 974). Language contributes to the social system with meanings contained in linguistic symbols (p. 976). Morphemic and lexical elements are also linguistic symbols, where symbols are defined as "objects with meaning on a particular minimum level of generality" (p. 975).

As long as Parsons' basic unit of analysis remains "subjective meaning" in the Weberian and Meadian sense of the term, he cannot incorporate into his framework the relational and transformational—hence "objective"—view of language developed by Saussure, Jakobson, and Chomsky. Having mentioned Jakobson and Halle's distinction between the message and code functions of language, Parsons states that "language is a code in terms of which the particular symbols constituting any particular message have meaning" (1969:407), but his analysis remains at the level of the message. This is so because the actor's orientation toward action remains a central focus of Parsons' perspective and this orientation is based on the meaning conveyed by messages. It is in this sense that, for Parsons, language "is the generalized mechanism mediating human communication" (Parsons et al. 1965:976).

An analysis of the most recently formulated notion of "generalized symbolic media of interchange" confirms the same point. I have mentioned that Parsons proposes the notion of code to explain the interchange between the hierarchically ordered four systems of action and between the four functions of each subsystem of action. Parsons argues that with a high degree of division of labor the interchange cannot take place on a barter basis but must be mediated by "some generalized mechanism" (1970:39). He initially proposed four such media for the social system—money, politics, power influence, and value commitment. Then he extended the notion of symbolic media to the general system of action, where intelligence, performance, capacity, affect, and definition of the situation perform the functions of adaptation, goal attainment, integration, and pattern maintenance, respectively.

It is undeniable that the symbolic media are "objectifications" of meaning embedded within interaction processes. However, such a notion of objective meaning presupposes the notion of subjective meaning; that is, subjective meaning remains the basic unit of sociological analysis, on the basis of which sociologically meaningful data are identified and analytical concepts are constructed. That Parsons' concept of symbolic medium is based on the notion of subjective meaning becomes immediately clear from his identification of the four generalized media with "the four wishes and the definition of the situation" of W. I. Thomas (Parsons 1970a:848). We all know that the definition of the situation proposed by Thomas is a characteristic contribution of the early tradition of symbolic interactionism, a tradition concerned with the process of construction of shared or "common meaning" (a Meadean term). For instance, Parsons argues that "money is a symbolic 'embodiment' of economic value" and signified commodities (1969:407); here Parsons deals with the content of symbol, that is, with meaning as understood by social actors. Power is a "generalized symbolic medium" of exchange because it "is effective only through communications that activate obligations to contribute to collective processes through compliance with collective decisions" (p. 446). In this text Parsons deals with ideas having motivational value and force, that is, with systems of meaning as understood by social actors. To make matters unequivocally clear, Parsons states that meaning understood in the Weberian and Meadean sense remains the focal point of his conception of the cultural system and symbolism. "The most important starting point in this area is the one associated especially with G. H. Mead—the involvement of the problems of meanings, and hence of the functions of signs and symbols in the elementary processes of social interaction. This is the focal point of departure for considering the cultural level of meaning" (1965, 1979).

The same level of analysis is evidenced in the more recently formulated "general action interchange system," where each symbolic medium of interchange is analyzed in terms of message and code and the code is discussed in terms of "value principle" and "coordination standard" (1970:67ff; see also Cartwright and Warner 1976). The whole context of Parsons' presentation indicates that the notions of "value" and "standard" still incorporate the notion of subjective meaning used in the voluntaristic formulation of the Theory of Social Action and in symbolic interactionism; this, of course, does not preclude their playing an objective and structural role in the conceptual scheme. One must conclude, then, that the notions of code, program, mediating agency, and binary and combinatory processes are used by Parsons as illustrative analogies and not in the relational and metaempirical sense of transformational structuralists.

At this point one question arises: why do transformational structuralists and Parsons use cybernetic and linguistic concepts in a so markedly different sense?

Epistemological Roots of Parsons' Empiricist Approach

Notwithstanding the exposure to modern cybernetic, biological, and linguistic thought, Parsons' framework has remained anchored on an empiricist notion of scientific activity. To be sure, Parsons rejected an extreme version of empiricism, i.e., the notion that scientific knowledge is "a total reflection of 'reality out there' " (1970a:830). However, Parsons did not avoid a more moderate version of empiricism, which in a variety of forms has permeated the interpretive and natural science paradigms as used in the classical sociological trandition.

The crux of the problem is that in Parsons' work the dualistic perspective that permeates objective and subjective empiricism is very prominent; by "objective empiricism" I refer to positivist, behavioral, and functional sociologies, and by "subjective empiricism" I refer to phenomenology and ethnomethodology. (See the Introduction to this volume.) Sociological dualism consists of the separation of the knower from the object known and of the related notion that sociological concepts have to be subordinated to empirical reality, be it observable behavior or subjective experience. Such a dichotomy is clear in Parsons' very rendition of the Kantian perspective as well as in his interpretation of transformational linguistics and Piaget.

Parsons presents the Kantian framework as producing such explanations as that the normality of death can be derived "from the combination of transcendental and empirical factors" (Parsons 1978:349). The notion of combination exemplifies the existence of two self-contained or separately constituted factors which come into interaction. This is a clear example of dichotomous and empiricist thinking. Lévi-Strauss is cognizant of this problem when he states that once a dichotomy is posited, one cannot bridge the gap. For this reason he posits the notion of isomorphic structural levels (Lévi-Strauss 1972, 1963).

The dualistic perspective is very much evident in some Parsonian thinkers. For instance, Victor M. Lidz argues that the categorization of the sentence into subject, object, verb, and modifier has a direct parallel in the categories of the action frame of reference: subject, object, mode of orientation of the subject to the object (verb), qualities of the object, and action or relation (modifier). Lidz sees the roots of this categorization in the Cartesian dichotomy of observer-object, a dichotomy which was continued by the positivist tradition (Lidz 1976:138–139).

Lidz's insight is correct, but it refers only to the system of categories of the analytical approach. The comparison between Parsons and Chomsky falls short on the key element of the latter's approach, i.e., the notion of deep structure from which an indefinite number of correct sentences is generated through precise transformational rules. I will come back to this crucial difference later on in this section. I should also add that the subject-object distinction is not understood by Chomsky as a dichotomy of two separate and independent entities as empiricists and positivists do. On the contrary, subject and object, deep and surface structures are understood to be in a trans-formational ánd constitutive relationship, the structure being the constitutive process of subjectivity. (The latter point has been vigorously pursued by poststructural semioticians.)

A similar line of reasoning also applies to the often spoken about similarities between Parsons and Piaget. Victor and Charles Lidz have argued that the Parsonian "behavioral system" should not include physiological processes, since they are not "meaningful" elements and therefore introduce a heterogeneous element in the action frame of reference. They propose to conceptualize the adaptive subsystem in terms of the cognitive function understood in the Piagetian sense of mental "schemas," which would control and coordinate behavioral processes (Lidz and Lidz, 1976:195–239). It is not surprising that Parsons has accepted this contribution as a highly original theoretical innovation (1975:81), considering his strong functional perspective. However, whereas it is true that both Piaget and Parsons (and Lévi-Strauss) accept the notion of self-governing systems, they conceptualize differently their adaptive function. Parsons conceives the adaptation of self-governing systems to the environment in an empiricist way, that is, as an adjustment between two separate and self-contained entities, whereas Piaget holds a transformational view of the adaptation of open systems to the environment. By this I mean that in the Piagetian perspective one does not deal with observable (hence empirical) patterns of interactions between two independently constituted entities—personality system and the environment; rather, the effort is focused on the formulation of transformational rules underlying the empirical patterns of transaction between personality and environment. On the other hand, Lévi-Strauss' attention is focused on the systemic laws or tendencies of a given set of phenomena. The environmental facts, be they ecological, historical, or psychological, are considered to be as many interferences with the internal tendencies of the system. To understand the concreteness of the phenomena one must take into account both the systemic tendencies and the contingent factors.

The dichotomous conceptualizations of sense impressions vs. conceptual representations, deep structure vs. surface structure, and system vs. environment are reflected in the basic dichotomy—and dilemma—which underlines all Parsons' sociological theorizing. For Parsons, sociological knowledge consists of the selective perception of essential "elements" of reality. As we have seen in part 1, he insists that concepts should be formulated "entirely out of accord with the facts" (Parsons 1961:287) and that concepts should adequately grasp aspects of the objective external world (p. 730). As I have mentioned, Parsons resolutely rejects the claim of the extreme empiricists that "any science has the task of delivering a full, complete, explanatory account of a given sector of concrete reality" (1935:420) because a complete account of a given reality in all its concreteness entails what Alfred Whitehead has called "the error of mistaking the abstract for the concrete" or the "fallacy of misplaced concreteness" (Whitehead 1925:74).

Parsons' contention that analytical realism avoids both nominalism and empiricism (or the extreme version of it) is based on a particular conception of concept formation. He holds that concepts are abstract in the sense that they refer only to some aspects of concrete phenomena and not others, and, therefore, concepts do not account for the totality of social phenomena in all their concreteness. In Parsons' view, social phenomena are to be understood as combinations of "aspects" ((1934:530) or abstract "elements" (1935:421) or analytical "factors" (1935a:646–647). Analytical elements are concepts which "correspond not to concrete phenomena but to elements in them which are analytically separated from other elements" (1961:739); analytical elements must be understood not as particles or parcels of reality but "as aspects of the systemic structure and connections of nature, as factors or variables in which by virtue of analytical abstraction every essence of systemic order can be grasped" (Schwanenberg 1976:40). Parsons holds a particular notion of abstraction. He claims that "the proper abstraction for the social sciences" consists of the process of formulating "abstract analytical systems each of which assumes as data the main outline of fundamental structure of concrete systems of action" (1961:465–466).

We can see here the theoretical roots of Parsons' systemic and highly "abstract" orientation. Parsons' conception of concept formation by abstraction is consistent with the classificatory mode of explanation, which consists of retaining only the essential characteristics of phenomena and ignoring the nonessential ones. The classificatory and essentialist notion of explanation is based on an Aristotelian view of the world composed of form and matter, essence and accidents, and it is in sharp contrast with Ernst Cassirer's constructivist notion of explanation, which is consistent with a Galilean view of the world (and with the perspective of transformational structuralism) (see Rossi 1974:74–75). The constructivist notion of explanation consists of using not essential but relational concepts whose meaning is determined by their relationships to other concepts that are part of the system. The particularity of an event is not ignored but interpreted in terms of the combinatory logic of the elements composing the totality; that is, a particular event is considered one among many other possible actualizations of the totality—a variant of the totality. In this way the particularity of an event is not ignored, by the process of selectivity, as it is in Parsons' notion of abstraction, but is accounted for (retained) in terms of the law of variation.

The classificatory notion of explanation has led Parsons to an impasse between an empiricist and a formalist mode of sociological analysis. His empiricist bias is evident, for instance, in his definition of social structure as "any set of relations among parts of a living system which on empirical grounds can be shown to be stable over a period of time" (1975:69). Here it is clear that for Parsons social structure refers to empirically observable patterns of interaction. Similarly, function is defined as "the consequences of the existence and nature of certain empirically observable structures and processes in such systems" (p. 70). At the same time, Parsons does not avoid the shortcomings of a quasiformalistic approach. In fact, for him sociological theory "does not refer to empirical generalizations about certain classes of concrete phenomena but to an abstractly analytical 'conceptual scheme'" (p. 73).

One must then raise the question of whether Parsons' theorizing is based on empirically observable regularities or on abstract conceptions about them. According to Parsons' thinking, a clear-cut distinction between the two levels of analysis is of crucial importance. In fact, he asserts that "the most important single proposition" about functional analysis is that it "will become intolerably confusing if there is not the best possible clarification of system references. This obviously has to be a problem concerning data about the objects of investigation 'out there.' At the same time, however, it must concern the theoretically defined cognitive system with which the investigator is working" (1975:71–72).

Besides making a clear distinction between the two levels of analysis (or "systems of reference" in his terminology), Parsons clearly states that both levels are essential components of a sound sociological theory. But in what sense must a sociologist deal with both levels "at the same time"? In the same essay, two pages earlier, Parsons tells us that his "term 'system' refers to classes of objects 'out there,' in the sense that they are not to be identified with the seeker of knowledge about them" (p. 70). To know something about objects, the investigator must "describe, conceptualize, and analyze data," i.e., form "cognitive maps" about them. However, "the cognitive products coming out of this process must not be identified with the objects themselves. They are entities of quite a different order" (p. 70). These Parsonian formulations do not clarify the relationship between two levels of analysis of different order. How can one be sure that cognitive constructs produce (true) knowledge of objects "out there"?

Parsons has tackled this issue in a reply to Thomas Burger's cogent critique of his analytical realism (1977). He admits that sociology has been for a long time caught in the dilemma of defining the subject matter in analytical terms or "in concretely empirical terms" (p. 335); although he concedes "there is simply no way of making the two match neatly so that it is possible to have the best of both worlds" (pp. 335–336), Parsons postulates a congruence between the theoretical order and the "socio-empirical" order, which includes the world of human action. But he cautions that congruence must "not be interpreted to imply a one-to-one correspondence" (pp. 338–339). Parsons' position boils down to reinstating a heterogeneity between the empirical generalizations and theoretical order and, at the same time, the need of dealing simultaneously with both levels; this need is stated although he does not have a formula to match them to each other. How can one postulate (or be sure of) a congruency between the two levels of analysis if a one-to-one correspondence between them is excluded? How and when, and between which elements of the two levels, does the congruence occur? Parsons does not offer a clear answer to these questions.

Moreover, the notion of generic congruity between the two levels of theorizing is incompatible with the principle of empirical verification or falsifiability, since this principle implies a one-to-one correspondence between theoretical concepts and empirical generalizations. Parsons never makes clear what he substitutes for the positivist notion of verifiability or falsifiability, which he resolutely (and I may add, rightly so) rejects (1977:338). In defense of his own position, Parsons states that analytical theories are as unfalsifiable as "the 'deep structures' of a language [which] cannot be demonstrated to be either *grammatical* or *ungrammatical;* they are *components* (his italics) on the basis of such judgments, not themselves constitutive of them. The judgments apply to sentences, not to deep structures" (p. 338). At this point intellectual uncertainty is transformed into intellectual confusion.

In the volume edited by Peter M. Blau and Robert K. Merton, I have argued that Parsons has unduly confused his own position with that of Chomsky (Rossi 1981). The point is that notwithstanding various elaborations of transformational grammar, Chomsky has remained faithful to the distinction between surface structure and deep structure; surface structure refers to actually occurring phonological forms and syntactical arrangements that are thought to derive from an underlying structure: "The fundamental idea is that surface structures are formed through the interaction of at least two distinct types of rules: basic rules, which generate abstract phrase structure representations, and transformational rules, which move elements and otherwise rearrange structures to give the surface structures" (Chomsky 1980:144). Chomsky concedes that there are two alternative ways to conceptualize the relations among these elements. However, he also states that "both answers accept the basic premise that has guided transformational grammar: namely, that the rules relating surface structures and logical forms should be factored into several components" (p. 153). Chomsky's key contribution is having shown that each one of these components relates with precision and predictability to the other components. In Chomsky one does not find the vague notion of congruence but a stepwise set of interconnected rules which govern the transition from one linguistic component to the next. As a result, we no longer find a dichotomy between the abstract and concrete, the general and the particular, as is the case in the positivist and empiricist perspectives. By the same token, the impasse between the empiricist and formalist levels of analysis is abolished.

In ultimate analysis, whereas Parsons has successfully shown that both the empiricist and formalist analyses are inadequate, he has not succeeded in formulating a viable alternative. (On the distinction between empiricist, theoretical, and structural concepts see Rossi 1975.) The outcome is that the sociologist is left with the problem of having to choose between two equally objectionable modes of theorizing.

The Lack of a Transformational and Truly Cybernetic Perspective

In the light of the previous discussion we must resolutely reject the contention that Parsons has delineated "the structure of action and society apart from any of its particular manifestations in the same manner that Chomsky" does (Alexander 1978:183). In Parsons' sociology there is no notion of deep structure in the Chomskian sense of the term, but only an abstract conceptual schema of functional relationships; in fact, Parsons defines the code as nothing but "the symbolic frame of reference within which meaningful utterances can be formulated" (1975:76). This frame of reference refers to an abstract scheme and not to a constitutive mechanism of specific meanings, because it lacks the transformational rules governing the production of meanings.

Let me succinctly show how some analogous applications of the notion of transformational rules could notably strengthen the analytical power of the four-function paradigm. One can accept Parsons' assumptions that the cultural system is grounded on deep symbolic codes and that the four subsystems of action are organized in a cybernetic hierarchy of control. If one introduces the additional assumption that the four subsystems of action are isomorphically organized, there emerges the need to formulate the following analytical components as indicated in figure 8.1: the code of each subsystem (column 2); the processes underlying the changes in each subsystem (column 3); and the intersystemic transformational links between the various subsystem composing the cybernetic hierarchy of control (column 1).

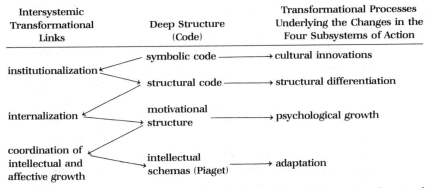

Intersystemic Transformational Links	Deep Structure (Code)	Transformational Processes Underlying the Changes in the Four Subsystems of Action
institutionalization	symbolic code ⟶	cultural innovations
	structural code ⟶	structural differentiation
internalization	motivational structure ⟶	psychological growth
coordination of intellectual and affective growth	intellectual schemas (Piaget) ⟶	adaptation

Figure 8.1. Paradigm for a structural reinterpretation of the action frame of reference.

Pure linguists might object to the use of notions of generativity and transformation. What I am here suggesting, however, are linkages which are only analogically, or perhaps improperly, called transformational. I am simply saying that if action theorists are serious about the Chomskian framework, they must find some linkage-mechanisms governing the transition of information from one cybernetic level to the next, rather than considering the relationship between the various levels as an empirical question.

One must also raise a word of caution against certain recent applications of structuralist concepts in the development of the theory of action. For instance, I see some serious problems in Lidz's reinterpretations of Parsons' behavioral subsystem in terms of Piaget's notion of intelligence (Lidz and Lidz 1976). It is not clear how the cybernetic hierarchy of control is preserved in the lowest two subsystems of the general action schema. Shall we give priority to intelligence (the behavioral system in Lidz's formulation), as Piaget does, or should we attribute an equal importance to the motivational structure (the "personality" of Parsons)? Since both motivational and intellectual processes are parts of the psychic functioning, isn't it arbitrary to reserve the adaptive function of the Parsonian behavioral system only to cognitive processes, with the exclusion of what Parsons calls the cathectic and evaluative modes of orientation? Lidz's formulation of the two different subsystems seems to imply, hence perpetuate, the dualistic perspective of empiricist positivism between intellectual and affective factors.

It is my contention that even the cybernetic perspective implies, or at least is compatible with, a decisive break away from empiricism and the dualistic perspective of positivists. In fact, the focus of cyberneticians is on context and not on content; Gregory Bateson has explained that the focus on relationships among data rather than on data themselves (content) gives a new meaning to the inductive and dialectic approaches. In cybernetic explanation what is crucial is "the relationship between context and content." For instance, the meaning of the phoneme derives from its combination with other phonemes; similarly the meaning of a word derives from its combination with the other words of the utterance. Therefore, not only the notion of context but also that of *hierarchy of context* is crucial in the cybernetic study of information (Bateson 1967:30). The notion of context, however, must be understood not according to the empiricist perspective. Empiricism leads one to conceive of the relationship between system and environment in terms of an interaction or adaptation between two separate entities. On the contrary, the system-environment relationship must be understood in terms of a mathematical function, that is, as a relationship between variables.[1] Cyberneticians conceive of the relationship between system and environment as "governed by a program, or to use an existentialist term, by meaning. Seen in this light, then, existence is a function (in the mathematical sense) of the relationship between the organism and the environment" (Watzlawick, Beavin, and Jackson 1967:259).

This switch from a subjective (content) to a mathematical and cybernetic view of meaning (program), from an empiricist to a mathematical notion of function is what is missing in Parsons' understand-

---

[1] We know that the modern psychology of perception has shown that the relationship among things, rather than isolated things, is the first datum of perception (see Lévi-Strauss 1971; Rossi 1978). This supports the structuralists' notion that invariant mathematical relationships and gestalt, rather than the individual terms, should be the units of analysis in psychological and social sciences.

ing and use of cybernetics. We know that the mathematical notion of group has produced the important notion of structure as a system of transformations, which has found further refinements in the generativity notion of Chomsky. Far from violating the Parsonian approach, this mathematical and relational perspective could bring to its fullest development the antiempiricist and mathematical thrust present in *The Structure of Social Action*, a thrust which has remained in an inchoate state because of Parsons' "analytical realism."

So far we have seen that Parsons' dualistic views have produced an empiricist notion of scientific activity and perpetuated a dichotomous view of the system-environment relationship. We shall now see that the dualistic perspective is also related to and responsible for the undialectical nature of Parsons' systemic approach.

The Systemic Bias of the Theory of Social Action and the Missing Dialectic

I have just argued that a fundamental aspect of Parsons' analytical realism is the construction of a classificatory scheme made up of abstract concepts. Whereas at the epistemological level Parsons has been led by his analytical realism to the dilemma of having to choose between empiricism or formalism, at the level of substantive analysis he has been led toward systemic and undialectic sociological thinking. Parsons has organized his analytical elements into a conceptual system and has assumed that the conceptual system is congruent with the objective world. Consistent with these theoretical premises, he has attributed systemic properties to the social world. It is, perhaps, at this fundamental theoretical level that one must look for the reasons why Parsons has progressively emphasized the systemic rather than the voluntaristic aspect of social action (although we have seen that the early theory of action is based on a set of elementary units which are "systematically" interrelated to one another).

The systemic bias is evident in Parsons' paramount concern with such issues as social equilibrium, adaptive function, consensus, and maintenance function (1970a:849). The notions of cybernetic hierarchy of control, cultural code, and symbolic mode of interchange (p. 846) are also derived from or consistent with Parsons' concern with the delineation and interrelationship of the four subsystems composing the general action system.

The systemic emphasis leads Parsons to a one-sided view of social life, emphasizing the cultural and, subordinately, the structural aspect of social life at the expense of the subjective (voluntaristic) aspect. This ultimately leads Parsons to a static and undialectical view of society.

Parsons himself argues that his functional approach is in line with Radcliffe-Brown's and not Malinowski's type of functionalism (1970a:849). Parsons explains the difference between these two approaches by noting that whereas for Radcliffe-Brown and Durkheim the system of reference was the social system, for Malinowski the system of reference also included the personality of the individual (1975:81).

One can argue, further, that even if it were included with the functional paradigm, Parsons' notion of personality would not permit an adequate understanding of the role of subjectivity in social life. Parsons describes the evolution of this thought as a "step from the conception of econonic activity as a *type* [Parsons' italics] of individual action . . . to the conception of economy as a social system of action, which could be conceived to be a primary functional subsystem of a total society" (1977:337). It is hard to see how the notion of personality type can do justice to the notion of subjectivity with its connotation of free and creative input into the processes of social interaction. This aspect of the subjectivity in social life cannot be ignored, especially after the legacy of the problems raised by poststructural semiotics.

In conclusion, if by dialectical paradigm we mean a paradigm which not only includes among the explanatory factors of social life both the subjective and the systemic factors but places them in mutual and constitutive relationships, then the Parsonian approach is an undialectical one for two reasons. First, the notion of personality as a type or role set does not give an adequate account of the innovative influence of individuals on social life. Second, the notion of a cybernetic hierarchy of control inevitably attributes an analytical priority to systemic factors over personality factors. In fact, the personality system is subordinated (cybernetically controlled by) the social system, which in turn is controlled by the symbolic code of the cultural system.

I realize that some action theorists might find the lack of dialectic perspective in Parsons not at all objectionable given his option for neo-Kantian methodology. However, the following question must be clearly answered: Does Parsons offer a fully satisfactory explanation of the dynamic of social life? We shall see in chapter 10 that semiotic Marxism and semiotic psychoanalytic thought contain elements of a more truly dialectical view of social life.

9

Semiotic Structuralism and the
Interpretive Paradigm

In discussing the relationship between phenomenology and structuralism I refer in this section mostly to Lévi-Strauss' semiotic structuralism. Lévi-Strauss' emphasis on universal and immutable structures has prompted phenomenologically and Marxist oriented social thinkers to label his structuralism a form of positivism. Yet phenomenology and semiotic structuralism agree on the principle that social phenomena must be explained in terms of "meaning" rather than in terms of causal relations or statistical regularities. In this sense, both phenomenology and structuralism appear to belong to the interpretive paradigm rather than to the natural science paradigm. There is another important affinity between semiotic structuralism and phenomenology—their common antiempiricist attitude. This is the reason for discussing phenomenology, after having introduced the reader to semiotic and genetic structuralism. I shall discuss first the antiempiricist and constitutive view of meaning of phenomenologists, then certain theoretical and methodological affinities between phenomenology and semiotic structuralism, and finally, I will show that phenomenology does not succeed in accomplishing a real break away from the empiricist orientation.

Phenomenological Sociology and the Constitutive View of Meaning

The most representative works of the phenomenological approach in American sociology have been written or prepared by the following authors: Peter Berger and Thomas Luckman (1966), Severyn Bruyn

(1966), Aaron Cicourel (1964, 1974), Jack Douglas (1970), Harold Garfinkel (1967), Burkart Holzner (1968), Hugh Mehan and Houston Wood
(1975), Maurice Natanson (1970, 1973), John O'Neil (1972), George Psathas (1973), David Sudnow (1971), Edward A. Tiryakian (1962, 1970),
and Roy Turner (1974). One cannot claim that all these works belong
to a well-delimited or homogeneous sociological orientation; however, all of them have been influenced to a greater or lesser degree
by phenomenological ideas in combination with ideas taken at times
from symbolic interactionism, at other times from modern linguistics,
and still other times from Marxism.

Heap and Roth (1973) have distinguished four meanings of the terms
"phenomenological sociology": first, and perhaps not totally appropriately, the term is sometimes used to indicate the emphasis placed
by Weber, Thomas, Cooley, and Mead on *subjective meaning* as the
key element in explaining social action and interaction. Secondly, and
more appropriately, the term is used to indicate the sociological approach of Schutz, Berger and Luckman, and Holzner, who apply with
varying degrees of approximation and analogy certain ideas of Husserl. Thirdly, the term is used to indicate the reflexive sociology of
O'Neil, who combines the phenomenological and Marxist perspectives. Finally, Heap and Roth consider ethnomethodology as a type
of phenomenological sociology, although some people might object
to such a characterization of ethnomethodology; Don H. Zimmerman, for instance, has recently argued that Garfinkel has greatly
transformed Schutzian ideas, hence one cannot characterize the intellectual content of his work as simply being a phenomenological
one (1978:6–8). Moreover, ethnomethodologists like Harvey Sacks and
Aaron Cicourel have borrowed some ideas from modern linguistics
and cognitive anthropology. The fact remains, however, that phenomenology has directly or indirectly played a crucial role in the
genesis of ethnomethodology and that certain phenomenological ideas
are used both by phenomenologically and linguistically oriented ethnomethodologists.[1]

[1] Heap and Roth do not mention the important branch of European phenomenology
developed by Alfred Wierkandt, Max Scheler, and Georges Gurvitch, who was influenced by Husserl. All these sociologists agree that the task of sociological analysis is
to study "essences," or social forms, underlying external and immediately observable
social facts.

Phenomenology as applied in sociology has been derived from the transcendental phenomenology of Husserl through the mediation and modifications introduced by the existential phenomenologies of Merleau-Ponty and Sartre and the sociological phenomenology of Schutz.

The Husserlian Perspective

It is well known that Husserl formulated his approach in reaction to the "natural attitude," or the application of the method of natural sciences to the study of psychological processes. Husserl believed that the method of natural sciences "objectivizes" psychic phenomena for being treated as if they were material objects located in space and time in the same sense that the bodies, connected with psychic processes, are located in time and space. Husserl strongly argued that psychic phenomena are different from natural phenomena because they consist of "streams of consciousness." By definition, *consciousness* means to be conscious of something; the objects we are conscious of are *meant*, that is, given meaning, by the intentionality of consciousness. Husserl contends that the natural attitude does not permit one to grasp the "sense" of experience of psychic phenomena because it imposes upon experience forms which are external or extraneous to it. The experiential sense of psychic phenomena can be captured only by intuitively describing the intentionality of consciousness without any presupposition or prejudices. Husserl wanted to achieve knowledge of the "things themselves," to discover the "essences" of the phenomena of consciousness, a phenomenon being what is immediately given in consciousness.

The goal of Husserl's phenomenological analysis was to clarify the essence of things through ideational intuition. He contrasted the science of essences (phenomenology) with the science of facts (psychology). The term "fact" refers to "individual form . . . having spatio-temporal existence . . . existing in this time-spot, having this particular duration of its own and a real content which in its essence could just as well have been present in any other time-spot" (Husserl 1962:46). On the other hand, essences are the necessary prerequisites of things; the term "essence" refers not to the necessary and defining features of empirical objects but to qualities of the intended object without which the latter cannot be thought to exist. Although the essences are embodied in empirical facts, they exist beyond time and space, because they are permanent and necessary forms for the existence of phenomena. In other words, the Husserlian essences are a priori and formal invariants which pertain to the realm of possibilities. It is only in this sense that "facts" connote the contingencies of things and essences their universal and invariant properties.[2] We will see that the distinction between the contingent and "necessary" principle of explanation and the definition of science as the quest for necessary, invariant, or common properties underlying a variety of observable events are important concepts in modern structuralism and structural Marxism.

To arrive at the *eidos*, or essence, Husserl has formulated the method of variation and permutation.

[Free variation] must be understood, not as an empirical variation, but as a variation carried on with the freedom of pure phantasy and with the consciousness of its purely optional character—the consciousness of the "pure" any whatever. Thus understood, the variation extends into an open horizon of endless manifold free possibilities of more and more variants. . . . What necessarily persists through this free and always repeatable variation comes to the fore: the invariant, the indissolubly identical in the different and ever again different, the essence common to all, the universal essence by which all imaginable variants of the example, and all variants of any such variant, are restricted. This invariant is the ontic essential form (a priori form), the *Eidos*, corresponding to the example, in place of which any variant of the example could have served equally well. . . . The concern is to take the particular as an example of some *Eidos*. (Husserl 1969:247–248, 267)

As we shall see, the method of free variation and the principle of interpreting the particular on the basis of the invariant are methodological milestones of the antiempiricist orientation of modern French structuralists.

―――――――――――

[2]For a discussion of the metaphoric usage of phenomenological ideas in sociology and the differences between Husserlian phenomenology, which is concerned with the realm of possibilities, and phenomenological sociology, which is concerned with the empirical realm, see Heap and Roth (1973:359) and their exchange with Burkart Holzner (1974:286–291).

The Sociological Phenomenology of Alfred Schutz

The antiempiricist attitude of phenomenology has influenced American sociology mostly through the interpretation and elaboration of the Husserlian ideas proposed by Alfred Schutz.[3] Schutz has taken the study of intersubjectivity away from the transcendental realm of possibilities to consider it as a category and precondition of all human experience. For Schutz the task of phenomenological sociology is to undertake the "exploration of the general principles according to which man in daily life organizes his experiences, and especially those of the social world" (Schutz quoted in Wagner 1971:44). To grasp the organizing principles of experience we have to practice the *épochè* of the natural attitude, which means to bracket common sense knowledge.

In the épochè I abstain from the belief in the being of this world, and I direct my view exclusively to my consciousness of the world. . . . All these experiences found in my conscious life, if they are not themselves originally giving and primarily founding experiences of this life-world, can be examined concerning the history of their sedimentation. In this way I can return fundamentally to the original experience of the life world in which the facts themselves can be grasped directly. To interpret all this by showing the intentional accomplishments of the (transcendental) subjectivity makes up the enormous area of work of constitutive phenomenology. . . . All cultural objects (books, tools, works of all sorts, etc.) point back, by their origin and meaning, to other subjects and to their active constitutive intentionalities. (Schutz 1940:455, 456)

The transcendental phenomenology of Husserl and the existential phenomenology of Sartre and Merleau-Ponty have proposed different conceptions of who is the subject of the "experience" and what is the content "experienced" by the subject. However, most of phenomenologists tend to agree that the essential task of phenomenology is "to give direct access to the world of immediate experience in terms of intending the acts of consciousness and the objects intended . . . through these acts" (Wieder 1977:4–5). Among the intended objects we must include the conscious experiences produced by social norms,

---

[3] I am, of course, aware that a serious discussion of Merleau-Ponty would open up an interesting discourse on the relationship between phenomenology and relational structuralism. Space considerations prevent such a discussion.

roles, institutions, and language. These objects are not "intended" in a sociological vacuum but in the course of social interaction. The task of phenomenological sociologists is to describe the intersubjective world of meanings and experience, the "life world" within which people carry out their daily interaction.

It becomes immediately apparent that there are obvious points of contact between the phenomenological notion of the intersubjective world of meaning and Weber's notion of "subjectively intended meaning." In fact, the subjectively intended meaning is the meaning individuals attach to the action in the process of orienting themselves toward the behavior of others. Schutz' ambition was to link the Weberian and Husserlian perspectives and, by so doing, to provide a phenomenological foundation to the sociology of "understanding." Schutz saw limitations in both thinkers and selected certain elements of their thought to blend into a new perspective. It is outside the scope of this volume to undertake a detailed discussion of the notions used by Schutz to describe the structure of the "life world," the inherent sociality of consciousness. I must mention that his notions of "reciprocity of perspectives," which implies the "interchangeability of standpoints," "congruency of the systems of relevance," "general thesis of the alter ego," and so on, are presently used, although in modified form, by ethnomethodologists (see, for instance, Cicourel 1974).

One should mention that the Schutzian conception of intersubjectivity is a refinement of the perspective of symbolic interactionists. This is not surprising since in the later period of his career Schutz was influenced by the works of Mead, Cooley, and Thomas. For instance, Schutz proposes the notion that in the direct and visual experience of the physical appearances and actions of others we see expressions of their conscious life and their "spiritual I," toward which we direct our behavior. This notion is clearly an expansion of the Meadian notion of I and Me.

There are many points of contact between Weber, symbolic interactionism, and phenomenology that could be discussed. From the point of view of this volume the crucial innovation introduced by the phenomenological paradigm in respect to symbolic interactionism is not so much the elucidation of various aspects of meaning, symbols, and language, but the notion that they cannot be properly understood without elucidating the processes by which they are produced.

It is the affinity between phenomenology and semiotic structuralism that most interests me. This affinity exists both in terms of substantive and methodological orientation.[4]

Substantive and Methodological Affinities Between Sociological Phenomenology and Semiotic Structuralism

To begin with the subject matter studied, both phenomenologists and semiotic structuralists emphasize the cognitive dimension of meaning. As Wagner states, Schutz deals with "sociological analysis from the cognitive angle" (Wagner 1971:38). In fact, Schutz's intent is to describe the cognitive structuring of daily experience, or the cognitive setting of the life world. Similarly, the cognitive emphasis is very prominent in Lévi-Strauss, who is concerned with the logical structures underlying systems of conscious meanings. Moreover, Lévi-Strauss attributes an analytic priority to intellect over affectivity and locates the origin of the structuring principles of experience in the a priori constraints of the human mind.

Phenomenologists maintain that intentionality gives origin to signs, symbols, and language. For this reason the study of language, signs, symbols, intercommunication, and gestural and visual expression is central in Schutz's works. Language, as the vehicle for communicating meaning, is the natural focus of analysis not only for phenomenologists, symbolic interactionists, and ethnomethodologists, but also for structuralists. We have seen that taking inspiration from Saussure, Lévi-Strauss has conceptualized culture as a system of signs so that signs are the subject matter par excellence of his investigation.

Besides sharing a common subject matter, phenomenology and

[4] I purposely use the term "methodological orientation" to differentiate the phenomenological and structuralist conceptions of methodology from the natural science definition of it. For behaviorists and operational sociologists, structural-functionalists, social exchange theorists, and other sociologists of natural science orientation, *methodology* refers to operational research techniques; for phenomenologists and structuralists methodology encompasses larger and more fundamental issues, such as the processes by which sociologists arrive at their interpretations of data and the relationship of interpretive processes to the data explained.

structuralism concur in a variety of methodological principles. First, both phenomenology and structuralism foster an antiempiricist attitude. We have seen that phenomenologists claim that the investigator must suspend spontaneous affirmations about the world and deal only with the intentional objects of "pure" consciousness: "Since (transcendental) phenomenology accepts nothing as self-evident, but undertakes to bring everything to self-evidence, it escapes all naïve positivism and may expect to be the true science of mind in true rationality, in the proper meaning of this term" (Schutz 1940:452). We have seen throughout this volume that the antiempiricist attitude is the whole raison d'être of Lévi-Strauss' and Piaget's approach.

Second, phenomenologists replace the empiricist notion that the object of scientific investigation is external to the mind, with a constitutive view of scientific activity. As Schutz states,

scientific thinking involves constructs (i.e., sets of abstractions, generalizations, formalizations, idealizations) specific to the respective level of thought organization. Strictly speaking, there are no such things as facts, pure and simple. All facts are from the outset selected from a universal context by the activities of our mind. They are, therefore, always "interpreted" facts, either facts looked at and detached from their context by an artificial abstraction or facts considered in their particular setting. In either case, they carry along their interpretational inner and outer horizon. (1962:4)

Lévi-Strauss' principle that empirical data must be broken down into their constituent elements in order to construct a table of their possible permutations and combinations is consistent with the constitutive notion of scientific activity. As we have seen, Jean Piaget has offered a masterful discussion of the epistemological foundations of the constructivist (to use his terminology) view of scientific explanation.

Third, there is apparently an affinity between the phenomenological and the semiotic notions of surface and deep structure. For phenomenologists, *surface rules* are the values and norms of traditional sociologists, whereas *basic rules* are the rationalities and other resources of common sense implicitly used to constitute the meaning of daily activity. Structuralists also emphasize the constitutive (deep) rules of social interaction, or in Lévi-Strauss' terminology, the need to discover the grammar of social life.

Fourth, both phenomenologists and structuralists make a distinction between form and content, a distinction analogous to that between basic and surface rules. Whereas conventional sociologists are interested in the *content* of surface rules, such as beliefs, ideologies, and social norms, phenomenological sociologists are primarily interested in the *form*, that is, the rules people follow in using the content of surface rules during the negotiation of meaning. In phenomenology the concern with form should not be separated from the concern with content because the basic rules must be located within the situational contexts of everyday interaction. This is an important methodological principle shared by structuralists who reject the accusation of formalism because their notion of structure refers to the empirical content apprehended in its logical organization (Lévi-Strauss 1976:113).

Fifth, the importance given to content and situational context is related to the importance attributed by both structuralism and phenomenology to the explanation of the *particular*. Phenomenologists must pay attention to the particulars contained in conscious experience to reach the essences of psychic phenomena. Structuralists account for particular phenomena in terms of relational and combinatorial principles that govern the realization of specific phenomena.

In the sixth place, we have seen that phenomenologists aim at discovering the "essential" characteristics of particular (intentional) objects through the method of free variation. The method of free variation is analogous to the mental experimentation with models carried out by structuralists in order to ascertain how a model will react when subjected to changes. Through this process structuralists can ascertain the relational constants of the system, that is, its structure.

A seventh methodological characteristic common to phenomenology and structuralism is suggested by Herbert Spiegelberg, who maintains that a distinguishing characteristic of the phenomenological method is the apprehension of "essential relationships among essences" (1965).[5] In the structuralist perspective the relational no-

[5] I ran across Spiegelberg's passage after I had written these pages and found it supportive of my conceptualization of phenomenological methodology. Spiegelberg, however, does not provide an exhaustive list of all the distinguishing characteristics of the phenomenological method nor a logically organized discussion of those characteristics.

tion of meaning is also crucial because the meaning of a given sign consists of its differential contrast with other signs. For structuralists, the deep structure consists of the invariant relationships uniting its elementary constituents.

Finally, in addition to the traditional criteria of logical consistency and adequacy, phenomenologists propose a new criterion of validation appropriate for phenomenological explanations. Phenomenological explanations are considered acceptable only when they can be translated back into the terms people use to give meaning to their actions. Similarly, structuralists maintain that structural analysis is valid when it permits one to reach back (to reconstitute, so to speak) all the observable data (or surface structures) from which the analysis started.

Yet we are not dealing here with two partners who possess all the ingredients to enter a marriage contract. The theoretical and methodological principles I have mentioned point out an affinity between phenomenological sociology and semiotic structuralism in so far as they both concur on the unacceptability of the empiricist approach. My contention is that phenomenology does not really succeed in presenting an alternative to empiricism.

The Persisting Empiricism in Phenomenological Sociology

As previously explained, the important contribution of phenomenology is the principle that to grasp the essences one must go beyond surface appearances, that is, beyond what is immediately observable and beyond common sense understandings. Consequently, the phenomenological conception of scientific analysis is different from that of traditional empiricist and positivist sociology. The real meaning of essences of phenomena cannot be grasped through empirical observation and analysis, but only through a synthesis of intuitively and intellectively grasped elements. This antiempiricist attitude is common to all the various forms of phenomenological sociology, which have shifted the focus of analysis from the realm of possibilities to that of empirical social phenomena. The European phenomenological sociology of Alfred Vierkandt purports to study the basic social dispositions of people, the inward social forms and essences that underlie society. These essences cannot be grasped by describing external manifestations but by participating in the "spirit" of human groups. As I have mentioned, a similar orientation is found in the sociology of Max Scheler and Georges Gurvitch, the other two major exponents of European phenomenological sociology.

Although praiseworthy for its programmatic, antinaturalistic, hence antiempiricist, attitude, the phenomenological effort falls short on three counts: on the very definition of the object of investigation, on the methodology used, and on the lack of adequate attention given to the structural constraints of the intersubjective communication.

Jack Douglas (1978), a proponent of existential sociology, has criticized phenomenological sociology for having emphasized the "conscious, cognitive, symbolically meaningful aspects of human experience" as the fundamental and primary aspects of experience, at the expense of "perception and feeling" (p. 9). Presumably, this is connected with Husserl's commitment to rationalism and his concern with the properties of the "transcendental ego." Husserl's philosophy was intended to be a philosophy of "intention and consciousness," i.e., "a philosophy of things to the human mind," rather than a philosophy of "the world out there" (p. 8). Husserl certainly does not deserve the label of idealist because he emphasized that all knowledge must originate from experience or from our intuition of experience. It is undeniable, however, that Husserl's phenomenology is rationalistic, in the sense that he attributes a predominance to cognitive activity. In fact, after having agreed with empiricists that knowledge must be grounded on experience, Husserl immediately adds: "Immediate seeing, not merely sensory seeing of experience . . . is the ultimate source of justification for all *rational* statements" (my emphasis) (Husserl 1962:74–76). It is undeniable, however, that the notions of a priori form and *eidos* betray an intellectualist bias, a bias against which existential sociologists react. It is not the intellectual or categorical aspect I object to (an aspect which is also fundamental in semiotic structuralism), but rather the a priori nature of the categorical. In fact, the latter introduces a dichotomy between the concrete and the abstract, the contingent and the universal, the intellectual and the affective.

The consequence of the intellectualist and dichotomous biases of phenomenology are clearly visible in Schutz's conceptualization of *meaningful experience* and in the methodology he proposes. Schutz criticizes Weber for not having shown what meaning is or how we come to have meaning. Schutz accepts Bergson's notion of the existence of a *stream of consciousness,* but for Schutz what constitutes meaning is not the stream of consciousness as such but rather the reflective activity upon it. "Schutz, then, defined meaning in terms of highly conscious, reflective experiences" at the expense of "feeling, emotion or simple perception, all of which may be subconscious or even conscious, but not reflective" (Douglas 1978:9). Such a cognitive bias was accentuated by Berger and Luckman (1966) since they focused on people's "knowledge of reality in their daily life" (Douglas 1967:9).

Schutz criticized Weber's notion of understanding and distinguished between subjective and objective meaning with the aim of pursuing the latter, which Weber had neglected. Schutz is not quite explicit in his definition of objective meaning, and Kurt H. Wolff takes it to mean the set of notions "generally accepted," "common sensical," "taken for granted" by the people living in a given culture (Wolff 1978:517).

For Schutz the key contribution of phenomenology to sociology is a methodological one. To describe the process of establishing meaning he used the "ideal type," with the intent of contrasting various possible courses of action and objectively classifying social acts. Schutz stated that the ideal type is used to interpret someone else's act, i.e., the motive behind the act: "[The interpreter] does this by interpreting the act within an objective context of meaning in the sense that the same motive is postulated as constant for the act regardless of who performs the act or what his subjective experiences are at the time. For a personal ideal type, therefore, there is one and only one typical motive for a typical act" (Schutz 1967:187).

It is paradoxical that the quest for objective meaning should have led Schutz to bypass the Weberian subjective meaning based on the personal experience of particular individuals in concrete situations. Schutz could not be more definite on this point: "The social scientist replaces the thought objects of common sense thought relating to unique events and occurrences by constructing a model of a section of the social world within which merely those *typified* events occur that are relevant to the scientist's particular problem under scrutiny" (my italics) (Schutz 1962:36). Consequently, the phenomenological quest for the unprejudiced assessment of subjective experience and consciousness ends up with a loss of concrete subjectivity and a focus on "models" of rational acts. Schutz deals not with the rationality of concrete daily experience but with typified rationality: "The concept of rationality in the strict sense already defined does not refer to actions within the common sense experience of everyday life in the social world: it is the expression for a *particular* type of constructs of *certain specific* models of the social world made by the social scientist for certain specific methodological purposes" (p. 42). Schutz's conception of the ideal type leads to the loss of subjectivity, which is one of the two indispensable elements of the dialectic perspective.

But does the structural perspective fare any better in Schutz's orientation? Schutz is concerned with regularities or invariants of social interaction: "[The scientist] ascribes to this fictitious consciousness a set of typical in-order-to motives corresponding to the goals of the observed course-of-action patterns and typical because motives upon which the in-order-to motives are founded. Both types of motives are assumed to be *invariant* in the mind of the imaginary actor-model" (Schutz 1962:40).

Thomas Luckman has pursued Schutz' quest for invariants by proposing a "mathesis universalis" of the social worlds, that is, "a programme of formalization (and a theory of measurement) that is appropriate to the constitutive structures of everyday life" (1973:236). Luckman's aim is to provide "a rigorous method that uncovers and clarifies invariant structures of the conscious activities in which human action is constituted" (p. 244). The end product of this effort is to provide a "formalization of a matrix of elementary and universal structures of human conduct" (p. 248). This can be accomplished only through "the phenomenological method of radical reduction and attention to the experience of intentional acts in originary evidence. It is this philosophically legitimated by a reflexive account of the knowledge of experience" (pp. 248–249). Apparently such a reflexive account is an antidote to the naturalist attitude of empirical sociology because it does not accept the notion of raw data and holds that the "interpretation of experience is a constitutive element of data" (p. 249). The end product of such reflexive, hence constitutive, activity would be to provide a "descriptive phenomenology of the invariant structures of everyday life, to provide the general matrix . . . for statements on human conduct articulated in historical vernaculars. Such a matrix offers a satisfactory solution to the problem of the comparability of historical data" (p. 249). Historically situated statements are translated into a metahistorical language in which all human actions must be presented and hence become comparable. However, Luckman immediately adds that such a metalanguage must "meet the criterion of subjective adequacy in the sense in which Weber introduced the term" (p. 249). The metalanguage would have to be "plausible in principle if not in immediate fact to the speakers-actors who produced the statements" (p. 250).

One can immediately see that our expectations have not been met for two reasons; in such a program there is no consideration of the structural constraints influencing subjective experiences; moreover, the phenomenological description of the invariants of daily interaction remains at the level of the concretely experienced and subjective meaning with all the ensuing empiricist pitfalls we have discussed apropos of Max Weber.[6] There have been attempts to reconcile the semiotic-structuralist perspective with the interpretative one.

Attempts to Integrate the Structural and Phenomenological Levels of Meaning

Whereas phenomenologists are concerned with subjective meaning and the constitutive principles of meaning, which are based on the processes of human intentionality, semiotic structuralists are concerned with objective (unconscious) meaning because they attempt to formulate the syntactical rules governing the formulation of subjective meanings.

---

[6] The same kind of criticism is also appropriate for the recently proposed existential sociology, whose aim is "to understand the total man in his total social environment." Existential sociologists "take the complete man and woman of flesh and bone in the concrete social situations in which we find them" (Douglas 1978:4; see also Fontana 1980).

Critics of structuralism, such as M. Dufrenne, H. Lefebvre, and J. Derrida, argue that the concrete meaning interpreted and exchanged by speaking people cannot be reduced to the study of the unconscious structures of language nor can it be explained by syntactic and transformational laws of combination and recombination of basic linguistic elements. The issue, however, is not whether structuralism implies the reduction of one level of meaning and constitutive rules to another. On the contrary, both conscious and unconscious meaning must be studied if one wants to carry out an adequate sociological analysis. This is true in the somewhat analogous sense that an adequate understanding of language is impossible without studying what Chomsky calls surface and deep structures. One cannot explain the variety of possible sentences without formulating the grammatical rules which govern their formulation. Similarly, one cannot fully account for the variety of subjective meanings without ascertaining the nature of the deep cultural code that makes it possible to interpret and produce a large variety of subjective meanings. In this sense the study of unconscious meaning provides the ultimate foundation of the phenomenologists' notion of presuppositionless "grounds" of meaning and of the ethnomethodologists' interpretive rules used by people to attribute meaning to situations.

Two relatively recent attempts aimed at showing the complementarity of the phenomenological and structural levels of analysis deserve a brief mention. Paul Ricoeur criticized the notion of meaning based on the combinatorics of signs because such a notion is incompatible with freedom and history and because it excludes from language "the intention of saying something about something" (1963). Later on, however, Ricoeur proposed a hermeneutic explanation of myths, that is, an interpretation of myth content in the context of the living cultural tradition carried out through a concrete reflection. In the conclusion of this volume we will see that Ricoeur considers hermeneutics the subjective stage and structural analysis the objective stage of the process of reconstruction of meaning. He conceives of language not as an object but as the medium by which we express ourselves and structure the world. Ricoeur asserts that we have to reintegrate the unity of language and speech, which were separated by Saussure, and that we must analyze the act of speech within the

context of language. He offers concrete suggestions on how to "articulate" the objective and subjective modes of analysis at the level of
the word and phrase (1967).

One may raise the issue of whether hermeneutic and structural
explanations are to be considered as complementary perspectives or
whether one perspective must be subordinated to the other. Phenomenologists and structuralists are likely to offer a different answer to
this question. After having expressed his opposition to a merely oppositional notion of meaning, Ricoeur has argued that the meaning
of a sign does not derive only or mainly from its position within a
system of signs. On the contrary, signs derive their meaning principally from the intentionality of the subject who uses signs to refer to
the outside world. Believing that the essence of signs is to refer to
external reality, Ricoeur argues that the integration of the semiological and semantic explanations can be achieved by subordinating the
signs to their symbolic function. Structuralists are likely to counter-
argue that the subject's use of signs is conditioned by the syntagmatic and paradigmatic relationships which exist among signs and
make of a set of signs a *system*. No one can deny that both the subjective intentionality and the systemic relationships among signs enter into the determination of meaning. Which one of the two sources
of meaning will be considered subordinated to the other depends on
the particular orientation of the social scientist and the analytical
scope of his or her analysis, and on the brand of phenomenology
one endorses (Schutz, Merleau-Ponty, and so on). It also depends on
whether one endorses the early, or systematic, structuralism or the
poststructural semiotic orientation.

Ricoeur is not the only author who has argued in favor of a complementary relationship between the phenomenological and structuralist perspective. Pierre Bourdieu proposed a "praxeological," or
dialectical mode of explanation, with the intent of avoiding both the
subjectivism of phenomenology and the objectivism of structuralism.
Praxeology means the study of the system of objective structures of
knowledge and of the dialectical relationship between the objective
structures and the structural "disposition" of people who actualize
and reproduce them. Since habits and dispositions are qualities of
individuals which originate from objective structures, they can be

considered the subjective but not subjectivized link between objective structures and situational contingencies (Bourdieu 1972).

Pierre Bourdieu's formulation has the merit of taking into account the influence of the situation into the determination of meaning; an influence which has been effectively studied by symbolic interactionists and ethnomethodologists, respectively with the notion of situational negotiation of meaning and interpretive rules of meaning.[7]

This brief excursus points at the need of reckoning a threefold layer of meaning or three codeterminants of meaning: 1) the system of objective relationships among signs, which is the focus of early semiotics or systemic structuralism; 2) the situational context of interaction, which is the focus of symbolic interactionism and ethnomethodologists; 3) the subjective intentionality, which is at the core of the traditional phenomenological perspective.

The issue of how to integrate these dimensions would take an entire volume by itself. In the conclusion to this work I will point out some directions one can pursue. One point is clear: a dialectical linkage among all these levels of meaning appears indispensable, and I will refer to it frequently.

My colleague Roslyn Wallach Bologh has argued that the antiempiricist attitude of phenomenological analysis consists of not taking data as "things in themselves," as apparently given objects; rather they are reflexively shown to be grounded in the social condition of their production. This reflexive activity would preserve the dialectical inseparability of object and subject (Bologh 1979:10–16). I agree that this kind of dialectical reflexivity is important, and that we must show the existential issues implied in the production of any human activity, "the struggle for self-conscious self-production" (p. 11); it is important to show that such existential issues are "internal to the knowing of the object" (p. 15). However, such a reflexive activity is still a predialectic activity if we take dialectic in the strong sense of the term. The ultimate aim of sociology is to show that the reflexive activity itself and the inseparability of subject and object as phenomenologically describable are based on relational and transformational

[7] Interesting perspectives on the relationship between hermeneutics and structuralism can be derived from Bleicher (1980) and suggestions on how to integrate "structural constraints and practical actions" can be found in Charles Lemert (1981:26ff).

mechanisms. My position is that the object and subject cannot be taken as concrete entities constituted independent of each other. On the contrary, symbolic and relational mechanisms are theoretical prerequisites and constitutive mechanisms of concrete subjects and objects. Moreover, the subject and object are not actualized or analyzable independent of the reciprocal influence on each other. We will see later on that this higher level of dialectic became possible only with the new set of theoretical issues opened by poststructural semiotics.

Where are we in our theoretical itinerary? We have seen that phenomenology has introduced a sharp methodological break by rejecting the taken for granted or natural attitude of the Weberian and interactionist perspectives. Both Weber and behaviorally oriented symbolic interactionists assume that social actors can spontaneously interpret one another's intentions and reach consensual agreements; both the Weberian and interactionist modes of analysis impose conceptual forms on meanings which are assumed to be negotiated in terms of common sense understandings. On the contrary, phenomenologists want to describe and analyze the ordering concepts and the forms of perception and reasoning used by social actors to construct the intersubjective world of meaning.

The constructivist view of meaning was continued by ethnomethodologists, whose main task is to discover the methods or strategies that people use to negotiate meanings in specific situations. However, ethnomethodologists, and we should add Goffman, are heavily influenced by Chomsky's transformational grammar; moreover, in Goffman's recent works one can clearly see traces of (or at least analogies with) Lévi-Strauss' thinking. For this reason it is appropriate to discuss the contribution of ethnomethodology and Goffman at this point.

The Constitutive and Situational View of Interaction: The Ethnomethodological Paradigm

When referring to phenomenology in the first part of this volume, I stated that there is a relationship of intellectual ancestry between

Schutz's phenomenology and Garfinkel's ethnomethodology. However, it would be simplistic and not quite accurate to label ethnomethodology simply as a form of phenomenology. In fact, different ethnomethodologists make different usage of phenomenological ideas. Moreover, some ethnomethodologists hardly use phenomenological ideas and others combine phenomenological ideas with ideas adapted from anthropological linguistics. It is beyond the scope of this section to discuss the various ethnomethodological orientations because I intend to deal only with the basic ethnomethodological attitude and compare it with the central thrust of the structural and phenomenological approaches.

A distinguishing feature of ethnomethodology is the elucidation of the intersubjective and contextual processes on which ordinary interaction and meanings as well as the daily language use are based. I will briefly discuss Garfinkel's conception of these intersubjective and contextual processes because he is the pioneer of the ethnomethodological movement, and because he makes an explicit attempt to adopt notions of generative grammar. By clarifying the differences in the way ethnomethodologists, like Cicourel, and quasi-structuralists, like Goffman, use certain ideas of generative grammar, one can better clarify the differences and complementarities between ethnomethodology and structuralism.

Harold Garfinkel

I have briefly mentioned that there is a relationship of intellectual ancestry between Schutz' phenomenology and Garfinkel's ethnomethodology. However, the content of Garfinkel's ethnomethodology cannot quite be called phenomenological. Like phenomenologists, Garfinkel is interested in studying the rationality of the social world, people's cognitive orientation. He is also interested in studying the people's essences as they are constructed in daily interaction. Unlike phenomenologists, however, the locus of Garfinkel's analysis is not consciousness, where intentionality originates, but the processes by which people continuously construct and maintain the sense of social structure. Rather than "meaning," ethnomethodologists prefer to speak of "rational properties of practical actions" and of the methods

used by people to construct the rationality of daily activity. Ethnomethodologists are concerned with "various policies, methods, results, risks and lunacies with which to locate and accomplish the
study of the rational properties of practical actions as contingent ongoing accomplishments of organized artful practices of everyday life"
(Garfinkel in Hymes and Gumperz 1972:309).

As is the case with phenomenology, ethnomethodologists reject the
normative view of social structure that is characteristic of most traditional sociological orientations. The structural functionalists, for instance, maintain that social actors are controlled by social norms that
are concretized in role expectations. Symbolic interactionists assume
that, once established, the system of shared meaning has an existence of its own; they also take for granted that such a system of
meaning is the framework by which social actors interpret their reciprocal expectations. Moreover, some symbolic interactionists hold
that certain aspects of social interaction are best understood as responses to existing structural constraints. Ethnomethodologists,
however, are far from taking for granted the existence of social structure, as they grounded it upon meanings continuously negotiated by
people interacting according to "interpretive rules"; not even symbols
are considered by ethnomethodologists to have an existence independent of the interpretive rules (Wilson 1970). Like phenomenologists and structuralists, ethnomethodologists shift their perspective
from content to rules and see in the interpretive rules the foundation
of culture.

The locus for studying the interpretive rules, which are constitutive
of the ongoing sense of social structure, is natural language. The emphasis on the study of language is common to ethnomethodology,
phenomenology, and structuralism. Ethnomethodologists consider
language an inextricable part of social interaction, and they focus on
the study of conversational analysis, language use, and the interpretive abilities revealed in the language use.

Garfinkel's notion of shared rules of interpretation and underlying
patterns of meaning has been compared by John J. Gumperz and
D. Hymes to the notion of competence, or the knowledge of unstated
assumptions that the members of a given culture must possess to be
able to function in it (1972:301). Hymes uses the notion of "speaker's

communicative competence" to refer to the rules by which deep structures of interpersonal relations are transformed into speech act or speech performance (Hymes 1972). Obviously, this notion is an application of Chomsky's distinction between linguistic performance, or usage of language, and linguistic competence, or knowledge of syntactic rules which enables one to interpret people's speech and to produce an unlimited number of correct sentences.

Aaron Cicourel

Aaron Cicourel, an ethnomethodologist who has worked with the linguists John Gumperz and Susan Ervin-Tripp, has made a systematic attempt to use notions of generative-transformational linguistics and has proposed a generative semantics of the structure of social interaction. He declares that the notion of deep structure is a useful model for explaining the contextual determination of meaning in everyday language (1974:108). However, Cicourel criticizes the notion of deep structure, as it entails the idea of a *given:* fixed and universal features of language; he prefers to use the notion of variable features on the basis of which meaning is determined. The same criticism is leveled by Cicourel (and, as we have seen, by phenomenologists and Garfinkel) against the normative view of social structure, that is, the notion that social structure is based on given conditions or events which are assumed to exist independent of the "negotiated interaction scenes in which social organization is produced" (p. 181). According to Cicourel, neither the normative nor the syntactic perspectives provide the means to assign meaning to concrete events, and neither view can account for the "emergent, negotiated nature of meaning over the course of social interaction" (p. 84). The reason is that both perspectives ignore the "interpretive procedures members use to make general (normative, syntactical) rules creatively relevant to concrete settings" (p. 81). In this sense, both paradigms lose "the semantically generative features of language production and comprehension" (p. 83).

In the place of the normative and syntactical views, Cicourel proposes a "generative semantics central for an understanding of all human communication" (1974:74). Because he rejected the notion of static and fixed linguistic features, one is surprised to see that Cicourel's generative semantics includes "invariant presuppositions basic to the production of everyday social activities" (p. 74). Cicourel suggests this notion precisely to establish a link between the contextual determination of meaning and general roles (p. 85). In fact, without the availability of general rules one does not explain how people agree in their negotiation of meaning in a variety of situations. Cicourel finds that some of these interpretive rules or "cognitive procedures" (p. 84) are clearly formulated by Schutz, especially in his notion of common scheme of reference. According to the Schutzian notion of reciprocity of perspectives, the participants in the encounter are instructed to disregard personal differences and to assume that the mutual experience of interaction is the same. Another interpretive procedure instructs people to treat a given item as a part of a larger set of meaning or to look for additional information before interpreting the meaning of the item. The interpretive procedure called normal form, also derived from Schutz, instructs interacting people to reduce the range of possible alternatives of meaning by accepting a particular event as a typification of a more general normative set. (A more complete list of interpretive principles can be found in various essays of Cicourel—see 1970 and 1970a:33ff.)

Cicourel has drawn a sharp distinction between the interpretive procedures he is interested in and surface rules, which refers to "prescriptive and proscriptive norms" of everyday life. Interpretive procedures enable social actors to recognize the relevance of surface rules and to convert them into behavior. In Cicourel's words, "the members of a society must acquire the competence to assign meaning to their environment so that surface rules and their articulation with particular cases can be made. Hence interpretive procedures are invariant properties of everyday practical reasoning necessary for assigning sense to the substantive rules sociologists usually call norms" (1970:146). In the distinction between deep (invariant) and surface rules we apparently have the central ingredients of a metaempirical structuralism à la Lévi-Strauss, Piaget, and Chomsky. However, we ought to carefully consider whether Cicourel (and also Garfinkel and Sacks) have really made the transition to a metaempirical level of analysis.

The Empiricist and Undialectic Nature of Ethnomethodology

The Empiricist Perspective. Cicourel maintains that the interpretive procedures have a generative power, because the "procedures are interacting together so as to produce instructions for the speaker-hearer for assigning infinitely possible meanings to unfolding social scenes" (1974:88). Again, one must carefully determine the meaning of the term "generative." "Everyday meanings are generative in the sense that interpretive procedures . . . rely on a common body of unstated knowledge that is socially distributed" (p. 96). It seems, then, that interpretive procedures, or rules or routines, are nothing but implicit meanings or shared notions used to interpret one another's responses, rather than Chomsky's formal rules, which, through precise operations, enable one to predict the totality of correct linguistic forms.

Does Cicourel's usage of transformational linguistics thus amount to a vague analogy and perhaps to an improper use of linguistic terminology? Like phenomenologists, Cicourel distinguishes between basic or interpretive rules and surface or normative rules.

Basic or interpretive rules provide the actor with a developmentally changing sense of social structure that enables him to assign meaning or relevance to an environment of objects. Normative, or surface rules, enable the actor to link his view of the world to that of others in concerted action and to presume that consensus or shared agreement governs interaction. . . . The basic rules activate short and long-term stored information (socially distributed knowledge) that enables the actor to articulate general normative rules with immediate interaction scenes. (1970a:29, 41)

This definition of interpretive rules does not seem to go beyond the phenomenological notion of deep rules.

Yet Cicourel argues that "basics of interpretive procedures are like deep structure grammatical rules; they enable the actor to generate appropriate (usually) innovative responses in changing situated settings (1974)." Implicit and shared meanings are necessary preconditions for the interpretation of situations, but they are not sufficient by themselves to produce meaning, like transformational rules are. Perhaps the present state of knowledge does not permit the formulation of precise transformational rules outside the field of linguistics. The point, however, is that the very notion of such rules seems to fall outside the scope of the ethnomethodological perspective. In fact, Cicourel "seeks to locate the comprehension of speech in an emergent interactional setting that makes speech production both a topic and a resource for the participants" (Cicourel 1974:110). This means that Cicourel deals with what Chomsky calls the level of performance rather than the level of competence.

Douglas states that ethnomethodologists are interested in the contextual determination of meaning or the situational aspects of everyday life (1970:37, 43). The metasituational rules of ethnomethodologists are not predictive transformational rules, but, as we have stated, only commonly shared notions (content) which make possible the determination of situational meaning. Douglas acknowledges that the transituational notion of meaning is of paramount importance, because people's symbolizing function transcends specific contexts. However, neither Douglas or Cicourel have determined a linkage between the situational and the metasituational analysis of meaning, because they lack transformational rules in the strict sense of the term. As a matter of fact, they reject the notion of transituational meaning as a characteristic of the absolutist (structural) sociology that is antithetical to the phenomenological and ethnomethodological perspectives.

Still, one can argue that structuralism and transformational grammar have notably stimulated the thinking of ethnomethodologists and contributed to a more articulate view of the constitutive study of meaning. Yet Garfinkel and Sacks themselves have also insisted on the need to discover the "formal structures of everyday activities." However, the purpose of studying these formal structures is to describe the "members'" accounts of formal structures (1970:346). This means that ethnomethodologists are not interested in mathematical—hence mataempirical—structures. In fact, Garfinkel and Sacks assert: "By formal structures we understand everyday activities" in so far as they have the properties of uniformity, repetitiveness, and standardization; moreover, these properties are independent of particular "production cohorts" and such independence is "a phenomenon for members' recognition" (p. 346). These "concerns" are very much within the domain of the traditional study of the regularities of empirically observable data.

Cicourel's explanation of interpretive procedures does not fare much better. In his own words, what he calls interpretive procedures and Garfinkel calls properties of practical reasoning are a "collection of instructions to members by members, and as a sort of continual (reflexive) feedback whereby members assign meaning to their environment. . . . The properties of interpretive procedures provide members with a sense of social order during periods of solitary living and they are integral to actual contact with others. . . . [They] operate to provide a continuous feedback to members about the *routine* sense of what is happening" (1970:149–150).

It is obvious that Cicourel refers to directions and instructions contained within cultural norms as traditionally understood. Since these instructions are directly understandable to social actors, one does not find any clue whatsoever that Cicourel is talking of mathematical and grammatical rules which are derivable through a stepwise process by the social scientist.

The empiricist level of analysis is also evident in the model of discourse Cicourel has recently proposed. According to Cicourel, such a model must "take into account how the propositional content of an utterance combines with its locutionary force or intention to act in the word by a promise, assertion, command and the like" (1981:99). The model must "reflect a wide variety of natural settings . . . [and] the fact that a listener understands a speaker partly by correlating speech acts with unspoken but apparent features of the environment. . . . The model must include the tide of intonational cues, stress, pitch, rhythm and nonverbal activities such as gaze, facial expressions and body movements" (*ibid.*). Obviously, this is a descriptive model which merely organizes whatever is immediately observable and documentable: again there is no clue of mathematical, or second order, generative rules such as in Chomsky.

The same critique applies to Cicourel's model of textual analysis, which is aimed at formulating rules describing the structure of the text. Cicourel's rules refer to a

summary created by using relatively simple elements or sentences to serve as arguments for complex predicates and more complex sentences. . . . Rumerlhart [the author Cicourel follows] provides a formal model for representing a story or summary of an activity or experience. He presents summarization rules that link the string of sentences used in a story and the summary of a story. The syntactic and semantic structures of the original stories can be mapped onto subjects' summaries of those structsres by using the summarization rules. (1981:102)

It could not be stated more clearly that the subject and subjective meaning remain the units of sociological analysis.

Analogous critical remarks are applicable to the conversational analysis of Zimmerman, Schegloff, Sachs, and so on, all of whom intend "to explicate structuring of resources that could have given rise to members' sense of what happened" (Frank 1979:181).

The Undialectic Bias. The undialectical character of ethnomethodology becomes immediately apparent if we consider that "like frame analysis, conversational analysis begins not with selves, but with structure. . . . Conversational analysis suggests that interaction emerges from the structure of conversation, and the study of interaction must begin with analysis of these structures" (Frank 1979:178).

Is there room for the role of subjectivity? Yes, but "in terms of constraints imposed on speaker-hearers by the properties and practices of natural language. . . . That reference to an individual necessarily implies a supraindividual system, a form or forms of social organization in terms of which the notion individual becomes intelligible" (Zimmerman 1978:9). We can see clearly that the individual is subordinated to the system and made intelligible only by reference to the system: "In this sense, members (or alternatively, speaker-hearers) are *agents* of the system in question. That is, the activities of individuals are of interest only insofar as their activities exhibit the workings of the system" (*ibid.*). Zimmerman allows for the role of creativity but creativity is understood in Chomsky's way; that is, Zimmerman recognizes the individual's ability to produce an indefinite number of sentences through the use of a finite set of rules. (For one interesting effort in this direction see Charles Lidz's essays in the volume of essays on structuralism—Rossi 1982.) "Creativity is both possible and occurs within the context of the constraints such rules provide" (*ibid.*). The systemic—hence undialectic—bias is here very explicitly stated.

Before we end the analysis of the interpretive paradigm we must pay attention to Erving Goffman, because he is a thinker who borrows ideas from phenomenology, ethnomethodology, and symbolic interactionism and tries to deal with the level of competence and the metasituational negotiation of meaning.

Goffman's Analysis of Daily Interaction

The Structuralist Perspective of Frame Analysis

Erving Goffman is considered a symbolic interactionist, but one can also detect in his works the influence of phenomenology and ethnomethodology. In one of his more recent works, Goffman refers to and quotes from thinkers representing a variety of perspectives, such as Alfred Schutz, Harold Garfinkel, Gregory Bateson, and the philosophers of language John L. Austin, Ludwig Wittgenstein, and Rudolf Carnap (Goffman 1974). However, Goffman cannot be neatly classified as a representative of one school of thought, since he is very selective in the ideas he borrows from a variety of disciplines and he combines those ideas in a highly personal way. He has called himself an independent thinker (p. 7), and certainly his approach to the study of face-to-face interaction is a distinctive one.

Goffman claims that social interaction occurs when people are accessible to each other's "naked senses," and observable interaction becomes a situation when interacting people are influenced by each other's naked senses. Goffman has furthered the sociological analysis of symbolic interaction by analyzing various determinants and consequences of situated conduct and by introducing important new concepts, such as layers of situated order, ritual exchanges, self-presentation, and identity.

A central thesis of Goffman's is that social interaction is built by and maintained through theatrical performances; this means that social actors "stage" their behavior in such a way as to control one another's definition of the situation. The staging of one's behavior is mostly accomplished by managing the impressions given to others through gestures, customs, and other forms of external appearances. A distinguishing characteristic of human actors is to communicate through language and to use language to influence and manipulate one another. Language is, therefore, the most important symbolic element of social interaction. Since his early works, Goffman has paid attention not only to what is said through language, but also to the style, or form of language as an important means to give credibility to what people communicate. Goffman has extended his concern with form to linguistic and nonlinguistic behavior and has offered a classic analysis of symptomatic and manipulative behavior. "Symptomatic behavior" refers to the use of "proper" style as a symptom of a valid performance; manipulative behavior refers to the manipulation of appearances with the intent of making other people perceive one's performance as a valid one.

The theatrical metaphor and the notion of dramatic performance are still fundamental in *Frame Analysis*, a work in which Goffman continues to use such concepts as "theatrical frame," "performance," "audience," "dramatic scriptings," manufacturing experience, demonstration, exhibition, fabrications, exploitation of directional tracks, personal-role formula, and role-character formula (1974). In these pages I intend to characterize the theoretical framework of this work.

It appears, at first, that Goffman simply continues the line of investigation begun by symbolic interactionists and then continued by phenomenologists and ethnomethodologists. Such a conclusion would be inescapable if one accepts the thesis that all that Goffman intends to show is that social structure is construed and sustained through symbolic performances. In fact, we already know that the central thesis of ethnomethodology and symbolic interactionism is that social situation and social reality are what people think they are, or what people construe them to be by what they say and how they say it. (This is true at least of those symbolic interactionists who emphasize situational negotiation as the key explanation of social interaction.) However, a close reading of *Frame Analysis* shows that Goffman brings a new perspective into the traditional concern of symbolic interactionists and ethnomethodologists. What Goffman calls frame analysis is nothing but a form of structural analysis that has some similarities to the Lévi-Straussian and Chomskian forms of analysis.

This thesis can be concisely and cogently argued by examining key passages of *Frame Analysis*, in which Goffman defines the perspective he uses. Goffman contends that people engaged in interaction ordinarily do not negotiate the definition of the situation totally from scratch, but rather they discover or assess what the situation is. "Those who are in the situation ordinarily do not create this definition . . . ordinarily all they do is to assess correctly what the situation ought to be" (1974:1–2). Goffman claims that the situation is "assessed in terms of a frame and this is why the first issue is not interaction, but frame" (p. 127). "My aim is to try to isolate some of the basic frameworks of understanding available in our society for making sense out of events" (p. 10).

It would seem that the term "frame" can be interpreted in an ethnomethodological sense: "I assume that definitions of a situation are built up in accordance with principles of organization which govern events, at least social ones, and our subjective involvement in them; *frame* is the word I use to refer to such of these basic elements" of the "organization of experience" (1974:10, 11). In 1961 Goffman defined frame as a world view or the "traditional equipment having a social history of its own in the wider society" (1961:27–28). Robert H. Lauer and Warren H. Handel have offered an interpretation of this notion which is consistent with the perspective of symbolic interactionists and ethnomethodologists: "A framework is a scheme of interpretations that renders observed events meaningful. . . . Frameworks constitute an important element of culture" (1977:414). In this interpretation the term "culture" refers to shared notions or ideals (*ibid.*), i.e., to cultural *content.*

Goffman, however, seems to go beyond the empiricist view of culture, which he defines as a set of rules. Goffman is not interested in detailed descriptions of culture, but in building a formal sociology, in discovering forms and signifying structures (1974:856). In Goffman's words, frame analysis is the study of the "structure of experiences individuals have at any moment of their social lives" (p. 12). The form and structure of daily experience is generated by rules underlying social situations, rules of operation and cognition. Like Cicourel, Goffman intends to use the term "rule" in the sense used by transformational grammarians. According to Goffman, the task of sociological analysis is determining "under what circumstances do we think things are real" (p. 2) and what are the "conditions that must be fulfilled if we are to *generate* one realm of reality, finite province of meaning" (my italics) (p. 3). Goffman "intends to look for rules which when followed, allow us to generate a world of a given kind" (p. 5). He wants to "uncover the informing, constitutive rules of everyday behavior" (ibid.). Like the rules of generative grammar, these rules constitute a code, i.e., "a device which informs and patterns all events that fall within the boundaries of its application" (pp. 7–8). For this reason sociological analysis is similar to the study of the "rules of the syntax of a language" and analogous to the linguist's concern with the forms of language (pp. 11, 12; also 236). On the basis of these quotes one could state that at least programmatically Goffman is a structuralist in the Lévi-Straussian, and perhaps even Chomskian, sense of the term; and I mean structuralist in a much more fundamental sense than understood by George Gonos' (1977) interpretation of Goffman's work.

I next focus on the conclusion of *Frame Analysis*, where Goffman systematically discusses his rereading of William James and Alfred Schutz (1974:560, 562; see also 10). I choose to systematize Goffman's exposition in ten points to demonstrate its parallelism with the transformational perspective of semiotic structuralism. 1) To carry out a frame analysis one must start from concrete and ordinary activity. This principle should spare Goffman the accusation of mentalism which is often—although unjustly—used against Lévi-Strauss. 2) Goffman wants to study "actual activity, activity that is meaningful in its own right" (p. 560). In this passage Goffman seems to echo the structural principle that the data must be explained not in terms of external factors but in terms of their internal organization (see the discussion on the notion of structural causality in the section on Piaget). 3) Goffman considers a given activity "as a model upon which to work transformations for fun, deception, experiment, rehearsal, dream, phantasy etc" (ibid.). This approach is consistent with the notion of structural model, which must be submitted to mental experimentation to see how the alteration of one element affects the whole system.

4) The various concrete activities are a "portion of the paramount activity" (the model, if I read Goffman correctly); the "resulting experiences (fun, deception, dream, etc) are derivative and insecure when placed against the real thing (the model)" (1974:560). This passage

seems to echo Lévi-Strauss' principle that structure does not refer to observable empirical relationships but to their underlying logical structure, which is formulated with the help of mechanical models. "When we decide that something is unreal, the reality it isn't need not itself to be very real, indeed, can just as well be a dramatization of events as the events themselves" (ibid.).

5) Consequently, "what is sovereign is relationship, not substance"; "real" is simply a "contrast term" (pp. 560–561). This formulation is consistent with the relational view of reality upheld by transformational structuralism. In fact, for transformational structuralists meaning is determined by the differential contrasts among the elements composing a given set of data.

6) Goffman also endorses a combinatory and permutational view of empirical phenomena, as Lévi-Strauss does. Every bit of interaction is one among many other possibilities; it is a "special variation on general themes" (1974:564). "Everyday life often seems to be a laminated adumbration of a pattern or model" (p. 562). The advantage of considering a particular event as one alternative among other possible ones (p. 563) is that "these expanded possibilities can be drawn upon in order to quicken our sense of what can unfold within an actual, fully sequestered, two-person talk" (p. 565). Structuralists also consider a particular event as one concrete realization among many other possible ones and attempt to formulate the combinatory rules governing the realization of concrete phenomena. The structuralist's concern with what is possible is more consistent with the nature of scientific inquiry than the concern of the empiricists with what exists and with causal relationships among things which exist. In fact, the formulation of universal propositions seems to connaturally imply a consideration of all the possible alternatives to what actually exists. Only when all possible variants are considered can one see the common structure of all possibilities.

7) The combinatory view of data permits a comparative analysis and "the comparative approach allows us to address assumptions about ordinary activity that would otherwise remain implicit" (1974:566). What remains implicit?

8) Goffman avoids the intellectualist bias of which presumably certain structuralists are victims. He remarks that a given item of behavior is "a direct instance, symptom of underlying qualities" which

consists in "cognition, intent, will, mood, character, status" (pp. 568, 569). Goffman emphasizes that "inside [human beings] there are information *and* effective states" (p. 572).

9) The notion of game and rule is paramount in Goffman's frame analysis, as it is in Lévi-Strauss: "We all have the capacity to be utterly unblushing, provided only a frame can be arranged in which lying will be seen as part of a game and proper to it" (p. 573). This means that there is a basic frame on the basis of which we interpret all the forms of behavior and that the notion of rule is a fundamental aspect of the frame; as in the case of the chess game, the power of daily interaction derives from its rules. "It appears, then, that normal honesty is a rule regarding the frame of ordinary literal interaction, which rules, in turn, is a particular phrasing of a more general structural theme, namely, that the parts of a play has something to conceal, has special capacity and incapacity for doing so, and labors under rulings regarding how he is to comfort himself in this regard" (p. 573).

10) Sociological analysis aims at formulating rules in the grammatical sense. Goffman maintains that even in the case of a variety of emotional behaviors "the difference is syntactical" (1974:571).

These quotes clearly demonstrate that the programmatic orientation of Goffman has a strong structuralist component. However, this essential characteristic could be easily overlooked by sociologists of traditional orientation, with the consequence that they would misread Goffman's real intent. One should add that such a structural perspective could extend the constitutive study of meaning up to the level of code. The constitutive rules of interaction are located by phenomenologists at the level of conscious intentionality and by ethnomethodologists at the level of situational processes. Goffman's programmatic intention seems to ground the intentional processes and interpretive rules of meaning at the level of competence or structural code. Such a program seems to go well beyond the scope of the interpretive paradigm of traditional (hence empiricist) orientation.

The Persisting Empiricism of Goffman's Structuralism

A careful examination of the substantive applications of *Frame Analysis* unequivocally shows that Goffman remains empiricist in orientation. In this section I intend to briefly show that Goffman's perspective is a structuralist one, and of an empiricist and undialectic kind.

First of all, it is quite clear that Goffman is a structuralist if we keep in mind his previously mentioned principle that social actors do not produce but only assess the situation on the basis of shared notions (frames) available to social actors in a given social milieu. Goffman's approach sharply differs from that of symbolic interactionists, who consider social interaction an ongoing definition of the situation being constructed by people in interaction and who focus on the motives which prompt people interact in the particular way they do. Goffman's approach also differs from that of phenomenologists, who are interested in the constitutive processes of interaction as they derive from the structure of experience and consciousness. Rather than focusing on the activities constituting the structure of experience, Goffman wants to know how the normative conventions which structure interaction work (Frank 1979:169).

However, Frank explains frame analysis as an "attempt to explicate resources of shared knowledge on the basis of which the accomplishment of intersubjective meaning becomes possible" (p. 175). We find here clearly stated the reasons why Goffman is an empiricist. Goffman is concerned with the structures which make understandable interaction at the level of subjective (intersubjective) meaning; that is to say, he is interested "exclusively in the member's sense of reality" (p. 176). As we know, subjective and intersubjective meaning as well as the actor's sense of reality have been the vantage point of interpretive sociologists of traditional (hence empiricist) orientation.

Goffman's empiricist perspective is clearly documentable in a recent work, *Forms of Talk* (1981), in which one can find applications and developments of the ideas proposed in *Frame Analysis* (1974). I limit my attention to chapter 3, entitled "Footing," which is described by Goffman as an "analytic and programmatic . . . very general statement" of his own position (1981:1). The notion of footing, first proposed in 1974, refers to "a change in the alignment we take up to ourselves and the others present as expressed in the way we manage the production or reception of an utterance" (p. 128). Footing is a "language-linked" phenomenon, and Goffman uses sociolinguistic ideas to determine the "structural underpinnings of changes in footing." He begins his analysis with a reexamination of the "primitive" notions of speaker and hearer; instead of taking these "folk categories" for granted, he dissects them "into smaller, analytically coherent elements" (p. 129).

The insistence on "primitive" and "smaller elements" has seemingly all the ingredients of a metaempiricist analysis of a semiotic kind. However, with the term "small elements" Goffman refers to the fact that the terms "speaker" and "hearer" do not entail sound alone but also sight and touch. In the paralinguistic function of gesticulation, gaze shifting, facial expression, etc., "it is apparent that sight is crucial, both for the speaker and for the hearer. For the effective conduct of talk, speaker and hearer had best be in a position to *watch* each other" (1981:130). It is quite clear that Goffman's analysis focuses on the level of ordinary interaction among people, and on sight, touching, sound, and similarly observable elements insofar as they are understandable to and by interacting individuals. Stated differently, Goffman's units of analysis are not "constructed" entities but small elements, as they are directly attainable through empirical observation. The same critical considerations apply to the notions employed by Goffman to analyze footing, such as participation framework, production format, and embedding (pp. 146–153).

The undialectical character of Goffman's approach is also easily demonstrable: "A frame is an a priori definition of reality, within which certain constructions of the situation (the reality having already been constructed) are taken for granted" (Frank 1979:176). Goffman is far from being interested in the constitutive processes by which subjectivity and structure mutually constitute each other through a dialectic relationship. People do not construct frameworks but only choose among alternative frameworks and perform variations on the primary frameworks, such as "keys" (Goffman 1970:43–44) and "fabrications," which, however, do not amount to a construction of reality but only to transformations of frameworks and strategies; therefore, their meaning depends on the primary frameworks. The constitutive contribution of subjectivity to social interaction is totally absent from Goffman's perspective. F. Jameson is correct in stating that "frame analysis offers a way of analyzing the phenomenological material of everyday life in impersonal terms. . . . Goffman's enterprise leads him to that decisive discovery . . . the revelation of the reality of the collective beneath the appearance of individual experience, the disclosure of the individual subject as a field of multiple forces, not a substance but a locus, a nexus, of sheer relationships" (Jameson 1976:131).

Besides neglecting creative subjectivity, Goffman is also trapped by the "taken for granted" normative frameworks. Does Goffman intend to rely on apparent or conscious shared meanings as if they were the authentic level of social reality to be analyzed by the social scientist? The theoretical debate generated by semiotic Marxism will permit us to see the frailty and unsophistication of such a position.

10

The Interface of Semiotic Structuralism and Marxism

Having discussed the interface of transformational structuralism with a systemic version of the natural science paradigm and the interpretive paradigm (subjective perspective). I next consider the interaction of structuralism with the critical paradigm. This is a logical progression of discourse because the critical paradigm is based on a dialectical way of thinking, and dialectical thought enables one to integrate the valid thrusts present in the systemic and subjective views of social life. However, there exists also a systemic and subjective notion of dialectic. In this section we shall determine the key ideas of these two views of dialectic with the intent of preparing the ground for the conclusion, where an attempt will be made to integrate the systemic and subjective views of social life that are found within the natural science, interpretative, and critical paradigms.

There are two delimitations in the scope of analysis of this section. The reader will remember that I have limited my attention to a few examples of the natural science paradigm. Similarly, in this section I will analyze not all forms of the critical paradigm but only those Marxist trends which have positively or negatively interacted with transformational structuralism. The reason is that the most important reactions to semiotic and transformational structuralism developed by social scientists of critical orientation are to be found among Marxist thinkers.

I have used the term "semiotic structuralism" to indicate another delimitation in the scope of analysis carried out in this section. We have seen that Parsons and interpretive sociologists (symbolic interactionists and ethnomethodologists) have made a selective usage of

certain ideas of Lévi-Strauss and Chomsky and that Parsonian sociologists have used some Piagetian ideas. For this reason part 2 of this
book and the first chapter of part 3 carry a title with the term "transformational structuralism." In this section I use the terms "structural
Marxism" and "poststructural semiotics" because the most important attempts to integrate Marxist and structural ideas have been put
forward by "linguistically" inspired structuralists. Two distinct periods of the interface between semiotic structuralism and Marxism
must be distinguished: that between Marxism and the first generation of semiotics, usually identified with the Saussurean and Lévi-
Straussian perspectives and that between Marxism and poststructural semiotics, which has been heavily inspired by the Lacanian synthesis of Freud and structural linguistics.

The most distinguished representatives of the first period are
Maurice Godelier and Louis Althusser. Godelier has begun with an
explicitly Lévi-Straussian theory and Althusser has dealt with a perspective consistent with, and at times complementary to, that of Lévi-
Strauss (although Althusser has also had some contact with Lacan's
ideas). The most distinguished representatives of the dialogue between poststructural semiotics and Marxism are Roland Barthes,
Jacques Derrida, and Julia Kristeva. There are many semiotic structuralists who deserve consideration. However, my discussion is selective on the basis of two criteria: I limit my attention to seminal thinkers and to those thinkers who have more directly dealt with those
issues which are the core issues of this book—the relationship between the structural (and systemic) approach, on the one hand, and
the subjective approach, on the other hand. As I have repeatedly
stated, my aim is to sound out the possibility of incorporating the
valid elements of these two approaches into a dialectic view of social
life.

Structural Causality and the Loss of Subjectivity

Next to existential and hermeneutic phenomenologists, some of the
most tenacious critics of structuralism are to be found among Marxist inspired social scientists. Since the early works of Lévi-Strauss,

such people as Henri Lefebvre, Lucien Goldman, and Jean Paul Sartre have attacked structuralism as a bourgeois ideology, with antihumanist, antihistorical, bureaucratic, and formalist biases. I cannot possibly deal with all the issues raised in the course of this complex controversy and many of these issues have been dealt with in another volume (Rossi 1974). I address those aspects of the structural Marxist controversy which are directly relevant to the key themes inherited from the classical sociological tradition. As mentioned previously, the discussion will center on the structural and subjective views of social life and related notions of structure, subjectivity, history, and dialectic.

Structure and History in Marx and Lévi-Strauss

Since Godelier has attempted to carry on a Marxist discourse starting from a Lévi-Straussian perspective, we must briefly discuss the relationship between Lévi-Strauss' and Marx's key ideas. Some exponents of historical and phenomenological Marxism (a term I shall explain in the next section) have argued that Lévi-Strauss' and Marx's positions are irreconcilable because Marx gives priority to the historical-perspective, whereas Lévi-Strauss' structuralism is primarily a form of synchronic analysis. Moreover, these critics argue that structuralists hold an inadequate conception of history and social structure. As to historical analysis, they argue that it is more than just a demonstration of how new structures originate from previous structures, which is what history is for structuralists. On the contrary, Lévi-Strauss claims that both the analytical perspective of his synchronic approach and the dialectical perspective are essential components of Marxist analysis. Lévi-Strauss has strongly argued with Sartre against giving priority to dialectic reason and has criticized the notions of homogeneous, continuous, and cumulative history and of totalizing historical consciousness as ethnocentric notions produced by the mythology of our times. (On the basic differences and certain complementarities between Sartre's and Lévi-Strauss' positions, see L. Rosen's essay reprinted in Rossi 1974:389.)

As to the conception of social structure, the Marxist critics of Lévi-Strauss argue that Marx finds the deep structure of social life in the economic infrastructure, whereas Lévi-Strauss finds it within the inner logic of the mind. The Marxist critics argue that Lévi-Strauss conceives of structure as a set of invariant logical relationships and dialectic as processes of universal logical contradictions. These two notions would amount to an "intellectualization" of Marx's position. According to historical Marxists, the socioeconomic structure of the capitalistic society is intrinsically dialectic because it is based on the fundamental contradiction of the capitalistic division of labor—the existence of capitalists and workers. As a consequence, the capitalist society inevitably tends toward the resolution of such a contradiction and therefore is undergoing a continuous and irreversible movement. Since the irreversible movement produces changes and alterations of the existing social structure, the notion of dialectic would be, according to historical Marxists, incompatible with the notion of universal and invariant structures.

On the contrary, Yvan Simonis has argued that Lévi-Strauss' notions of unconscious, synchronic, and logical structures are complementary with Marx's dialectical notion of economic infrastructure (1968). Other scholars have argued that Marx's position is not a clearcut one and leaves room for controversial interpretations (Pouillon 1965).

In the next section I shall discuss in detail Marx's notion of dialectic. Here I limit my remarks to two points, one concerning Marx's position, the other concerning Lévi-Strauss'. Firstly, many differences among various interpretations of Marx depend on differences in the epistemological positions of the Marxist interpreters. Marx was a pioneer thinker concerned with the analysis of specific historical situations rather than with the formalization of theoretical positions. As a pioneer and articulated thinker, he has used a variety of ideas, some of which can be read and developed from a historical-dialectical perspective and others from a structural-dialectical perspective. Insofar as Lévi-Strauss' position is concerned, much of what has been said about the incompatibility between structural analysis and the specificity of historical analysis is a result of superficial reading or misreading of Lévi-Strauss' works. Lévi-Strauss reminds his critics that he gives precedence to form over content (1963:204) to place into evidence the interrelationships and transformations among various levels of structures and infrastructures. He is interested in "systems of differences" and contradictions which are present within and between concrete social structures. This analytical level of analysis does not imply an intellectualization of Marxist thought or a neglect of historical specificity. Rather, the aim of structuralists is to formulate the common principles which make possible the various societal transformations.

As we shall see in the following section, Lévi-Strauss claims that structuralists and Marxists have in common the task of interpreting the dynamics of different types of societies on the basis of their specific transformations. It is precisely on the basis of specific historical analyses that Lévi-Strauss moves one step further to the level of formalization of common transformational relationships. Interestingly enough, such an interpretation of the relationship between Lévi-Strauss' and Marx's historical analysis is consistent with some interpretations of Marx proposed by contemporary American sociologists. For instance, Michael Burawoy has stated that "Marxists constitute the. history of the capitalist totality out of its essence or underlying structures. . . . Marxists conceive the history of capitalism as the unfolding of some irrevocable logic or combination of logics" (1977). Structural Marxists must be given credit for trying to unravel the properties of this combinatory logic and the transformational aspects of the underlying economic infrastructure.

But Lévi-Strauss has cautioned his critics that "form and content are of the same nature, susceptible to the same analysis. Content draws its reality from the structure and what is called *form* is the *structural formation* of the local structure forming the content" (1976:131). Since 1960, Lévi-Strauss has been explicit in his rejection of formalism and similar kinds of "intellectualizations." He has stated that "unless the event is surreptitiously reintegrated into the form, the latter is condemned to remain at such a level of abstraction that it neither signifies anything any longer nor has any heuristic meaning. Formalism destroys its object" (p. 132). Lévi-Strauss' criticism of the application of structuralism by certain literary critics and historians of the literature seems applicable to the historical Marxists we are dealing with here. Whereas literary critics are "seeking recurring contents under variable forms," Lévi-Strauss is seeking "invariant forms within different contents" (p. 274). This task is not by any means incompatible with the historical analysis of specific contents and forms and their particular transformations.

It is the merit of structural Marxists to have systematically elaborated and carried out the application of Marxist and structuralist ideas. In discussing their contribution we shall add depth and specificity to the question of the relationship between historical and structural analyses.

Althusser's View of Marxist Dialectic

The Marxist movement has proliferated into a variety of orientations, ranging from the so-called crude materialism of Frederick Engels (1940) and the early Lenin (1927), to the interest-based reductionism of Edward Bernstein and Karl Kautsky, to the humanist and historical marxism of Antonio Gramsci, George Lukàcs, Henri Lefèbvre, and Lucien Goldman, and to the antihumanist and antihistoricist Marxism of Louis Althusser and other modern French structural Marxists such as Etienne Balibar, Maurice Godelier, and Nicos Poulantzas. The humanist and structural forms of Marxism are of direct interest to the central theme of this volume because they hold a contrasting view on the relative importance of structure and subjectivity in the study of social life.

Historical and humanist Marxism is a quite heterogenous orientation since it encompasses a long list of scholars who have made different use of ideas taken from Hegel, Marx, Gestalt psychology, Sartre, Piaget, and other thinkers. Within humanist and historical Marxism one can distinguish the following trends: Hegelian Marxism, phenomenological and existential Marxism, the Marxism of the Frankfurt school, and the genetic Marxism of Lucien Goldman. All these varieties of humanist Marxism are opposed to the so-called crude Marxism as well as to recent structural Marxism.

A form of crude Marxism is found by some critics in certain works of Frederick Engels (1940) and the early Lenin (1927), where the superstructure is mechanically derived from the economic infrastructure. One can find some followers of this form of crude Marxism even in contemporary American sociology (see Van den Berghe 1963).

Two important exponents of humanist Marxism are George Lukàcs and Antonio Gramsci, who, in reaction to a purely economico-deterministic interpretation of Marx, have attempted to integrate both the objective and the subjective element of social dynamics, that is, the role of the economic infrastructure and people in the dynamics of social life. The Marxists who emphasize the role of people give a primary place in sociological analysis to the concepts of alienation, praxis, and negation. This is the case not only of Lukàcs and Gramsci but also of Marcuse, Lefèbvre, Goldman, and, most importantly, Sartre, who considers people as the makers of history.

Other Marxists maintain that one should reject any humanist or "voluntaristic"—in Burawoy's terminology (1977)—interpretation of Marxism as an ideological position. Louis Althusser is a preeminent exponent of this view. He has energetically reacted against the humanist and, in his words, "idealistic" and "historicist" interpretations of Marx, which are based on the ideology of philosophical humanism, an obstacle to a scientific interpretation of Marx. A philosopher by training, Althusser draws his notion of scientific perspective from the French philosopher of science Gaston Bachelard and to a certain extent from Spinoza and Freud. Common to these three thinkers is the notion that immediate or spontaneous evidence and experience do not provide a reliable source of genuine knowledge. This notion is fundamental also in Marx's and Lévi-Strauss' approach to social phenomena. Bachelard argues that in any field of investigation one must "break" (*coupure*) away from the empiricist mode of knowledge and establish a "scientific" mode of thinking. For Bachelard, science is a process of production in the sense that science proceeds by constructing its own concepts rather than abstracting them from observations as empiricists do. At the same time, Bachelard claims to avoid an idealist position because in his view the very notion of "scientific process" guarantees the reality of the external world. I do not enter into the discussion of the merits of Bachelard's position, but it is important to notice that his rejection of both empiricism and idealism is a cardinal point of both Althusser's and Lévi-Strauss' approaches.

Althusser uses Bachelard's notion of "epistemological break" (Althusser 1970:32) to describe the "theoretical and historical discontinuity" (p. 168) he sees between the ideological and the scientific stage of Marxist thought (p. 185). After several years of study, Althusser has reached the conclusion that already in the *Theses on Feurerbach* and more clearly in *The German Ideology* (p. 33) Marx introduced a new philosophy (dialectical materialism) and a "science of history" (historical materialism). Althusser argues that the ideological period of Marx's thought was based on a Kantian-Fichtean perspective first and on a Feuerbachian one next. Central to the liberal rationalism of Kant and Fichte was the notion that human beings' essential characteristics are liberty and freedom. According to the communalist rationalism of Feuerbach, history is the realization of the human essence through alienated labor; therefore, humankind must regain its own essence by becoming the subject of history. Notwithstanding their differences on other issues, both the Kantian-Fichtean and the Feuerbachian perspectives assume the existence of a universal human nature (a notion called by Althusser "idealism of the essence") and they consider human nature an attribute of each individual (called by Althusser "empiricism of the subject"). The epistemological break introduced by the scientific stage of Marx's thought implies the rejection of both the empiricism of the subject and the idealism of the essence (p. 228). Given the fundamental importance of the theory proposed by Althusser in the contemporary structural Marxist debate, I will attempt to determine the precise meaning of Althusser's dialectical view of history (and hence of a structure and subjectivity) through a direct and contextual reading of some of his key texts.

It is Althusser's contention that the scientific perspective of Marx can be best understood precisely as antithetical to the "idealism of essence" and the "empiricism of the subject." Althusser counteracts the widespread notion that Marx was ever a Hegelian thinker. He argues that the Hegelian criticism found in the early works of Marx was based on a Feuerbachian perspective, a perspective which largely consists of an inverted form of the Hegelian perspective. According to Althusser, Marx began a genuine critique of Hegel when he became aware of the Hegelian assumptions present in Feuerbach's thought; at that point Marx began to formulate his own "scientific problematics" (Althusser 1970:48) in antithesis to the Hegelian position.

The Althusserian view of the difference between Marx's scientific perspective and Hegel's perspective can be best understood by examining the difference Althusser sees between Marx's and Hegel's notion of dialectic. Althusser argues that Hegel's dialectic is based on the concepts of "simplicity, essence, identity, unity, negation, fission, alienation, opposites, abstraction, negation of the negation, supersession, totality" (1970:196). He sees traces of this Hegelian conception of dialectic in the *Manuscripts*, written in 1844, where the concepts of "Human Essence, Alienation, Alienated Labor" have a great importance (1976:109). Althusser contends that after 1845 Marx formulated a theory of history based on radically new concepts, such as "social formation, productive forms, relations of production, superstructure, ideological determination in the last instance by the economy, specific determination of the other levels, etc" (1970:227). To this first list of key concepts Althusser later on added the following ones: "ruling class/oppressed class, ruling ideology/oppressed ideology, class struggle" (1976:108–109).

The notion of totality is a convenient starting point to understand what Althusser means by "scientific" theory of historical materialism. Marxists define historical materialism as the science of "social formation," a term by which they indicate that society is a complex totality composed of "economic, political, ideological practices at a given place and stage of development (Althusser 1970:251). The concept of totality implies that no aspect of social organization can be understood independently of other aspects of social organization. According to Lukàcs, "the essence of the method" Marx derived from Hegel consists of the "all pervasive supremacy of the whole over the parts. . . . In Marx the dialectical method aims at understanding society as a whole" (Lukàcs 1971:27). Lukàcs sees in the notion of totality the principle which distinguishes the dialectical from the positivist method, which explains particular phenomena independently of each other. Following Hegel and Lukàcs, Lucien Goldman makes the notion of totality the cardinal principle of his theoretical orientation. For Goldman totality and identity are two cardinal dialectical principles, and totality implies the notions of structure and history (1959, 1970). We can perhaps see in Goldman's conception of totality the promising auspices of a much needed synthesis in view of the debate between Marxists and supporters of Lévi-Strauss on the question of the analytical priority of structure or history.

How does Althusser use the notion of totality? In particular, does his notion of totality imply an opposition or a synthesis between structure and history? Althusser states that Hegel, Marx, Gestalt psychologists, and Sartre use the term "totality" in a different sense (1970:203); in particular, he sees a clear-cut difference between Marx and Hegel's notions of totality, since Marx's notion of totality entails new terms, and new relations among the terms. For Hegel, totality implies an initially posited "simple" unity and history is the alienated development of the original unity (idea) (*ibid.*). Consequently, the Hegelian dialectic is a dialectic of a principle internal to each society, a dialectic of the "idea," and of people's consciousness of themselves; i.e., ideology (p. 107). Such a simple and monistic dialectic implies a splitting of a simple principle in two opposites and therefore a simple contradiction; as a result, historical diversity is reduced to a simple internal principle (p. 103). Social totality is explained on the basis of one major contradiction, that between the essence (idea) and its phenomenon (social reality). Similarly, political society or the state is a mere epiphenomenon or manifestation of the essence (civil society) (pp. 108, 111).

Althusser argues that the Marxist position is not produced by a mere inversion of the Hegelian position, an inversion which consists of deriving history from economics by virtue of a simple internal contradiction. For Althusser such a position is an unacceptable form of "economism" and "technologism" that merely inverts, and therefore retains, the terms of the Hegelian dialectic (1970:108). Althusser shows that Hegel's notion of civil society was based on relations among individuals which were defined in terms of their particular needs. On the contrary, Marx has criticized the presuppositions of the notion of "homo economicus" and has considered "civil society" (the sphere of individual economic behavior) "as the effect of a deeper and more concrete reality: the mode of production of a determinant social formation"; "the degree of development of the forces of production, the state of the relations of production" became the central concern of Marx (p. 110). Althusser argues that Marx has also transformed the Hegelian notion of the state because the latter has been conceived of as an instrument of coercion in the hands of the ruling class (p. 111).

We have also stated that, for Althusser, Marx changed not only the terms of the dialectic but also the relationship among the terms. By this Althusser means that the relationship between structure and superstructure is no longer conceived of as a simple and oneway relationship, as is the case, for instance, of the relationship between essence and its phenomenon. On the contrary, the relationship between infrastructure and superstructure is a complex and multidimensional one, and it is a relationship governed by two principles: "on the one hand, [the] determination in the last instance by the (economic) mode of production; on the other hand, the relative autonomy of the superstructures and their specific effectivity" (1970:111). These two principles are at the heart of what Althusser considers to be the scientific phase of Marxist thought.

For Althusser, Marxist dialectic is based on an originally complex totality where "a structure with multiple and uneven determinations intervene primitively, not secondarily" (1970:195). "The capital-labor contradiction is never simple, but always specified by the historically concrete forms and circumstances in which it is exercised" (p. 106). Althusser's list of historically specific circumstances includes the various forms of superstructures as well as internal and external historical situations and national traditions. This notion of multiple and uneven determinations is expressed by Althusser by the term "overdetermination" (pp. 101, 106).[1] Each one of the various forms of superstructure, such as state, ideology, religion, and political movements, has its specific effect or influence on the class struggle (pp. 111, 112); these forms of superstructure can survive beyond the immediate life context and can "recreate and substitute conditions of existence temporarily" (p. 116). The economic situation is the basis of the class struggles but the various elements of the superstructure also influence their course "and in many cases preponderate in determining their form"—this is quoted from Engels (Althusser 1970). Far from being a pure epiphenomenon of the structure, the superstructure is the "condition of existence" (p. 205) of the structure. The

[1] Althusser remarks that this notion comes from linguistics and psychoanalysis (1970:206). For refinements and clarifications of the notion of overdetermination, see Althusser 1976:181–185.

specific and autonomous role of the superstructure is universally found in all historical situations and, therefore, "the economic dialectic is never active in the pure state; . . . the lonely hour of the *last instance* [of the economic determination] never comes" (p. 113). From these notions Althusser logically concludes that the overdetermination of the basic contradiction is "based primarily on the existence and nature of the superstructures" (p. 114).

At this point a question arises. For Althusser a given social formation is composed of "various levels and instances" (1970:101), each one of which has its specific determination on the totality; this means that the structured totality is composed of many contradictions; moreover, all these contradictions are essential because the secondary contradictions are not pure epiphenomena of the main one (p. 205). How can such an heterogeneous and multidimensional totality function as an integrated totality? The unity of the totality is guaranteed by the dominance of the principal contradiction, that is, by the "structure in dominance" (p. 204). All contradictions mutually condition each other's existence (p. 205) and each contradiction reflects in itself the structure of dominance (p. 207). Once again, overdetermination is the term Althusser chooses to express the "complexly-structurally-unevenly determined" character of the totality. Althusser also borrows other Freudian notions, such as displacement and condensation, to explain the dialectical development implied by the notion of overdetermination (p. 211 ff).

The discussion of the synthesis that Althusser operates between Marx and Freud would take us far afield. Jean-Marie Benoist (1978) has provided a cogent critique of Althusser's usage of Freudian notions, especially the notion of "denial." According to Benoist, Althusser would have brought Freud back into the metaphysical realm of the logic of truth. The primacy attributed by Althusser to the scientific perspective is considered by Benoist a positivist scientism which replaces dialectic with logical and formal simplicity, the latter being incompatible with the notion of "otherness" and negation. More directly relevant to our discussion is Benoist's criticism that Althusser's concept of overdetermination pluralizes and therefore destroys the notion of dialectic, which would be replaced with a Heracletian logic of becoming based on heterogeneity; heterogeneity in turn exceeds contradiction and mediation. Benoist's criticism might be well taken from a metaphysical (and Hegelian) point of view, but as sociologists we are interested in the preservation of a dialectical mode of thinking which accounts for the complexity and dynamics of social life. This is precisely what Althusser has attempted to do. The directionality of Althusser's dialectic is guaranteed by the "structure in dominance" and the continuance of the dialectical process by the uneven and partially autonomous nature of feedback relationships between infrastructure and superstructure and among the various superstructures. The metaphysical stringency of thinking in terms of a thesis and antithesis (negation) would imply a return to a monistic (and Hegelian) thinking, which is not too useful in sociological analysis.

We shall discuss later the question of the absence of the subject from the "objective" dialectic of Althusser—a dialectic, that is, based on contradictions inherent within the structure of society. At this point the question arises of whether the dialectic of a multilevel and unevenly determined totality has affinities with Lévi-Strauss' notion of dialectical relations between dominant and subordinated structures.

Lévi-Strauss' and Althusser's Structural Perspectives: A Converging Problematic?

Althusser concedes to have flirted with structural terminology but he argues that the usage of this terminology was meant as a parody. His proof that his own perspective is radically different from that of Lévi-Strauss is that the notions of "determination in the last instance" and "domination and subordination" are alien to structuralism (1976:126–127).

It would be untenable, if not naïve, to argue that Lévi-Strauss actually anticipated the Althusserian interpretation of Marx. Yet one can argue that Lévi-Strauss and Althusser share in common basic views of social totality. Lévi-Strauss refers to the notion of "a coordinated whole" that insures the permanence of social groups (1963:309). He views "the whole social fabric as a network of different types of orders" (p. 312) and he is concerned with "social dynamics" (p. 309) and with "showing the kind of relationships which exist among them [the various orders composing the social fabrics]" (p. 312).

Admittedly, these ideas are too generic to be considered as distinguishing features of Althusser's perspective. However, many Althusserian notions can be seen as providing plausible, although tentative and questionable, answers to certain basic questions that Lévi-Strauss raises apropos of the study of social dynamics. This is not a far-fetched notion considering Lévi-Strauss' statement that he has set out for himself the task of integrating anthropological knowledge with the Marxian tradition. He has also claimed to have borrowed the notion of structure from Marx and Engels, a notion which has "a primary" (1963:343) or "essential" role (according to the French original 1958:364) in his own structural approach. Lévi-Strauss describes his analysis of the Caduveo and Bororo tribes as "efforts to interpret native superstructures based upon dialectical materialism" (1963:344). He stresses the importance of ideological systems in social life; the reasons why different societies use or reject certain natural products and the way they use them "depend not only upon the intrinsic properties of the products but also on the symbolic value ascribed to them. . . . Marx himself suggests that we uncover the symbolic systems which underlie both language and man's relationships with the universe" (p. 95).

The infrastructure, however, must be accorded a fundamental importance in social life: "Far from the forms of social existence being determined by political systems, it is they which give meaning to the ideologies by which they are expressed" (Lévi-Strauss 1974:148). Ideological transformations do not give origin to social ones but the reverse: "Men's conception of the relations between nature and culture is a function of modifications of their own social relations" (1966:117). Lévi-Strauss argues that we must accord to the infrastructure "its rights" because we cannot understand the various versions of myths without understanding the modifications the infrastructure imposes on them. Myths are "temporal and local responses to specific problems and contradictions" present within the infrastructure; the infrastructure itself belongs to the living order and is always in a state of tension and disequilibrium (1971:562). "Myths choose this or that formula in function of the techno-economic infrastructure, or rather they cumulate them when the infrastructures permit them to do so" (1966a:241–243). "We are not in a position to free ourselves completely from the patterns and rhythm [of human experience]" (1974:123).

The point to be made is that Lévi-Strauss seems to have somewhat anticipated the notion of "determination in the last instance" by the mode of production when he recognizes that "kinship structure does not exhaust social structure" (1963:309) and that, as a consequence, one may want to "attempt to correlate the phenomena belonging to the order first studied, that is, kinship, with phenomena belonging to the new order but showing a direct connection with the former" (p. 310).

For Lévi-Strauss the study of the infrastructure belongs to the realm of history, whereas "it is to this theory of superstructures, scarcely touched on by Marx, that I hope to make a contribution" (1963:130). The relationship between the infrastructure and superstructure is not mechanistically conceived as a one-way determination by the economic or technological factors. On the contrary, Lévi-Strauss holds a dialectical conception of complex totality which is strikingly consistent with that of Althusser. The first level of the social totality consists of such "natural conditions" as geographical, climatological, and biological. However, the natural conditions never "exist in their own right for they are a function of the techniques and way of life of the people who define them and give them a meaning by developing them in a particular direction." These techniques and way of life correspond to Marx's notion of forces of production and relations of production. It is at this second level of the social formation that one encounters contradictions, because human activities and interpretations vary according to specific historical circumstances and their own position in the social hierarchy (p. 133).

It is the task of ideological systems, the third level of social totality, to reconcile these contradictions. The ideological systems are never mechanically predetermined but they are, we could say in Althusserian terms, "relatively autonomous": "man's relations with his natural environment remain objects of thought: man never perceives them passively; having reduced them to concepts, he compounds them to arrive at a system which is never determined in advance: the same situation can always be systematized in various ways" (Lévi-Strauss

1966:95). Lévi-Strauss uses the following metaphor to explain the relationship among the three levels: the primacy of the infrastructure is like having to play a card game set at a table within the limitations imposed by two contingent but unavoidable facts. To begin with, the player does not invent the card game but has to accept it "as a datum of history and civilization." Secondly, the player must accept each deal, which is the result of a contingent distribution of the cards; similarly, the various social interpretations are contingent and historically specific. The primacy of infrastructure means having to accept as given these two contingent and historically specific facts (*ibid.*). Then it is up to the player to use his or her imagination and expertise to structure each game: here is where the relative autonomy and specific effectiveness of superstructure come in.

Lévi-Strauss' notion of dialectic is also a multidimensional and complex one, like that of Althusser: "Infrastructures and superstructures are made up of multiple levels and there are various types of transformations from one level to another" (1963:333). These various levels are in dialectical relation to each other, as "they may be—and often are—completely contradictory; however, it should always be possible to proceed, by transformation, from economic or social structure to the structure of law, art, or religion" (p. 333).

Lévi-Strauss goes on to say that "Marx never claimed there was only one type of transformation—for example that ideology was simply a 'mirror image' of social relations. In his view, these transformations were dialectic, and in some cases he went to great length to discover its crucial transformation which at first sight seemed to defy analysis" (1963:333). This notion of crucial transformation seems consistent with the Althusserian notion of structure in dominance.

These brief quotations show that the Althusserian notion of overdetermination is consistent and perhaps can be considered as one possible development of Lévi-Strauss' notion of dialectical transformation between various levels of social structure.

Besides a relationship of consistency and, possibly, logical development, there also exists a basic methodological convergence between Lévi-Strauss and Althusser on the notion of structural causality. Althusser calls this notion the "effectivity of an absent cause"; by this he means that the "contradiction determinant in the last instance is never present in person" nor can be grasped directly as one can grasp a person physically present. It is a cause in a dialectical sense in that it refers to the "decisive link" in the class struggle (Althusser 1976:126). The decisive link is, of course, the "determination in the last instance" by the mode of production. For Althusser, structural causality is a "dialectical materialist causality" and, therefore, a concept discovered by Karl Marx. Yet Lévi-Strauss developed such a concept into a major analytical approach. One should add that the shared notion of structural causality entails the common rejection by Lévi-Strauss and Althusser of the conscious subject as the motor of history. In this sense both Lévi-Strauss and Althusser give a priority to the structural (systemic) over the subjective view of social dynamics.

In all likelihood, Althusser would totally disassociate himself from this present discussion. He sees validity in the antipsychological and antihistoricist posture of such "good structuralists" as Saussure. However, he finds that contemporary structuralism is an approach ill-defined and impaired by rationalist, mechanistic, and formalist biases. Althusser finds unacceptable Lévi-Strauss' idea that "the production of the real [is] an effect of a combinatory of elements." This is "a crazy formalist idealism" totally alien to Marx's notion of "combination" of the elements of the structure of the mode of production (Althusser 1976:129). Althusser claims that Lévi-Strauss pretends to construct a priori the mode of production through the formal play of combination of elements (ibid.); Althusser rightly argues that such an approach makes concrete realities disappear.

However, this is a gross misrepresentation of Lévi-Strauss' position. Lévi-Strauss is interested in the "formal properties of the whole made up of subwholes" and the "homologous relationships between the different structural levels" (1963:334, 335). But formal analysis is not synonymous with a formalist and idealist approach or with an a priori construction of the mode of production. This latter point should be obvious from Lévi-Strauss' insistence that the infrastructure is a datum of history which imposes modifications on ideological systems. Surely Lévi-Strauss holds a combinatory view of social reality, but in the methodological sense that he intends to apprehend the empirical content in its logical organization. He recently stated that a given cultural datum "is not first of all what it represents but what it transforms, i.e., what it has chosen not to represent" (1979:144). This is all but consistent with the syntagmatic and paradigmatic determination of meaning proposed by Saussure, the structuralist he admires. We know that Lévi-Strauss finds the determinants of empirical events in the interaction of internal and external constraints. The notion of internal determinants refers to the creative activity of mind, a notion which seems consistent, if not explanatory, of the autonomous role attributed by Althusser to ideology.

Althusser argues that another crucial difference between Lévi-Strauss and Marx is that Marx attributes a primacy to contradiction over process and structure (Althusser 1976:130). Lévi-Strauss attributes a central role to the dialectic of logical contradictions. But we have also seen that Lévi-Strauss' notion of dialectic has been attacked by many Marxists. The efforts to determine the true meaning of the Marxist dialectic is at the heart of the present efforts of many structural Marxists. Among them, Maurice Godelier has a prominent place because of his declared intent to overcome the deficiencies of Lévi-Strauss' perspective with a "genuinely" Marxist dialectic.

The Structural Marxism of Maurice Godelier

The Early Lévi-Straussian and Althusserian Perspective. The work of Louis Althusser has emerged in the context of the Marxist debate that was in vogue in the postwar French cultural milieu, a debate concerned with establishing a scientific and critical interpretation of Marx. The major issues underlying the new Marxist debate can be found in the works of Althusser and his critics; they center on the "scientificity" or "historicity" of the Marxist approach, the notion of dialectic and humanism, the role of theory, and the role of the intellectuals. Underlying these Marxist concerns is the epistemological reaction, so marked in Lévi-Strauss and Althusser, against both empiricism and idealism.

Godelier's works also have emerged from the postwar French Marxist debate and are based on the new epistemological perspective. Godelier describes the itinerary of his thought in the 1972 "Forward" to the English edition of *Rationality and Irrationality in Eco-*

nomics (1972). He started out in 1958 as a philosopher concerned with epistemological issues, and especially with the questions of the foundation of reality and our knowledge of it (p. viii). Working at a time when, in the name of Marx, Nietzsche, and "science," many intellectuals had declared the death of philosophy, Godelier intended to clarify the relation between philosophy and science by examining the conditions of the "rationality" of economic systems, i.e., the conditions of their hidden logic and necessity. Having begun his scientific itinerary with the discipline of economics, he soon turned to anthropology because he could not have adequately assessed the rationality of capitalism and socialism without undertaking a comparative study of economic systems, including the most primitive ones (pp. vii–viii, 1–5).

The critical edition of Marx's *Economic and Philosopic Manuscripts* by E. Bottigelli—a publication discussed by Althusser (1970:153–160)— was the occasion for Godelier to express his views on the position of the young Marx, on Marx's transition from an idealist to a materialist notion of dialectic, and on the scientific nature of the analysis proposed in *The Capital*. Godelier's interpretation of the evolution of Marx's thought is consistent, if not a variant formulation, with Althusser's notion of "epistemological break," discussed by Althusser in his famous 1963 essay "Marxism and Humanism" (reprinted in Althusser 1970:219ff). In an article published four months later, Godelier argues that the critique of theoretical economy presented in the 1844 *Manuscripts* is still based on the philosophical notion of human essence. In fact, communism is presented as the means to realize authentic human nature through the abolishment of alienating social conditions; communism is a "political instrument of victorious humanism" (Godelier 1972:129). After *Manuscripts*, Marx based "the necessity" of the Communist revolution "in history itself, in its real contradiction, as the inner contradiction between the productive forces and the relations of production. The resolving of this contradiction will no longer be the victory of the essence, but the *bringing into correspondence of* the productive forces and the relations of production. Analysis will lose its speculative character and be based henceforth on the scientific knowledge of the law of necessary correspondence between productive forces and relations of production"

(p. 126). Short of the usage of the term "epistemological break," this passage posits the same contrast that Althusser posits between the philosophical (ideological) and the scientific phases of Marx's thought. Does this mean that Godelier has the same conception of historical materialism as does Althusser?

Godelier's original Marxist perspective was very close to Lévi-Strauss' perspective. Godelier argues that some of the conditions of the rise, functioning, and evolution of economic systems derive from people's intentional activity; however, other conditions "of more decisive importance" are inherent within the nature of social relations rather than in people's intentionality (Godelier 1972:viii). We can see that Lévi-Strauss, Althusser, and Godelier concur in rejecting a key idea of humanist Marxism—the priority of conscious subjectivity in the dynamic of historical formations. Noticing that social and economic systems are at times "mutually contradictory," Godelier formulates the question of the reproduction and disappearance of social and economic systems as follows: some systems can reproduce themselves only "by way of transformations that are compatible with the unintentional properties of its inner structures. . . . It was therefore necessary to bring these concepts of compatibility, incompatibility and limits into relation with the concept of contradiction and the concepts of system-theory and cybernetics" (ibid.). All these notions also are basic in Lévi-Strauss' perspective.

Godelier states that his position is opposed to "dogmatic Marxism and the other form of vulgar materialism" according to which economy, reduced to a relationship between technology and environment, gives rise to social relations as its own "epiphenomena" (1972:ix–x). This formulation closely reflects or is squarely consistent with Althusser's rejection of "economism and technologism" (Althusser had published For Marx and Reading The Capital seven years before Godelier's "Foreword." Godelier articulates his antidogmatic Marxism in quasi-Althusserian terms; he raises the question of the "ultimate reason" for the transformation of economic systems and states that such a reason must be looked for "from within the various types of relations that obtain among men"; the analysis of the internal determinations of social systems is consistent with Lévi-Strauss's and Althusser's points of view. For Godelier the question is to determine "which, among these relations, are the ones that bear primary responsibility for the major transformations that occur in the history of mankind, determining them in the last analysis" (p. ix).

According to Marx, the material conditions of social existence determine the compatibility or incompatibility "between all levels of social life"; consequently, these material conditions are what "determine, in the last analysis, the outstanding transformations that occur in the forms and functions of the other *levels* of social life (political, ideological etc.)" (my italics). To endorse the view of "dogmatic Marxism" means to deny the "irreducible differences between the *levels* and structures of social life, the reason for the *relative autonomy* with which they operate" (my italics) (p. x). For instance, kinship relations can never be reduced to or deduced from economic relations. Godelier wants to reject "vulgar materialism" and approach in a correct way the analysis of "the relations between determination and dominance, and to establish the working of the structural causality of various modes of production in relation to their organization and evolution" (p. x). The reader will remember that the notions of levels of structures, relative autonomy, dominance, determination in the last analysis, and structural causality are key notions of Althusser's perspective.

Althusser's scientific career differs from Godelier's in that the latter left philosophy and became an anthropologist because of his desire to study the largest possible number of economic and social systems, including those different from capitalism. Godelier did so with the acknowledged assistance of Lévi-Strauss.

However, Godelier soon found out that structuralism could not account for history or the historical appearance of some systems more than functionalism could (1972:xi). His avowed intent has been "to carry out a theoretical revolution in the human sciences" on the basis of Marxism (we can see here echoed again the Althusserian notion of epistemological break). To accomplish this, he shows first the weakness of dogmatic Marxism and the helplessness of structuralism and functionalism in the face of history. He starts his task by reanalyzing Hegel's dialectic (which was also Althusser's starting point for the reconstructing of the genuine Marxist thought). Like Althusser, Godelier distinguishes a philosophical from a scientific element, but here the similarity between the two thinkers ends. Godelier relegates to metaphysics the first principle of the identity of opposites: matter is thought-in-itself which doesn't conceive itself, i.e., thought is both itself and its opposite. However, the Hegelian principle of the unity of opposites belongs to science because it permits one to grasp both the complementarity (compatibility) and conflict (incompatibility) of the opposites as well as the reproductive capacity of a given unit within certain limits (p. xiii). At variance with Althusser, Godelier rejects as ambiguous the formulations of Lenin, Mao Tse-tung, and Lucian Sève; Althusser's notion of overdetermination has a positive but marginal value because it doesn't show the metaphysical character of the first principle of Hegel's dialectic.

Godelier argues that we need to return to the "facts of reality" but not as they are conceived of by abstract empiricism or functional empiricism"; these two approaches, present in an idealist form in cultural anthropology and in a materialist form in the cultural ecology of Marvin Harris, are found by Godelier to be totally inadequate. The inadequacy of abstract empiricism is demonstrated through a discussion of the empiricism of the classical economists Walras and Pareto and the Marxist economic anthropologists (to which we may add natural science sociologists). All these thinkers base their analysis on the notion of abstract and equal individuals, i.e., "individuals which are embodiments of the 'theoretical fetish' called 'homo oeconomicus' " (Godelier 1972:xv); by the latter term Godelier refers to the notion that people cannot but compete with one another and they do so with equal resources and equal share of information.

Godelier contends that all three—functionalism, structuralism, and Marxism—refuse to study the relations among individuals in an "abstract" social space. One can dispute the validity of this assertion in so far as functionalism (at least) is concerned; but what is important to us is not the details but rather the main thrust of Godelier's argument. The relationships among individuals are not "direct" relations among equal individuals; on the contrary, they are mediated by social relations of a "capitalist" nature. In a capitalist society every social transaction and every product, labor included, is treated as an exchangeable commodity; the relations among individuals are also treated as relations of commodity-exchange, and exchange-relations are competitive and unequal. The inequality between the two classes is the necessary mechanism through which society reproduces itself. It is this unequal, competitive, and commodity-exchange quality of social relations that must be the explicit focus of social scientists and the starting point of their analysis (Godelier 1972:xiv–xvii).

Godelier offers a systematic and clear discussion of the similarities and differences of approach among empirical functionalism, Lévi-Strauss' structuralism, and Marxism (or his own version of Marxism). Godelier accepts three methodological principles of functionalism: 1) sociological analysis must focus on the *relations* between individuals rather than on "abstract" individuals; 2) social relations must be studied as a totality, i.e., as forming a system; and 3) the study of the structure of social relations must precede the study of their origin and evolution (1972:xviii, xxi). These three methodological principles are also fundamental in modern linguistics, Lévi-Strauss' structuralism, and Marxism; however, these three approaches differ from empirical functionalism in that they maintain that the structure is not directly visible and observable, as Radcliffe-Brown maintains, but has to be found in the "underlying logic of the system, the subjacent order by which the apparent order is to be explained" (p. xix). Godelier claims that this principle also is fundamental in Marx, for whom the structure is not immediately visible or an object of "direct cognition through experience" (p. xxviii). For Marx the mode of production is the ultimate determinant of all social relations, including political and religious relations; in the mode of production one finds "the underlying logic" (p. xxviii), the "inner relations" of the functioning of the whole society. The empirical functionalism of Parsons, however, perceives only "*the apparent form* of the social relations of capitalist society" because it studies economics, religion, and politics as systems which are autonomous and function independently of each other. Moreover, empirical functionalism reduces the mode of production to mere subsistence activity (p. xxvii).

Godelier dispels a frequent misconception about the notion of a "not immediately visible" structure. To conceive of social structure as the underlying logic of the social system is not the same as saying that social structure exists only as a logical construction of the anthropologist, which is Leach's contention (Leach 1954:5). There is no doubt that, for Marx, structure is "real" because Marx's notion of structure refers to the ultimate determination of all social relations by the mode of production. Godelier rightly rejects the "idealist and formalist interpretations of structuralism" because they "keep intact the empiricist view of reality as a multiform, unstructured flux" (Godelier 1972:xx, xxi).

All Godelier's ideas so far discussed are explicitly and implicitly contained in Lévi-Strauss' works. Godelier's position becomes original when he criticizes Lévi-Strauss' empiricist notion of history and infrastructure.

At this point we are facing an apparent contradiction; how is it possible that both Marx and Lévi-Strauss partake of an antiempiricist and antiformalist notion of structure and then part from each other on the conception of infrastructure? We have seen that Lévi-Strauss is mostly interested in the structure of ideological systems, but we have also seen that he establishes a dialectical relationship between superstructure and infrastructure and that he relegates the study of infrastructure to the study of history. How do Lévi-Strauss and Godelier conceive of the relationship between structure and history?

Godelier's Criticism of Levi-Strauss. Godelier maintains that to be a true Marxist one must go beyond the discovery of mythical representations and discover the mechanisms external to thought which impose upon the latter illusory concepts of reality. Marxists must be concerned not only with the study of the forms of mythical representations but also with "their content and their historical necessity" (1972:xxvi). It is a cardinal principle of Marxism that the conditions of production and reproduction of the material basis are the ultimate determinants of the inner logic of the functioning of society; the material conditions of production are the ultimate determining "constraints" of all levels of society, levels which are in a hierarchical relationship of causality (p. xxviii).

Godelier intends to recapture the functional perspective, which is donwplayed in Lévi-Strauss' works. To study a society one must start from a structural analysis of the functions of structures and then determine the basis, reasons, forms, and conditions of their existence (1972:xxiii, xxviii). These two programmatic statements are the gist of

Godelier's approach. Like Lévi-Strauss, Godelier criticizes empirical functionalism, but for different, although complementary, reasons. Godelier finds that British functionalists have either undervalued the analytical power of the Marxist approach (as in the case of Leach) or have not explained why economics has a decisive influence on the structure of social relations (as in the case of Firth). Godelier also finds that cultural ecologists, such as A. D. Vayda, R. A. Rappaport, and Marvin Harris are exponents of various forms of "vulgar materialism" because they reduce economics to technology and explain people-nature relationships in terms of the ecological environment. Rightly Godelier considers this position a new form of "economism" in the sense that social structure is treated as an epiphenomenon of economics and is understood as a function of environmental adaptations. The notion of functional adaptation is ultimately based on truisms (and here Godelier's criticism concurs with that of Lévi-Strauss) and on the notion of probabilistic correlations among structures; moreover, functionalists reduce history to a series of events of greater or lesser frequency (p. xxxiv).

On the notion of history, Godelier departs not only from functionalists but also from Lévi-Strauss: "History as a reality can no longer be reduced to a succession of purely accidental events. Events have their own necessity which expresses the objective properties of social relations, properties of compatibility and incompatibility, which underlie the limited system of their possible transformations" (1972:xxix). Godelier's notion of internal constraints, which set the limits of alternative possible actualizations of empirical systems and their transformations, is certainly consistent with Lévi-Strauss' notion that cultural systems are the result of a double determinism or sets of constraints; they are compelled by "mental laws" to become organized according to certain "recurring patterns" and transformational rules of "inverted symmetry"; at the same time, cultural systems are determined also by the ecological environment, techno-economic activities, and sociopolitical conditions (Lévi-Strauss 1972:9). This distinction between mental and material constraints seems to be implied in Godelier's refusal to explain the dominance of kinship or religious relations by considering them (or reducing them) to mere "epiphenomena of material life" (Godelier 1972:xxix). Lévi-Strauss would wholeheartedly concede the latter point: "When confronted with a given ecological and techno-economic situation, the mind does not stay inactive. It does not merely reflect it, it reacts to it and works it out into a system" (Lévi-Strauss 1972:10).

Godelier, however, insists that his notion of history is decisively different from that of Lévi-Strauss because, like empiricists and reductionist materialists, Lévi-Strauss cannot explain "the fundamental necessity of what exists"; he cannot explain the reasons for the history of society, the reasons why societies are not always totally integrated but provisionally stable effects of compatibilities between structures (Godelier 1972:xxxv). In my opinion, Godelier's notion of the necessary existence of a society is weak and not carefully spelled out. Once more, the issue comes down to the explanation of the relation between economics and the rest of society. On this point Godelier finds Lévi-Strauss' position deficient. Notwithstanding his opposition to empiricism, and the primacy he attributes to the infrastructure, Lévi-Strauss endorses an empiricist notion of "history as a succession of accidental events." Godelier refers to Lévi-Strauss' statement that the transition to philosophy and science in Western culture was not a "necessary transition" because it did not occur among preliterate people (p. xxxvi).

In reality Lévi-Strauss doesn't reduce history to a "succession of accidental events." In that passage, which occurs at the end of *Du Miel aux Cendres* (1966a), Lévi-Strauss rejects the notion of universal and unilineal evolution according to which the stages of thought succeed each other spontaneously and by "inevitable causality." For him "an historical occurrence only means that an event is produced in this place and at this time" (p. 408). In my opinion this statement does not amount to saying that a given historical event is simply an "accidental" event. Lévi-Strauss distinguishes between structure and historical analysis as two analytical principles which are both needed to explain historical events: "Structural analysis does not reject history; on the contrary, it gives to it a place of first rank, that which rightfully belongs to the irreducible contingencies without which one could not even conceive of necessity" (*ibid.*). Lévi-Strauss is speaking here about the inseparability of two correlative analytical principles and not about "two irreducible realities," as Godelier claims

(1972:xxxvii). Structural analysis is possible or rather is made necessary precisely by a careful analysis of the heterogenity of historical data. Lévi-Strauss never states that structuralists ignore the heterogeneity and apparently contingent character of data. On the contrary, the heterogeneity and apparent contradictions of data are the very reason for the structuralists' quest of fundamental and common properties which underlie "apparent diversity." To say "apparent diversity" is not the same as saying "illusory diversity." Lévi-Strauss carefully analyzes in its ethnographic context the diversity which "appears first" and then attempts to formulate the invariant laws governing its dynamics. He has done so not only in *The Elementary Structures of Kinship*, as Godelier himself states, but also in the *The Mythologiques.*

Lévi-Strauss' position is that structural analysis cannot explain why certain particular events instead of many other possible ones are realized (1966a:408). This aspect of the events cannot be explained in terms of the structural tendencies of the system and therefore is referred to as their "contingent" aspect. It remains true, however, that any concrete event must be explained in terms of both the structural and the contingent principle. Truly, the particularity of an event can be called an "inanity" (*ibid.*) in the sense that the event could be replaced by many other possible ones. The particularity of the event, however, is also "structurally necessary" because it cannot be fully accounted for unless one considers the structural tendencies of the system that define the limits of compatibility of various possible realizations of an event.

I also find questionable another criticism that Godelier levies against Lévi-Strauss. Godelier claims that Lévi-Strauss' analysis is a formalist one, or at least is concerned only with the formal grammar of social relations (Godelier 1972:xii), with forms and not with content (p. xi). Lévi-Strauss never "meets history in its concrete diversity and reality" (p. xxxix) because he does not analyze the functions of those forms. In actuality, Lévi-Strauss is interested in forms but not in a formalistic sense; he clearly states that structure is not to be understood as a form opposed to content but as the logical organization of content. He considers the ethnographic and historical context of cultural data in their most minute details (see 1979:19) but he does not explain them only in terms of the principle of contingency. Like Godelier, Lévi-Strauss also downplays the usefulness of studying empirical functional relations, which for Lévi-Strauss are nothing but truisms based on psychological and biological considerations (1963:14). For Lévi-Strauss what is important is to deal with "the fuctional permanence of systems of reciprocity," that is, with the ever-present form organizing the "contingency of the institutional matter placed at [its] disposal by history" (1969:76). We can see that structure and contingency are inseparable analytical concepts and, moreover, that the notion of totality of functions lends support to the notion of structure (Lévi-Strauss 1963:391).

Having dealt with Godelier's criticism of Lévi-Strauss, we deal now with his concept of the "necessity" of historical occurances.

The Structural Necessity of Historical Contingencies: The Wanting Explanation. For Godelier, a truly Marxist analysis should be concerned with the study of the conditions of the forms, functions, and articulations and transformations of social structure "within concrete societies." These conditions are to be explained on the basis of the determination in the last analysis by the mode of production (Godelier 1972:xli–xlii). This notion seems to echo the Althusserian approach. However, Godelier clarifies that one must show that the fetishization of social relations have the quality of "necessity" because of the determination of the mode of production. Godelier has developed this concept in various essays collected in *Perspectives in Marxist Anthropology* (1977).

The study of the religion of Mbuti pygmies made Godelier realize that religious representations and practices draw their content and reason of existence from the hidden articulation of their mode of production (1977:61). This still sounds very much like Lévi-Strauss' notion that the infrastructure imposes modifications on mythical thought. However, Godelier argues that a true Marxist analysis "goes beyond a structural analysis of kinship forms and the uncovering of formal codes and grammar of Amerindian myths. These structural analyses may be indispensible, but they are not sufficient in themselves" (p. 49).

Marxism, Godelier contends, does not limit itself to extracting "formal systems" from "concrete facts" but studies "real societies . . . to account for their diversity or internal complexity." The originality of Godelier's position is the ambitious goal of explaining under which circumstances political or religious or ideological relations became dominant over kinship relations. This means that one must explain the historical emergence of societies, in contrast to Lévi-Strauss' contentions that historical occurrences must be taken as given. Godelier states that for Marx, history cannot be taken as a given but must be explained. Starting from the "hypothesis about the articulation of [society's] inner levels," Godelier intends to unravel "the specific hierarchical causality of each of these levels" and "the types and mechanisms of this causality and articulation." Godelier proposes a kind of "morphological analysis" aimed at discovering "the intrinsic connections between form, funtion, mode of articulation and conditions for the appearance and transformation of these social relations" (ibid.).

Lévi-Strauss shows that the functioning of "the formal logic of analogy" is the activity through which mind "organizes the control of experience in nature and society into symbolic forms of metaphor and metonymy." One must also show the nature of the "articulation of form and content," the functions of symbolic representations and the circumstances under which function and content are transformed (Godelier 1977:50). Godelier concedes that few Marxists have attempted to undertake such a task, which demands "the continuation of multiple theoretical practices."

Godelier uses Colin Turnbull's material on the Mbuti pygmies to propose a concrete example of the kind of relationships he suggests. He argues that the conditions of production determine three types of internal constraints, which simultaneously act as a system on "all other instances [Godelier's term] of Mbuti social organization" (Godelier 1977:53). This system of constraints simultaneously acts on all levels of society, including kinship and religious relations, without reducing them to economic relations; in this way the specificity and relative autonomy of the various levels of strata is preserved (pp. 53,54). Mbuti religion is an ideological instance which represents the conditions of the mode of production upside down, that is, in "fetishized" or "mythical" forms; for instance, the forest, and not the hunter, catches the game (p. 39). Mythological representations or fetishizations have the function of broadening and heightening all aspects of social relations and attenuating all the contradictions contained within social relations under the determination of the mode of production. Religion, then, becomes a form of "genuine labor" under contradictions determined by the mode of production and other social relations; religion becomes "one of the essential conditions for the reproduction of the relations of production as well as other social relations" (p. 60). Religion is not just a system of representations but also a social practice which is totally oriented toward the conditions of reproduction (pp. 9, 59). The representational element ("phantasma") is not a reflection of reality but is itself part of the content of social relations (p. 9). Religious, economic, and political relations are nothing but forms of one and the same process; they are elements of the same content, existing simultaneously on several levels (p. 10).

Apparently this kind of reasoning is consistent with holistic perspective. However, one finds a certain slip of logic in Godelier's argument; he states that "religious representations and religious observances draw their contact, the very weight of their existence and the efficacy of their presence from the central join, from the hidden articulation of their mode of production and the instances corresponding to it" (1977:61). Here Godelier intends to explain the concrete content of mythical representations, or what Lévi-Strauss calls the contingent material presented by history to mythical thought. Godelier argues that on the basis of the system of the three constraints revealed by the Mbuti's mode of production one can "account and reveal the *necessity* of all *major facts* observed" (p. 53). "We must discover scientifically the raisons d'être and the inevitability of history's multiple momentum which provides new subject matter for human thought" (p. 219). One wonders whether to carry out the "analyses of unintentional inevitability which are manifest in history" (p. 219) is equivalent to demonstrating the necessity of specifically different contents. When Godelier analyzes the effects of the three structural constraints on the political relations, he argues that "these effects are different in their content because they have an effect on a different aspect, irreducible to elements of the process of production, but they are isomorphic to the effects produced on other instances of Mbuti society. The isomorphic relations derive from the fact that all the different effects come from the *same* cause acting simultaneously on all levels of society" (p. 55).

A question must be raised: on the one hand, differences in content are related to different aspects of social relations (which is an apparent tautology). On the other hand, different effects are explained on the basis of the same cause (which is an apparent contradiction). What is Godelier really saying? The influence of the system of the three internal constraints "on all other instances of Mbuti organization" has to be understood in the following way: "All these effects consist in the determination of the elements of content and form of instances which are compatible with these constraints, therefore assuring the reproduction of the Mbuti mode of productign" (1977:53). Godelier has only shown the relations of compatibility between certain forms and functions of religious, political, and economic relations; he has shown "the internal constraints" (p. 52) or "internal conditions," or perhaps limits, within which the simultaneous and multilevel structural causality can take place. What I am saying is that the system of internal constraints guarantees the conditions within which the reproductign of the mode of production can take place but not the necessity of this or that particular realization of the mode of production. Stated differently, the internal constraints are the necessary but not sufficient conditions for the reproduction of the mode of production. The internal constraints are the "channels by which the mode of production determines, in the final analysis, the nature of the different instances of Mbuti society" (p. 53). More precisely, the internal constraints are the limits within which alternative realizations of the mode of production are possible.

In the same passage one reads: "By the action of the system of constraints, the mode of production determines the relations and articulations of all instances. . . . It determines the general structure of the society" (1977:53). The notion of determination must be understood here from the perspective of the structural and not efficient causality; this means that Godelier speaks of the determination of the limits of compatibility of alternative possible realizations and not of the determination of which specific realizations will occur. Godelier's formulations become more clear a few pages later, where he states that the system of constraints "condition the reproduction" of the modes of production (p. 61).

Ultimately, my criticism is that Godelier does not succeed in demonstrating the necessity of contingencies because he does not explain which one of the various concrete modes of production possible within the limit of compatibility will materialize. All Godelier has succeeded in accomplishing is the elaboration of Lévi-Strauss' notion of internal constraints along the lines of a multilevel and hierarchical causality of the same basic structure. However, he has not eliminated the need for the notion of "contingency" as an analytical principle of explanation.

This point has been made by Lévi-Strauss himself in a debate with Godelier and M. Augé (Lévi-Strauss et al. 1976). There Lévi-Strauss argued that "history constantly confronts us with irreducible phenomena" (p. 49) in the sense that things could have happened in an entirely different way from the way they happened; it is not possible to discover a law accounting for the "inevitability" of the occurrence of a phenomena which happened in history once: "Once the event has occurred we can understand it, but we cannot discover a law, i.e., we can't be certain that under the same conditions the same thing wguld happen elsewhere" (p. 61). Godelier has conceded to Lévi-Strauss that the kind of predictive laws Lévi-Strauss mentions are beyond the realm of possibilities and that all he has tried to do is to study "the problem of the properties of compatibility among social relations" (p. 51). But these are the very same terms of the initial perspective of *The Elementary Structure of Kinship* (Lévi-Strauss 1969). One cannot find traces of the theoretical advances beyond the notion of history as a contingency, which Godelier had so forcefully promised.

Infrastructural or Superstructural Dominance? The Missing Dialectical Link. We have so far dealt with Godelier's notion of the necessity of historical occurrences. Another of his ideas also deserves close scrutiny: the simultaneity of functions of a given social institution. How is this notion reconcilable with the notion of the primacy of infrastructure? In a recently published paper, Godelier (1982) argues that the forms and contents of ideological representations are in a relationship of expression rather than structural causality with the forms and contents of the infrastructure (p. 230). At the same time, he argues that ideology is simultaneously an internal component of social relations. We remember that for Lévi-Strauss the infrastructure has a primacy in that it confronts thought with contradictions to be resolved. For Godelier the matter of contradictions orients thought in specific directions; the content (matter) of infrastructure not only gives to thought the form of its contradictions, but also determines the necessity of religious institutions through the mediation of representations (p. 240, also 230). Godelier goes as far as saying that the matter of contradiction determines the kind of solutions proposed by thoughs (p. 236). The forms, function, and reproduction of ideology largely depend on the nature of social relations brought into play by the content of productive forms (p. 241–242).

Here Godelier seems to go beyond the position elaborated in *Perspectives in Marxist Anthropology* (1977). Structural causality means more than a relationship of compatibility; it means order of priority, hierarchical order of various functions, all of which simultaneously exist within one structure. The novelty of Godelier's position lies in attributing a structural priority (dominance) to the content of material and intellectual relationship with nature. Such a content at times determines the dominance of mythical representations and, through them, determines social relations (Godelier 1982:242). Ideology is simultaneously the expression and interpretation of productive forces and the necessary mediation for the appearance of social relations whose finality they define (p. 243). Consequently, ideology is not a superstructure located at the vertex of the pyramid, so to speak, but is an internal component of social relations (p. 244) (see also Godelier in Lévi-Strauss et al. 1976:46).

The strong point of Godelier's position is that structure and infrastructure should not be conceived of as two separate institutions, as Lévi-Strauss and Althusserians, Terray, Meillassoux, and Rey do. Godelier shows that in Murngin and Greek societies kinship and political institutions functioned both as relations of production and as superstructure.

A given social institution can assume more than one function and to the extent that it functions as a relation of production that institution becomes a dominant one. We can no longer recognize here the Althusserian point of view. It is no longer true that the infrastructure determines which superstructure becomes dominant; rather, the superstructure becomes dominant because it assumes in and by itself the function of relation of production (Godelier in Rossi 1982: 29).

Has Godelier succeeded in demonstrating the "necessity" of historical occurrences? As far as I have read, nowhere had Godelier shown why in Murngin society it was kinship and in Greek society politics rather than other social institutions that functioned as a relationship of production. This means that, like Lévi-Strauss, whom he is criticizing, Godelier also takes historical contingency as a given. Moreover, whereas Godelier argues that the matter of "contradictions" suggests solutions to thought, in reality all he succeeds in showing is that a particular "matter" is what is being thought about. However, there exist many ways to think about it, many types of solutions which can be proposed, and in thinking about a given matter or resolving certain contradictions, the mind can propose a variety of messages or deal with a variety of existential issues. As far as I have read, nowhere does Godelier explain why mythical thought chooses one type of solution or elaborates one type of mythical system rather than another, all of which are compatible with a given infrastructure. Finally, if Godelier had succeeded in demonstrating his thesis, what would happen to the thesis of the primacy of infrastructure? How can this thesis remain valid, if the superstructure assumes in and by itself the function of mode of production?

Godelier has tried to clarify his thought on this matter. A social activity can be said to play a dominant role in society if it "functions directly and internally as a relation of production" (1978:765). The reason why kinship or religion come to function as relations of production is found in some state of the productive forces, i.e., in the relations of present and past labor (p. 766). For instance, the fact that in Athenian society political relations functioned as relations of production made it unthinkable for the slaves to wage a political struggle. The various thinkable and doable possibilities "cannot escape [go beyond] the nature of the relations of production and the productive forces in a given society. It is perhaps this that is meant by historical necessity" (p. 768).

This formulation seems to deny the position that Godelier had previously announced, i.e., that the superstructure assumes in and by itself the function of mode of production. At the same time, Godelier seems to go back to the Marxist-Althusserian thesis of the primacy of the economic infrastructure; all this is to be understood in the sense of the determination of "limits of compatibility." Godelier seems to be shifting between the theses of the dominance of infrastructure and the dominance of superstructure.

Perhaps this ambivalence in Godelier's thought can be resolved with the Althusserian (and Lévi-Straussian?) notion of the ultimate determination of the infrastructure and the relative autonomy of the superstructure. However, Godelier's efforts to clarify his own position seem to have produced more and more ambivalent statements. He criticizes the Althusserian conception of infrastructure and superstructure, and in doing so he seems to run the risk of reducing them to the same logical order. He states that the notion of infrastructure entails a combination of three elements: ecological and geographical conditions, social relations of production, and productive forces. Productive forces include "the material and intellectual means" that the members of a society use to transform nature; within the notion of "intellectual" means one must include all knowledge of nature, technical processes, rules governing the manufacture of tools and the use of body, ideas, taxonomic principles, etc.: these are "ideal" realities which are inseparable from material processes. In this way thought and language become part of the infrastructure, of the notion of forces of production (p. 764). Godelier's position is that "all social relations arise and exist simultaneously both in thought not ideal and outside of it; all social relations contain from the outset, an "ideal" element which is not a posteriori reflection of it, but a condition for its emergence and ultimately an essential component. . . . Thought not only interprets reality, but actually organizes every kind of social practice on the basis of this reality." Godelier concludes that "social relations are simultaneously a material and 'ideal' reality" (pp. 766–767).

These principles are well taken and, as remarked by a commentator on Godelier's article, are already contained, at least implicitly, in Durkheim. Moreover, they have been explicitly put forward by Lévi-Strauss himself when he stated that in a "given ecological and techno-economic situation, the mind does not stay inactive. It does not merely reflect it, it reacts to it and works it out into a system" (Lévi-Strauss 1972:10). Lévi-Strauss, however, made the following cautionary remarks in reaction to Godelier's notion that the objects of the Kula King had in reality a phantasmagoric value since they represented political, religious, and social relations: "One shouldn't get carried away in this directign, for taken to its limits, anything can serve as anything" (Lévi-Strauss et al. 1976:55).

Moreover, it is not sufficient to state the simultaneity of the material and ideal elements of social life; one must also clearly formulate their interrelationship. We have seen that Godelier asserts that the matter of contradicitions determines the solution of thought. Lévi-Strauss more accurately states that mind does not react only to the particular environment perceived through senses. "It also keeps aware of environments which are not experienced in a direct way, and it keeps aware of the ways in which other people react to them. All these environments, both present and absent, are integrated into an ideological system" (1972:10). This principle spells out the reasons for the relative autonomy of ideological systems, while at the same time not loosing sight of the "interlocking of external and mental constraints" (Lévi-Strauss 1972:12). At the same time, Lévi-Strauss avoids a dualistic perspective with the notion of the structural homology of neurological, psychological, and mental processes.

Godelier does not satisfactorily deal with the issues of the dialectics between the ideal and material components of social life. He has repeatedly attempted to reckon with this issue, which seems to have become his nemesis. Since 1966 he has expressed his dissatisfaction with the inadequacy of Althusser's notion of overdetermination of the basic contradiction and has referred to a twofold contradiction. First, there exists the contradiction internal to the structure of relationships of production—an intrasystemic contradiction. Such a contradiction does not contain within itself all the elements for the needed resolution; in fact, the resolution of the contradiction cannot take place without the intervention of political and cultural superstructures, which are, of course, outside the structure of relations of production. Consequently, the solution of the intrasystemic contradiction depends on the intersystemic contradictions between forces and relations of production (Godelier 1972:85–86, 78). Jonathan Friedman states that the intrasystemic contradiction (class struggle) contains within itself its laws of development and therefore must be considered a positive form of causality. However, this contradiction is insufficient to explain the breaking up of the system without referring to intersystemic contradictions. Friedman calls the causality of intersystemic contradictions a "negative causality" to express the notion that the intersystemic contradictions only set the limits of the development and stability of the system, the limits of the possible variations of the system (1974:447–448, 452).

This line of reasoning leads us to the same conclusion: notwithstanding his intention to explain the contingency of historical occurrences and their development, Godelier is caught within the limitations imposed by the structural notion of limits of compatibility of various historical developments. The originality of Godelier's approach lies in his having perceived the need for referring to factors "external" to the contradiction as necessary elements of a dialectical explanation. However, this line of reasoning turns out to be irreconcilable with his proclaimed intention of demonstrating the necessity of historical occurrences. Godelier states that the ultimate reason why a given superstructure functions as relations of production must be searched for in "some given state of the productive forces" (1978:766). Here Godelier reverts to the principle of the dominance of the infrastructure and neglects his intention of demonstrating the necessity of historical occurrences. In fact, when he refers to "some given state of the productive forces," he seems to accept the contingencies of historical occurrences as given.

In view of the criticisms I have proposed, one cannot accept Godelier's contention that his analysis makes "all distinctions and oppositions between anthropology and history disappear." Godelier wants to avoid a mechanistic conception of the relationship between superstructure and infrastructure, but he ends up formulating an ambivalent position. On the one hand he postulates the dominance of the infrastructure and the notion that it explains the "necessary" quality of history. On the other hand, he must reckon with the autonomous role of the superstructure, and he argues that superstructure takes "in and by itself" the function of the mode of production: to explain why and when this happens he refers to the infrastructure *tout court* and therefore accepts the contingent notion of history he intended to refute. The roots of Godelier's dilemma seem to lie in his reductionist or extremist structural orientation. Having eliminated contingency as an analytical principle, he remains imprisoned within the realm of structural determinism and is left with the option to either demonstrate the structural necessity of history through some sort of Hegelian dialectic or to accept the contingency of history as given. Moreoever, Godelier has not resolved the problem of whether superstructure or infrastructure is the ultimate motor of dialectic, since he has not shown under what circumstances ideal factors assume the function of the mode of production and under what circumstances they are confined to playing the function of superstructure: how can we account only in terms of the systemic tendencies of a given social formation that one structure plays different functions in different places and times in history?

Where Are We At with Structural Marxism? To summarize, Godelier began his career with a typical Lévi-Straussian perspective (i.e., a concern with social forms of production and social morphology) and then switched to the study of the physiology of social forms. Throughout this itinerary, Godelier has kept at least the following elements of the Lévi-Straussian approach: a metaempirical focus on relations rather than concrete and observable facts; the notion of transformation as a set of structural variation; and the notion of structural causalty as a set of constraints or internally generated limits of possible variations. On this structural matrix Godelier has elaborated a more specific Marxist perspective—a concern with the conditions and distribution of social forms and their transformations. For this reason he has tried to recapture the specificity of history understood as a historical necessity, the importance of content in addition to form, and the concept of function. To explain the emergence and transformation of a variety of forms and functions in terms of the content of social relations, he as added the perspective of intersystemic contradictions to Lévi-Strauss' notion of intrasystemic contradictions. (On the latter, see Lévi-Strauss 1967:45–46.)

Godelier has switched from the Hegelian notion of identity of opposites to that of the unity of opposites (1972:88) and has reinterpreted the notion of internal constraints in terms of the law of correspondence between structures and limits of their functional compatibility. Like Althusser, he has made use of the notion of structural dominance, relative autonomy of superstructure, and determination in last analysis of the infrastructure. The substitution of the word "analysis" to the Althusserian term "instance" is not a casual occurrence. Godelier sees in Althusser's theory of instances a distinction between institutions rather than between functions; for Godelier this means to fall back into empiricism.

Unfortunately, Godelier's antiempiricist attitude does not go as far as elaborating a truly dialectic perspective because of his one-sided structural perspective and his shifting conceptions of the relationships between superstructure and infrastructure. As a consequence, Godelier cannot cope with the problem of history in terms of the notion of structural necessity, as he has promised. Where does structural Marxist theory leave us? With Lévi-Strauss and Althusser we are witnessing the abolishment of subjectivity as an explanatory element of social dynamics. Althusser has reintroduced a dialectic perspective but only an objective dialectic that excludes subjectvity. Godelier refines the notion of objective dialectic but he cannot offer a dialectic theory of history; having abolished contingency and subjectivity he remains imprisoned within the notion of structural necessity.

One is thus not surprised to have witnessed a strong anti-structuralist reaction by existential Marxists, who intend to recapture the notions of contingent history and conscious subjectivity as the dominant factors in the dynamics of history.

The Subjective Interpretation of History: Sartre's Critique of the Notion of Structural Causality

Godelier could have not been more explicit in denying the role of subjectivity in the dynamics of social life: "Marx brings out the existence of aspects of reality that do not relate to any consciousness and are not explicable by consciousness." In fact, the fundamental contradiction of capitalism "appears without anyone having willed its appearance. It is thus unintentional, based on the "intrinsic" limits of the capitalistic structure, on "objective characteristics of the capitalistic mode of production" (1972:80–81). We have seen that Lévi-Strauss has adopted the same position, and the same is true of Althusser, as we shortly see. This fundamental position of structuralists has been strongly attacked by Jean-Paul Sartre, in debate with Lévi-Strauss (Sartre 1966; see also Lévi-Strauss 1966, ch. 9) and with Althusser and Michel Foucault (Sartre 1966).

Jean-Paul Sartre is a complex and multiform thinker (philosopher, novelist, political writer) who has been influenced by various thinkers, principally Husserl, Jaspers, Heidegger, Freud, and later on Karl Marx. Hence, Sartre's intellectual itinerary evolved from a phenomenological-existentialist phase to a Marxist-existentialist one. I briefly touch upon the phenomenological-existentialist phase to provide a background for understanding his debate with Lévi-Strauss, Althusser, and Foucault. Sartre was attracted to Husserl's "philosophy of the concrete" since his years at the French Institute of Berlin (from 1933 on) and remained strongly committed to the rationalist spirit ever since; it is no wonder that Sartre rejected Freud's notion of the unconscious as a threat to freedom.

In *Being and Nothingness*, Sartre (1943) declared himself a phenomenologist and was very much interested in Heidegger's attempt to unite subject and object in the totality of human endeavor. The reader will remember that the dialectical integration of subject and object is at the center of Marx's programmatic notion of dialectic. At that point, however, Sartre was not seriously influenced by Marxist thought, and having made a distinction between consciousness ("for-itself") and the phenomenal world ("in-itself"), he strongly advocated consciousness' attempt to emerge at the center of the world as a genuine subject. For Sartre such a committment is inevitable if one seriously wants to make the world intelligible and human. Consciousness is radically free, the only limitation being external circumstances and other people's freedom. One can speak of authentic freedom and of dialectic development in history only on the basis of consciousness' attempt to achieve a central place in the world. Sartre's theory of history derives from his theory of consciousness and is antithetical to Hegel's theory of history, which is conservative and acritical.

At first Sartre tried to reject the label of existentialist and was forced to explain the humanistic implication of his position. His "philosophy of existence" was humanism, but not in the old sense of bourgeois conscience or categorical imperative; in fact, he was strongly reminding people of their responsibility not only to themselves but to all humanity. If we are in good faith, we must agree that every person's quest for freedom is a quest for the freedom of everybody else (Sartre 1946). Two principles appear very clearly in Sartre's lengthy 1946 essay: the sovereign role of subjectivity in social life and an attempt to reintegrate subject and object, which in Sartre's earlier work (1943) had been radically separated from each other.

How did the Sartrean synthesis of subject and object differ from the programmatic synthesis proposed by Marx (see part 1 of this volume)? In 1946 Sartre criticized Soviet and French Marxism's materialism because it was denying subjectivity by declaring it an "object" or a subject matter of science. Sartre argued that consciousness has its source only in itself and therefore is not reducible to material sources; hence only his own position could provide a rational basis to human beings. Sartre rejected Engel's conception of natural or objective dialectic because in his opinion, no dialectic is possible without human intentionality. We are here at the heart of Sartre's humanist conception of history, which puts him at odds not only with materialist or "vulgar" Marxism but also with Lévi-Strauss' notion of natural dialectics (Lévi-Strauss 1971): "History cannot be characterized by change nor by the pure and simple action of the part. It is defined by the deliberate resumption of the past by the present; only human history is possible" (Sartre 1946:206). Sartre had first anticipated this theme in *Being and Nothingness*, where he concurred with Marx that consciousness is inevitably oriented toward the transformation of the world. We acquire knowledge of the world precisely by entering into interaction with it and acting on it. Through this process the material world and consciousness are reunited and a totality in becoming is reconstituted. Hence, history is the demonstration of how the transformation of the world by human activities is taking place; the urgent task of existentialism is to reinsert consciousness into the historical process. Only in this way we can make the world "human and intelligible" and only in this way we can speak of a dialectic of history and human freedom.

This 1946 thesis was continued in the *Critique de la Raison Dialectique* (1960). There Sartre presented dialectical rationalism not just as a form of inquiry but also as a form of ongoing interaction between people and their environment. Without denying the possibility that dialectic processes are inherent within material objects, Sartre insisted that dialectic is mostly evident in the conscious and purposeful activity of people. People always strive to transcend the practico-inert and the existing state of being by moving forward to a "truer" state of being. Hence, dialectic is not a phenomenon of nature but the process through which people confront nature; people unify or "totalize" things by placing them into purposeful relationships to one another. Dialectic is a relational phenomenon in that it presupposes people's mediation between their personal situation and the one they have to confront. Purposeful human action is the mediating link between people and their situations; this is an important point to which we shall come back in the conclusion. Thus Sartre's attention is always on people's continous effort to ward "totalization" or providing a unifying frame of meaning to every aspect of the world they come into contact with.

Given his homocentric and totalizing view of people, it is not surprising that Sartre has strongly rejected the primacy attributed by Lévi-Strauss to "analytical reasoning," which dissects people and human activities into constituent parts in an effort to find their underlying determining relationships (Lévi-Strauss 1966). To be sure, Lévi-Strauss does not deny the role of dialectic but he intends only to detect its structural regularities. However, for Sartre such an attempt does not make sense because it is based on the notion that people can be broken down into structural components, whereas for Sartre people are a basic and irreducible unity. Much has been written about differences, possible complementarities, and misunderstandings between Sartre and Lévi-Strauss on the notions of history, human nature, and freedom. A large section of the first volume I have edited (Rossi 1974) deals precisely with these issues (see also Pouillon 1965) as they are conceptualized by Sartre and Lévi-Strauss in *La Critique de la Raison Dialectique* (Sartre 1960) and *The Savage Mind*, originally written in 1962 (Lévi-Strauss 1966). Here I briefly discuss Sartre's reaction to structuralism subsequent to the controversy generated by those two works.

Sartre has made clear that he is not for a total rejection of structuralism as long as it "remains aware of its methodological limitations" (Sartre 1966:111). He accepts the usefulness of the synchronic approach in the study of language conceived as "a network of oppositions" and "relations of difference" (*ibid.*) However, he considers the synchronic approach only one moment of analysis, the moment of structure and the "inert." Sartre argues that structure is worked out by people, by "praxis as a totalizing process" (*ibid.*). The understanding of praxis as a totalizing process goes beyond the scope of structural analysis; the realm of "dialectical comprehension" alone can account for historical developments. For Sartre the moment of praxis is essential because language is not a static, inert system but rather "exists only as spoken, that is in action" (*ibid.*).

Sartre contends that to explain the system in action or evolution, one must consider the forces which are "external" to the system. This position is radically different from that of structuralists. To study forms external to the system means to study history, but for Sartre history is not a matter of uncertainty or contingency. Sartre complains that for structuralists (and here he refers mostly to Lévi-Strauss) "history appears as a purely passive phenomenon," as a contingency, because for structuralists either structure contains in itself the seed of its own destruction "within it from the beginning" or it is destroyed by "an external event" (1966:111), that is, by a contingent event.

It seems that Sartre's critique applies also to Godelier, who intends to explore the reproduction or disappearance of the capitalist society in terms of properties intrinsic to its structure. We have seen that Godelier intends to show the necessity of history by relating particular events to the internal contradictions of the system—both intrastructural and interstructural contradictions. The criticism raised by Sartre against Jean Pouillon seems applicable to Godelier's approach also. Sartre argues that Pouillon derives a structural model defining "a certain number of possibilities" from the differential distribution of political and religious functions in different societies (1966:111–112). What Sartre finds wanting in this approach is an explanation of why not all the possibilities are realized. Structuralists explain specific realizations or disintegrations of structure by invoking the interference of accidental or contingent events. Sartre reacts against this kind of reasoning with a protest: to structuralists and structural Marxists, "it is never men themselves who modify it [structure] because it is never they who make it: they are on the contrary, made by it" (p. 112). Far from contesting the existence of structure and "the necessity of analyzing its mechanism," Sartre argues that "structure is only a moment of the practico-inert," a "moment of history" (*ibid.*). Surely "man is in some way developed by the development of structure; . . . man receives structures, and in a sense it can be said that they make him" (*ibid.*). However, this is only one side of the story; structure is a moment of passivity and passivity cannot perpetuate itself. As it is true that people receive structure, it is equally true that they go beyond structure. People receive structures because they are "engaged in history," but their involvement in history is such that they "cannot fail to destroy [structures], to constitute anew that which in turn will condition [them]" (*ibid.*).

Not only do Sartre and the structuralists differ on the issue of the priority of structure over history, but also on the very notion of history. Sartre argues that for structuralists history is order, history is reducible "to the development of structure," to an internal process; history is a succession of strata, and each stratum "conditions" other strata as well as certain types of thought (1966:111). At this point Sartre extends his criticism to Michel Foucault; Foucault does not explain how each thought is constructed out of historical conditions, how people make a transition from one type of thought to another; to Sartre this means that history is denied and "movement" is replaced "by a succession of immobilities" (*ibid.*). What is missing from the structural perspective is the intervention of praxis or history. For Sartre history is not order but disorder, "a rational disorder. At the very moment when it maintains order, i.e., structure, history is already on the way to undoing it" (p. 112). The central motor of historical dialectic is the "class struggle" which creates structures without ceasing "simultaneously to overcome them" (*ibid.*); class struggle is for Sartre

inseparable from the notion of praxis. On this point, humanist Marxism radically differs from structural and Althusserian Marxism. Sartre
does not deny that "superstructures constitute regions of relative autonomy," but he insists that we must place at the primary level "the
material elements of men's lives" and determine "the relations of
production and praxis" (p. 111).

Althusser has proposed an alternative explanation of the class
struggle. In his well-known reply to John Lewis, Althusser stressed
the Marxist-Leninist notion that class struggle is the motor of history
(Althusser 1976:49). The class struggle is rooted in the material basis,
in the unity of relations of production and productive forces: "History
is an immense natural-human system in movement" (p. 50). But Althusser cautions that "history is a process without subject" (p. 51).
Already in 1969 Althusser had expressed this view. He had argued
then that in 1844 Marx held that history was the process of the alienation of the subject, whereas in *The Capital* he proposed the notion
that history was a process without a subject, a thesis clearly present
in Hegel (Althusser 1971:121ff). Althusser concedes that society is not
made of abstract individuals but of "historically and socially determined individuals" (1976:53). He concedes also that social individuals
act in history as subjects, "as agents of the different social practices
of the historical process of production and reproduction." But "they
work in and through the determinations of the forms of historical
existence of the social relations of production and reproduction." Social relations comprise "ideological relations which in order to function impose the subject-form on each agent-individual" (p. 95).

This Althusserian view does not make individuals the subject of
history. For Althusser the notion of an origin or cause as a subject
"existing in the form of the unity of an internality and . . . thus ac-
countable, thus capable of accounting for the whole of the phenomena of history" is a notion derived from idealist and Feuerbachian
philosophy. Althusser maintains that a Marxist should not think in
terms of origin, cause, essence, but in terms of relations, contradictions, determinations in the last instance (1976:96). By the same token
Althusser criticizes Sartre for making of "concrete individuals" the
"transcendental, constitutive" subjects of history. Althusser contends
that Sartre brings Kantian categories down to the level of "a vulgar

philosophical psychosociology" which is untenable and has nothing to do with the true Marxism (p. 98).

Althusser backs up his own position with quotes taken from *The Eighteenth Brumaire of Louis Bonaparte:* "Men make their own history, but they do not make it out of freely chosen elements, under circumstances chosen by themselves, but under circumstances directly encountered, given by and transmitted from the past. . . . I show something quite different, namely how the class struggle in France created the circumstances and the relations which allowed a person (a subject) so mediocre and grotesque to play the role of a hero."[2] Althusser's position is that we shouldn't speak of a subject but of a motor of history—and "the class struggle is the motor of history" (1976:99, 48). The class struggle is adequately explained by the material basis and the social relations of the mode of production without the need for "an absolute point of departure." What determines social relations is not a "chimerical human essence," not "a relation between persons nor an intersubjective or psychological or anthropological relation, but a relation between groups of men concerning the relation between these groups of men and things, the means of production." What determines social relations is not only relations among people but also relations among things (p. 202).

Althusser finds the conditions for an organization of the class struggle in the superstructure of the capitalistic society; "the legal, political ideological relations can contribute to its [class struggle] and consciousness" (1976:204). By referring to consciousness does Althusser mean to recognize the role of subjectivity and freedom (the "practico-inert" in Sartre's terminology) in the dynamics of social life? He does not totally reject these notions, but he argues that if we start with people, we end up believing in the omnipotence of liberty or of creative labor; this would mean falling into the traps of bourgeois ideology, which masks reality by giving it the illusion of freedom (p. 205). In reality, people are determined both by the infrastructure and superstructure: "All these relations [ideological relations] determine and brand men in their flesh and blood, just as the production relation does" (p. 204).

[2]Althusser also criticizes Sartre on pages 43, 45, and 60. He contends that Sartre hinders rather than helps Marxist thought.

Sartre is not as radically negative toward Althusser's position as Althusser is toward Sartre's position. For instance, Sartre agrees with Althusser's rejection of "historicism," the notion that "man is as history requires him. . . . [H]istory must designate to man the work it requires of him." However, Sartre finds equally unacceptable the opposite extreme proposed by Althusser, that "it is not history which requires man, but the whole structure in which he is situated which conditions him. History is lost in structures" and "man makes history without knowing it" (Sartre 1971:114). The basic fault of structuralists (and here Sartre refers to Lévi-Strauss, Foucault, Lacan, and Althusser) is that they "don't want a dépassement or at any rate a dépassement made by man" (*ibid.*). With structuralism "we return to positivism. But it is no longer a positivism of facts but a positivism of signs. There are totalities, structural wholes which constitute themselves through man; and man's unique function is to decipher them" (*ibid.*).

What is the alternative proposed by Sartre against the total subordination of people to structure? "What is essential is not that man is made, but that he makes that which made him. That which made man are structures, the meaningful whole studied by the humanities (and the analytical method of science). What man makes is history itself, the real overcoming of these structures in totalizing praxis" (1971:115). Sartre defines his own method as a dialectical method and finds it antithetical to the analytical method followed by the practitioners of science as well as structuralists. The term "dialectic" is not as self-clarifying or uncontroversial as is the term "history." In fact, even Althusser claims to follow a dialectical perspective, but, of course, his notion of dialectic is different from that of Sartre. The Sartrean dialectic is based on the notion of totalizing praxis, which gives a primary place to the activity of people as a conscious subjectivity: "If one admits, as I do, that historical movement is a perpetual totalization, that each man is in all moments totalizing and totalized, then philosophy represents the effort of totalized men to regain the meaning of totalization" (*ibid.*). It is not the totalized aspect of people, but people as the totalizers and shapers of the totalizing process which is at the center of Sartre's interest: "Philosophy . . . is the questioning of man, that is, of the totalizing historical subject" (*ibid.*). Sartre accuses structural Marxists of having failed to incorporate the role of praxis into their analysis, with the result that they have impoverished Marxism.

Does Althusser really neglect the moment of praxis and the role of concrete individuals? He counterargues that only Marx (the "Althusserian" Marx, of course) is a true humanist. But in Marx we meet people at the end and not at the beginning of analysis; we meet, however, real people rather than the abstract people of bourgeois ideology (Althusser 1976:52–53). People are "the bearers of a function in the production process, determined by the production relation." The capitalistic mode of production reduces people to an exploitative relation, to antagonistic class relations. Capitalism submits individuals to a "terrible practical reduction" as it treats them "only as bearers of economic functions and nothing else"; capitalism reduces people "to nothing, but appendices of the machine" (pp. 202, 203).

We can see, then, that "if Marx does not start out from man . . . it is in order finally to reach living men; if he makes a detour *via* these relations of which living men are the bearers, it is in order finally to be able to grasp the laws which govern both their lives and their concrete struggle" (Althusser 1976:205–206). Marx's intent was "to aid the working class to understand the mechanisms of capitalistic society . . . in order to reinforce and orient its struggle" (p. 206).

This conception is not contrary to Sartre's notion that Marx has to regain control of history, since the purpose of helping "the working class to make revolution and . . . to suppress the class struggle and classes" is to aid people in regaining control over their own destiny (Althusser 1976:206). In this sense Sartre is not quite correct when he states that Althusser "renounces the understanding of transition. But we are always in transition, always in the act of producing to separate, and separating to produce. Man is perpetually dephased in relation to structures which condition him because he is something other then what makes him what he is. Therefore I do not understand how one can stop at structures" (Sartre 1971:115). Actually, Althusser does not stop at structure but he begins from the analysis of structure to make people understand its functioning and therefore overturn it. But the transition to new structures derives, first and most of all, from laws immanent to structure, independent of people's conscious effort. This is the very same position as Godelier's.

In reality, neither Sartre or Althusser can afford to ignore either structure or subjectivity; they differ only in which should be considered the principal force of historical dialectic. Whereas Althusser (and Godelier) proposes an objective dialectic, Sartre proposes a human-centered dialectic.

In my view, both Sartre's and Althusser's positions are objectionable in that they assume an opposition between object and subject, structure and subjectivity. Such a dichotomy is based on the dualistic perspective typical of positivist thinking. Because of this dichotomy neither Althusser nor Sartre can propose a truly dialectic view of the interaction of the objective and subjective forces of social dynamics. On the contrary, they hold on to a monistic theory, since they choose one of these two social forces as the adequate motor of the dynamics of history. For the same reason Piaget is not a true dialectician either; although he attributes a priority to genesis over structure, he explains genesis in terms of transformations of structures without recognizing any role of the conscious subject.

The Production of the Subject by Structure in Poststructural Semiotics

The Production of the Subject by the Signifying Chain: Lacan's Perspective

At this point in our theoretical journey we must raise the question of whether we can overcome the impasse between the objective and subjective interpretation of Marxist dialectic and integrate key elements of both perspectives. My concern is not with determining the real Marxist thought but rather with integrating all the valid insights Marx has suggested so as to formulate an adequate sociological approach. Sartre and Althusser take for granted the priority of human subject and structure, respectively, in the dynamics of history. We need a theory which overcomes this dichotomous thinking and accounts for the origin and combined influence of both of these two forces in society.

At this point our attention must turn to Lacan for reasons indicated by Althusser himself. Althusser has sought in Lacan support for his notion that the center of history is structure and not the human subject. In his essay "Freud and Lacan," Althusser argues that Freud discovered that the "real subject . . . has not the form of an ego, centered on the 'ego,' on 'consciousness' or on 'existence' . . . that the human subject is de-centered, constituted by a structure which has no 'center' either, except in the imaginary misrecognition of the 'ego,' i.e., in the ideological formation in which it 'recognizes' itself" (Althusser 1971:218–219).

What interests me in Althusser's statement is not the decentered and objectivized notion of subject but the notion that the subject is constituted by structure. This notion seems useful to overcome the structure vs. subjectivity conflict and to establish the needed dialectical linkage between them. Besides, Jacques Lacan's thinking has influenced the works of poststructural semioticians who have attempted to work out an integration of Marxist and Freudian thought from a linguistic perspective. This shows how important it is to briefly examine those key ideas of Lacan which have a direct bearing on the relationships between structure and subjectivity.

Jacques Lacan offers an unorthodox interpretation of Freud—it was rejected by the International Psychoanalytical Association—that stands in opposition to the so-called neo-Freudianism. Yet Lacan's intention has been to work out the scientific development of psychoanalysis, a development based on Freud's "genuine" thinking. Lacan's undertaking is similar to the one Althusser wants to carry out in regard to Marx's thought. The aim of the psychoanalyst is unquestionably to study the unconscious, but the unconscious can be studied only in the patient's verbal report of dreams. Lacan finds that the Freudian terminology and categorizations are directly translatable into those of the linguistics of Ferdinand de Saussure, whose lectures were published in 1916, sixteen years after *The Interpretation of Dreams*. Lacan contends that the verbalizations of unconscious dreams have a structure similar to that of language: "The psychoanalytic experience discovers in the unconscious, the whole structure of language" (Lacan 1970:103).

Lacan's notion of structure is very similar to that of Lévi-Strauss;

this is no surprise since they both draw heavily from Saussurean linguistics. Lacan starts from Saussure's distinction between signifier and signified and explains the function of the former "in the birth of the signified" (1970:105). He goes beyond the notion of a mere "bi-univocal correspondence between the word and the thing" and "the illusion that the signifier answers to the function of representing the signified" (p. 106). For Lacan the "signifier intrudes into the signified" (p. 108) and "by its very nature, always anticipates on meaning by unfolding its dimension before it" (p. 110). The signifier cuts out and articulates the signified in relation to the system of other signifiers; the signifiers combine "according to the laws of a closed order" so that they form a "signifying chain" (p. 110).

Lacan does not hold a static conception of meaning (meaning presupposed as given in the structure of the sentence): "It is in the chain of the signifier that the meaning 'insists' but none of its elements 'consists' in the meaning of which it is at the moment capable. We are forced, then, to accept the notion of an incessant sliding of the signified under the signifier" (1970:111). However, how do we explain that notwithstanding this continuous sliding of the signified, each signifier has a definite meaning?

Lacan reverses the traditional (ideological) way of thinking; the signifier operates not because there exists a subject who knows or because the word "disguises" the thought of the "indefinable" subject: "The structure of the signifying chain makes evident the possibility . . . to use it in order to say something quite other than what it says. . . . The function of the word . . . is no less than the functioning of indicating the place of the subject in the search for the truth" (1970:113). This means that the signifying chain cannot produce meaning without constructing the subject. The elements of the signifying chain achieve their own identity through relationships of differences among each other; but it is through the subject that they can represent themselves as different from the rest of the signifying system. Without the subject the signifier cannot have directionality and, therefore, identity.

The same point can be expressed as follows: language cannot be used without determining the positioning of the speaking subject, that is, without constituting an "I" who makes the predication. It is precisely at this point that psychoanalysis comes in and shows that the "subject is constituted in the positions that enable predication precisely through the limitation of the productivity of the signifying chain; . . . a subject is produced in this movement of productivity. Man is constructed in the symbol, and is not pre-given or transcendent" (Coward and Ellis 1977:23).

The theory of the construction of the subject fills a gap in Sartrean thought in which subjectivity is assumed as constituted; it also fills a gap in Althusser, for whom the subjectivity is secondary and dispensible in respect to the explanatory power of structure. For this reason Lacan's theory has the potential of integrating the notions of subject, language, and ideology; we know that in Marx there is no theory of language; it is collapsed into ideology.

To determine whether Lacan's perspective permits one to accomplish a synthesis of the structural and subjective views of dialectics, we must clarify Lacan's notion of subjectivity. Basic to the Freudian theory of the development of the ego is the concept of reality rejection. In the early stages of development the child substitutes for the reality of the world an image of a controlled and obedient self; this narcissistic attitude underlies all his or her relationships with others. Lacan finds a parallel mechanism in the linguistic process; language imposes forms on a variety of experiences and perceptions to enable us to control the environment. This process is analogous to the denial of reality governed by the pleasure principle; this denial gives origin to a forgotten language, the unconscious, and to an illusion of objectivity and stability; the purpose of psychoanalytic intervention is to recover the original (archaic) language.

Lacan shows with a detailed analysis how the structural activity of the signifying chain is paralleled and completed by the structural activity of the unconscious. The signifying function in language takes place through a process of metonymy and metaphor (Lacan 1970:114). Similarly, the dreams function through a distortion, a notion similar to that of the continuous sliding of meaning within the chain of signifiers. The unconscious process functions through the process of condensation, which is equivalent to metaphor, and through displacement, which is equivalent to metonymy (p. 119). Primary processes are based on the mechanisms of displacement and condensation and, therefore, on a free flow of energy. The secondary processes, however, are characterized by control or regulatory functions, which give rise to the construction of the ego.

That the construction of the ego takes place through a process similar to the construction of language is shown as follows: the ego is constructed through three processes of separation; first from its mother, then from its own ideal image, and finally from the system of symbols. Through this process both the subject and the unconscious are created, the unconscious being what refuses to enter into consciousness. To represent itself the subject must experience another separation; it must be at the axis of differentiation between the signifier and the signified. The metaphor accomplishes the substitution of the signifier for the signified (and in this arises poetic or creative language). The passage from the signifier to the signified gives origin to meaning; meaning is created when the signifier is barred from entering into consciousness. This is the very place where the subject is posited (Lacan 1970:124).

The subject, then, is determined by the signifier: "Its cause is the signifier without which there would be no subject in reality, and it wouldn't know how to represent anything except another signifier" (Lacan 1966:835); "the register of the signifier institutes itself, in that a signifier is what represents the subject to another signifier (p. 840). The subject is not ontological, a completely self-defined entity with a positive psychological identity. On the contrary, it is the material and effect of language (p. 689).

The notion of subject implies the notion of object—"the other"—as a precondition for self-identification and as a precondition to the signifying activity of the signifier: the "other" is the place of the signifier and the language of the unconscious (Lacan 1970:133). "The signifier producing itself in the place of the other, which is not yet marked out, makes the subject surge up there" (Lacan 1973). The subject, then, is the nodal point without which no signifier, no predication or object, is possible. Subject is an "objectivized" entity in the relational and differential sense of the term. We are far from the

Sartrean humanist notion of the subject; as a matter of fact, such a notion is totally rejected (Lacan 1970:137).

Lacan has the merit of having shown that the productivity of the subject is inherent in the social process of communication. The Lacanian subject, however, is not a unified subject. For this reason one must qualify the judgment that Lacan has resolved the ambiguity of traditional Marxism on the conception of the subject as both the maker and the product of history. The same is true of the judgment that Lacan has overcome the positivist subject-object dichotomy (Coward and Ellis 1977:8). What we find in Lacan is a distinction between the object and an objectivized and relational subject.

Lacan also has been credited with developing a theory of the articulation between language and ideology (Coward and Ellis 1977:9) and of the role of ideology in the functioning of the unconscious (Althusser 1971:190). Althusser also claims that Lacan has raised the important issue of the relationship between the structure of language, kinship structure, and the ideological formation in which the functions of kinship structures are lived (p. 217). Yet all these notions are based on the notion of a decentered subject or a structure without center, the structure consisting of an infinitely creative chain of signifiers whose meaning is continuously sliding.

The positive aspect of Lacan's contribution is his proposal of a dynamic conception of structure, a conception which in a sense parallels and extends Althusser's notion of an objective dialectic, a dialectic generated by the contradictions inherent in the structure of capitalist society. But the notion of the infinite productivity of the signifying chain does not permit us to recapture the notion of conscious subjectivity and its dialectic relation to structure, because we are left with a decentered structure activated by unconscious mechanisms.

We now turn our attention to those semioticians who have used Lacanian ideas to offer correctives to the static and closed conception of structure proposed by Saussure and Lévi-Strauss. The contribution made by poststructural semioticians deserves special attention because these thinkers have tried to integrate the Marxian and Freudian perspectives by using Lacan's notion of the construction of the subject in the signifying chain.

The Infinite Productivity of Structure and Subjectivity: The Contribution of Roland Barthes and Jacques Derrida

By "poststructural semiotics" I mean those thinkers closely associated with the periodical *Tel Quel* who have formulated their semiotic approach in reaction to the first phase of semiotics—the structural approach of Saussure and Lévi-Strauss. Their perspective is, therefore, first of all a linguistic one, but one heavily influenced by Lacan's reinterpretation of Saussure's approach; the Lacanian notion that the structure cannot function without constructing the speaking subject is a fundamental notion of poststructural semioticians.

These semioticians argue that the notion of the productivity of structure is already contained, at least implicitly, within the synchronic study of language proposed by Saussure. According to Saussure, the meaning is produced by the systems of differences among linguistic signs rather than by the conscious intentionality of the subject; the subject is subordinated to the structure and finds its experiences set up by the structure.

The shortcomings of Saussure's approach are to be found in his basic assumptions; Saussure assumed linguistic signs as given and focused on the systematic relationships of differences between the given signs. Furthermore, Saussure assumed as given the existence of "real referents" of signs, the arbitrary relations between signifier and signified and the existence of some sort of natural bond between mind and referent (Coward and Ellis 1977:22). Not only the structure but also the subject is assumed as given in the Saussurian perspective.

In opposition to these presuppositions, poststructural semioticians argue that in reality the signifier articulates the signified and "cuts out" meaning by its very relationships to other signifiers. Stated differently, the signifier is not just a manifestation and an expression of the signified but its producer. This conception implies a total rejection of the mechanistic conception of the activity of structure proposed by Saussure, who has separated the product from the process of productivity. Poststructural semioticians argue that a mechanistic conception of structure is antithetical to the perspective of dialectical materialism, whereas their own semiotic approach extends the Marxist approach and complements it by proposing a "dialectic view" of linguistic "productivity," which is missing in Marx.

Roland Barthes is an important semiotician who has made a clear-cut transition from a structural to a poststructural semiotic view.

The Multidimensional Productivity of Structure in Roland Barthes.

The structural phase of Barthes' semiotics, which consisted of an extension and systematization of Saussure's and Lévi-Strauss' semiotice, has been discussed in part 2 of this volume. Here we discuss the reasons for his transition to a poststructural orientation, which is evident in *S/Z*, a work published in 1974. This is how Barthes explains the change of perspective in relationship to his early structural orientation (see especially in 1966 and 1966a):

> In the former text I appealed to a general structure from which would be derived analysis of contingent texts. In *S/Z* I revised this perspective: there I refused the idea of a model transcendent to several texts . . . in order to postulate that each text is in some sort its own model, that each text . . . must be treated in its difference, 'difference' being understood here precisely in a Nietzchean or a Derridean sense. . . . The text is ceaselessly and through and through traversed by codes, but it is not the accomplishment of a code . . . it is not the parole of a narrative language. (1971:44)

Barthes' passage contains an explicit challenge not only to the Saussurean perspective but also to the Chomskian notion of linguistic competence and the related notions of universal structure and transformational rules as well as the key role accorded to the intuition of the native speaker. Barthes considers all these notions ideological ones because they are based on a static and closed conception of structure which excludes creativity, especially the creativity of new rules.

A few quotes from Barthes will clarify the precise meaning of his position: Some semioticians "context the hierarchy of denotated and connotated; language, they say, the raw material of denotation, with its dictionary and its syntax, is a system like any other; there is no reason to make this system the priviledged one. . . . To reduce language to the sentence and the lexical and syntactical components . . . is to return to the closure of Western discourse" (1974:7). To

Barthes it is important that we respect "the plurality of text" and stop "structuring" it. There is "no construction of the text: everything signifies ceaselessly and several times, but without being delegated to a great final ensemble, to an ultimate structure" (p. 12).

The one text is not an (inductive) access to a model, but entrance into a network with a thousand entrances; to take this entrance is to aim, ultimately, not at a legal structure of norms and departures, a narrative or poetic law, but a perspective (of fragments, of voices from other texts, other codes) whose vanishing point is nonetheless ceaselessly pushed back, mysteriously opened; each (single) text is the very theory (not the mere example) of this vanishing of this difference which indefinitely returns, insubmissive. (ibid.)

Barthes substantiates his conception of literary text through an analysis of the poetic language. S/Z is an analysis of Sarrasine, a short story by Balzac. Barthes divides the text into 561 lexias (reading units) and analyzes them in terms of the hermeneutic, semic, symbolic, proiaretic, and cultural codes. The text is analyzed according to the development of a plot (proiaretic code), problem (hermeneutic code), character (semic code), the way it refers to conventional and ideological knowledge (cultural code), and the changing positionalities it creates (symbolic code). The ceaseless and simultaneous employment of these codes even in the same lexias has the effect of showing a text liberated from cultural traditions, literary context, and so on. The text turns out not to be a "realist" text.

"Realists" assume that the signifier preexists and has a one-to-one relationship to the signified; they assume also that language is merely an expression or communication (as opposed to production) of concepts. A realist text stands for (and is identical with) the world (a notion called *mimicry*). Accordingly, the realist conception of narrative is based on an instrumentalist view of language; the word is supposed to speak of reality, to be the voice of reality rather than the voice of the author. The narrative, then, is supposed to reveal the "true" world, a world of true essences which are immediately evident in what spontaneously appears to us. Moreover, this true world of essence is assumed to be without contradictions.

Such a realist view of the world presupposes a parallel ideological conception of the subject. There cannot be a precise intelligibility of the text without presupposing the existence of a subject at a precise position. Stated differently, the identification of a signifier with a signified is possible only if the reader takes a precise position in relationship to the text. Moreover, as the world is presumed homogeneous and without contradictions, so the subject is presumed to be homogeneous, not submitted to the flux of events.

It is not so, says Barthes, who pretends to refute the realist (and traditional) view by reading a presumably realist text with the help of the five codes. The symbolic code especially is most telling (a notion he has borrowed from Lacan). The text is not developed around "normal" sexual positionalities; on the contrary, they are ideological positions constructed around the masculine-feminine antithesis based on the presence or absence of the phallus (signifier). *Sarrasine*'s personages are not characterized or defined on the basis of the presence of given characteristics, but on the basis of active/passive and power/subservience dimensions. Sex positionality is not established positively (having a phallus or not), in terms of fullness, identity, and exchange, but negatively (being castrated or not), in terms of lack, difference, refusal. All the normal positions and equivalencies of bourgeois ideology are disturbed and new positions are continuously produced.

Using an interrupted and intersecting application of the five codes, Barthes concludes that the text is an interweaving of voices and codes (1974:160); it is like a stereophony and polytonality (pp. 28–29); the meaning of the text appears full of multivalences and uncertainties (pp. 76ff, 78ff, 163) as well as ambiguities (pp. 80, 88). The notion of subject, which parallels this notion of text, is of particular importance to us. As there is no identification or interchangeability of signifier and signified, so there are no logically fixed and clearly identifiable roles. The fixed scheme of individualities appears to be a mere presupposition of a consumeristic and bourgeois society, which does not correspond to a close reading of the text: "the text, in its mass, is comparable to a sky, at once flat and smooth, deep, without edges and without landmarks. . . . [T]he commentator traces through the text certain zones of reading, in order to observe therein the migration of meanings, the outcropping of codes, the passage of citations" (p. 14).

The ultimate thrust of Barthes' position is not to propose a relativistic notion of meaning, but the notion of the plurality of the text. Plurality of text means more than multiplicity of meanings; it means simultaneity and interdependence of meanings. Barthes' position can be summed up by saying that he is not interested in structure but in structuring, he is not interested in a finalized organization of meaning but in the fullest productivity of various tonalities of meaning and in continuous redefinitions of the subject.

Jonathan Culler has rightly argued that Barthes' position is an ambiguous one since his antistructuralist argumentation is based on the very same notion of code he wants to replace. Barthes involves the reader with the text and produces a variety of meanings with the usage of many codes; but the production of a variety of meanings and structures is based on the structural procedures he wants to dismantle (Culler 1975:243). This criticism is well taken in relationship to the question of the continuity or discontinuity between structural and poststructural semiotics. What is important, however, for the aim of this volume is the notion that the text is not a static but a dynamic structure whose meaning is made possible by the production of the subject, a subject whose positionality is continuously redefined. Structure and subjectivity are two inseparable analytical principles whose structure and functioning depend on their dialectical interrelationship. Such a dialectical view, which can be at least indirectly inferred from Barthes' position, seems to provide valid elements for the integration of the subjective and objective views of social life in a dialectic perspective. However, dialectic concepts are not useful if they remain merely abstract tools; they must be rooted in an adequate conceptualization of the psychodynamics of the individual and social structure. Pioneer efforts in this direction have been made by Jacques Lacan and Julia Kristeva.

Language as a Structuring Activity in Jacques Derrida. Jacques Derrida is an important figure who has elaborated not only the theory of the primacy of the signifier but also of its materiality in relation to the idealist notion that the signified is independent of and interior to the signifier, a notion implicit in Saussure's approach.

Derrida has dismantled the ideological notion of the existence of fixed events and meaning. According to Derrida this notion is based on the "metaphysics of presence," that is, on the illusion that there exist an objective real world and objective people, and that people "come face to face" with the world without mediation. This is a distorting humanist view and one which upholds a necessary connection between signifier and signified (Derrida 1967a:41–44, 409–11). The analysis of writing shows the nonexistence of a transcendental ultimate meaning; writing is not a transparent window or a substitute for the real world, but rather a system with its own properties, a signifier in search of a signified. Language works through the principle of *difference* (differentiation). Difference is an extension of the Saussurean notion of differential contrasts, and also includes the notion of *deferment* and *postponement.* The very notion of writing refers one back to the spoken word and produces a separation from it. In turn, speech refers to a prior act of signification. We can, then, see that there is an infinite regression to a previous moment of signification, that meaning is something which has always happened. There exists no origin of meaning, or an absolute presence of meaning or an ultimate and unitary meaning. Writing and language itself are not specific and closed structures but rather structuring processes: "The absence of an ultimate meaning opens up an unbounded space for the play of signification" (Derrida 1967a:411).

"Writing" is not a reproduction of reality but a production of a new reality and new meanings. "We are from the beginning caught up in the play of the unmotivated developing of the symbol. . . . The non-motivated character of the *traces* [3] must be understood not as a state but as an operation, not as a given structure but as an active movement, a process of demotivating" (Derrida 1967:94). This seems to echo the Nietzchean conception of pure becoming, an affirmation of a world without origin or truth and the notion of active interpretation as a "creative function and joyful process without looking backwards" (1967a:427).

What, then, is language? Language is the activity of differing or structuring rather than a structure. Jacques Derrida, here quoted by

---

[3] "Trace" or "gramme" is a key word which refers to the notion that there is no pure or transparent sign. Symbol refers to something which has already happened and meaning is always a "trace" of something which has already occurred.

Barthes, has explained that the notion of structure is based on an intuitive (and arbitrary and ideological—see Kristeva's *Semiotikè* 1969:30–31) assumed center or origin of the text. Only by assuming a definite meaning or end or effect of the text can one establish what is the structure or arrangement of the text intended to produce the end. As Derrida says, the metaphysics or structuralism is based on the "concept of centered structure," which permits only a limited number of combinations and therefore gives a closure to the text (1967:41, 410). Derrida calls the attention to the notion of *structuralité de la structure* (structured structure) (p. 411), a notion he wants to replace with that of *système décéntré* (decentered system). The center of the system is continuously displaced during the analysis, so that the analysis must encompass a critic of the center itself.

There exists another important notion in Derrida, that the signified and the signifier are two aspects of one single production (Derrida 1972:27). Derrida stresses the importance of analyzing the actual production of signification in speech usage, the temporal construction or spacing through which language generation and transformation take place.

The ongoing productivity of meaning needs to be analyzed from a materialistic and Lacanian point of view. This is the task Julia Kristeva has set out for herself to accomplish. Whereas in Lacan and Derrida the subject is trapped within a decentered structure, Kristeva makes an attempt to recapture the importance of the speaking subject.

The Positioning of the Subject in the Signifying Practice: The Negative Dialectic of Julia Kristeva

Julia Kristeva has clearly explained her own semiological perspective in a review essay prepared for a survey of semiotics (Kristeva 1975:47–55). For her, the semiotics of Saussure, Peirce, the Prague school, and structuralism are the first phase of semiology, a phase which has revealed "the immanent causality and/or the presence of a social systematic constraint in each social functioning" (p. 5). This phase of semiotics represented a healthy reaction against both idealism and "mechanistic sociologism." Idealism neglects the historical socializing of the role of the symbolic and, therefore, the issue of the external determination and internal adjustment of meaning (p. 3). Mechanistic sociologism suppresses the specificity of symbolism and its logic and it reduces ideology (superstructures) to external determinants.

Kristeva considers Chomsky's generative grammar a synthetic approach that replaces the analytical approach. Whereas the followers of the analytical approach break down the sentences into components, Chomsky connects the components into a syntagmatic structure and provides the transformational rules by which a variety of structures can be produced out of a basic structure. Chomsky's view of language is based on the intuition of the speaker as the criterion for finding the grammaticality of an indefinite number of sentences. This means that Chomsky's notion of language is based on "the Cartesian conception of language as an act carried out by a subject" (Kristeva 1975:5). Seen from this perspective, language is a process of production centered on the consciousness of the speaking subject. However, recent linguists (from Jakobson to Kuroda) have shown that the speaking subject might turn out to be the transcendental ego of Husserl. Kristeva is firm in stating that the notion of transcendental ego is far from being essential to the semiotic perspective; moreover, if based on the perspective of generative grammar such a notion will only produce "a reduction . . . of signifying practices to their systematic aspect" (ibid.).

Kristeva is clearly influenced by the Husserlian perspective, of which she proposes a materialist rereading with the help of Lacan's notion of language. In his search for the ultimate presuppositions of Kant, Husserl was led to focus on the intentionality of consciousness that takes place in the act of judgment. The judging consciousness of the transcendental ego is produced in the act of predication; the subject is the subject of predication and judgment. Kristeva's attention is drawn to this object-producing subjectivity, which is given in the act of predication (thetic process).

In this context we should remember that the French linguist Emile Benveniste had already called attention to enunciation as constituent of subjectivity; by its very definition subjectivity implies the notion of otherness and of relations between speakers. The subject is constituted in language where one can refer to oneself as "I." By positing an "I" automatically one posits "another" who is external to oneself and to whom one refers as "you." Benveniste conceives of these functions as the deep structure of interspeakers' relations (1971). This kind of reasoning makes social transaction and interpersonal communication an essential element in understanding the structure and dynamics of language.

Yet Benveniste is directly or indirectly attached to the notion of transcendental subject. Kristeva believes she can avoid this hurdle by adopting a Lacanian perspective. What we need is a "theory of the speaking subject as a divided subject (conscious/unconscious) and go on to attempt to specify the types of operation characteristics of the two sides of this split; thereby exposing them to those forces extraneous to the logic of the systematics." We have to expose them to the biophysiological process implied in the signifying process, which are related to both Freudian drives and to the social constraints imposed by family structures and modes of production (Kristeva 1975:6). The attempt to integrate the Marxist and the psychoanalytic perspectives is the distinguishing feature of the new semiotics, which Kristeva calls semanalysis.

We remember that Lacan has established the existence of parallel processes in the functioning of language and in the development of personality. Kristeva utilizes Lacan's interpretation of the primary processes of displacement, condensation, metonymy and metaphor, projection, expulsion, and so on to explain the production of the subject and meaning in language.

We do not need to enter into a detailed discussion of Kristeva's theory of signification, as a brief examination of her notions of structure and subjectivity provide sufficient material to conclude our discussion of poststructural semiotics. The materialist theory of signification is a dialectic process which originates from the unconscious and simultaneously produces in the judgment (sentence) meaning and the holder of meaning, i.e., the subject. Such a process is "also a dialectic of the bond between the subject and its heterogeneous outside" (1971:101). The notion of heterogeneity is related to the Freudian notion of drives, which implies a duality (life and death) and also a contradiction of negativity. In this context one should refer to the "introjection and expulsion" mechanisms of the ego, which are related to linguistic processes of affirmation and negation. Language operates a split within the signifying body between the symbolic order and the work of libido (the latter being heterogeneous in respect to the former). This duality introduces a split and a continuous shift in the speaking subject. Being under the constraint of signifying systems and social norms (socio-family), on the one hand, and of biological constraints, on the other hand, the speaking subject is pushed by the latter to renovate and break the normative constraints; this breaking activity provides the subject with pleasure (Kristeva 1975:7–8). Drives produce continuous changes and dissolution of structural arrangements and new rearrangements; these movements and rearrangements produce the positioning of the predicating subject. The heterogeneity of signifying practices is best perceived in drug usage, in the arts oriented toward the reorganization of psychic drives, and in poetic language, especially in the works of Sollers, Lautréamont, and Joyce.

What is the nature of the predicating subject produced by heterogeneous contradictions and negative dialectics? Kristeva presents a dynamic notion of subject. The subject "accentuates not identification but process, not desire but projection, not the signifier but the heterogeneous, not structure but struggle" (1974:161). This subject, however, is far from being a unified, psychological subject but is "a subject which cannot be grasped since it is a transforming reality" (ibid.). The reality of the subject consists of the activity of signifying what is negatively understood: "The subject never is, but is only the process of signification and exhibits itself only as a signifying practice, namely when it is absent from the position where the historical-social-signifying activity unfolds itself" (p. 188). The signifying practice is not a practice of a subject but an objective activity whose discontinuity is conceptualized as a positioning of the subject.

We have here again a negative and objectivized notion of subjectivity that makes of the unconscious the motor of history. In fact, the dialectic heterogeneous process is dominated by the death drive and its self-reproductive reiteration: "The moment of practice places the subject in relationship to and in a position negating objects and other subjects in the social environment, with which it comes into antagonistic or nonantagonistic contradiction. Although it is located out-

side the subject, the contradiction internal to social relationships de-
centers the subject, suspends it and articulates it as the transitional
place where opposed tendencies come into conflict." These tendencies emerge in family relations as much as in the class struggle (pp.
179–180).

We can see that with Kristeva we have a complete opening up and
breaking up of structure and an atomization of the subject, the latter
term implying discontinuity and dialectic heterogeneity. The subject
seems to be reduced to an analytic function, to a negative moment
which permits the signifying of the system, a system motivated by
the negative forces of the death instinct.

Kristeva contends that semanalysis can be considered as the suc-
cess of dialectic method since it permits one "to rediscover practice
by way of the system, by rehabilitating what is heterogeneous to the
system of meaning" (1975:9). The semanalysis permits one to recognize the materiality and heterogeneity of negativity, whereas this was
not possible in the mechanistic and humanist version of Marxism.
Marxism "is not the theory of meaning or of the subject" (ibid.). This
conceptualization echoes Althusser's position with an aggravated
negative psychological overtone.

Surely, Kristeva presents a truly dialectic perspective centered on
negativity, but it is a negativity based on heterogeneous and unconscious impulses; the unconscious becomes the motor of history. Kristeva's dialectic incorporates both a materialist and a psychological
principle and produces a conception of an open and dynamic structure and subjectivity. But one is troubled by the heavy emphasis on
the relativistic and psychological character of this dialectic, and by
the disintegration of conscious subjectivity. Subjectivity, in fact, is reduced to a signifying practice, i.e., to an open and relativistic structuring activity. Kristeva reaches dialectic at the expense of and on the
basis of the dissolution of both structure and subjectivity, which are
reduced to a negative and heterogeneous signifying practice.

There exists, however, an important message in the works of poststructural semioticians—the need to recapture the structural and
subjective principles of social dynamics and to conceive of them as
interdependent and reciprocally constitutive mechanisms.

Conclusion: Toward a Dialectical Conception of Structure and Subjectivity

Besides many methodological differences and discontinuities, one can also detect a continuity of substantive concerns between the sociological paradigms analyzed in this volume. By substantive concerns I refer to the central place that symbolic systems and meaning hold both as subject matter of analysis and as explanatory variables in the sociological paradigms we have examined. By methodological differences I refer to a variety of orientations, such as empiricism, positivism, formalism, subjectivism, transformationalism, and dialectic thought, which have interacted or replaced one another as alternative orientations in the development not only of traditional natural science, interpretive, and critical paradigms, but also of semiotic paradigms. Concomitant with a continuity of substantive concerns, one can detect in the various paradigms a remarkably persistent dichotomy of a shifting focus on either the objective (or structural, or systemic) aspect of symbolic systems or on their subjective interpretation and the creative input of the individual. In this conclusion I deal with the implications of this persistent conflict or alternating focus of analysis, which cuts across a large variety of theoretical paradigms in social sciences.

After a very brief overview of the continuity of substantive concerns and of the methodological discontinuities, I will argue that the conflict between the objective and subjective approach is not to be construed as a radical or totally irreconcilable dichotomy but rather as suggesting the need to integrate the two focuses of analysis. My argument is that both the objective and subjective focuses ought to be indispensible components of a holistic and dialectic approach because they refer to two facets of the organization and functioning of symbolic systems. I will not argue in favor of a multidimensional and integrated paradigm, but in favor of a dialectic mode of analysis which permits one to use the valid elements of various paradigms and account for both the objective, or structural, and subjective aspects of symbolic systems.

Continuity of Substantive Concerns: The Central Importance of Symbolic System's in Traditional and Semiotic Paradigms

That symbolism and meaning hold a central place in the interpretive and critical paradigms is quite obvious from the fact that they focus on meaning and ideology, respectively, as the key reference points for understanding the nature and dynamics of social life. Max Weber has attributed a primary role to ideas, Pitirim Sorokin to cultural systems, Karl Mannheim to culture and situational meaning, symbolic interactionists to the negotiation of meaning, phenomenological sociologists to conscious intentionality and intersubjective communication, which generate meaning, and ethnomethodologists to the rational methods used by social actors to interpret and negotiate meaning. Marxists emphasize the role of ideology, social praxis, and alienation in the dynamics of social life. In the natural science paradigms of Pareto, Durkheim, and Parsons a primary role is attributed to derivations, collective representations, and the cybernetic control of the cultural system, respectively.

Transformational structuralists and poststructural semioticians have continued to consider symbolic systems the central subject matter of sociological analysis, although they have done so on radically different theoretical and methodological bases. The semiotic structuralism of Lévi-Strauss has considered symbolism as the generative matrix of social life and has extended the notion of meaning to a metaempirical and objective level of analysis. Structural Marxists have shown the autonomous (Althusser) and at times predominant (Godelier) role of ideology in the objective dialectic of capitalist systems. Poststructural semioticians have added to Marxist theory the notion of the constitutive role of language in the dynamics of social praxis and ideology. It is precisely with the works of semiotic Marxists that the clash between the structural (objective) and subjective explanations of symbolic systems has assumed a new significance. In fact, semiotically oriented Marxists have called attention to new aspects of the structural and subjective aspects of symbolism and formulated new conceptualizations which point to the need for a dialectical integration of the structural and subjective approaches.

Structural vs. Subjective Explanations of Symbolic Systems

The contrast between the objective and subjective focus has been very much in evidence since the very beginning of the sociological tradition. Durkheim and Parsons have focused on the integrative function and constraining role of symbolic systems in the maintenance of society and the behavior of people. Weber, symbolic interactionists, and phenomenologists have focused on the role of the individual in the construction and maintenance of the social structure. The objective approach has produced systemic formulations of mechanical (Durkheim) and cybernetic (Parsons) types. The systemic bias has been perpetuated and extended to a metaempirical level by the transformational structuralism of Lévi-Strauss and strengthened with a developmental and generative perspective by Piaget and Chomsky, respectively.

We have seen that transformational structuralism can provide the methodological tools to overcome the impasse between a formalistic and empiricist explanation. Yet the conflict between the objective (structural) and subjective approach has remained. To be sure, the notion of deep structure provides the constitutive mechanism to explain (and therefore link) behavioral structures and the production of subjective meaning to symbolic systems. However, the conflict of the structural versus subjective approach has reemerged at the metaempirical level. In fact, Lévi-Strauss, Piaget and Chomsky are thinkers with a clearly structural and systemic bias, and within the Marxist and dialectical paradigm we have detected a split between the supporters of an objective (Althusser and Godelier) and subjective (Sartre) dialectic. Semiotic Marxists have formulated the notion of a decentered structure producing the positionality of the subject, but they do not deal with a conscious subject, rather with the notion of signifying practice understood in a relational and negative sense (Lacan, Kristeva). It is incumbent upon us to draw the full implications of these intellectual concerns inherited from the classic sociological tradition and redefined by semiotic structuralism.

Dialectic Approach vs. Multiple Paradigm

The succession and progressive refinements of sociological paradigms have been paralleled by a progressive refinement of the structural and subjective approaches to the analysis of symbolism. These parallel developments can be summarized as shown in Figure C.1.

I have placed Piaget, Lacan, and Kristeva in side slots to indicate that these structural thinkers have attempted to somewhat integrate the notion of subject within their structural perspective. Their attempt, however, is not satisfactory because they have not dealt with the role of conscious subjectivity but only with an epistemic (Piaget), structural (Lacan), and negative and relational (Kristeva) subject. The two arrows at the bottom of the diagram indicate the thrust of my

	Objective Approach (Systemic)		Subjective Approach
Empiricism	Durkheim Parsons		Weber Interactionists Phenomenologists
Transformationalism	Lévi-Strauss Chomsky	Piaget → Lacan →	
Marxism	Althusser Godelier	Kristeva →	Sartre Humanist Marxists

Dialectic Approach

Figure C.1. Sociological paradigms and the analysis of symbolism.

thesis, the need to balance out the objective (systemic) and subjective perspectives with a truly dialectic approach, which has been missing not only from the natural science and interpretive paradigms, but also from the critical (Marxist) paradigm, including the paradigms of structural Marxists and semiotic Marxists of poststructural orientation.

I am not suggesting that we should work out a multiple paradigm which would synthesize elements of the various paradigms as well as their versions of the subjective and systemic perspectives. Rather than a multiple or universal or integrated paradigm, I am proposing a dialectical mode of thinking that uses both the objective and subjective perspectives but keeps them distinct and in a complementary relationship.

Some sociologists argue in favor of a multiple paradigm or in favor of building a bridge between various paradigms (Ritzer 1975). Such attempts may well succeed in demonstrating elements of complementarity and continuity as well as ways of developing and extending key concepts of sociological paradigms. However, we will never be able to produce a truly integrated paradigm because "there are no scientific or logical criteria for a choice between the competing" paradigms (Klima 1972:89). Not even a true "theoretical pluralism" is possible because there exists no "methodological consensus on the rules according to which the process of elimination has to be organized. It is precisely this consensus among sociologists which is lacking" (p. 74).

The need, however, for systematically relating the structural and subjective focuses of analysis remains important since it is not merely a domestic issue among structural Marxists. On the contrary, it is an issue related to (and an extreme test case of) the larger issue of the relationship between society and individual, which Simmel already had conceived of in a conflicting and dialectical relationship (1950 and 1968). In one form or another the question of the place of the individual in society has permeated the whole sociological (and anthropological) tradition (see Hawthorn 1976:255ff) and has been dealt with in terms of two opposing perspectives, called by Tiryakian *Sociologism* and *Existentialism* (1962).

In an issue of *The American Sociologist* dedicated to contemporary social theory, Scott G. McNall recognized that "there have been, and continue to be, heroic efforts to bridge objective/subjective gaps in social theory" (1978:4). Outside of a passing reference to Marx's position, McNall does not discuss any such specific effort, although he suggests that to bridge the epistemological gaps present within sociology, he would propose "a combination of critical theory and Marxist structuralism" (p. 6). Not all social scientists would agree with him that Marx's "concept of praxis specifically bridges the gap between the objective and subjective realm" (ibid.). But I certainly concur with McNall on the need to bridge the objective and subjective approach, not with the intent of amalgamating them into a monolithic approach, and therefore abolishing their distinctiveness, but with the intent of showing their complementarity and dialectic relationship. In this sense I agree with McNall that Marx's "images of human beings are not as valuable as its dialectic, which could provide a means of understanding how total systems operate" (p. 5).

However, we have seen that Marx's dialectic leaves room for at least two contrasting interpretations. The issue comes down to determining what we should mean by dialectic in view of the fact that Marxists have proposed different notions of dialectics and that Louis Schneider has listed as many as seven usages of the term "dialectic" among sociologists of various orientations (1971).

On Substantive and Methodological Dialectic

We can distinguish between a dialectical view of social reality and a dialectic method. It is the second aspect which directly interests me; however, the choice of an appropriate dialectic method must be based on an adequate dialectic conception of reality. A dialectic view of social reality implies that we consider society as a totality and as a dynamic and ongoing totality. A dynamic view of social totality is not necessarily based on a dialectic of oppositions (as in Lévi-Strauss) or contraries or conflicts (Marx). George Gurvitch (1962) has pointed out that there exists a dialectic of mutual involvement, a dialectic of ambiguity and ambivalence, a dialectic of polarization, and a dialectic of reciprocity of perspectives.

In my view the notion of dialectic of reciprocity of perspectives must be considered as a core element of sociological dialectic. A true dialectic should preserve a "dialectic relationship established between the object constructed by science, the method used and the respective reality" (Gurvitch 1962:179ff). It is essential that the "object" constructed by the sociologist, or sociological conceptualizations, reflects the dialectic nature of social reality, especially the tension between the structural and subjective aspects of social reality. In this way one can avoid the shortcomings of analytical, formalistic, systemic, and subjectivist explanations. Not only are dialectic concepts the only concepts which can render the dialectic of social reality (ontological dialectic), but they are also the only concepts which permit the development of a dialectic method. Transformational structuralism can be considered to have prepared the foundations for the dialectical method in the sense that it avoids the limitation of formal and empirical analysis and offers the premises for conceiving the formal and empirical levels of analysis in transformational relationship. Transformational structuralism also achieves the unity of method and reality, but a reality understood in a systemic and, therefore, undialectic sense. Marxism is based on a dialectic view of social totality but it has produced an impasse between the proponents of an objective dialectic and the proponents of a subjective dialectic; moreover, within the objective dialectic of Godelier we have detected a lack of a dialectic relationship between the ideal and real elements of social reality. Poststructural semioticians have formulated a position based on a negative dialectic that has dissolved conscious subjectivity.

To avoid these impasses I propose to consider structure and subjectivity as related by a dialectic of complementarity and a reciprocity of perspectives, to use Gurvitch's terminology. The soundness and, in a sense, logical inevitability of the dialectical relationship between structure and subjectivity can be demonstrated both in terms of a phenomenological analysis of language and a Marxist inspired (although modified) dialectical conception of history.

On the Dialectic Between Structure and Speech Event in Discourse

The phenomenologist Paul Ricoeur has proposed a decisive argument in favor of the inseparability of the notions of "structure" and "event" to explain the nature of "discourse." He argues that the traditional structural perspective has unilaterally emphasized *langue* (structure) and neglected *parole* (event) and therefore it cannot provide intelligibility to the acts and operations contained in discourse (1967a:801ff). If, however, one goes beyond the level of *sign*, that is, the semiotic level of analysis, and locates the analysis at the level of the word, one sees that structure and event are not in antinomic but in a mutually constitutive interrelationship. At variance with the empiricist position, Ricoeur argues that language must not be approached as an object but as a "mediation" through which we express ourselves and things. He argues that we must recuperate speech and understand the operation of speaking as a dialectical production (p.808ff); in this way we are able to perceive "the system as act and the structure as event" (*ibid.*). Alternatively, one can argue that we ought to perceive the system as generating events and events as restructuring systems. Rightly, Ricoeur states that "we need analytical tools to master the phenomenon of language which is not structure or event but the increasing conversion of one into the other in the discourse" (p. 813). In this sense, language is more appropriately conceived of as a "structuring operation" rather than as a "structured inventory" (p. 816).

This way of thinking adds important correctives to Kristeva's notion of language as a signifying practice, insofar as it explicitly recognizes the role of contingent event and, by implication, of the conscious subject. It is important that we preserve the contingent aspect of the event and the conscious aspect of subjectivity together with the "constructive" power of structure (and here Piaget's notion of structure as a system of transformations is useful). This is at the heart of Ricoeur's concern. Moreover, we ought to realize that the demonstration of the interaction or mutually constitutive relationship of structure and event depends on one's level of analysis. Ricoeur finds in the "word" the locus of intersection of *langue* and *parole*, synchrony and diachrony, structure and event (1967a:816ff); similarly, Ricoeur considers "usage" the crossroads of *langue* and *parole* (p. 816).

In the process of discourse, the word passes from the level of the system to that of the event and therefore brings structure to the act of speech. By going back from the event to the system, the word brings contingency, and disequilibrium to the latter (1967a:810). On the basis of this and similar kinds of phenomenological analysis, Ricoeur has suggested the existence of a dialectic interrelationship between explanation and understanding (1971).

Praxis as the Locus of the Dialectic Relationship Between Structure and Subjectivity

Analogous principles can be used to demonstrate the inevitability of the dialectical relationship between "structure" and "subjectivity" and to resolve the controversy between Sartre and Althusser, two thinkers who propose the thesis of subjective and objective dialectic, respectively. We can begin from the notion that the dialectical perspective is antithetical to the concept of closed structure but not to the notion of structure per se. As Sartre states, structure is a moment of the dialectic process and, as Kristeva says, structure posits the subject and constitutes its activity. The arch of dialectic thought is completed by adding the other side of the dialectic relationship—the conscious activity of the subject, which contributes to the production of changes in the structure or produces new structures; without the subject's activity there would be no structure or adaptation of structures.

I consider *praxis* as the interaction between structure and subjectivity, rather than are mere subjective activity. This represents a radical departure from the Marxist notion of dialectic in its objective and subjective version. First of all, I cannot accept the position of those Marxists who endorse the notion of objective dialectic while totally dismissing the role of subjectivity as a motor of history, to use Althusser's expression. I cannot accept either the Sartrean notion of dialectic, which makes the individual the locus and motor of history. For similar reasons I do not accept Karel Kosik's "dialectical rationalism," which "takes the category of the concrete in the dialectical sense of that which came to be known by the active transformation of nature and society by human purposive activity" (Kosik 1976:v). Such a definition of dialectical rationalism is obviously very close to Sartre's notion of dialectical reason, which we have previously discussed. As in the case of Sartre, Kosik's dialectical rationalism is both a form of inquiry (and an epistemological position) as well as a theory of history. Kosik seems to reject what I have called in the introduction the objective and the subjective forms of empiricism; he especially rejects positivism, phenomenalism, and metaphysical rationalism (ibid.). Such a programmatic statement would certainly please Lévi-Straussean and Piagetian thinkers: "The structure of the things, that is the thing itself, can be grasped neither immediately, nor by contemplation or mere reflection, but only by a certain activity" (p. 9).

However, the similarity between Kosik and the structuralists' theory of knowledge ends with their common rejection of the antiempiricist and antinaturalistic attitude. Kosik's theory of knowledge is not based on the notion of structural activity (Barthes 1967a) but on the notion of praxis as "the historically determined, one-sided and fragmentary praxis of individuals" (Kosik 1976:2): "In its essence and generality, praxis is the exposure of the mystery of man as an auto-formative being, as a being that *forms* the (socio-human) reality and *therefore* also grasps and interprets it (i.e., reality both human and extra-human, reality in its totality)" (p. 137). Kosik clearly echoes Sartre's contention that people must be the center of history and totalizers: "Praxis is active and self-producing in history, i.e., it is a constantly renewing, practically constituting unity of man and world, matter and spirit, subject and object, products and productivity" (ibid.).

The issue in contention here is precisely how the unity (in Kosik and Sartre's language) or dialectical linkage between subject and object, subjectivity and structure is to be understood. For Kosik (and Sartre) the unity is guaranteed by the totalizing activity of the subject; for me the unity is produced by a dialectic surpassment of the object, whereby surpassment entails the preservation of the subject-object alterity as a condition and guarantee of continued social dynamics. What I find objectionable in Kosik's position is the virtual elimination of the object by the activity of the subject (praxis). Kosik argues that praxis is "the foundation of a real active center, as the real historical mediation of spirit and matter, culture and nature, man and the universe, theory and action" (1976:139). But such a mediation nullifies the subject-object alterity. In fact "in praxis and on the basis of praxis, man transcends the closed character of animality and of inorganic nature and constitutes his relationships with the world in its totality" (p. 140). It is Kosik's position that "Marx found that history does exactly nothing, and that everything in it, including history itself, is the doing of man. . . . History is made by people" (p. 143). After praxis only people and human totalizations are left: "In history, man realizes himself . . . man realizes himself, i.e., humanizes himself in history" (p. 145).

Totalizing praxis abolishes not only the metaphysical world of Providence (Kosik 1976:44) but also the nonsubjective (structural) dimension of social reality. Surely, "the objective social substance, in the form of materialized production forces, language and forms of thinking is independent of the will and consciousness of individuals, but it exists only through their activity, thinking and language" (p. 146). By this Kosik means that they "exist as the continuity of history only in connection with the activity of people" (ibid.). Kosik admits the object-subject duality only as a precondition of dialectic activity: "Conditions do not exist without people or people without conditions. This is the basis for the development of a dialectic between conditions that are given for every individual, for every generation, epoch and class, and action that unfolds on the basis of ready-made and given prerequisites" (p. 147). Since people's activity invests the objective conditions with meaning, the conditions lose their objective character: "People enter conditions independently of their consciousness and of their will but once there they transform these conditions." In Kosik's words, conditions are transcended: "Conditions stand out as prerequisites of this action; the action in turn invests them with a particular sense. Man transcends conditions not primarily in his consciousness and intentions, in his ideal project, but in his praxis. . . . It is in this action that man inscribes meanings into the world and forms a structure of meanings in it. . . . [C]onditions and man are constitutive elements of praxis which is in turn the fundamental prerequisite for transcending conditions" (p. 147).

It is apparent that for Kosik human activity (praxis) transcends or surpasses the nonhuman aspects of conditions, and therefore it eliminates the alterity of objective conditions. I consider this position another expression of a dichotomous and positivist thinking that takes for granted the subject-object duality. In other words, subject and object are considered self-constituted, already made, entities which enter into interaction with each other after they have been in existence as independent and separate entities. Were this premise accepted, dialectic could logically be understood only as the attempt by the subject to transcend the object or vice versa. On the contrary, I maintain that neither the subject nor the object (and I am more precisely interested in social structure) are constituted or even conceivable independent of each other. This means that we have to reckon both with a structural as well as a subjective principle when we deal either with empirical social structures or subjective activity. There is nothing mysterious about this, considering that symbolic interactionists have abundantly demonstrated that the self cannot emerge apart from primary group interaction.

I understand social praxis as the acting out of the dialectic tension between the subjective and objective principle, an acting out which does not eliminate one of the two principles but reproduces their tension at a higher level. The permanence of such dialectic tension is the key explanatory variable of social dynamics. The dialectic tension, however, is not produced by contradictory principles but by mutually constitutive, although different principles; by their very nature these principles perpetuate the alterity or heterogeneity by reproducing higher forms of it. I interpret Lévi-Strauss' statement that the "difference" is the first datum (Lévi-Strauss 1971) in a dialectic rather than analytic sense; that is, for me difference is not an analytical statement but a constitutive dialectic principle.

One might argue that my position amounts to a platitude or a reinstatement of the obvious facts that there cannot be personality without culture, nor culture without personality, or society without individuals and vice versa. To this criticism I reply that I am not talking of empirical entities but of dialectical principles. Structure by definition connotes regularities and constraints, but there cannot be constraints without subjects being constrained and trying to overcome the constraints; by very definition neither one of the two principles can exist without the other. This is why the structural or objective element is much more than just a "practico-inert" element; it is the very constitutive condition of the active subject.

Since my argument is couched in logical terms, one might suggest that I propose a purely logical notion of dialectic. Far from it—I refer to objective elements of social processes as they have been conceptualized by either interpretative sociologists or structural sociologists. I want to clarify that I do not use the term "element" in the Parsonian sense of abstraction and separation of certain aspects from the complexity of eternal reality. We have seen that the Parsonian perspective entails a dichotomous and empiricist orientation, which violates the very notion of constitutive dialectic relations.

Perhaps my position can best be expressed as an attempt to preserve the permanent and always productive relationship between structuring activity and structured subjectivity. By "structuring activity" I mean subjective praxis, which structures the practico-inert and the continuously emerging elements extraneous to and infringing upon existing structures. By "structured subjectivity" I mean that no subjective praxis would be possible without the existence of structural constraints. The latter is true in a twofold sense: the fact of constraints generates a pressure toward surpassment by human creativity and freedom. At the same time, the latter would not be possible without the formation of self and positive identity, which, in turn, is not possible except within primary group (structured) settings. In this way, one can preserve both the input of structure and structural transformations, on the one hand, and the input of the conscious and free activity of the subject as well as historical events, on the other hand.

Seen from this perspective, particular events are not merely contingent events but outcomes of the combined influence of structuring activity and structured subjectivity. That is, events cannot be understood without reference to both structure and subjectivity. A dialectical relationship is, then, established between event, history, and subjectivity, on the one hand, and structure and systems, on the other hand, as shown in Figure C.2. With the term "historical events" I refer to the realm of empirical observations, which can be alternatively conceptualized as the realm of historical events, social interaction, society, and so on. This represents the static (for the lack of a better term) moment of social totality, the moment when we take cognizance of the existence of social relations and we account for their nature, either in terms of structural and functional principles (see the

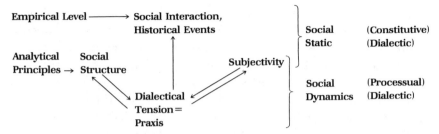

Figure C.2. Dialectic view of social totality.

Durkheimian notion of social integration and the AGIL functional scheme of Parsons) or in terms of their meaning for the social actors (see W. I. Thomas' definition of the situation, Weber's subjective meaning, Parsons' systems of meaning).

Social dynamics refers to the dynamic moment of social totality, the moment when we take cognizance of the social changes and conflicts that produce a reorganization of the social totality or new totalities. This dynamic aspect is conceptualized as praxis in the sense previously discussed of a joint output of the subject's activity that takes place within structural constraints, which has been conceptualized in alternative ways in terms of the notions of social structure and social function or in terms of the Marxist notions of capitalist contradiction and ideological superstructure.

The notion of contradiction and "determination in the last instance" by ideology points at the active and dynamic aspect of the structural principle (as distinct from social integration, or the static aspect of social structure). The existence of a twofold aspect of structure and subjectivity (i.e., their static and dynamic aspects) and of a dialectical linkage between the two aspects is indicated in the diagram by two double arrows. The dynamic aspect of social structure, which constitutes the positionality of the subject (see Lacan and Kristeva), can be conceptualized as the dynamic tendency of the structure toward the production of the subjectivity. The dialectical linkage of this subject-structuring aspect of social structure with the subject as conscious activity is operated through praxis, which we have described as the output of the tension between the structural and subjective principles.

In a similar manner, within subjectivity we can distinguish a static and a dynamic aspect. The static aspect, so to speak, consists of the moment when, in Lacan's term, the subject is constituted by the structure. Alternatively, in Meadean terms, we may refer to the formation of the "me" through the process of social interaction. In interactionist terms the active aspect of subjectivity refers to the definition of the situation or, in Marxist terms, to the process of becoming aware of one's alienated position and state of false consciousness. This latter process is a prerequisite for alienated social individuals to contribute to social conflicts and class struggle or to the resolution of the capitalistic contradiction.

At this point I reiterate that the dialectic approach here proposed does not aim at producing a theoretical integration of theoretical perspectives generated by different and often, at times, contrasting paradigms. Such an enterprise might easily lead to a misuse of concepts taken out of their own theoretical context or to reducing fundamentally different paradigms to one another, with the end result of producing a meaningless eclecticism or an extremely vague and abstract scheme. More fruitfully, the dialectical approach proposed here permits one to establish a dialectical linkage, and especially linkages of complementarity and reciprocity, between different and often competing explanatory variables proposed by contrasting paradigms. This point could be illustrated by proposing dialectic linkages (not a synthesis) between such different notions as social integration, AGIL functional scheme, definition of the situation, and alienation.

At the same time, the dialectic approach presented here permits one to fill gaps existing in traditional sociological paradigms. For instance, the "facticity" and static aspect of Durkheim's position and the systemic bias of Parsons and early structuralists can be balanced out and complemented with a dialectical (and constitutive) linkage to the notion of subjective meaning, definition of situation. The bias of interpretive sociologists can be avoided through a dialectical and constitutive linkage to structural principles. By the same process we can bring a remedy to the shortcomings of structural Marxism and poststructural semiotics. For instance, Godelier's notion of the structural necessity of contingent history becomes superfluous or even a contradictory notion. In fact, in our dialectic perspective, history is by definition the outcome of the combined interaction of a necessary principle (structure) and a contingent principle (subject's activity). Any particular event is a moment of the self-realization of the totality and, therefore, it cannot be conceived of independent of the structural and subjective principles of social totality. Moreover, the dialectic approach here proposed does not make use of a negative notion of dialectic or of a decentered (and relativized) subject. To fully understand the dynamics of social structures we need to preserve both the decentering and centering aspects of structure, the first referring to the notion of subject, the second to the notion of structural constraints.

I conclude this volume with the consideration that the dialectic approach here suggested is both a substantive and methodological approach. It is a substantive approach because it programmatically accepts and intends to account for the multiplicity of the forces of social dynamics and because it approaches society as a totality. It is a methodological dialectic because it conceives of the relationship between the structural and subjective principles as constituting each other; it takes into account both the surface and deep levels of structure and subjectivity and places them into a transformational relationship; and it operates on the unity of method and reality, that is, it dialectically links the structural and subjective principles based on the recognition that they are constitutive principles of social totality.

The dialectic approach here proposed is not based on the notion of a universal and deterministic dialectic, like the Hegelian dialectic, but it is firmly anchored in the analysis of historical specificity; in fact, its aim is to explain the specific features of particular social formations in terms of the mutually constitutive interaction of structural and subjective forces. Throughout this volume I have attempted to show how this approach can bring out the constructive potential of interpretive and system-oriented sociologies and permits one to recapture and develop dormant elements present in their classical formulations. I have also suggested the existence of deep sociological continuities where we have been trained to see irreconcilable differences. It is up to others to systematically elaborate on these suggestions, which I could merely adumbrate in this volume. As a matter of fact, all I have aimed at was to initiate a new sociological discourse and indicate some of its preliminary directions.

References

Alexander, Jeffrey C. 1978. "Formal and Substantive Voluntarism in the Work of Talcott Parsons: A Theoretical and Biological Reinterpretation." *American Sociological Review* 43(2):177–198.

Althusser, Louis. 1970. *For Marx.* Translated by Ben Brewster. New York: Random House.

—— 1971. *Lenin and Philosophy and Other Essays.* Translated by Ben Brewster. New York: Monthly Review Press.

—— 1975. "Est-il Simple d'être Marxiste en Philosophie?" *La Pensée,* October.

—— 1976. *Essays in Self-Criticism.* Translated by Grahame Lock. Atlantic Highlands, N.J.: Humanities Press.

Ardener, Edwin. 1971. "The New Anthropology and Its Critics." *Man* 6(3):449–467.

Aron, Raymond. 1967. *Main Currents in Sociological Thought.* Vol. 2. New York: Basic Books.

Badcock, C. R. 1975. *Lévi-Strauss Structuralism and Sociological Theory.* New York: Holmes and Meier.

Barthes, Roland. 1964. *On Racine.* New York: Hill and Wang (French orig. 1963).

—— 1964a. *Essais Critiques.* Paris: Seuil. Translated as *Critical Essays.* Northwestern University Press, 1972.

Barthes, Roland. 1966. *Critique et Verité.* Paris: Seuil.

—— 1966a. "Introduction à l'Analyse Structurale des Recits." *Communications* 8:1–27.

—— 1967. *Elements of Semiology.* Translated by A. Lavers and C. Smith. New York: Hill and Wang (orig. 1964).

—— 1967a. "The Structuralist Activity." *Partisan Review* 34(1):83–88.

—— 1967b. *Système de la Mode.* Paris: Editions du Seuil.

—— 1970. *Writing Degree Zero.* Boston: Beacon Press (French orig. 1953; 1972).

—— 1971. "A Conversation with Roland Barthes." *Signs of the Times.* Granta, Cambridge; 41–55.

—— 1974. *S/Z.* Translated by Richard Miller. Paris: Seuil.

—— 1975. *The Pleasure of the Text.* Translated by Richard Miller. New York: Hill and Wang (French orig. 1973).

Bateson, Gregory. 1967. "Cybernetic Explanation." *The American Behavioral Scientist:* 29–32.

Beck, Robert N., ed. 1969. *Perspectives in Philosophy.* New York: Holt, Rinehart and Winston.

Bellah, R. N. 1973. "Introduction" to *Emile Durkheim on Morality and Society.* Selected and edited by R. N. Bellah. Chicago: University of Chicago Press.

Benoist, Jean-Marie. 1978. *The Structural Revolution.* New York: St. Martin's Press.

Benveniste, Emile. 1971. *Problems in General Linguistics*. Vol. 1. Miami: University of Miami Press (French orig. 1966).

Berger, Peter and Thomas Luckman. 1966. *The Social Construction of Reality*. Garden City, N.Y.: Doubleday.

Bever, T. G., J. J. Katz, D. T. Langendoen, eds. 1976. *An Integrated Theory of Linguistic Ability*. New York: Crowell.

Blau, Peter, ed. 1975. *Approaches to the Study of Social Structure*. New York: Free Press.

—— 1981. "Introduction: Diverse Views of Social Structure and Their Common Denominator." In Blau and Merton, eds., *Continuities in Structural Inquiry*, pp. 1–23.

Blau, Peter M. and Robert K. Merton, eds. 1981. *Continuities in Structural Inquiry*. Beverly Hills, Calif.: Sage.

Bleicher, Joseph. 1980. *Contemporary Hermeneutics as Method, Philosophy, and Critique*. Boston: Routledge and Kegan Paul.

Blumer, Herbert. 1980. "Comment: Mead and Blumer: The Convergent Methodological Perspectives of Social Behaviorism and Symbolic Interactionism." *American Sociological Review* (June), 45:409–419.

—— 1962. "Society as Symbolic Interaction." In Arnold M. Rose, ed., *Human Behavior and Social Processes*, pp. 179–192. New York: Houghton Mifflin.

Bober, M. M. 1965. *Karl Marx's Interpretation of History*. New York: Norton.

Bologh, Roslyn Wallach. 1979. *Dialectical Phenomenology; Marx's Method*. Boston: Routledge and Kegan Paul.

Bottomore, Tom and Robert Nisbet, eds. 1978. *A History of Sociological Analysis*. New York: Basic Books.

Bottomore, Tom and M. Rubel, eds. 1963. *Karl Marx: Selected Writing in Sociology and Social Philosophy*. London: Watts.

Boudon, Raymond. 1970. *The Uses of Structuralism*. London: Heinemann.

Bourdieu, Pierre. 1972. *Esquisse d'une Theorie de la Pratique*. Geneva: Librairie Droz.

Brown, E. Michael. 1979. "Sociology as Critical Theory." In Scott G. McNall, ed., *Theoretical Perspectives in Sociology*, pp. 251–275. New York: St. Martin's Press.

Bruyn, Severyn. 1966. *The Human Perspective in Sociology: The Methodology of Participant Observation*. Englewood Cliffs, N.J.: Prentice-Hall.

Buckley, Walter. 1967. *Sociology and Modern Systems Theory*. Englewood Cliffs, N.J.: Prentice-Hall.

Burawoy, Michael. 1977. "Marxism and Sociology" *Contemporary Sociology* 6(1):9–17.

Burger, Thomas. 1977. "Talcott Oarsons, The Problem of Order in Society, and the program of analytical sociology" *American Journal of Sociology* 83(2):320–34.

Cartwright, Bliss C. and R. Stephen Warner. 1976. "The Medium Is Not the Message." In Loubser et al., *Explorations on General Theory in Social Science*, 2:639–660.

Cherry, C. 1957. *On Human Communication*. Cambridge, Mass.: M.I.T. Press.

Chomsky, Noam. 1957. *Syntactic Structures*. The Hague: Mouton.

—— 1965. *Aspects of a Theory of Syntax*. Cambridge, Mass.: M.I.T. Press.

—— 1972. *Studies on Semantics in Generative Grammar*. The Hague: Mouton.

Chomsky, Noam and M. Halle. 1965. "Some Controversial Questions in Phonological Theory." *Journal of Linguistics* 6(2):97–138.

—— 1968. *The Sound Pattern of English*. New York: Harper and Row.

Cicourel, Aaron V. 1964. *Method and Measurement in Sociology*. New York: Free Press.

—— 1970. "The Acquisition of Social Structure: Toward a Developmental Sociology of

Language and Meaning." In Jack Douglas, ed., *Understanding Everyday Life*, pp. 136–168. Chicago: Aldine.

—— 1970a. "Basic and Normative Rules with Negotiation of Status and Role." In Hans P. Dreitzel, ed., *Recent Sociology*, 2:4–48. New York: Macmillan.

—— 1974. *Cognitive Sociology*. New York: Free Press.

—— 1981. "The Role of Cognitive-Linguistic Concepts in Understanding Everyday Social Interactions." *Annual Review of Sociology* 7:87–106.

Clarke, Simon. 1981. *The Foundations of Structuralism: A Critique of Lévi-Strauss and the Structuralist Movement*. Sussex: Harvester Press. New York: Barnes and Noble.

Collins, Randall. 1980. "Weber's Last Theory of Capitalism: A Systematization." *American Sociological Review* 45(6):925–942.

Cooley, Charles Horton. 1926. "The Roots of Social Knowledge." *The American Journal of Sociology* (July), 32:59–79.

—— 1964. *Human Nature and the Social Order*. New York: Schocken.

Coser, Lewis. 1965. *Georg Simmel*. Englewood Cliffs, N.J.: Prentice-Hall.

—— 1976. "Sociological Theory from the Chicago Dominance to 1965." *Annual Review of Sociology* 2:145–160.

Coward, Rosalind and John Ellis. 1977. *Language and Materialism: Developments in Semiology and the Theory of the Subject*. Boston: Routledge and Kegan Paul.

Crick, F. H. C. 1966. "The Genetic Code: III." Reprinted in *Biology and Culture in Modern Perspective*, pp. 59–65. Readings from *Scientific American* edited by J. G. Jorgensen. San Francisco: W. H. Freeman.

Culler, Jonathan. 1975. *Structural Poetics: Structuralism, Linguistics and the Study of Literature*. Ithaca, N.Y.: Cornell University Press.

Derrida, Jacques. 1967. *De la Grammatologie*. Paris: Minuit.

—— 1967a. *L'Ecriture et la Différence*. Paris: Seuil.

—— 1972. *Positions*. Paris: Minuit.

Deutsch, Karl W. 1963. *The Nerves of Government*. New York: Free Press.

Douglas, Jack D. 1967. *The Social Meaning of Suicide*. Princeton: Princeton University Press.

—— 1970. "Understanding Everyday Life." In Jack Douglas, ed., *Understanding Everyday Life*, pp. 3–34. Chicago: Aldine.

—— 1978. "Existential Sociology." In J. Douglas and J. M. Johnson, eds., *Existential Sociology*, pp. 3–73. New York: Cambridge University Press.

Duncan, H. D. 1969. *Symbols and Social Theory*. New York: Oxford University Press.

Durkheim, E. 1885. Review of Schäffle: "Bau und Leben des Socialen Körpers." *Revue Philosophique* 19:84–101.

—— 1887. "La Science Positive de la Morale en Allemagne." *Revue Philosophique*, vol. 24.

—— 1897. "Labriola, Antonio—Essai sur la Conception Materialiste de l'Histoire." *Revue Philosophique* 44:645–651.

—— 1898. "Representations Individuelles et Representations Collectives." *Revue de Metaphysique et de Morale* 6:273–302.

—— 1911. "Jugements de Valeur et Jugements de Realité." *Revue de Metaphysique et de Morale*.

—— 1954. *Sociology and Philosophy*. New York: Free Press (French orig. 1924).

—— 1961. *The Elementary Forms of the Religious Life*. Translated by Joseph W. Swain. New York: Collier (French orig. 1912).

—— 1963. *Suicide*. Translated by J. A. Spaulding and G. Simpson. New York: Free Press (French orig. 1897).

—— 1964. *The Rules of Sociological Method*. 8th edition. New York: Free Press (1950) (French orig. 1895).

Durkheim, Emile and Marcel Mauss. 1963. *Primitive Classifications*. Translated by R. Needham. London: Cohen and West (French orig. 1903).

Easton, Lloyd D. and Kurt H. Guddat, eds. 1967. *Writings of the Young Marx on Philosophy and Society*. Garden City, N.Y.: Doubleday.

Eco, Umberto. 1973. "Social Life as a Sign System." In D. Robey, ed., *Structuralism: An Introduction*, pp. 57–72. Oxford: Clarendon Press.

—— 1976. *A Theory of Semiotics*. Bloomington: Indiana University Press.

Effrat, Andrew. 1972. "Power to the Paradigms: An Editorial Introduction." *Sociological Inquiry* 42:3–33.

Eisenstadt, S. N. 1981. "Some Observations on Structuralism in Sociology, with Special, and Paradoxical, Reference to Max Weber." In Peter M. Blau and Robert K. Merton, eds., *Continuities in Structural Inquiry*, pp. 165–176. London/Beverly Hills: Sage.

Eisenstadt, S. N. *with* M. Curelaru. 1976. *The Form of Sociology—Paradigms and Crisis*. New York: Wiley.

Ekeh, Peter P. 1974. *Social Exchange Theory: The Two Traditions*. Cambridge, Mass.: Harvard University Press.

Engels, Friedrich. 1940. *Dialectics of Nature*. New York: International Publishers.

Evans-Pritchard, E. E. 1965. *Theories of Primitive Religion*. Oxford: Clarendon Press.

Feuer, Lewis S., ed. 1959. *Karl Marx and Friedrich Engels: Basic Writings on Politics and Philosophy*. Garden City, N.Y.: Doubleday.

Fontana, Andrea. 1980. "Toward a Complex Universe: Existential Sociology." In J. D. Douglas et al., eds., *Introduction to the Sociologies of Everyday Life*, pp. 155–181. Boston: Allyn and Bacon.

Frank, Arthur W. 1979. "Reality Construction in Interaction." *Annual Review of Sociology* 5:167–191.

Friedman, Jonathan. 1974. "Marxism, Structuralism and Vulgar Materialism." *Man* 9(3):444–469.

Friedrichs, Robert W. 1970. *A Sociology of Sociology*. New York: Free Press.

Fromkin, V. and R. Rodman. 1974. *An Introduction to Language*. New York: Holt, Rinehart and Winston.

Fromm, Erich. 1968. *Marx's Concept of Man*. New York: Ungar.

Gardner, Howard. 1973. "Structure and Development." *Human Context* (Spring), 5:50–67.

Garfinkel, Harold. 1967. *Studies in Ethnomethodology*. Englewood Cliffs, N.J.: Prentice-Hall.

Garfinkel, Harold and Harvey Sacks. 1970. "On the Formal Structures of Practical Actions." In John C. McKinney and E. A. Tiryakian, eds., *Theoretical Sociology*, pp. 337–364. New York: Appleton-Century-Crofts.

Geertz, Clifford. 1966. "Religion as a Cultural System." In Michael Banton, ed., *Anthropological Approaches to the Study of Religion*, pp. 1–46. London: Tavistock.

Gerstein, Dean Robert. 1976. "A Note on the Continuity of Parsonian Action Theory." *Sociological Inquiry* (Winter), vol. 46.

Gerth, H. H. and C. Wright Mills. 1958. *From Max Weber: Essays in Sociology*. New York: Oxford University Press.

Glucksmann, M. 1974. *Structuralist Analysis in Contemporary Social Thought.* Boston: Routledge and Kegan Paul.

Godelier, Maurice 1966. "Système, Structures, et Contradictions Dans le Capital." *Les Temps Modernes* 246:828–864.

—— 1970. "Logique Dialectique et Analyse des Structures. Reponse a Lucien Sève." *La Pensée* (February), vol. 149.

—— 1972. *Rationality and Irrationality in Economics.* Translated by Brian Pearce. New York: Monthly Review Press (French orig. 1966).

—— 1977. *Perspectives in Marxist Anthropology.* Translated by Robert Brain. New York: Cambridge University Press (French orig. 1973).

—— 1978. "Infrastructures, Societies, and History." *Current Anthropology* 19(4):763–771.

—— 1982. "Myths, Infrastructures and History in Levi-Strauss" in Rossi 1982b:232–261.

Goffman, Erving. 1961. *Encounters.* Indianapolis: Bobbs-Merrill.

—— 1974. *Frame Analysis.* New York: Harper and Row.

—— 1981. *Forms of Talk.* Philadelphia: University of Pennsylvania Press.

Goldmann, Lucien. 1959. *Recherches Dialectiques.* Paris: Gallimard.

—— 1970. *Marxisme et Sciences Humaines.* Paris: Gallimard.

Gonos, George. 1977. "Situation versus Frame: The Interactionist and Structuralist Approaches of Everyday Life." *American Sociological Review* 42(6):854–867.

Granger, G. G. 1960. *Pensée Formelle et Sciences de l'Homme.* Paris: Aubier.

Greimas, A. J. 1976. *Semiotique et Sciences Sociales.* Paris: Seuil.

Gumperz, John J. and D. Hymes. 1972. *Directions in Sociolinguistics: The Ethnography of Communication.* New York: Holt, Rinehart and Winston.

Gurvitch, George. 1962. *Dialectique et Sociologie.* Paris: Flammarion.

Habermas, Jurgen. 1970. "Toward a Theory of Communicative Competence." In Hans Peter Breitzel, ed., *Recent Sociology,* 2:114–148. New York: Macmillan.

—— 1971. *Knowledge and Human Interests.* Translated by J. J. Shapiro. Boston: Beacon Press.

Hawthorn, Geoffrey. 1976. *Enlightenment and Despair: A History of Sociology.* New York: Cambridge University Press.

Hayes, Adrian C. 1974. "A Comparative Study of the Theoretical Orientations of Parsons and Lévi-Strauss." *Indian Journal of Social Research* 15(2–3):101–111.

Heap, James L. and Phillip A. Roth. 1973. "On Phenomenological Sociology." *American Sociological Review* (June), 38:354–367.

Hill, Lester and Douglas Lee Eckberg. 1981. "Clarifying Confusions about Paradigms: A Reply to Ritzer." *American Sociological Review* (April), 46:248–252.

Hinkle, Roscoe C. and Gisela J. Hinkle. 1954. *The Development of Modern Sociology: Its Nature and Growth in the United States.* Garden City, N.Y.: Doubleday.

Hjelmslev, Louis. 1959. *Essais Linguistiques.* Copenhagen: Cercle Linguistique de Copenhague.

—— 1961. *Prolegomena to a Theory of Language* Translated by Francis J. Whitfield. Bloomington: Indiana University Press (Orig. 1943)

Holzner, Burkart. 1968. *Reality Construction in Society.* Cambridge, Mass.: Schenkman.

—— 1974. "Comments on Heap and Roth" on Phenomenological Sociology" *American Sociological Review* 39(2):286–289.

Homans, George C. 1964. "Contemporary Theory in Sociology." In R. E. L. Faris, ed., *Handbook of Modern Sociology.* Chicago: Rand McNally.

—— 1975. "What do We Mean by Social Structure?" In Peter M. Blau, ed., *Approaches to the Study of Social Structure*, pp. 53–65. New York: Free Press.

Householder, F. W., ed. 1972. *Structuralists*. Baltimore: Penguin.

Howe, Richard Herbert. 1978. "Max Weber's Elective Affinities: Sociology Within the Bounds of Pure Reason." *American Journal of Sociology* 85(2):366–385.

Husserl, Edmund. 1962. *Ideas*. Translated by W. Boyce-Gibson. New York: Macmillan.

—— 1969. *Formal and Transcendental Logic*. Translated by Dorion Cairns. The Hague: Nijhoff.

Hyman, Larry M. 1975. *Phonology: Theory and Analysis*. New York: Holt, Rinehart and Winston.

Hymes, Dell, ed. 1972. *Towards Communicative Competence*. Philadelphia: University of Pennsylvania Press.

Israel, Joachim. 1971. *Alienation: From Marx to Modern Sociology*. Boston: Allyn and Bacon.

Jakobson, R. 1968. *Child Language: Aphasia and Phonological Universals*. The Hague: Mouton (German orig. 1962).

Jakobson, R. and M. Halle. 1956. *Fundamentals of Language*. The Hague: Mouton.

Jameson, F. 1976. "Review Article: On Goffman's Frame Analysis." *Theory and Society* 3:119–133.

Jenkins, Alan. 1979. *The Social Theory of Claude Levi-Strauss*. New York: St. Martin's Press.

Jorgensen, J. G., ed. 1972. *Biology and Culture in Modern Perspective: Readings from Scientific American*. San Francisco: Freeman.

Kalberg, Stephen. 1980. "Max Weber's Types of Rationality: Cornerstones for the Analysis of Rationalization Processes in History." *American Journal of Sociology* 85(5):1145–1179.

Kaplan, Abraham. 1964. *The Conduct of Inquiry: Methodology for Behavioral Science*. San Francisco: Chandler.

Katz, Fred E. 1976. *Structuralism in Sociology: An Approach to Knowledge*. Albany: State University of New York Press.

Katz, J. J. and P. Postal. 1964. *An Integrated Theory of Linguistic Descriptions*. Cambridge, Mass.: M.I.T. Press.

Klima, Wolf. 1972. "Theoretical Pluralism, Methodological Dissension and the Role of the Sociologist: The West German Case." *Social Science Information* 77(3/4):69–108.

Kosik, Karel. 1976. *Dialectics of the Concrete: A Study on Problems of Man and World*. Dordrecht, Holland: Dreidel.

Kristeva, Julia. 1969. *Semiotikè: Recherches pour une Sémanalyse*. Paris: Seuil.

—— 1971. "Objet, Complément, Dialectique." *Critique* 285:99–131.

—— 1974. *La Revolution du Langage Poetique*. Paris: Seuil.

—— 1975. "The System and the Speaking Subject." Thomas A. Sebedk, ed., In *The Tell-Tale Sign: A Survey of Semiotics*. Lisse: Peter De Ridder Press.

Kuhn, Thomas S. 1970. *The Structure of Scientific Revolutions*. 2d ed. Chicago: University of Chicago Press.

Lacan, Jacques. 1966. *Écrits*. Paris: Seuil.

—— 1970. "The Insistence of the Letter in the Unconscious." In Jacques Ehrman, ed., *Structuralism*, pp. 101–127. Garden City, N.Y.: Anchor Books. (Originally published in *La Psychanalyse*, vol. 3, 1957).

—— 1973. *Le Quatre Concepts Fondamentaux de la Psychanalyse.* Vol. 11 of *Le Séminaire.* Paris: Seuil.

Lauer, Robert H. and Warren H. Handel. 1977. *Social Psychology: The Theory and Application of Symbolic Interactionism.* Boston: Houghton Mifflin.

Lazarsfeld, Paul F. and Morris Rosenberg, eds. 1955. *The Language of Social Research: A Reader in the Methodology of Social Research.* New York: Free Press.

Leach, Edmund R. 1954. *Political Systems of Highland Burma.* Cambridge, Mass.: Harvard University Press.

Lemaire, Anika. 1977. *Jacques Lacan.* Translated by David Macey. London: Routledge and Kegan Paul.

Lemert, Charles C. 1979. *Sociology and the Twilight of Man: Homocentrism and Discourse in Sociological Theory.* Carbondale, Ill.: Southern Illinois University Press.

Lemert, Charles C., ed. 1974. "Beyond Mead: The Societal Reaction to Deviance." *Social Problems* 21:457–468.

—— 1981. *French Sociology: Rupture and Renewal Since 1968.* New York: Columbia University Press.

Lenin, V. I. 1927. *Materialism and Empirocriticism.* New York: International Publishers.

—— 1972. "Philosophical Notebooks." In *Collected Works,* Vol. 38. London: Lawrence and Wishart.

Lévi-Strauss, Claude. 1953. "Comments." In Sol Tax, ed., *An Appraisal of Anthropology Today.* Chicago: University of Chicago Press.

—— 1954. "Place de L'Anthropologie dans les Sciences Sociales et Problèmes Posés par son Enseignment." In *Les Sciences Sociales dans L'Enseignement Supérieur.* Paris: UNESCO. (Reprinted in Lévi-Strauss 1963.)

—— 1955. "The Structural Study of Myth." *Journal of American Folklore* 67(270).

—— 1958. *Anthropologie Structurale.* Paris: Plon.

—— 1960. "L'Analyse Morphologique des Contes Russes." *International Journal of Slavic Linguistics and Poetics* 3:141–143.

—— 1960a. "La Gêste d'Asdiwal." *Annuaire de l'E.P.H.E.* (Sciences Religieuses).

—— 1963. *Structural Anthropology.* Translated from the French by Claire Jacobson and Brooke Grundfest Schoepf. New York: Basic Books (French orig. 1958).

—— 1965. *Tristes Tropiques.* New York: Atheneum (French orig. 1955).

—— 1966. *The Savage Mind.* Chicago: University of Chicago Press (French orig. 1962).

—— 1966a. *Du Miel aux Cendres.* Paris: Plon.

—— 1967. *Totemism.* Translated by R. Needham. Boston: Beacon Press (French orig. 1962).

—— 1969. *The Elementary Structures of Kinship.* Translated by J. H. Bell and J. R. Von Sturmer under the editorship of Rodney Needham. Boston: Beacon Press (French orig. 1949).

—— 1969a. *The Raw and the Cooked.* New York: Harper and Row (French orig. 1964).

—— 1971. *L'Homme Nu.* Paris: Plon.

—— 1972. "Structuralism and Ecology." Gildersleeve lecture delivered at Barnard College, in *Barnard Alumnae* 72, (Spring):6–14. Reprinted in *Social Sciences Information* 12(1):7–24

—— 1973. "Reflexions sur L'Atome de Parenté." *L'Homme* 13(3):5–30.

—— 1974. *Tristes Tropiques.* Translated by John and Doreen Weightman. New York: Atheneum; 2nd edition.

—— 1976. *Structural Anthropology*. Vol. 2. Translated by Monique Layton. New York: Basic Books.

—— 1979. *La Voie des Masques*. Revised and augmented edition. Paris: Plon.

Lévi-Strauss, Claude, M. Augé, and M. Godelier. 1976. "Anthropology, History and Ideology." *Critique of Anthropology* 2(6):44–55. A debate originally published in *L'Homme* 15(3–4):177–188.

Lewis, J. D. 1979. "A Social Behavioral Theory of the Meadian I." *American Journal of Sociology* (September), 85:261–287.

Lidz, Victor Meyer. 1976. "Introduction." Part II in J. J. Loubser et al., 1976:124–150.

Lidz, Charles W. and Victor Meyer Lidz. 1976. "Piaget's Psychology of Intelligence and the Theory of Action." In J. J. Loubser et al., 1976:195–239.

Loubser, Jan J. 1976. "General Introduction." In J. J. Loubser et al., 1976; 1:1–23.

Loubser, Jan J., et al., eds. 1976. *Explorations on General Theory in Social Sciences: Essays in Honor of Talcott Parsons*. New York: Free Press.

Luckman, Thomas. 1973. "Philosophy, Social Sciences and Everyday Life." In M. Natanson, ed., *Phenomenology and the Social Sciences*, pp. 43–85. Evanston, Ill.: Northwestern University Press. Reprinted in Thomas Luckman, ed., *Phenomenology and Sociology*, pp. 217–253, Baltimore: Penguin.

Lukàcs, Georg. 1971. *History and Class Consciousness: Studies in Marxist Dialectics*. London: Merlin Press.

Lukes, Steven. 1972. *Emile Durkheim: His Life and Work. A Historical and Critical Study*. New York: Harper and Row.

McLellan, David. 1971. *The Thought of Karl Marx: An Introduction*. New York: Harper and Row.

McNall, Scott G. 1978. "On Contemporary Social Theory." *The American Sociologist* 13(1):2–6.

McPhail, Clark and Cynthia Rexroat. 1979. "Mead vs. Blumer: The Divergent Methodological Perspectives of Social Behaviorism and Symbolic Interactionism." *American Sociological Review* (June), 44:449–467.

—— 1980. "Rejoinder: Ex Cathedra Blumer or Ex Libris Mead?" *American Sociological Review* (June), 45:420–430.

Maines, David R. 1977. "Social Organization and Social Structure in Symbolic Interactionist Thought." *Annual Review of Sociology* 3:235–259.

Manis, Jerome G. and Bernard N. Meltzer, ed. 1967. *Symbolic Interaction: A Reader in Social Psychology*. Boston: Allyn and Bacon.

Mannheim, Karl. 1967. *Essays on the Sociology of Culture*. Edited by Ernest Manheim. London: Routledge and Kegan Paul.

Manning, Peter K. 1978. "Structuralism-Survey Review." *Contemporary Sociology* 7(2):139–143.

Mao Tse-Tung. 1968. "On Contradiction" and "On Practice." In *Four Essays on Philosophy*. Peking: Foreign Language Press.

Marc-Lipiansky, Mireille. 1973. *Le Structuralisme de Lévi-Strauss*. Paris: Payot.

Martindale, Don. 1960. *The Nature and Types of Sociological Theory*. Boston: Houghton Mifflin.

Marx, Karl. 1904. *A Contribution to the Critique of Political Economy*. Translated by N. I. Stone. Chicago: C. H. Kerr.

—— 1932. *The Capital, the Communist Manifesto and Other Writings*. Edited by M. Eastman. New York: Modern Library.

—— 1932a. *Theses on Feuerbach*. Published in *Marx-Engels Gesamtausgabe*, ABT.1, Band 3. Berlin: Verlag.

—— 1932b. *Economic and Philosophical Manuscripts*. Published in *Marx-Engels Gesamtausgabe*, ABT.1, Band 3. Berlin: Verlag.

—— 1971. *The Early Texts*. Edited by David McLellan. London: Oxford University Press.

—— 1972. *The Grundrisse*. Edited and translated by David McLellan. New York: Harper and Row.

Marx, Karl and Friedrich Engels. 1970. *The German Ideology*. London: Lawrence and Wishart.

Mead, George H. [922. "A Behaviorist Account of the Significant Symbol." *Journal of Philosophy* 157–163.

—— 1934. *Mind, Self and Society*. Edited by Charles W. Morris. Chicago: University of Chicago Press.

Mehan, Hugh and Houston Wood. 1975. *The Reality of Ethnomethodology*. New York: Wiley Interscience.

Merton, Robert K. 1968. *On Theoretical Sociology*. Part 1 of *Social Theory and Social Structure*. New York: Free Press.

—— 1975. "Structural Analysis in Sociology." In Blau 1975:21–52.

Mounin, Georges. 1970. *Introduction à la Semiologie*. Paris: Minuit.

Natanson, Maurice, ed. 1970. *Phenomenology and Social Reality: Essays in Memory of Alfred Schutz*. The Hague: Nijhoff.

—— 1973. *Phenomenology and the Social Sciences*. Evanston, Ill.: Northestern University Press.

O'Neil, John. 1972. *Sociology as a Skin Trade: Essays Toward a Reflexive Sociology*. New York: Harper and Row.

Overton, Willis F. 1975. "General Systems, Structure and Development." In Klaus F. Riegel and George C. Rosenweld, eds. *Structure and Transformation: Developmental and Historical Aspects*. New York: Wiley.

Pareto, Vilfredo. 1963. *The Mind and Society: A Treatise on General Sociology*. Translated by Andrew Bongiorno and Arthur Livingston. New York: Dover.

Parsons, Talcott. 1934. "Some Reflections on the Nature and Significance of Economics." *Quarterly Journal of Economics* (May), 48:511–545.

—— 1935. "Sociological Elements in Economic Thought, I." *Quarterly Journal of Economics* (May), 49:414–453.

—— 1935a. "Sociological Elements in Economic Thought, II." *Quarterly Journal of Economics* (August), 49:646–667.

—— 1945. "The Present Position and Prospects of Systematic Theory." In G. Gurvitch and W. A. Moore, eds., *Twentieth Century Sociology*. New York: Philosophical Library.

—— 1951. *The Social System*. New York: Free Press.

—— 1961. *The Structure of Social Action*. (1st edition 1937; 2nd edition 1949). New York: Free Press.

—— 1963. "On the Concept of Political Power." *Proceedings of the American Philosophical Society* 107, reprinted in Parsons 1969:352–404.

—— 1964. *Essays in Sociological Theory*. (1st edition 1949; 2nd edition 1954). New York: Free Press.

—— 1966. *Societies: Evolutionary and Comparative Perspectives*. Englewood Cliffs, N.J.: Prentice-Hall.

—— 1969. *Politics and Social Structure*. New York: Free Press.

—— 1970. "Some Problems of General Theory in Sociology." In John C. McKinney and E. A. Tiryakian, eds., *Theoretical Sociology*, pp. 27–68. New York: Appleton-Century-Crofts.

—— 1970a. "On Building Social System Theory: A Personal History." *Daedalus* 99(4):826–881.

—— 1971. "Comparative Studies and Evolutionary Change." In Ivan Vallier, ed. *Comparative Methods in Sociology*, pp. 97–139. Berkeley: University of California Press.

—— 1971a. *The System of Modern Societies*. Englewood-Cliffs, N.J.: Prentice-Hall.

—— 1973. "Cultural and Social System Revisited." In L. Schneider and Charles M. Bonjeau, eds., *The Idea of Culture in the Social Sciences*, pp. 33–46. Cambridge, England: Cambridge University Press.

—— 1973a. "Durkheim on Religion Revisited: Another Look at the *Elementary Forms of the Religious Life.*" In C. Y. Glock and P. E. Hammond, eds., *Beyond the Classics: Essays in the Scientific Study of Religion*. New York: Harper and Row.

—— 1975. "The Present Status of Structural-Functional Theory in Sociology." In L. A. Coser, ed., *The Idea of Social Structure: Papers in Honor of Robert K. Merton*, pp. 67–84. New York: Harcourt Brace Jovanovich.

—— 1975a. Comment on "Parsons' Interpretation of Durkheim," and on "Moral Freedom Through Understanding in Durkheim." *American Sociological Review* (February), 40:106–110.

—— 1977. Comment on "Burger's Critique." *American Journal of Sociology* 83(2):335–339.

—— 1978. "A Paradigm of the Human Condition." In T. Parsons, *Action Theory and the Human Condition*, pp. 352–433. New York: Free Press.

—— 1982. "Action, Symbols, and Cybernetic Control." In Ino Rossi, ed., 1982. *Structural Sociology*, pp. 49–65.

Parsons, Talcott, Robert F. Bales, and Edward Shils. 1953. *Working Papers in Theory of Action*. New York: Free Press.

Parsons, Talcott, R. C. Fox, and V. M. Lidz. 1972. "The Gift of Life and Its Reciprocation." *Social Research* 39:367–415.

Parsons, Talcott and Edward Shils, eds. 1951. *Toward A General Theory of Action*. Cambridge, Mass.: Harvard University Press.

Parsons, Talcott, E. Shils, K. D. Naegele, and J. R. Pitts, eds. 1965 *Theories of Society*. One volume edition. New York: Free Press (orig. 1961).

Pettit, Philip. 1975. *The Concept of Structuralism: A Critical Analysis*. Berkeley: University of California Press.

Phillips, Derek L. 1973. *Abandoning Method: Sociological Studies in Methodology*. San Francisco: Jossey-Bass.

Phillipson, Michael. 1972. "Phenomenological Philosophy and Sociology." In Paul Filmer, Michael Phillipson, David Silverman, and David Walsh, eds., *New Directions in Sociological Theory*, Cambridge, Mass.: MIT Press.

Piaget, Jean. 1950. *Introduction à L'Epistemologie Genetique*. 3 volumes. Paris: Presses Universitaires de France.

—— 1967. "Le Structuralisme." *Cahiers Internationaux de Symbolisme* 15–16:73–85.

—— 1969. "Discussion" of "On Voluntary Action and Its Hierarchical Structure." By Jerome S. Bruner in Arthur Koestler and J. R. Smythies, eds., *Beyond Reductionism: New Perspectives in the Life Sciences*, pp. 181–191. New York: Macmillan.

—— 1969a. "Genetic Epistemology." Reprinted in Richard I. Evans, *Jean Piaget: The Man and His Ideas*. New York: E. P. Dutton, 1973, pp. xlii–lxi.

—— 1970. *Structuralism*. Translated by C. Maschler. New York: Basic Books.

—— 1970a. *Genetic Epistemology*. Translated by Eleanor Duckworth. New York: Columbia University Press.

—— 1973. *Main Trends in Interdisciplinary Research*. New York: Harper and Row.

Piaget, Jean, ed. 1967. *Logique et Connaissance Scientifique*. Paris.

Pope, Whitney. 1973. "Classic on Classic: Parsons' Interpretation of Durkheim." *American Sociological Review* 38(4):399–415.

Pouillon, Jean. 1965. "Sartre et Lévi-Strauss." *L'Arc* 26:55–60.

Prieto, Luis. 1968. "La Semiologie." In *Le Langage: Encyclopedie de la Pleiade*. Paris: Gallimard.

Propp, Vladimir. 1970. *The Morphology of the Folktale*. Austin: University of Texas Press (Russian orig. 1928).

Psathas, George, ed. 1973. *Phenomenological Sociology: Issues and Applications*. New York: Wiley Interscience.

Radcliffe-Brown, A. R. 1940. "On Social Structure." *Journal of the Royal Anthropological Institute* 70:1–12.

—— 1965. *Structure and Function in Primitive Society*. New York: Free Press (orig 1952).

Remotti, Francesco. 1971. *Lévi-Strauss. Struttura e Storia*. Torino: Piccola Biblioteca Einaudi.

Rex, John. 1961. *Key Problems of Sociological Theory*. London: Routledge and Kegan Paul.

Reynolds, J. and L. Reynolds. 1973. "Interactionism, Complicity and the Structural Bias." *Catalyst* 7:76–85.

Reynolds, L. 1969. *The Sociology of Symbolic Interactionism*. Ph.D. thesis. Columbus: Ohio State University.

Ricoeur, P. 1963. "Response à Quêlque Questions." *Esprit* 31(322):628–653.

—— 1967. "New Developments in Phenomenology in France: The Phenomenology of Language." *Social Research* 34:1–30.

—— 1967a. "La Structure, le Mot, l'Evénément." *Esprit* 35:801–821.

Riegel, Klaus F. and George C. Rosenwald, eds. 1975. *Structure and Transformation: Developmental and Historical Aspects*. New York: Wiley.

Ritzer, George. 1975. *Sociology: A Multiple Paradigm Science*. Boston: Allyn and Bacon.

Robey, David, ed. 1973. *Structuralism: An Introduction*. Oxford: Clarendon Press.

Rossi, Ino. 1973. "The Unconscious in the Anthropology of Claude Lévi-Strauss." *American Anthropologist* 75(1):20–49.

—— 1973a. "Verification in Anthropology: The Case of Structural Analysis." *Journal of Symbolic Anthropology* 1(2):27–55.

—— 1975. Comment to "Dominant Epistemological Presuppositions in the Use of the Cross-Cultural Survey Method" by C. J. J. Vermeulen and A. De Ruijeer. *Current Anthropology* 16(1):45–46.

—— 1977. "Reply to Cohen." *American Anthropologist* 79(1):114–115.

—— 1977a. "On the Notion of Social Structure: A Mental or Objective Reality?" *American Anthropologist* 79(4):914–916.

—— 1978. "Toward the Unification of Scientific Explanation: Evidence from Biological, Psychic, Linguistic, Cultural Universals." In Marvin D. Loflin and James Silverberg, eds., *Discourse and Inference in Cognitive Anthropology*, pp. 199–228. A volume in the "World Anthropology" series. The Hague: Mouton.

—— 1978a. "On Theoretical and Technical Incompetence: The Case of Needham." *American Anthropologist* 80(3):675–676.

—— 1981. "Transformational Structuralism: Lévi-Strauss' Definition of Social Structure." In Peter M. Blau and Robert K. Merton, eds., *Continuities in Structural Inquiry*, London: Sage Publications.

Rossi, Ino, ed. 1974. *The Unconscious in Culture: The Structuralism of Claude Lévi-Strauss in Perspective*. New York: Dutton.

Rossi, Ino, ed. 1982. *Structural Sociology: Theoretical Perspectives and Substantive Analyses*. New York: Columbia University Press.

Rossi, Ino, ed. 1982a. "On the Scientific Evidence for the Existence of Deep Structures and Their Objective and Mathematical Nature: A Training Session for Rodney Needham, Ronald Cohen, Peter Caws, Paul Chaney." In Rossi 1982b:265–293.

—— 1982b. *The Logic of Culture: Advances in Structural Theory and Method*. South Hadley, Massachusetts: J. F. Bergin.

Rossi-Landi, Ferruccio. 1973. *Semiotica e Ideologia*. Milano: Bompiani.

—— 1968. *Il Linguaggio come Lavoro e Come Mercato*. Milano: Bompiani.

Roth, Guenther. 1977. "Review Essay: On Recent Works Concerning Max Weber." *American Journal of Sociology* 82(6):1350–1355.

Sartre, Jean-Paul. 1943. *L'Etre et le Néant*. Paris: Gallimard.

—— 1946. "Materialism and Revolution" *Les Temps Modernes;* quoted as translated by Annette Michelson in *Literary and Philosophical Essays*. New York, 1962.

—— 1960. *Critique de la Raison Dialectique*. Paris: Gallimard.

—— 1966. "Jean-Paul Sartre Repond." *L'Arc* 30:87–96. Here quoted as translated in *Telos* 9:111–115 (1971).

—— 1971. "Replies to Structuralism: An Interview with Jean-Paul Sartre." *Telos* 9:111–115. Originally published in *L'Arc* 30.

Saussure, Ferdinand de. 1966. *Course in General Linguistics*. Edited by C. Bally and A. Sechehaye. Translated by W. Baskin. New York: McGraw-Hill (orig. 1916).

Schneider, Louis. 1971. "Dialectic in Sociology." *American Sociological Review* 36(4):667–678.

Schutz, Alfred. 1940. "Phenomenology and the Social Sciences." In Marvin Farber, ed., *Philosophical Essays in Memory of Edmund Husserl*. Cambridge, Mass.: Harvard University Press. Reprinted in Joseph J. Kockelmans, ed., *Phenomenology: The Philosophy of Edmund Husserl and Its Interpretation*. Garden City, N.Y.: Doubleday.

—— 1962. *Collected Papers*. Vol. 1. Maurice Natanson, ed. The Hague: Nijhoff.

—— 1967. *The Phenomenology of the Social World*. Translated by George Walsch and Frederick Lehnert. Evanston, Ill.: Northwestern University Press.

Schwanenberg, Enno. 1976. "On the Meaning of the Theory of Action." In Loubser et al., 1976:35–45.

Scott, Joseph F. 1969. "The Changing Foundations of the Parsonian Action Scheme." *American Sociological Review* (October), 28:716–739.

Seuren, P. A., ed. 1974. *Semantic Syntax*. New York: Oxford University Press.

Sheridan, Alan. 1981. *Michel Foucault: The Will to Truth*. London: Travistock.

Sherman, L. W. 1974. "The Uses of the Masters." *American Sociologist* 9:176–181.

Simmel, Georg. 1950. *The Sociology of Georg Simmel*. Translated and edited by Kurt H. Wolff. New York: Free Press.

—— 1968. *The Conflict in Modern Culture and Other Essays.* Translated by K. Peter Etzkorn. New York: Teachers College Press.

Simonis, Yvan. 1968. *Claude Lévi-Strauss ou la "Passion de L'Inceste": Introduction au Structuralism.* Paris: Aubier Montaigne

—— 1968a. "Echange, Praxis, Code et Message." *Cahiers Internationaux de Sociologie* 45:117–129.

Slabert, F. Van Zyl. 1976. "Functional Methodology in the Theory of Action." In Loubser et al., 1976; 1:46–58.

Sorokin, P. A. 1928. *Contemporary Sociological Theories.* New York: Harper and Row.

—— 1966. *Sociological Theories of Today.* New York: Harper and Row.

Spiegelberg, Herbert. 1965. "The Essentials of the Phenomenological Method." In *The Phenomenological Movement: A Historical Introduction,* 2:655–701. 2nd edition. The Hague: Nijhoff.

Stark, Werner. 1958. *The Sociology of Knowledge.* London: Routledge and Kegan Paul.

Steinberg, D. D. and L. A. Jakobovitz, eds. 1971. *Semantics: An Interdisciplinary Reader in Philosophy, Linguistics and Psychology.* Cambridge: Cambridge University Press.

Stent, Gunther S. 1975. "Limits to the Scientific Understanding of man" *Science* 187 (4181):1052–1057.

Stinchcombe, Arthur L. 1975. "A Structural Analysis of Sociology." *The American Sociologist* 10(2):57–64.

Sturrock, John, ed. 1979. *Structuralism and Since: From Lévi-Strauss to Derrida.* New York: Oxford University Press.

Sudnow, David. 1971. *Studies in Social Interaction.* New York: Free Press.

Swanson, Guy E. 1973. "Framework for Comparative Research: Structural Anthropology and the Theory of Action." In Ivan Vallier, ed., *Comparative Methods in Sociology,* pp. 141–203. Berkeley: University of California Press.

Timasheff, Nicholas. 1967. *Sociological Theory: Its Nature and Growth.* 3rd edition. New York: Random House.

Tiryakian, Edward A. 1962. *Sociologism and Existentialism.* Englewood Cliffs, N.J.: Prentice-Hall.

—— 1970. "Structural Sociology." In J. C. McKinney and E. A. Tiryakian, eds., *Theoretical Sociology: Perspectives and Developments.* New York: Appleton-Century-Crofts.

Turner, Jonathan H. 1978. *The Structure of Sociological Theory.* 2nd edition. Homewood, Ill.: Dorsey Press.

Turner, Jonathan, H. and Leonard Beeghley. 1974. "Current Folklore in the Criticism of Parsonian Action Theory." *Sociological Inquiry* (Winter), 44.

Turner, Roy, ed. 1974. *Ethnomethodology.* Baltimore: Penguin.

Van den Berghe, Pierre. 1963. "Dialectic and Functionalism: Toward a Theoretical Synthesis." *American Sociological Review* 28:695–705.

Viet, Jean. 1969. *Les Méthodes Structuralistes dans les Sciences Sociales.* 2nd edition. Paris: Mouton.

Wagner, Helmut R. 1963. "Types of Sociological Theory." *American Sociological Review* (October), 28:735–742. Reprinted in R. Serge Denisoff, Arerl Callahan, and Mark H. Levine, eds., *Theories and Paradigms in Contemporary Sociology,* pp. 41–52. Itasca, Ill.: Peacock, 1974.

—— 1971. "Introduction." In H. Wagner, ed., *Alfred Schutz on Phenomenology and Social Relations,* Chicago: University of Chicago Press.

Walls, David S. 1979. "Dialectical Social Science." In Scott G. McNall, ed., *Theoretical Perspectives in Sociology*. New York: St. Martin's Press.

Warshay, Leon H. 1975. *The Current State of Sociological Theory: A Critical Interpretation*. New York: McKay.

Watzlawick, P., J. H. Beavin, and D. D. Jackson. 1967. *Pragmatics of Human Communication: A Study of Interactional Patterns, Pathologies, and Paradoxes*. New York: Norton.

Weber, Max. 1949. *The Methodology of the Social Sciences*. New York: Free Press.

—— 1958. *The Protestant Ethic and the Spirit of Capitalism*. New York: Scribner's.

—— 1964. *The Theory of Social and Economic Organization*. Translated by A. M. Henderson and T. Parsons. New York: Free Press.

—— 1978. "Anticritical Last Word on *The Spirit of Capitalism*." Translated by Wallace M. Davis in *American Journal of Sociology* 83(5):1110–1131.

Whitehead, Alfred. 1925. *Science and the Modern World*. New York: Macmillan.

Wieder, D. L. 1977. "Ethnomethodology and Ethnosociology." *Mid-American Review of Sociology* 2:1–18.

Wiener, Norbert. 1954. *The Human Use of Human Beings: Cybernetics and Society*. New York: Avon.

—— 1955. *Communication*. Cambridge, Mass.: M.I.T. Press.

—— 1961. *Cybernetics*. Cambridge, Mass.: M.I.T. Press (1st edition 1948).

Wilson, Thomas P. 1970. "Normative and Interpretive Paradigms in Sociology." In Jack D. Douglas, ed., *Understanding Everyday Life*, pp. 57–79. Chicago: Aldine.

Wolff, H. Kurt, ed. 1971. *From Kark Mannheim*. New York: Oxford University Press.

—— 1978. "Phenomenology and Sociology." In Bottomore and Nisbet 1978. 499–556.

Zaret, David. 1980. "From Weber to Parsons and Schutz: The Eclipse of History in Modern Social Theory." *American Journal of Sociology* 85(5):1180–1201.

Zeitlin, Irving M. 1968. *Ideology and the Development of Sociological Theory*. Englewood Cliffs, N.J.: Prentice-Hall.

—— 1973. *Rethinking Sociology: A Critique of Contemporary Theory*. New York: Appleton-Century-Crofts.

Zimmerman, Don H. 1978. "Ethnomethodology." *The American Sociologist* 13(1):6–15.

Znaniecki, Florian. 1934. *The Method of Sociology*. New York: Holt, Rinehart and Winston.

——1978. "Ethnomethodology." *The American Sociologist* 13(1):6–15.

Index

Action Theory, structural reinterpretation, 203
Alienation, 249
Althusser, L., 1, 249; and class struggle as the motor of history, 288; and destruction of dialectic, 254; and dual determination by infrastructure and superstructure, 288; and Hegelian dialectic, 252; and history as process without subject, 287; and John Lewis, 287; and Marxist dialectic, 252; and monistic dialectic, 252; and objective dialectic, 255; and relations and contradictions, 287; and overdetermination, 253; and primacy of superstructure, 254; and relationship between structure and superstructure, 253; and structure in dominance, 254; and totality, 251; as positivist, 254; as critic of Lévi-Strauss' formalism, 259; subject as constituted by structure, 290
Anthropology, as a semiological science, 139
Augé, M., 274

Bachelard, G., 249
Badcock, C. R., 25
Balibar, E., 248
Barthes, R., 1, 138, 147; and Brecht, 151; and creativity of rules, 298; and plurality of the text, 301; refutes the realist view of narrative, 300; challenges Saussure and Chomsky, 298, 300; and surface structures, 147; structural (early) phase of, 151, 298; and text as dynamic structure, 301; and the text as an inter-

weaving of voices and codes, 300; and transition to a poststructural orientation, 298
Bateson, G., 204; and semiotics, 132
Bellah, R. N., 119
Benoist, J. M., 1, 254
Benveniste, Emile, 304
Berger, P., 208, 219
Berlin, P., 13
Bernstein, E., 248
Binet, A., 153
Blau, Peter M., 119
Bleicher, J., 224
Bloomfield, L., 138
Blumer, H., 84
Boas, F., 138
Bourbaki School of Mathematics, 19
Bourdieu, P., and praxeology, 223
Bruyn, S., 208
Burawoy, M., 247

Cannon, W. B., 126
Carnap, R., 18; and semiotics, 132
Cartesian dichotomy, 5
Cartesian dualism, 14
Cartesian thought, 18
Cassirer, E., 18
Chomsky, N., 25; and Cicourel and Goffman, 165; and deep structure, 172; and extended standard theory, 168; and generative model of language, 169; and generative semantics, 168; and "grammar," 165; and linguistic competence, 164; and linguistic performance, 164; and phrase structure rules, 165; and Piaget, 163; and primacy of syntax, 167;

Chomsky, N. (*Continued*)
and priority of structure over transformation, 172; and selectional rules, 167; static and descriptive rules, 176; and surface structure and deep structure, 201; and transformation, 172; and transformational grammar, 164; and transformational rules, 166, 176, 201

Cicourel, A., 209, 228; and Chomsky, 232; and empiricist level of analysis, 232; and generative semantics of social interaction, 228; and performance, 231; and Schutz, 229

Code: of commodities, 150; in cybernetics, 187; of language, 189; in linguistics, 187; in semiotic structuralism, 187; as a set of relations, 187

Communication theorists and linguistics, 187

Communicative competence, 228

Comte, A., 3

Comtean method, 15

Comtean positivism, 2, 3, 4

Connotation, 148; and ideology, 149

Connotative system, 148

Constructivist notion of explanation, 199

Cooley, Charles H., 22; and human knowledge, 81; and the knowledge of external traits, 81; language in, 82; and "mental" aspect of social interaction, 81; and "sympathetic introspection," 82

Coser, L., 86

Crick, F. H., and code, 187

Culler, J., 301

Cultural sociology, Mannheim's, 22

Cultural "texts," 146

Culture as rules for communication of signs, 142

Cybernetic perspective, 186

Deep structure, 141

Deleuze, G., 152

Derrida, J., 222, 301; and decentered system, 303; and difference, 302; and language, 302; and materiality of the signifier, 301; and notion of writing, 302; and primacy of the signifier, 301

Descartes, R., 6

Descriptive linguistics, 138

"Determination," 46

Dialectic: between event, history, and subjectivity, 321; vs integrated paradigm, 313; as methodological approach, 324; of reciprocity, 35, 314; and reflexive activity, 224; strong sense of, 224; as substantive approach, 324

Dialectic approach, 32, 35, 310

Dialectic method, 315

Dialectic, ontological, 315

Dialectic perspective, 35

Dialectic view of social reality, 314

Dichotomies: mind-external world, 14, 15; subjective-objective reality, 14

Dichotomus thinking, 16, 319

Difference, as constitutive dialectic principle, 320

Dilthey, W., 80

Distinctive features, 137, 138

Douglas, Jack, 209, 218, 231

Dualism, 12

Dufrenne, M., 222

Durkheim, E., 2, 4, 14, 15, 21, 25, 31; ambivalent between a Kantian and positive attitude, 96, 98; collective representations and social organization, 110, 111; continuity with the semiotic perspective, 119, 121; and distinction between surface and deep structure, 117; elementarist and relational perspective, 116; empiricism of, 5; empiricist interpretation of, 94; essential idealism of, 106; as essentialist, 110; evolution from a morphological to a symbolic perspective, 104; and immanent explanation, 114; influence on Saussure, 133; as intellectualist, 111; and Lévi-Strauss as neo-Kantian, 111; logical and methodical method, 99; methodological positivist, 98; not a behaviorist or empirical structuralist, 119; as organistic and utilitarian thinker, 97; partial autonomy of collective representations, 102; as positivist, 4, 100; as precursor of semiotic approach, 113; representation in, 95; social life as representations, 105; social morphology in, 103; and structure as first and self-explanatory datum, 160; symbolic realism in, 109; symbols and collective representations, 108; and synchronic explanation, 115; and total social fact, 114; the unconscious as a source of social phenomena, 112; vs. Chomskian and Piagetian conception of morality, 163; as voluntarist and idealist, 97

Durkheimian positivism, 3

Dynamic structuralism, 146

Eco. U.: and culture as communication process, 150; and the early Barthes, 146

Eisenstadt, S. N., 71

Emerson, A., 126, 189

Empirical knowledge, 3, 5

Empiricism, 3, 10; abstracted, 6; and behaviorism, 85; crude, 182; functionalism as, 5; objective, 7; and phenomenology, 85; persisting in phenomenological sociology, 217; rejected by phenomenological sociology and semiotic structuralism, 139; subjective, 7, 8; in traditional sociology, 5

Engels, F., 248

"Epoché," 8

Ervin-Tripp, S., 228

Ethnomethodology: and interpretive rules, 227; and metaempirical structures, 231; and natural language, 227; and transformational rules, 230; and undialectic bias, 233

Existential phenomenology, 210

Existential sociology, 221

Evaluative sociology, 28, 32

Evans-Pritchard, E. E., 97

Falsifiability, 3

Feuerbach, L., 250

Fillmore, C., and case grammar, 169

Formal validity, 29

Foucault, M., 1

Fox, R. C., 190

Frankfurt School, 248

Friedman, J., and negative causality, 279

Garfinkel, H., 209; and the rationality of the social world, 226; and Schutz, 226

Genetic Epistemology, 10

German positivism, 17

Gertz, C., 23

Gestalt psychologists, 18; and priority of gestalt over transformation, 170

Godelier, M., 1, 248; against dogmatic Marxism and vulgar materialism, 262; against Marvin Harris, 264; against vulgar materialism, 170; and Althusser's epistemological break, 261; and compatibility between forms and functions of social relations, 273; and critic of Lévi-Strauss, 266, 269; deficient dialectic of, 278; and determination in last analysis, 270; and dominant superstructure, 276; and early Lévi-Straussian perspective, 260; and historical contingency, 276; and ideology, 275; imprisoned within structural determinism, 280; and infrastructure and superstructure as the same logical order, 277; and internal constraints, 273; and intrasystemic contradictions, 279; and Leach, 265; and Marxist perspective, 280; notion of history, 267; and philosophical vs. scientific phases of Marx, 262; rejects conscious subjectivity with Althusser and Lévi-Strauss, 262; rejects empirical functionalism, 265; rejects Lenin, Mao, Lucian Sève, and Althusser, 264; rejects structuralism and functionalism, 263; representations as part of social relations, 272; shares elements of Lévi-Strauss' approach, 280; and shifting dominance between infractructure and superstructure, 277; and similiarity with Lévi-Strauss, 266; and simultaneity of functions, 274; and social relations as both material and idea, 277; and structure-infrastructure relationship

Goffman, E.: and Chomsky, 225; code in, 237; as empiricist, 240; and formal sociology, 236; frame (notion of), 236; and Lévi-Strauss and Chomsky, 237; neglects creative subjectivity, 242; similarities with Lévi-Strauss and Chomsky,

Goffman, E. (*Continued*)
235; structuralist component in, 239, 240; and transformational grammarians, 236; and the transformational perspective, 237
Goldman, L., 248, 251; structure and history, 251; totality and identity, 251
Gramsci, A., 248
Greimas, A. J., 147
"Group," definition of, 171
Gumperz, J. J., 227
Gurvitch, G., 209, 218; and dialectic, 314

Habermas: "communication competence" in, 51; intersubjectivity in, 51; reflection as a motive force of history, 50; subjectivity in, 51; symbolic communication in, 50
Halle, M., 137, 193
Handel, W. H., 236
Harris, M., 267
Harris, Z., 138, 175
Heap, J. L., 209
History, definition, 324
Hjelmslev, L., 138, 148; and glossematics, 148
Holzner, B., 209
Homans, G. C., 27
Humanist marxism, 49
Humanistic coefficient, 31
Husserl, E., 210, 219; and intellectualist bias, 218; method of variation and permutation, 211; and rationalistic phenomenology, 218; science of essences, 210
Husserlian perspective, 210
Hymes, D., 227

Ideal typical explanation, 4
Ideological systems, logical structure of, 150
Ideology, sociology of, 151
Individual and society, 32, 51
Information, 187
Interparadigmatic linkage, 36
Interpretation, 4
Interpretive paradigm, 31
Interpretive sociology, 28, 32

Introspection, 2
Isomorphic structural mechanisms, 14

Jakobson, R., 136, 193; offers a synthesis between Piaget and Lévi-Strauss, 80
James, W., and Alfred Schutz, 237
Janet, P., 153

Kant, I., 6, 80
Kantianism, 17
Kaplan, A., 29
Kautsky, K., 248
Kay, B., 13
Knowledge, constructivist notion of, 13, 18; as reconstruction, 12; as system of transformations, 10
Koffka, K., 170
Köhler, W., 170
Kosik, K., and dialectical rationalism, 317
Kristeva, J., 1; and atomization of the subject, 307; and Chomsky, 304; and dissolution of both structure and subjectivity, 307; and Husserl, 304; and Joyce, 306; and Lautréamont, 306; and materialistic theory of signification, 305; and negative and objectivized notion of subjectivity, 306; and negative dialectic, 303; and the production of the subject and meaning in language, 305; and semanalysis, 305; and Sollers, 306; and subjectivity as signifying practice, 307; and the unconscious as motor of history, 307
Kuhn, T. S., notion of paradigm, 27

Lacan, J., 1; and construction of subject by the signifying chain, 293; and decentered subject, 296; and dynamic conception of meaning, 293; fills gaps in Sartre and Althusser, 294; and Freud, 292; and language and ideology, 296; and linguistic interpretation of Freud, 292; notion of structure, 292; and objectivized and relational subject, 296; and poststructural semiotics, 297; and the structural activity of the unconscious, 294
Lakoff, G., and generative semantics, 168

Language: as foundation of meaning, 152; as mediation, 316; and social praxis, 53; as structuring operation, 316

"Langue," 133, 134

Lauer, R., 236

Lefebvre, H., 222, 248

Leibniz, G. V. (von), 18; and semiotics, 132

Lemert, E., 86

Lenin, V. I., 248; early phase of, 148; international negativity in, 52

Lévi-Strauss, C., 1, 3, 11, 255; and affinity with Piaget's perspective, 173; and Althusser, 244; and Althusserian notion of overdetermination, 258; and Althusser's notion of structural causality, 258; and analytical and dialectical perspectives, 245; and the "atom of kinship," 145; and Chomsky, 170, 174; combinatory approach of, 143; consistent with Althusser, 257; and complementarities with Chomsky and Piaget, 169, 173; critics of, 146; and cybernetics, 141; and determination in the last instance, 257; and the elementary structure of exchange, 145; and empiricist notion of history, 268; as extension of Durkheim and Mauss, 145; and Godelier, 244; influenced by Durkheim, 139; intellectual antecedents of, 139; and infrastructure, 256; and infrastructure-superstructure relationship, 257; and Marx, 245, 256; and notion of dialectic, 258; overture to a dynamic perspective, 174; and paradigmatic analysis, 140, 171; and Piaget, 10, 160, 174; as positivist, 3; and positivist dichotomies, 139; and precedence of form over content, 246; and primacy of infrastructure, 258; and priority of structure over transformation, 171; and rejection of formalism, 245, 247, 259; and rejection of the conscious subject, 259; reverses Durkheim's perspective, 143; and Russian formalists, 140; and Sartre, 245; social structure in, 171, 245; and society as a system of communication, 141; and structure and historical analysis, 268; and the theory of "group," 171; and transformational approach, 172; and Troubetzkoy's phonological method, 144; and the unconscious system of relational constants, 144; and verification of explanation, 172; and Weberian, Kantian, and neo-Kantian thought, 74

Lidz, V. M., 190; and development of the theory of action, 203; dualistic perspective, 196; and Piaget, 203

Linguistic code, 137

Locke, J., and semiotics, 132

Luckman, T., 208, 219, 220; and empiricist pitfalls, 221

Lukàcs, G., 249; dialectical vs positivist method, 251

Mach, E., 18

MacIver, R. M., 82

Macrosociological perspective, 24

Maines, D. R., 86

Mannheim, K., 22; and combinatory view of social phenomena, 79; conscious and unconscious meaning in, 77; situational meaning in, 77; and structural analysis, 78; transformational structuralism, 76

Mao, principal contradiction (notion of), 52

Marc-Lipiansky, M., 1

Marx, K., 37-53, 150, 246; alienated language in, 43; commodity as fetishism, 41; and consciousness, 44; contradiction (notion of), 48, 51; dialectic, 39, 52; economic infrastructure, 46; economic structure of society, 44; externalisation, 42; false consciousness, 40, 42; history (conception of), 44; ideology, 21, 41; language, 43; mode of production, 40, 45, 46; notion of totality, 44; opposition to bourgeois materialism, 48; positivist interpretation of, 49; "practice" in, 48; rejects economic determinism, 46; scientific stage of, 250; scientific vs Hegelian perspective, 251; social praxis, 41; superstructure (notion of), 40, 44; superstructure and infrastructure, 46; unity of thought and being, 45; and Weber, 55

Marxism, 248, 249

Martinet, A., 147
Mathematical concepts, in Saussure, Lévi-Strauss and Chomsky, 175
Mathematical knowledge, 10
Mauss, M., 2, 4, 9, 25
McCawley, J., and generative semantics, 168
McNall, S. G., 314
Mead, G. H., 22, 83, 195; definition of meaning, 84; notion of "I" and "me," 213; significant symbols, 84; symbolism, 84
Meaning: constructivist view of, 225; in phenomenology and semiotic structuralism, 208; objective, 24, 132; threefold layer, 224; transituational, 231; in Weber and Mead, 131
Mehan, H., 209
Meillassoux, C., 275
Merleau-Ponty, M., 210
Merton, R. K., 27, 29, 119
Metaphoric relationships, 137
Methodology, definition of, 29, 30, 214
Metonymic relationships, 137
Microsociological perspective, 24
Morphemes, 137
Morris, C., and semiotics, 132
Mounin, G., 147

Natanson, M., 209
Natural attitude, 225
Natural science paradigm, 31
Naturalist attitude, 7
Negation, 249
Neo-Kantian perspective: and Lévi-Strauss, Parsons, Weber, 183; neopositivist philosophers, 122
Nietzsche, F. W., 60

Objective approach, 311
Objectivism, naïve, 17
O'Neil, J., 209

Paradigm, 27, 29
Paradigmatic analysis, 141
Pareto, V.: circulation of lions and foxes, 92; derivations, 91; logical actions, 89; nonlogical actions, 90; notion of elite, 92; rationalizations, 90; residues of action, 90; social strata as constellations of consciousness, 93; symbolism, 90; and transformational structuralism, 93
"Parole," 133, 134
Parsons, T., and the binary principle, 190; and Chomsky, 127, 196, 201; and classificatory mode of explanation, 198; critical of positivism, utilitarianism, and idealism, 123; and cultural code, 185; culture in, 124; and cybernetic view, 126, 185; and Deutsch, 186; and dichotomous conceptualizations, 197; and dilemma between analytical terms and empirical terms, 199; dualistic perspective, 196; on Durkheim, 103; as empiricist, 7; and empiricist notion of code, 192; and empiricist notion of scientific activity, 195; and empiricist view of language, 193; empiricist vs. formalist level of analysis, 70; evolution and the genetic code, 189; and formalist mode of sociological analysis, 199; and Freud, 125; as functionalist, 184; and generalized symbolic media of interchange, 188; and Halle, 187, 192; homeostatic view of the system, 126; and the "interpretive" and "natural science" approaches, 127; and Jakobson, 187, 192; and Kant and Chomsky, 184; Kantianism of, 7, 11, 16; and lack of transformational perspective, 202; and Edmund Leach, 190; and Lévi-Strauss, 127, 190; shares with Lévi-Strauss a classificatory elementary and combinatorial perspective, 190; and linguistic code, 185; and linguistics, 185; and mathematical notion of structure, 2024; and Mead, 125; mechanical notion of system, 126; mind-reality dichotomy in, 11; and moderate empiricism, 182; and the natural science paradigm, 12; and notion of linguistic code, 137; and observable regularities vs. abstract conceptions, 199; organic perspective of the system, 126; and Pareto, 122, 126; and Piaget, 125, 127, 197; and Radcliffe-Brown, 206; and rejection of extreme empiricism, 195; and Schumpeter, 126; and similarity between the

role of the genetic code and the cultural system, 189; and subjective meaning as focus of analysis, 191, 193; and symbol, 192; and symbolic medium, 194; symbolic orientation, 123; symbolism in, 123; and systematic bias, 205; systemic view, 121, 123, 125; theoretical order vs. "socio-empirical" order, 200; and traditional sociological categories, 125; and transformational structuralism, 125; and undialectic sociological thinking, 205, 206; and Weber, 125; and Wiener, 186

Parsons, T., 124

Peirce, C. S., and semiotics, 132

Permutation, 171

Phenomenological sociology: and intersubjective world of meaning, 213; four types of, 209

Phenomenology: and antiempiricist attitude, 214; and constitutive view of scientific activity, 215; and distinction between form and content, 216

Piaget, J., 1, 9, 10; against Lévi-Strauss' dismissal of functionalism, 161; antiempiricist conception of scientific explanation, 155; complementarity with semiotic structuralism of, 162; and the constructive laws of structure, 160; concept of group, 159; and his opposition to Chomsky, 161; cybernetic aspect of, 158; and dynamic perspective, 176; and genetic epistemology, 155; knowledge as a system of transformations, 157; links the functional to the structural perspective, 161; logic of thought and logic of action, 156; not a true dialectician, 291; organismic and formal assumptions, 153; and priority of genesis over structure, 158; reverses Lévi-Strauss' and Chomsky's notion of deep structure, 173; and structure as a construct, 162; and structure as a dynamic link between subject and object, 161; structure as a system of transformations, 158; structuralism of, 156

Poincaré, H., 18

Popper, K., and neopositivism, 3

Positive sociology, 28

Positivism: dualistic perspective of empiricist positivism, 204; as naturalism, determinism, phenomenalism, 94; structural and empiricist version of, 181

Positivist methodology, 15

Pouillon, J., 285

Poulantzas, N., 248

Praxis, 249, 317, 320, 322

Propp, V., 140

Psathas, G., 209

Radcliffe-Brown, A. R., 97, 100; and Durkheim, 125, 206

Rappaport, R. A., 267

Rationalism, and Lévi-Strauss, Piaget, Chomsky, 183

Realism, analytical and radical, 6

Reflexive sociology, 209

Relational invariants, 24

Relational perspective, 20

Relational thinking, 19

Rey, P. P., 275

Ricoeur, P., 222, 315; and dialectic between explanation and understanding, 317; and integration of semiological and semantic explanations, 223

Ritzer, G., 27

Rossi-Landi, F., and semiotic study of ideology, 152

Roth, P. A., 209

Ruesch, J., and semiotics, 132

Sapir, E., 138

Sartre, J. P., 210; vs. Althusser, Foucault, Lévi-Strauss, 282; at odds with vulgar Marxism and Lévi-Strauss' natural dialectic, 283; and dialectical method, 289; and dialectic of history and human freedom, 284; and dialectical rationalism, 284; and Foucault, 286; and Freud, 282; and Heidegger, 282; and human-centered dialectic, 291; and humanism, 282; and Husserl, 282; and Jaspers, 282; and Marx, 282; as phenomenologist, 282; reintegration of subject and object in, 283; rejection of analytical reasoning, 284; rejection of structuralism, 285; and sovereign state of subjectivity, 283; and

Sartre, J. P. (*Continued*)
structuralism as a positivism of signs, 289; and the structuralist notion of history, 286; theory of history and consciousness, 283; and totalizing praxis, 289

Saussure F. (De), 19; diachronic linguistics, 136; language as system of relational contrasts, 135; paradigmatic relationships, 135; permutation, 136; positivist perspective of, 134; relational value of signs, 135; shortcomings of, 297; sign (definition of), 135; signifier and signified, 135; synchronic linguistics, 136

Semiotics, 132; poststructural, 35, 152; poststructural and dialetic view of linguistic productivity, 298; and structuralism, 153; and the study of ideology, 146, 152

Semioticians, 1

Sign, 148

"Sign Function," 148

Simmel, G., 80; and dialectic, 313; and pure form, 80

Simonis, Y., 1, 246

Social behaviorist, 27

Social definitionist, 27

Social dynamics, 322

Social factist, 27

Social structure, as simultaneously a producer and a product, 86

Sociological phenomenology, 210

Speaking, as a dialectical production, 316

Spiegelberg, H., 216

Spinoza, B., 249

Structural Marxism, 1, 23

Structural phonology, 136

Structuralism: as antihistorical and antihumanist, 20, 245; classical French, 2; complementary with phenomenological, 222; and invariant relationships, 217; modern French, 2, 3, 17; relationaL, 2, 21, 22, 24, 33, 34; semiotic, 16, 19
—modern, supported by neurology and modern scientific thought, 13, 176
—static: in Durkheim, 159; in Gestalt Psychology, 159

—transformational, 2, 71

Structure: as constitutive condition of the active subject, 320; mathematical, 9

Structure and event, as mutually constitutive, 316

Structure and subjectivity, in dialectical relationship, 315

Structured subjectivity, 321

Structuring activity, 321

Subject and object, 6, 49, 224
—and object in Habermas, 51; and superstructure, 52; as materialistic process, 53; dialectically linked to object, 318; notion of contradictory subject needed, 52

Subjectivity, active aspect of, 323

Sudnow, D., 209

Sullivan, H. S., and semiotics, 132

Superstructure, mechanistic interpretation of, 52

Symbolic interactionism, "structural bias" of, 86

Symbolism, in classical sociology, 34

Symbols, threefold function of, 84

Terray, E., 275

Thomas, W. I., 22; and the identification of the situation, 82, 194

Tiryakian, E., 109, 209, 313

Todorov, T., 147

Totality of social phenomena, 9

Transformation, in the works of Lévi-Strauss and Piaget, 169

Turnbull, C., 271

Verification, 4, 201

Vierkandt, A., 217

Vulgar materialism, 46

Wagner, H. R., 28, 32, 33

Weber, M., 21; centrality of symbolism in, 56; class interests and origin of religious ideas in, 59; duality of perspective in, 62; elective affinity in, 74; empiricist conceptualization of historical data, 69; empiricist position of, 68; and the ethics of entrepreneurs, 56; function of religion in, 60; functional analysis in, 65, 67; ideal type, 64, 69, 76; and interpretive sociology, 55; and Marx, 55; and relational structuralism, 71; and religious rationalism, 56; and social strata, ideas, and social interests, and social action, 61; interests and ideologies in, 60; interpretive understanding and causal explanation, 64; lack of correspondence rules, 69; methodological psychologism, 66; orientation to social action in, 72; people's orientation toward normative structures in, 65; priority of ideas, 55; sociology of symbolic forms, 73; and the structural perspective, 58; structural orientation in, 62; structural prerequisites of capitalism, 57; substantive psychologism, 66; symbolic forms and social stratification, 71; and transformational structuralism, 71; verification in, 68; and the verstehen approach, 60; *Wirtschaftsethik*, 71; "world images," 75

Weberian perspective, and formal structuralism, 71
Wertheimer, M., 170
Western epistemology, 6
Whitehead, A. N., and fallacy of misplaced concreteness, 198
Whorf hypothesis, 193
Wiener, N., 141, 187
Wierkandt, A., 209
Wolff, A., 209
Wood, H., 209

Zeitlin, I., 55
Znaniecki, F., 22; and "humanistic coefficient," 82